99
5c95

350

LIBRARY

This book is due for return on or before the last date stamped below

WITHDRAWN
Leeds Trinity University

D0767516

T.A.S.C. LIBRARY LEEDS

181828 5

THEMES IN FOCUS

Published

Jonathan Barry and Christopher Brooks (*editors*)
THE MIDDLING SORT OF PEOPLE
Culture, Society and Politics in England, 1550–1800

Tim Harris (*editor*)
POPULAR CULTURE IN ENGLAND, *c.* 1500–1850

Forthcoming

Jacqueline Eales and Christopher Durston (*editors*)
THE CULTURE OF ENGLISH PURITANISM, 1560–1700

Paul Griffiths, Adam Fox and Steven Hindle (*editors*)
THE EXPERIENCE OF AUTHORITY IN EARLY MODERN
ENGLAND

Bob Scribner and Trevor Johnson
POPULAR RELIGION IN GERMANY AND CENTRAL EUROPE,
1400–1800

Series Standing Order
If you would like to receive future titles in this series as they
are published, you can make use of our standing order
facility. To place a standing order please contact your bookseller or, in case of difficulty, write to us at the address below
with your name and address and the name of the series.
Please state with which title you wish to begin your standing
order. (If you live outside UK we may not have the rights for
your area, in which case we will forward your order to the
publisher concerned.)

Customer Services Department, Macmillan Distribution Ltd,
Houndmills, Basingstoke, Hampshire RG21, 2XS, England

Popular Culture in England, c. 1500–1850

Edited by

TIM HARRIS

MACMILLAN

BRU 92825
181828
306.40942 HAR

Editorial matter, selection and Preface © Tim Harris 1995

Chapter 1 © Tim Harris 1995; Chapter 2 © David Underdown
1995; Chapter 3 © Susan Dwyer Amussen 1995; Chapter 4
© Jonathan Barry 1995; Chapter 5 © Martin Ingram 1995;
Chapter 6 © Roy Porter 1995; Chapter 7 © Patty Seleski 1995;
Chapter 8 © John Rule 1995; Chapter 9 © Bob Bushaway 1995

All rights reserved. No reproduction, copy or transmission of
this publication may be made without written permission.

No paragraph of this publication may be reproduced, copied or
transmitted save with written permission or in accordance with
the provisions of the Copyright, Designs and Patents Act 1988,
or under the terms of any licence permitting limited copying
issued by the Copyright Licensing Agency, 90 Tottenham Court
Road, London WIP 9HE.

Any person who does any unauthorised act in relation to this
publication may be liable to criminal prosecution and civil
claims for damages.

First published 1995 by
MACMILLAN PRESS LTD
Houndmills, Basingstoke, Hampshire RG21 2XS
and London
Companies and representatives
throughout the world

ISBN 0–333–54109–X hardcover
ISBN 0–333–54110–3 paperback

A catalogue record for this book is available
from the British Library

10 9 8 7 6 5 4 3 2 1
04 03 02 01 00 99 98 97 96 95

Printed in Malaysia

5C95
£12.99

For Peter Burke

Contents

viii   Contents

Preface

Over the past few decades there has been a great expansion of interest in studying history 'from below'. More and more scholars have begun to shift their focus from the learned and educated few at the top of society and started to pay greater attention to exploring the ideas, values, assumptions and aspirations of ordinary people. As a result, a whole new field of enquiry has opened up, namely the study of what has come to be labelled 'popular culture'. Scholars working in this field have laid down a powerful interpretative paradigm concerning what was happening to popular culture in early modern England. The period between *c.* 1500 and 1850, it has been argued, saw an increasing polarisation between the culture of the elite and that of ordinary people, with the result that by the middle of the nineteenth century a great cultural chasm existed between the upper and lower classes, the high and low, the respectable and the vulgar. Two broad forces have been identified as responsible for bringing about this transformation: first, the attack on popular culture from above, by moral and religious reformers; and second, the transforming effect of certain social and economic changes, such as the rise of literacy, the commercialisation of society, the enclosure movement, the rapid growth of cities, and the impact of the Scientific Revolution. In recent years, however, historians have become increasingly critical of this interpretative framework: some have questioned the appropriateness of the two-tier model of cultural conflict, which seems to obscure the important place occupied by the middling sort in English society; others have pointed to the diversities within popular culture itself (such as regional diversities), which seem to make it difficult to talk of 'a popular culture' in the singular; still others have raised questions about the alleged chronology of cultural transformation during the early modern period. There has also emerged a recognition that more attention needs to be paid to the cultural space occupied by women, for it is by no means clear that women experienced or participated in popular culture in the same way as did men from similar social backgrounds. As our revisionism proceeds, some historians have even begun to doubt whether the term 'popular culture' is a particularly meaningful analytical category.

The time was thought ripe, therefore, for a volume which would explore some of the major issues about 'popular culture' in early modern England in the light of recent critical trends. Given the broad nature of the field, it was thought wiser to put together a collection of essays on specific themes written by experts in particular areas of research, rather than for one author to attempt a broad work of synthesis; we felt that the end-result would offer more in-depth analyses and more penetrating insights into what are unquestionably very complex historical problems than could ever be achieved by an individual working on his or her own. It is true that as recently as 1985 Barry Reay published an excellent collection of essays exploring various aspects of popular culture in his *Popular Culture in Seventeenth-Century England* (London: Croom Helm, 1985), but his edition focused exclusively on the seventeenth century. Many of the interesting questions about popular culture that still need to be addressed centre on changes that happened over the longer time period, from (broadly speaking) the Reformation to the Industrial Revolution. This volume has been assembled, therefore, not as an alternative to Reay's, but rather as a complement to it, building on that book's important findings, but exploring issues which it was unable to address because of its more limited chronological time frame.

Contributions have been solicited from those who could draw on their own scholarly expertise to investigate certain key themes in early modern English popular culture which, we thought, had either been insufficiently explored or were in need of fresh examination. David Underdown, for example, looks at regional variations in popular culture. Two of the chapters – those by Susan Amussen and Patricia Seleski – focus on women. Three chapters look at what have been identified as some of the crucial agencies of change, and seek to reassess their impact: Jonathan Barry looks at literacy and popular literature and examines whether it is appropriate to talk of a growing divide between a literate, respectable culture and the oral world of popular tradition; Martin Ingram explores the enormous sea-changes effected in the religious culture of English society by the Reformation and its aftermath; Roy Porter investigates certain aspects of the impact on popular culture wrought by both the alleged rise of scientific rationalism and the commercialisation of society in Georgian England in his chapter on the hitherto largely neglected field of medicine. The last two chapters look at different aspects of the culture of the lower orders towards the end of the early modern period, to shed light on the issues of how much had changed and how resilient to change that culture proved to be. John Rule takes an urban perspective, looking at custom and resistance in the workplace between 1700 and 1850, whilst Bob Bushaway takes us into the countryside with his examination of alternative belief in nineteenth-century rural England. My own introductory chapter seeks to raise critical questions about our conceptualisation of popular culture and the way we should approach its study, in the hope of providing an appropriate context for the essays which follow.

As editor of this volume I have accumulated numerous debts along the way. I am particularly grateful to Peter Burke, who initially suggested the idea of putting this volume together. Despite certain differences of opinion which will emerge in my own chapter, I trust our friendship will survive this book; my personal debts to him will ever remain immense. Martin Ingram provided much intellectual input and constructive advice; if in the end I was not as radical as he perhaps would have liked in my attack on the notion of 'popular culture', my own thinking about these issues has certainly been sharpened as a result of our discussions. I should also like to thank Keith Wrightson for many stimulating conversations over the years on the subject of early modern English social history more generally, in places as far afield as Cambridge (England), the other Cambridge (Massachusetts) and Claremont (California). In addition, Bob Scribner has been very influential in shaping the way I think about popular culture in early modern Europe; what I owe to him will be apparent from the pages of my chapter. I benefited enormously from the discussions I had with the students in my graduate seminar on a number of the topics explored in this volume; in particular I am indebted to Susannah Ottaway, who not only read a number of draft chapters, but even carried various materials back and forth across the Atlantic for me on one of her trips to England. Above all, I need to offer my deepest thanks to my contributors and the publishers for their patience and support whilst I was putting this collection together. As these things always seem to, the whole process took much longer than I thought; I apologise for the long delay and hope they feel that, in the end, it was worth it.

Providence TIM HARRIS

1. Problematising Popular Culture[1]

TIM HARRIS

All students of popular culture would acknowledge the intellectual debt they owe to Peter Burke's seminal study *Popular Culture in Early Modern Europe*. In this impressively wide-ranging work, Burke laid down a powerful model of cultural change in early modern Europe. Culture he defined as 'a system of shared meanings, attitudes and values, and the symbolic forms (performances, artifacts) in which they are expressed or embodied'; by popular culture he meant the culture of 'ordinary people' or the 'subordinate classes', those below the level of the elite (though not necessarily excluding the elite). In the Europe of 1500, according to Burke, 'popular culture' was everyone's culture. Although there existed a separate culture of the learned and educated few – the 'great tradition' – the elite at this time also participated in the 'little tradition' of the rest. The following three centuries, however, saw an increasing polarisation between these two traditions, with the result that by 1800 European elites 'had abandoned popular culture to the lower classes, from whom they were now separated, as never before, by profound differences in world view'. Burke identified two broad forces responsible for this transformation: first, the attack on popular culture from above (the clergy and lay reformers), motivated by the desire for moral and religious reform; and second, the transforming effect of social and economic changes, such as the divisive impact of the spread of literacy, the commercialisation of society, the impact of the Scientific Revolution, and the rise of a culture of manners which caused the elite to withdraw from what they saw as the 'uncouth' practices of the lower orders. By the early nineteenth century the gap had become so large that the elite needed to rediscover popular culture, and some educated men began to collect and record popular songs, beliefs and festivals which appeared both exotic and quaint, belonging to a world that was now totally alien to them.[2]

1

Burke's account is tempered by an awareness of the complexities of regional variations and of specific exceptions to the rule, but on the whole he feels that the model he develops is generally applicable to all of Europe, including England. Indeed, much of the specific scholarly work into various aspects of popular culture in early modern England seems to confirm Burke's picture. In their detailed reconstruction of life in the Essex village of Terling between 1525 and 1700, Keith Wrightson and David Levine documented an increasing socio-economic polarisation between the village elite and the village poor which was accompanied by a concomitant cultural polarisation: 'new distinctions of education and religion, of attitudes and manners' emerged, and as the parish notables, many of whom are known to have been Puritans, 'gradually withdrew from traditional popular culture', they 'attacked it', attempting 'to impose a new form of social discipline that would reinforce their own position' and using the courts 'to redefine and mark out anew the boundaries of permitted behaviour'.[3] In his influential textbook on English society, Wrightson argued more generally that by 1680 'The poor had become not simply poor, but to a significant degree culturally different':

> At the time of the Armada, rural England possessed a vigorous popular culture of communal recreations and rituals. By the time of the Exclusion Crisis this traditional culture had been greatly impoverished, while its surviving manifestations were discountenanced by respectable society and participation in them was largely confined to the vulgar.[4]

Eighteenth- and early nineteenth-century scholarship has also served to endorse the appropriateness of Burke's model for England. Robert Malcolmson has shown how traditional recreations were gradually undermined in the period 1700–1850 (especially from the later eighteenth century), partly as a result of social and cultural changes, such as the enclosure movement and the rapid growth of cities, and partly as a result of attempts at suppression by 'respectable society' – evangelical reformers and those concerned with imposing a more rigorous labour discipline. In addition, 'enlightened' opinion became increasingly hostile to certain traditional pastimes, in particular cruel animal sports such as bull-baiting and cock-fighting, whilst there was also growing alarm amongst local elites at the disorders that might be promoted by popular recreations, particularly so after the outbreak of the French Revolution.[5] Other important studies have also identified changes in the structure and organisation of leisure occurring during the Industrial Revolution, related to attempts to impose greater social discipline and adapt to the conditions of industrial production.[6] Reviewing the state of the field in an essay published in 1985, Anthony Fletcher and John Stevenson were able to conclude that between 1500 and 1800 'a polarisation was occurring that detached the gentry and some of the middling ranks from labourers and the poor, finally leaving the traditional culture, a culture imbued with symbolism, magic and superstition, high and dry ... By the end of our period a chasm had opened between the mentality of the gentry and the people that was not apparent at its beginning'. As a result of 'a process of withdrawal by the gentry and middling sorts', they continued, we can detect 'a whole series of developing polarities – of speech, dress, manners, living conditions, leisure pursuits and literary interests'.[7] And more recently still, Peter Borsay, from his work on English provincial towns in the period 1660–1770, has concluded that 'from the very end of the seventeenth century there was a marked acceleration in the rate at which the privileged and affluent withdrew from traditional beliefs and activities', with the consequence that 'a widening cultural gap emerged between polite society and the majority of ordinary people'.[8]

However, as our explorations in the field of early modern popular culture have become more advanced – as we move from the stage of 'pioneers' to 'settlers', to employ Peter Burke's metaphor[9] – some of our received wisdom about both the nature of popular culture and what was happening to it during this period has come under increased critical scrutiny. Part of the discussion has centred on the problem of methodology, and the extent to which it is possible, from the available sources, to recreate the contours of the culture of the subaltern classes. Even more critical attention has been paid to conceptual problems. What precisely do we mean by the term 'popular culture'? What is meant by culture, and what range of phenomena should be included within this category? What precisely does the term 'popular' signify, and who were the popular classes who were supposed to have inhabited this particular cultural space? Some have questioned the appropriateness of the two-tier model of cultural conflict, others would point to the diversities within both elite and popular culture themselves, whilst still others have noted the continued interaction of the popular and elite spheres throughout this period. Questions have also been raised about the alleged chronology of cultural transformation during the early modern period, with some now coming to place greater emphasis on continuity rather than on change.[10] One glaring weakness with existing scholarship is that it has largely focused on the culture of men. Burke candidly confessed that he had 'too little to say about women, for lack of evidence'.[11] In the light of recent important developments in women's history, this omission can no longer be acceptable.

The time was thought ripe, therefore, for a volume which would explore these issues in the light of recent critical trends. All of the essays compiled here, in their different ways, offer important critical perspectives on the model of cultural transformation offered by Burke and others, some challenging the validity of seeing a simple polarisation between elite and popular cultures, others the chronology and extent of change during this period. However, there has been no attempt to impose a particular editorial line, because the aim of this volume has been to open up critical debate by exploring the complexities of the cultural dynamics of early modern England, rather than foreclose it by attempting to establish a new consensus. The purpose of this introductory chapter, therefore, is to set the context for the following essays, not by trying to develop an alternative interpretative paradigm, which the various contributors may or may not endorse, but rather by raising critical questions about our conceptualisation of popular culture and the way we should approach its study.

It will be argued here that the initial formulation of the concept of popular culture by pioneers in the field was extremely fruitful, since it forced scholars to pay more attention to the humbler ranks of society and the cultural framework within which they experienced their world and acted out their daily existence. However, as our enquiries progress, the concept of popular culture itself has become constraining, because it fails to problematise certain areas of historical enquiry which are now in need of further investigation. The language we use often limits the questions we ask and structures the way we conceive the phenomena and processes we are seeking to understand. The use of the term 'popular culture' in the singular encourages us to think of the culture of those below the elite as if it were a coherent whole, and directs our attention away from a consideration of the diversities within popular culture itself. Similarly, the way our approach has been conceptualised in terms of a dichotomy between popular and elite culture encourages us to see the subordinate classes as an undifferentiated group, which clearly does an injustice to social, economic and cultural realities. Did all of those below the level of the elite really inhabit the same cultural world, or do we need to introduce more sophisticated distinctions, dependent upon social status, geographic location, religious affiliation and gender? Likewise, formulating the question in terms of a conflict between elite and popular culture which the elite eventually (and inevitably) won distracts us from considering the degree of interaction between the cultural worlds of the educated and the humbler ranks of society as well as the degree of resistance to pressure from above exhibited by those from below. It is true that many of the pioneers in the field of early modern popular culture, Burke included, were aware of these issues. My point, however, is that the language of Burke's conceptual model does not invite us to identify these complexities as central areas for historical investigation.

This introduction therefore seeks to unpack the concept of 'popular culture' in order to problematise those issues which need further enquiry for our understanding in this field to progress. I shall start with a consideration of the problems of the sources, before moving on to an examination of the meaning and usefulness of our central terms 'culture' and 'popular'. I shall then explore the question of the alleged elite/popular dichotomy, suggesting that it is unhelpful to think in terms of a bi-polar model of cultural relations in early modern England. A final section will consider the extent to which the culture of the subordinate classes was transformed during the early modern period, and the mechanisms by which this was achieved, where I shall warn against the view which sees 'popular culture' as being perpetually impoverished as a result of attacks from the elite. Some of the efforts to reform 'popular culture' came from those who themselves were below the level of the elite. Moreover, whereas some elements of traditional culture did disappear, many aspects survived the attempts at reform, whereas in other areas the culture of the ordinary people can seen to have become enriched, as it developed in new ways and met changing situations and needs.

At the heart of any discussion of 'popular culture' must lie a consideration of what this critical term means. Yet in many respects, the quest for popular culture began as an attempt to identify a field of enquiry rather than as a search for a clearly defined structure that was believed to exist: the aim was simply to shift attention away from the learned and educated few, and invite more scholarly enquiry into the cultural world of ordinary people. For this reason, we should start with a methodological question, and ask whether the sources exist which might enable us to explore this cultural world, before moving on to the question of how we categorise the cultural system that emerges as a result of our enquiries.

The source problems, however, are quite severe. Ordinary people in the early modern period seldom left direct evidence of their own beliefs, values or attitudes; our access to the culture of the subordinate classes is therefore normally indirect, mediated through sources produced by those who belonged to the learned culture of the elite. What becomes difficult is to discern the extent to which the historical record of this popular culture has been contaminated by these elite mediators. The risk of contamination is most apparent when dealing with elite descriptions of popular activities and practices. For instance, accounts of riots and demonstrations by those in positions of authority who were responsible for maintaining peace and order often give a somewhat tainted view of the activities they were purporting to describe. As John Morrill and John Walter have recently shown, much of the evidence upon which historians have traditionally relied to investigate the nature and extent of agrarian unrest in England in the 1640s 'reveals more about the propertied classes' fears than the rioters' intent'.[12] Likewise, descriptive accounts of lower-class religious movements or radical groups from contemporary observers who sought to distance themselves from the attitudes and beliefs they were recounting have to be treated with extreme caution, as the recent debate over whether the Ranters existed has shown.[13] These are stark examples, but the difficulty persists – perhaps in less obvious but nevertheless in equally problematic forms – with many of the sources on which historians of popular culture have to rely. We must not confuse what the elite perceived and feared with what ordinary people actually believed and practised.

A variety of approaches have been suggested for gaining more direct access to what was authentically popular. For instance, we can exploit those sources that can be said to have been 'popular' in the sense that they had a mass consumption. Here we might include cheap printed wares, such as illustrated broadsides, ballads and chapbooks, which were accessible to those on the margins of literacy or even people who were illiterate: pictures could be viewed, ballads could be heard, and chapbooks were written in a simple enough style that they could be read aloud to those who could not read themselves. Because publishers had to make a living, what was printed, and especially what was reprinted, must to some degree have represented consumer choice, and therefore might tell us something about the values and tastes of the consumers. The trouble is, as Tessa Watt has recently shown, the idea that such cheap print was 'aimed at and consumed by a definable social group may be a myth'. Gentry and people from the more prosperous middling ranks of society accounted for a significant proportion of the buyers of such material. It may be that in some cases such sources tell us not so much about popular culture as about a tradition of popularised learned literature.[14] 'Popular' devotional literature is a case in point: to what extent does this tell us about popular piety, and to what extent does it reflect elite notions of piety targeted at a mass audience? The same observation would be pertinent to all forms of moralistic and prescriptive literature. It would be wrong, of course, to assume that the more humble consumers did not internalise the values contained in such material – although it is virtually impossible to know how they did internalise them. The point, however, is that the values being internalised often came from 'outside'; at best such sources tell us about the interaction between the culture of the elite and that of ordinary people.

Some 'popular' printed material was of a deliberately propagandistic nature. During the Exclusion Crisis at the end of Charles II's reign, for example, a number of prints and illustrated broadsides were produced in order to represent the dangers posed by the Popish Plot and the evils that might befall the nation should the Catholic heir become king. This material was certainly targeted at a mass audience, and it clearly sought to exploit what was perceived to be a deep-seated hostility towards popery amongst the English population. To a certain extent, therefore, such propaganda must have reflected the sentiments and anxieties of the audience it was seeking to reach. Yet it was also designed to

persuade, to shape or even re-direct opinion – in this case, to con-
vince people of the necessity of excluding the Catholic heir from
the succession. As a result, it becomes very difficult to distinguish
between what was genuinely popular sentiment and what was the
propagandist's opinion, which he hoped his audience would come
to share. In this particular case we in fact know that many people
did not buy the argument of the propaganda; there is quite considerable evidence now emerging of 'popular' opposition to the
policy of exclusion.[15]

Another approach is to search for what appear to be vestiges of a
traditional oral culture, such as ballads, folk-songs, folk-tales and
proverbs. Many of these have been transcribed into printed
sources, some of them in major collections assembled by folklorists and antiquarians in the nineteenth and early twentieth centuries. Even when we can feel confident that the collectors merely
recorded what they took to be oral tradition, and did not introduce any distortion of their own, we cannot readily assume that
here we have firm evidence of authentic popular culture. For
example, it has now been shown that the vast majority of folk-
songs gathered in the great compilations at the turn of the last
century can be traced back to printed broadsides. Whilst some of
these might represent an early recording of an oral tradition,
many such ballads owed their origins to musical hacks or even professional composers who published for a living.[16] Folk-tales and
proverbs present similar problems. The origins of many of the
Luther folk-tales collected in Germany at the beginning of the
twentieth century, for example, can be traced back to the hand of
a pious Lutheran pastor, and some of them appear to have been
deliberately created for a propagandist function.[17]

A third line of enquiry has been to exploit court records (both
ecclesiastical and secular), to discover what infractions of the
social and legal norms established by the elite can tell us about
popular beliefs and attitudes. Here, so it seems, in the accusations
of seditious words, in the allegations of witchcraft, in matrimonial
disputes, and so on, we can find the authentic voices or actions of
ordinary people: we can hear what people said about politics, for
example, or discover what they thought about the power of maleficent magic. A large number of excellent studies, on a wide range
of subjects, have been undertaken using such sources, and there
can be no doubting that valuable insights into the world of

ordinary people can be gained through an exploration of court records. Yet as a means of gaining access to popular culture, the sources are problematic. Court records do not tell us, in unmediated form, what ordinary people said or thought; they tell us what some legal official, given his own prejudices and his own understanding of the law, thought worthy of recording in order to initiate legal proceedings. Indictments for seditious words, for example, record those words allegedly spoken which were regarded as legally seditious; they do not necessarily record the whole of the speech, nor tell us how such a seditious conclusion was reached, nor perhaps even what the accused regarded as the most important points of his speech. The degree of filtering that went on can be seen when we can compare indictments with depositions, which are often much fuller and typically provide much information that never found its way into the indictment. Unfortunately depositions do not always survive, especially before the eighteenth century; but even when they do, we have to realise that the justice of the peace who took the deposition might have been writing down only selective parts of the allegations, those which struck him as legally significant.[18] The methodological problems of using court records as a way of gaining access to popular culture have been exposed by Clive Holmes in an essay on early modern English witchcraft. Although English witchcraft accusations were predominantly initiated from below, and to that extent reflect popular beliefs and concerns, they found expression, as Holmes put it, through 'a complex machinery staffed by members of the elite who might shape those concerns in the light of their own attitudes'. These sources, in the end, tell us not, in any simple way, about popular culture, since they are 'the product of a complex interweaving of the concerns of the elite and those of the populace'.[19]

We should not paint too bleak a picture. Historians always have to confront the methodological problems of their sources, and although the difficulties facing the student of popular culture might be particularly extreme, with the right approach and with sensitive handling the sources can be extremely revealing. On the other hand, it must be recognised that trying to reconstruct something we might label popular culture in early modern England is an extremely difficult task. Rather than struggling to overcome the limitations of the sources, which might not, in the end, be particularly productive, a better approach could be to play to the sources' strengths. That is, since the sources tell us about the interaction of elite and popular culture, maybe we should make the nature of that interaction the focus of our study, rather than the attempt to isolate what was purely popular, which could end up being a futile endeavour.

Having considered some of the methodological difficulties involved in reconstructing the culture of those below the level of the elite, let us now turn to definitional problems, and confront the issue of whether the concept of 'popular culture' is a particularly meaningful one. What do we mean by 'culture' in this context? In the seventeenth century culture carried the meaning of cultivation, whether of plants (as in agriculture), or of the mind, faculties, manners, and so on. When applied to human beings it was synonymous with improvement or refinement through education or training. As Thomas Hobbes put it in *Leviathan,* 'The education of children [is called] a culture of their minds'.[20] To early modern English people, then, 'popular culture' would have been a contradiction in terms: by definition there was no culture of the unrefined and ill-educated masses. The modern usage of the term as applied to human societies did not emerge until after 1750, and initially was confined to the German language; it was first used in the English language in the modern anthropological sense in 1871 by E. B. Tylor. Today the term itself has become rather broad, possessed with a variety of meanings: a semantic history written in the early 1950s identified close to 300 definitions of culture as applied to discussions of human societies.[21] Even if we agree to work with Burke's definition of 'a system of shared meanings, attitudes and values, and the symbolic forms in which they are expressed or embodied', it is a definition which embraces a wide range of phenomena for the historian to investigate, and seems capable of almost indefinite expansion. Popular culture is not just what ordinary people did to amuse themselves whilst the toffs went to the opera; it is about how they saw their world, how they lived, worked, worshipped, what they believed, their attitudes towards the law, politics, the church, the supernatural, their family, marriage, in short, perhaps about everything. Ludmilla Jordanova has argued that '*all* history is cultural history, since there can be no processes, whether economic, social or political, which are not mediated through ideas, concepts, theories, images or languages'.[22]

This broadening of the concept is to be welcomed. What we might broadly term cultural considerations must surely be placed alongside other factors, such as material circumstances, in explaining both how people experienced their world and the way they reacted to it. Yet the broader the concept becomes, the less coherence it is likely to possess as an analytical category. Does it make sense to talk about 'a popular culture' in the singular, or are we going to see a variety of different 'popular cultures' – or at least a variety of sub-cultures – depending on which different aspects of human existence we choose to focus on?

An earlier generation of structural anthropologists tended to view 'an individual culture as a coherent whole', as Malinowski put it, as an integrated and internally consistent belief system which formed, in Mary Douglas's words, 'one single, symbolically consistent universe'.[23] Such a conceptualisation has been particularly influential in shaping historians' thinking. For example, Robert Muchembled, in his important study of popular culture in early modern France, insisted on the need to 'seek out the *internal coherence* of this system of explaining the world'.[24] The value of such an approach is that it can help reveal why it made sense for a particular people to hold beliefs which by modern western standards seem irrational and superstitious. As Bob Bushaway shows in his chapter on alternative belief in nineteenth-century rural England, by seeing alternative belief as a coherent and holistic structure, we can free ourselves from the view, adopted by contemporary elite commentators, that the rural poor were essentially stupid and held slavishly to popular delusions, and begin to comprehend the meaning and significance such a belief system had for many labouring families. But Bushaway's essay also makes it clear that not all people below the elite subscribed to this value system and, of those who did, not all related to it in exactly the same way.

The danger of the holistic approach, with its stress on cultural integration, is that it can tend to imply an over-consensual view. Cultures are seldom monolithic, even in primitive societies; they are certainly not so in complex, hierarchically structured and regionally diverse societies such as early modern England. Instead, as many historians and even anthropologists would now warn us, we need to recognise the existence of cultural pluralism, and of various oppositions and contradictions which create fractures and tensions within the whole.[25]

The question of pluralism becomes immediately apparent when we consider the issue of regional variation. Contemporaries were well aware of the difficulty of generalising about the culture of England as whole. As one observer put it in 1672:

> has not every county their particular rites and customs, not only different, but even contrary? He therefore that shall ascribe the particular customs of any one county, as Yorkshire, or Devonshire, to England in general, does he not expose himself to the just censure and indignation of those ... that have better knowledge of the country?[26]

Historians would now place greater emphasis on the geographical determinations of culture: cities, towns and villages might all have distinctive cultures of their own, as might also different agrarian and economic regions in the countryside. Jonathan Barry's work on Bristol, for example, has pointed to the existence of an indigenous social and political culture in what was at this time one of England's major provincial urban centres. With regard to the countryside, David Underdown has identified important cultural differences between the 'chalk' and the 'cheese', that is, between the communal culture of the densely settled, open-field parishes of the arable villages, and the more individualistic culture of the scattered parishes of the wood–pasture areas.[27] Underdown picks up this theme of regional variation in his contribution to this volume, where he evaluates the usefulness of a number of analytical categories for making sense of the many local variations in cultural forms. Distinctions need to be made between town and country, between large, imprecise regions such as the North, the West Country and East Anglia, between smaller ones such as counties, and of course, between the arable and wood–pasture areas which, in a slightly modified form from his earlier work, he still insists to be a particularly useful conceptual model. From his essay it becomes clear that there was no singular culture of the non-elite in early modern England: different parts of England had their own distinctive cultures; 'Cornish tin-miners inhabited a different culture from that of East Anglian fen-dwellers' (below, p. 29).

The extent to which we can talk about a single culture of those below the level of the elite becomes even more questionable once we introduce the category of gender into our analysis. In the light of recent research in women's history, the assumption that men and women from similar social backgrounds and geographical environments inhabited the same cultural space seems highly doubtful. Amongst other things, culture influences how individuals behave towards other individuals and also what is expected from them. In that sense, it has been said, 'any culture is a system of expectancies' – about what type of behaviour might be deemed appropriate, for example, or might be condoned or condemned.[28] It is undoubtedly the case, however, that the way women were expected to behave, and the way they were treated when they did not conform to expected norms, was very different from men's experience. Women were supposed to be subordinate, scolds were liable to be prosecuted at law, wives who beat their husbands were likely to be subjected to village shaming rituals known as skimmingtons or charivaris. There was a double standard with regard to sexual behaviour: a man was expected to be sexually experienced, a woman was expected to be chaste: adultery may have been regarded as a sin, but a sin much more readily forgiven in a man than in a woman.[29]

Many scholars would now recognise that men and women experienced popular culture in very different ways and that they did not occupy the culture of their class in the same way.[30] Susan Amussen, in her chapter in this volume, explores the critical role the values and cultural assumptions of the lower orders played in sustaining gender relations in early modern society, and emphasises the way that gender affected the meaning given to the behaviour of women and men in virtually every aspect of their daily lives. She also shows, however, that cultural conceptions of gender were not fixed. Although the core values of the culture of the masses were deeply misogynistic, stressing women's subordination, in practice the extent of women's subordination was sharply contested, allowing women a certain degree of authority and respect. The cultural space occupied by women, and the way issues of gender and class interacted, are themes explored by Patty Seleski in her chapter on domestic servants in eighteenth- and early nineteenth-century London. The eighteenth century saw the articulation of a new domestic ideology, especially powerful amongst the middle class, which posited certain natural differences between men and women and which sought to restrict women to the private world of the household, with women being seen as the 'natural' managers of family life. Yet this contemporary project of dividing the world by gender, Seleski reminds us, should not cause us to lose sight of the question of class relations, and the differentials of wealth, status, and power that divided women amongst themselves. As is clearly brought out in her study, domestic servants experienced this new definition of womanhood differently from their female employers, and the feminised household was often itself an arena of cultural confrontation between the differing value systems of different classes of women.

The problems involved in talking about 'popular culture' in the singular become even more apparent when we scrutinise the other term in this formulation, and consider exactly what is meant by the term 'popular'. Most scholars have defined 'popular' in juxtaposition to what it is not – it is not official culture, it is not the culture of the elite, or the educated classes. Such a strategy has led to the development of a bi-polar frame of analysis. As a result, we have come to think in terms of a series of dichotomies: between elite and popular; patrician and plebeian; high and low; rulers and ruled; learned and unlearned; literate and illiterate; godly and ungodly. Under critical examination, however, many of these alleged dichotomies break down.

Let us first ask whether the bi-polar model does justice to the sociological realities of early modern England. It is true that members of the elite did sometimes embrace an 'us' and 'them' vision of society. They often described the subordinate classes in contemptuous terms, referring to them variously as the vulgar, the rabble, the many-headed monster, the giddy multitude, and, from the later seventeenth century, as the mob.[31] The high-church Tory, Charles Leslie, discussing the partisan allegiances of the electorate in the Parliamentary elections of 1705, made a distinction between 'the principal gentry, both for estates and reputation', and 'the refuse and scum, the beasts of the people' (the latter of which, not surprisingly, Leslie thought supported the Whigs).[32] A few years later, the high-Tory cleric, Francis Atterbury, could maintain that 'the voice of the people is the cry of hell', and that 'the people are by the voice of heaven declared foolish, sottish, void of understanding, wise for wickedness, and senseless for good'.[33]

We need to be careful about how we treat such remarks, however. There was often a polemical purpose behind statements which posited a sharply polarised view of social relationships, with the dichotomy between the worthy 'us' and the unworthy 'them' being deliberately overdrawn in order to achieve a desired effect or make a particular point. Contemporaries typically had a more subtle conceptualisation of the sociological make-up of their society.[34] The best-known contemporary commentators on the social hierarchy of early modern England never adopted a bi-polar model. William Harrison, writing in 1577, stated that 'We in England divide our people commonly into four sorts'. The four groups consisted of first gentlemen (which could be further differentiated into the titular nobility, knights, esquires and simple gentlemen), second the citizens and burgesses of the cities and towns, third the yeomanry of the countryside, and finally a group embracing day labourers, poor husbandmen, artificers and servants.[35] The late seventeenth-century demographer Gregory King divided England into twenty-six 'ranks, degrees, titles and qualifications' of people, though these in turn could be grouped into three broader 'classes' which he described as 'the poorest sort ... the middle sort ... the better sort'.[36] All sorts of evidence, from formal works of social and economic analysis to more casual remarks in writings and speeches, suggests that for the seventeenth and eighteenth centuries contemporaries most commonly embraced a three-tier view of their social hierarchy. The mid-seventeenth century radical, George Foster, when he spoke of a vision he had about the levelling of social hierarchies, did not talk of 'us' becoming equal with 'them', but rather reported a vision in which he saw a man on a white horse 'cutting down all men and women, that he met with, that were higher than the middle sort', and who 'raised up those that were lower than the middle sort and made them all equal'.[37] In a speech in Parliament in November 1761, Member of Parliament William Beckford made it clear that when he spoke of the people he meant neither those at the top nor the bottom of society (and certainly not 'the mob'), but rather 'the middling people of England, the manufacturer, the yeoman, the merchant, the country gentleman'.[38]

Social historians have seldom found a bi-polar description of early modern English society subtle enough for their analytical purposes. Wrightson and Levine, in their study of Terling between 1525 and 1700, thought it most useful to employ four broad categories in order to make sense of what they termed 'the finely graded hierarchy of wealth and social position within the village'.[39] Most seventeenth- and eighteenth-century historians would at least wish to adopt a three-tier hierarchy, stressing the importance of the 'middling sort' – those engaged in the professions, commerce or business (from doctors, lawyers and merchants through to the more prosperous local tradesmen and shopkeepers) and the yeomen farmers and richer husbandmen in the countryside.[40] This was not an insignificant group. One historian has estimated that in the eighteenth century the middling sort accounted for over 30 per cent of the population and were in receipt of nearly 60 per cent of the national income.[41]

The existence of this middle layer not only questions the validity of thinking in terms of a basic social polarity, but it also provides problems for the posited dichotomy between rulers and ruled, since at the local level the middling sort played an important role in the governance of the realm. They filled many of the local offices of the parish or ward, serving as churchwardens, vestrymen, constables and beadles, and on the night watch. They also played a vital part in local regulation and the administration of justice by serving as jurors: whilst the grand juries of the assizes were composed mainly of gentry, men of lesser status got to sit on the quarter sessions grand jury, trial juries, hundred presentment juries and coroner's juries.[42] The potential for involvement in some of the processes of government at the local level extended fairly far down the social scale, as contemporaries themselves recognised. In a tract of 1686, Nathaniel Johnston, a fairly extreme Tory who believed that the kings of England were absolute, wrote of the 'common people':

> They have according to their several capacities and abilities, a participation of offices in their particular hamlets, parishes, wapentakes, or counties, either relating to the assistance to the justice of the land in juries, or conserving of the peace, in being petty, or chief constables, or other officers.[43]

Some historians who recognise the existence of these middle ranks would nevertheless persist in the view that a process of cultural polarisation was taking place, maintaining that culturally the middling sort came to identify themselves with the values of the elite. This is what Wrightson and Levine argue in their study of Terling.[44] Likewise Morrill and Walter have maintained that those from the middle ranks of society who dominated their local communities in their capacity as parish or manorial officeholders allied themselves firmly with the gentry as magistrates, an alliance which was 'eased by an identity of economic interests in service of the market, facilitated by the trend towards enclosure by agreement and cemented where there occurred a shared religion and literate culture'.[45] Edward Thompson, defending his categorisation of eighteenth-century English society as divided between patricians and plebs, has recently asserted that 'in between, where the professional and middle classes, and the substantial yeomanry, should have been, relations of clientage were so strong that, at least until the 1760s, these groups appear to offer little deflection of the essential polarities'.[46]

It is certainly true that the middling orders often sought to create social and cultural distance between themselves and those beneath them, and that they could be highly critical of the mores, manners, customs and disorders of the poor. We also find plenty of evidence of the middle ranks 'straining to imitate their betters', as Lord Chesterfield put it in the eighteenth century.[47] Yet it is by no means clear that we should invariably locate the middle ranks of society on the elite side of the cultural divide. It is revealing, in this respect, that Barry Reay's recent collection of essays on popular culture in seventeenth-century England encompasses both the 'middling' and the 'lower sort of people'; indeed, the middling sort have a high profile in the various contributors' investigations into the culture of the non-elite.[48] In his study of fenland riots in the later seventeenth century, Clive Holmes has shown that the middling sort allied themselves with the landless poor and took a prominent role in organising local opposition to the drainage and enclosure of the fens.[49] Recent work on the law has shown that the middling sort often played a powerful role as mediators in the exercise of justice, and that they did not automatically or instinctively adopt the values of the governing elite. Trial juries (composed, as we have said, largely of those from the middle ranks of society) frequently failed to convict those with whom they felt themselves in broad sympathy, a notable example being those who had offended against the game laws, which explains why gentry game preservers were often forced to use summary conviction instead.[50] We can discern a definite anti-aristocratic flavour within the value system of the emerging middle class. For example, the middle-class emphasis on thrift and condemnation of extravagant expenditure on leisure reveals as much a sense of cultural distance from those above as from those below.[51] Similarly, the Wilkite reform movement of the 1760s and 1770s, which was spearheaded largely by men of middling status, took on a distinctively anti-aristocratic tone, as John Brewer has shown.[52]

Many of the other alleged dichotomies implied by our traditional conceptual framework also appear difficult to sustain. The view, once commonly held, that popular culture was essentially oral and that a fundamental cultural fissure developed in early modern England between the literate and illiterate classes, can no longer be readily held, as Jonathan Barry's contribution to this volume makes clear. There was a substantial overlap between the oral and literate worlds.[53] Although it is true that illiteracy rates get higher the further one goes down the social hierarchy, some humble types could read and write, with the result that literacy and the world of print had already begun to penetrate the culture of the lower orders. Indeed, literacy and illiteracy might even co-exist within the same families.[54] Besides, there were many ways of bridging the gap between the literate and oral worlds, such as by reading newspapers or printed tracts aloud, or even singing published ballads. Furthermore, as Barry points out, to make a basic distinction between those who were literate and those who were not is too simplistic, since there are qualitative dimensions to consider, such as how well one could read or write, what sort of reading material one had access to, and how one read (whether privately or publicly).

The alleged dichotomy between a godly elite and an irreligious multitude is another that does not bear up to critical scrutiny. It is true, as many historians have shown, that for the late Elizabethan and early Stuart England the hotter sort of Protestants were particularly visible amongst the more prosperous middling sorts and the upper ranks of society, whilst throughout the early modern period we can find many traces of religious ignorance or scepticism and superstitious practices amongst the mass of the population (especially in the countryside). But there is also evidence to suggest that as a result of the Protestant Reformation of the sixteenth century and the political and religious struggles of the seventeenth, the religious divisions that emerged in England cut vertically through this society rather than horizontally. The elite became divided, between those who wanted to continue the Reformation further (Puritans), and those who remained attached to the established church of bishops, prayer book and the thirty-nine articles. In addition, not all those below the level of the elite can be styled 'ungodly'. Recent research has shown that, even before the Civil War, Puritanism was not without its appeal to the poorer sort, whilst some of the more radical religious movements which emerged during the 1640s and 1650s – such as the Baptists, Fifth Monarchists and Quakers – generated much of their support from plebeian types. Studies of Restoration nonconformity have shown that dissenters were drawn from all sections of society, including the very poorest. And if we look at the evangelical revival of the eighteenth century, we find that Methodists drew many of their supporters from the middling and lower ranks of society. Of course, such religious 'enthusiasts' were a small minority of the population, but even if we look at the conforming majority, we can uncover evidence of popular Anglican piety and even a zealous attachment to episcopacy and the prayer book. Indeed, it is arguable that poor Anglicans possessed a stronger sense of cultural identity with upper-class Anglicans – and likewise poor dissenters or poor Methodists with their more well-to-do counterparts – than they did with people from a similar social background who did not share their religious leanings. There is plenty of evidence of plebeian hostility towards Puritan, sectarian, nonconformist and Methodist groups in seventeenth- and eighteenth-century England, manifesting itself in various forms, from peaceful petitions and addresses to ritualised demonstrations, and even physical attacks on individuals or property. Such religious tensions tended to translate into vertical political allegiances, particularly during the turbulent seventeenth century. Under the later Stuarts, as has now been well documented, nonconformists and those sympathetic to dissent tended to ally with the Whigs, whilst high-Anglicans sided with the Tories; even the 'London crowd' was divided.[55]

We must nevertheless remain alert to the possibility that the way people understood or internalised their religious culture might have varied according to social and economic status; or, in other words, a poor Anglican might have experienced his religion differently from a rich one. The theme of 'popular religion' between *c.* 1540 and 1690 is addressed by Martin Ingram in his contribution to this volume. He stresses that popular religion can only be understood in relation to the official or dominant religion, emphasising the need to explore the degree of mismatch between official prescription and popular practice. What he uncovers is a range of overlapping popular religious cultures, which were not necessarily separated off from those of the upper ranks of society, and which interacted in complex ways with official precepts and doctrines which themselves were neither unitary nor unchanging.

The previous sections have stressed the problems involved in thinking in terms of an elite/popular dichotomy, suggesting that such a model is not sophisticated enough to make sense of the complex social and cultural realities of early modern England. In particular, it has been shown that more attention needs to be paid to regional variations, the issue of gender and the position of the middling sort. At the same time, attention has been drawn to the considerable degree of interaction between the high and the low and the fact that cultural tensions could sometimes divide this society vertically rather than horizontally. When taking on board these critical reflections, we must be careful not to lose sight of the fact that there clearly was a considerable degree of cultural conflict between the upper layers of society (those in positions of power and authority) and the subordinate classes. There undoubtedly were attempts to reform the traditional culture of the masses in early modern England, and the culture of the non-elite was certainly transformed in many significant respects during this period, as the researches of Wrightson, Malcolmson and others have shown. But in turning to the question of transformation, a number of observations need to be made, which taken together invite further refinements to the received model of cultural conflict.

In the first place it is worth re-emphasising that the attack on the culture of the subaltern classes was not continuous throughout this period, although this is a fact that has long been recognised by scholars. Distinct phases can be identified. The first occurred in the later sixteenth and early seventeenth centuries, and was associated with the desires of religiously inspired reformers, especially Puritan, to create what they thought to be a more godly society, and also those of the magisterial classes and local elites to regulate the disorders of the poor at a time when the pressures of inflation and rapid population growth seemed to be posing a threat to the stability of society. Following the defeat of the mid-century Revolution, however, there was a reaction against these attempts at repression, and in the century after the Restoration of 1660 many traditional recreations and pastimes (such as maypole dancing, cock-fighting and various holiday festivities) seem to have continued to flourish. Members of the elite showed a willingness to tolerate popular pursuits and amusements, and even, on occasion, to patronise and sponsor them themselves. Although hostility can still be detected in some quarters (note the campaign against vice and immorality conducted by the Societies for the Reformation of Manners in the 1690s and early eighteenth century), it was not until the second half of the eighteenth century that a more concerted attempt to reform popular pastimes began to pick up again.[56]

Even in the periods of most intense pressure for reform, we should not assume that the elite were unanimously hostile towards the culture of those below them. During the earlier phase, as David Underdown's work has shown, considerable numbers of the upper classes remained sympathetic to and even protective of traditional recreations; hostility appears to have been greatest in those areas which were most infected by Puritanism. James I's *Book of Sports* of 1617–18, which was reissued by Charles I in 1633, and which defended the right to participate in certain sports on Sundays after divine service and condoned the custom of holding parish feasts, made it quite clear where the state stood on these issues at this time.[57] Similar divisions amongst the elite can be detected during the later period. In early nineteenth-century Lancashire, for example, many of the employers in the cotton firms came from landed backgrounds, and they often retained a paternalistic attitude, remaining happy either to tolerate or even extend open patronage to traditional sports and holidays.[58] At the national level, paternalist members of parliament often complained of the attempts to deprive the poor of their recreations, claiming that rural sports served several important purposes, not least of which was keeping the poor content.[59]

A third point to consider is that hostility towards the traditional culture of the masses was not an exclusive preoccupation of the elites. Some of the most aggressive attempts to reform popular manners were initiated by reformers who are perhaps better described as middle-class, such as the Methodists and other evangelicals from the middle of the eighteenth century onwards, who began their campaign at a time when many members of the upper classes still retained a paternalistic tolerance towards the lower orders.[60] And we have to recognise that certain of the ideals and preoccupations of the moral reformers might have been shared by some of the lower orders themselves. For example, whilst we see various attempts 'from above' to reform sexual mores during the early modern period, we should not assume that vice was of concern solely to puritanical elites. The lower orders had their own ways of dealing with sexual transgressions: those guilty of blatant sexual immorality might be the victims of community shaming rituals such as skimmingtons, which seem to have been predominantly plebeian affairs; they might even become the subjects of locally circulated mocking rhymes or satirical libels.[61] Members of the lower classes can be found participating in later reformist movements, such as Methodism or teetotalism, actively engaged in the campaign to promote the virtues of sobriety and industry.[62] By the end of the period covered by this book, many lower-class radicals had come to shun many aspects of traditional culture, seeing certain forms of pastime and recreation as dangerous distractions which diverted the working classes from paying attention to what was really in their best interests, namely self-improvement and the promotion of political reform. And by the middle of the nineteenth century it is clear that a distinctive working-class concept of respectability had emerged; not that all members of the lower orders shared this ideal, but clearly the old, traditional culture had begun to fracture from within. All these examples go to show that what was hostile to what has been called popular culture might not have been elite culture but another culture with a popular purchase.[63]

Another warning is that we should not exaggerate the transformation that had occurred by the end of the early modern period. Nineteenth-century historians have pointed to the evidence

of significant continuities with the past which needs to be balanced with the evidence for change. For example, wakes and other
traditional festivals survived in the cotton districts of south and
east Lancashire well into the Victorian era, although in recognis-
ing this we need to be sensitive to possible changes in context and
content, and not confuse the apparent continuity in form with a
continuity of function and meaning.[64] The question of survivalism
is the central theme of Bob Bushaway's chapter below, where he
documents the persistence of a range of alternative beliefs and
unorthodox practices in many parts of the English countryside
well into the nineteenth century, showing that these helped give
the rural labourer not only a sustaining philosophy which enabled
him to cope with his lot, but also 'a sense of cultural self-respect
and self-awareness'.

Such observations raise one final concern about how we conceptualise cultural change during this period. There has been a
tendency to see what has been labelled popular culture as the passive victim of the historical process, undermined and impoverished by various attempts at reform or suppression, or eroded by
the effects of social, economic and intellectual changes. Historians
interested in tracing long-term cultural change have often started
by trying to identify what 'popular culture' was like before the
changes began to have their effect, with the result that that culture
is represented as a static structure, or almost as a reified object.
Thus we start with some *thing* identified as the traditional culture
of the subaltern classes in, say, 1500, and over time certain facets
of this culture are seen to disappear – such as bull-baiting, cock-
fights, village festivals, and so forth. Adopting this conceptual
approach it is inevitable that this traditional culture is always going
to appear to be shrinking.

Rather than seeing culture as a thing or a structure, we should
see it as a process, constantly adapting itself to new developments
and new circumstances.[65] Some older customs and pastimes might
have disappeared because they were willingly abandoned by the
lower orders in a changing world, or were successfully suppressed
because those from the subaltern classes saw no need or had no
desire to offer resistance. Those customs and practices which continued to serve a valuable function, however, were often vigorously
defended, whilst structures of belief which continued to make
sense of their everyday existence were often stubbornly adhered

to.[66] The question of custom and resistance is one that is addressed by John Rule in his chapter on custom in the workplace. The insistence on customary work practices, Rule shows, enabled artisans to keep a considerable degree of control over the labour processes, and any attempts to undermine such customs were likely to meet with resistance. But to represent artisanal culture as being purely defensive and traditionalist would be misleading. Customary culture was not necessarily in opposition to market culture, and innovations introduced into the workplace could be embraced, so long as they were seen as advantageous. Moreover, what was defined as customary could itself often be of recent origin; as Rule reminds us, 'the language of custom does not necessarily indicate an unchanging reality' (below, p. 187).

We must also warn against seeing a perpetual impoverishment of the culture of the non-elite. Some forms of popular recreation were able to withstand attempts at suppression by the elite; others, which had at one time enjoyed the patronage of the rich, were able to survive after the withdrawal of that patronage, with sponsorship often being taken over by the local alehousekeeper or publican. The commercialisation of society, which we normally date from the eighteenth century, had the effect of opening up new cultural horizons, and of making available pursuits and leisure activities which had hitherto been the preserve of a select few – first for the middling ranks of society, but gradually over the course of the eighteenth and early nineteenth centuries for the lower orders as well. Here we might point to developments such as the explosion in publishing (novels, chapbooks, provincial newspapers, the popular press) and the concomitant emergence of circulating libraries, the rise of the provincial theatre (which came to pander increasingly to lower-class audiences), and the growth of spectator sports, such as horse-racing, boxing and cricket. Such expansion did not go uncontested, and there were various attempts to preserve the social exclusivity of certain types of fashionable leisure pursuits (such as horse-racing and the theatre), but over the longer term the process of commercialisation and the emergence of an entertainment industry made available a whole new range of recreational opportunities for those from lower down the social scale.[67] One aspect of the impact of commercialisation is explored by Roy Porter in his contribution to this volume, where he shows that traditional oral lore about healing the sick was in part elbowed aside by the remarkable growth of 'popularised' medical knowledge. The old remedies lost much of their appeal once people could easily purchase special preparations and patent medicines at the market or through newspapers, gain ready access to surgeon-apothecaries and general practitioners who were setting themselves up in every market town and large village, or discover how to heal themselves by buying works of domestic physic aimed at the common reader.

In seeking to highlight some of the problems involved in our approach to the study of popular culture in early modern England, this introduction might seem to have come close to explaining popular culture away. It may be wondered whether anything which might meaningfully be described as popular culture ever existed in the centuries between the Reformation and the Industrial Revolution. Does this mean that the concept 'popular culture' should now be jettisoned as an unhelpful analytical category? Perhaps this is a question best left to the reader to decide, after he or she has read all the essays in this volume; the contributors themselves would undoubtedly offer different answers.

Whatever the problems with the notion of 'popular culture', it would be excessively pedantic to insist that henceforth scholars desist from using the term; it can at times be a useful form of shorthand, and it is often difficult to think what alternative descriptive label could be employed. I would go further and suggest that the coining of the term 'popular culture' was invaluable, since it forced historians to turn their attention away from the elite, and focus on those lower down the social scale, and also to think more about the cultural forces which helped shape society and social relationships in the past. Enormous advances have been made in our understanding of the past as a result of the identification of something which was given the label 'popular culture'; a whole new area of historical enquiry was opened up, and the results have been highly fruitful and intellectually stimulating. It may be true that as research continues and our understanding deepens, our initial formulation might appear to present more difficulties than once thought, but this is surely a healthy sign; what cannot be forgotten is that we would never have got this far without formulating the concept of popular culture in the first place.

Furthermore, the positing of a dichotomy between elite and popular culture forced us to think terms of the power relationships that existed in early modern English society, and kept the question of social hierachy to the fore in our investigations. This is something which must not be lost sight of as our revisionism proceeds. For all the evidence of cultural overlap and interaction we might uncover, for all the signs of the resilience of plebeian culture in the face of attack, and for all the examples that point to the fact that hostility to plebeian culture could come from below as well as from above, it must not be forgotten that early modern England was a hierarchically structured society, with enormous differentials in wealth, power and education, and where the balance between different social forces was very unequal. As Burke himself highlighted in his seminal study, cultural historians have to address questions about the relationship between the official and unofficial culture, between the dominant (or hegemonic) and the subordinate, between those who have more and those who have less power.

Yet it is by no means the case that these power relationships invariably cut horizontally through early modern English society, and this is where some of the greatest problems in terms of elite versus popular, or high versus low, emerge. Against the horizontal divisions that undoubtedly existed, we need to set other divisions in the cultural relationships of power which dissected English society somewhat differently. There could be regional power relationships, perhaps between a dominant metropolitan culture and provincial sub-cultures (in this respect more needs to be learnt about the cultural influence of London). Likewise, there were clearly gender imbalances in the distribution of power, though ones which were affected, in complicated ways, by considerations of social status. Or, if we take the example of religion, we clearly cannot lose sight of the conflict that existed between the official or dominant religious culture and various forms of dissenting or unorthodox practice, but again we see a power hierarchy here which resulted in no simple horizontal split, but which often helped encourage vertical ties of allegiance.

At the same time, it is not enough just to look at different cultural spheres; we also need to ask more probing questions about degrees of cultural integration. To return to an example already mentioned, it may be true that lower-class Anglicans had more in common with upper-class Anglicans than with lower-class dissenters, yet on another level of analysis we might find that lower-class Anglicans experienced their faith very differently from their elite co-religionists. To put it more generally, we might find people who in many respects identified with the official, or dominant, or hegemonic culture, and yet who at the same time were not fully integrated within it. Finally, we need to think more carefully about the issue of national culture, and how that fits into our picture. Although regional attachments could be powerful, at some levels most seventeenth- and eighteenth-century English people would identify themselves as being English: they shared a common language, they shared a common law, the overwhelming majority were Protestant; they were not like the Spanish or French, they were not Catholic, and they came to see themselves as having a common vested interest in wanting to defend the security of their realm, the reformed religion, and the liberties guaranteed them at law and by Magna Carta, against the threat posed by the tyrannical, Catholic superpowers of Europe.[68] On this very basic level, it could be suggested that early modern English people shared the same culture (however striking their cultural differences might be in many other respects), and that this common culture fundamentally affected the way they identified themselves and interpreted the world around them.

It is not the intention of this chapter to try to offer easy answers to the questions raised here. Rather, the purpose has been to identify issues that remain to be addressed, and areas that require further research and exploration. The chapters presented in this volume reflect an ongoing process of research into a very lively and intellectually challenging field. Not all the questions raised will be answered by this volume. And no doubt further questions will emerge as a result of the studies offered here. But taken as a whole it is hoped that these essays will add significantly to our understanding of popular culture – or whatever we choose to call it – in early modern England.

2. Regional Cultures? Local Variations in Popular Culture during the Early Modern Period

DAVID UNDERDOWN

Regional differences remain one of the unsolved mysteries of popular culture.[1] Why do we find one cultural form – a shaming ritual, perhaps, or a popular sport – in one region, another in another? In early modern England there were many locally specific customs which were maintained by people of all ages. Keith Thomas has pointed out that in some areas schools had annual rituals which are rarely found elsewhere. In one such custom the boys once a year 'barred out' the masters and took over their school for the day. This custom was confined to northern England, and rarely occurred in the South. Why was this? Thomas has to confess that he is baffled, and falls back on the consoling reflection that the problem has defeated folklorists and anthropologists just as much as it has historians.[2]

In this essay I shall examine some other examples of ritual forms associated with specific localities of England, in the hope that they will tell us something about the culture of the regions involved. Before we start, though, we ought to define our terms and confront some theoretical problems. The difficulties inherent in any definition of culture, and of 'popular culture' in particular, have been sufficiently outlined in Chapter 1 of this collection. Here we need only a couple of broad working definitions. By 'culture', I mean the sets of norms and values underlying a community's social existence, and the verbal, visual and ritually symbolic means by which those beliefs are expressed (often unconsciously) and transmitted over time.[3] By 'popular', I mean the culture pertaining primarily to people below the level of the educated social and political elite – in early modern England, broadly speaking, those

below the level of the gentry, clergy and prosperous urban bour-
geoisie. There are problems with both of these definitions, and
some historians nowadays call the whole concept into question, in
so far as it rests on an absolute polarity between the elite and the
popular levels. Bob Scribner has argued for the existence of a
single national culture, in which multiple sub-cultures express the
identities of classes and regions. Many elements of culture were
shared by both elite and plebeians – there was in certain respects a
common culture – but there were other elements that were *not*
shared, and were primarily the preserve of either educated or
uneducated, as the case might be.[4]

Instead of the binary model, it is more useful to think about
popular culture, as both Scribner and Peter Burke have urged us
to do, in terms of a spectrum of overlapping sub-cultures. We
make distinctions between different classes or status groups, just as
we do between different geographical regions, so why should it be
surprising that both regions and status groups in some respects
had their own cultures? The illiterate labourer did not share the
cultural universe of the minister who preached to him on the sabbath, or the squire who governed him as lord of the manor and
justice of the peace. It seems just as reasonable to suppose that
Cornish tin-miners inhabited a different culture from that of East
Anglian fen-dwellers.[5]

A couple of other preliminaries should be noted. First, historians of popular culture inevitably have to start with the forms in
which culture is expressed – the mask, the ritual, the dance –
rather than the underlying norms and values which make up that
culture. But the object of the exercise is to get at the values, and
we can only do this by decoding the expressive forms. A second
point: some of the cultural forms that will be discussed in this essay
were certainly expressions of attitudes more strongly held by the
common people, or by certain other sub-groups – women or
young people, for example – than by the gentry. But the gentry
often had access to them as observers or patrons. They might
benignly preside over their villagers' festivals, and pay for the
cakes and ale, and sometimes they wrote down descriptions of
local customs, as a good many local antiquaries were beginning to
do. As magistrates they might also have to record them in formu-
laic legal depositions when boisterous rituals like church ales or
skimmington rides got out of hand and the law was broken. The

observer, patron or magistrate may well have looked at these rituals very differently from the participants, and have given them
very different meanings. Much of our information about popular
culture is filtered by observers of this kind; we need to try to put
ourselves into the place of the people whose customs are being
written down in a form largely shaped by the questioning of their
betters.[6]

Interrogation of popular culture requires us to adopt analytical
categories. One obvious set of such categories is town and country.
The inhabitants of both urban and rural communities were conscious of living in different cultural environments, and the sense
that London in particular was unique – uniquely civilised and
sophisticated, uniquely vicious and corrupt, according to taste –
was as much a commonplace as the sense that Court and Country
were distinct cultural and political entities. The barely suppressed
suspicion and hostility between town and country affected many
other places much smaller than London. It was very pervasive in
Dorset, for example, where Dorchester townspeople felt themselves to be inhabitants of a beleaguered bastion of godliness in
the midst of a sea of popery and moral corruption, and the neighbouring rural gentry in turn resented the vigour with which plebeian urban magistrates pursued them when they came drinking
and wenching in the county town. Richard Carew noted the same
sort of antagonism between the small Cornish towns and their
rural hinterlands.[7]

But we should not exaggerate the depth of the cultural rift
between town and country. Richard Gough's description of his
rural Shropshire parish contains many references to neighbours
who spent part of their lives in Shrewsbury or even in London, and
there was similar mobility in small towns and villages closer to the
capital, like Romford or Terling.[8] Although they may have been
weakening by the eighteenth century, in earlier times the cultural
ties between town and country were very close. John Stow's *Survey
of London* describes a metropolis with many sports and rituals –
Shrove Tuesday football matches, May-games and midsummer
bonfires – which would have been familiar to newcomers from the
countryside.[9] And these urban rituals often fulfilled the same

functions as their rural counterparts. In both town and country parish bounds were perambulated to define the territorial identity of the community, and if townspeople encountered physical obstacles along the perambulation way, so too did country people in many parishes after enclosures. There were bull-baitings and cock-fighting matches in town as well as country; football and other sports were played in such urban settings as Chester and Derby with just as much vigour as they were in rural areas.[10] Facilities such as wells, which provided resource vital to human survival, were treated with respect and honour in urban and rural parishes alike. The mayor and burgesses of Shaftesbury had their annual procession on Holy Cross Day to decorate a nearby spring, and give ceremonial presents to the officers of the parish where the spring was situated. Londoners were equally dependent on a regular water-supply. Even during the Puritan Commonwealth, when such rituals were officially frowned on, the London water-carriers still decorated the Gracechurch Street conduit with flowers and garlands at midsummer. In 1654 there was a great drought, so they dressed the conduit with mourning cloths, and held a mock funeral procession headed by a 'lord and lady' in black. Rituals like this were also common in places where salt wells or pits were vital to the local economy. At Nantwich the ancient salt pit known as 'old Biat' was annually decorated with green boughs and flowers, and the young people had music and dancing around it. There were similar celebrations at Droitwich. When the local Puritans tried to stop them at the end of the Civil War, the well dried up, 'to the great loss of the town', John Aubrey tells us. The next year the townspeople sensibly ignored the prohibitions, and the well immediately gushed forth again.[11]

One thing that distinguished urban from rural rituals, however, was their greater richness and elaboration. There is nothing surprising about this: towns had money, skills and other resources that could be devoted to putting on a good show for the honour of the parish or guild. The struggles between Puritan reformers and traditionalists at Chester over whether to permit the giants, 'naked boys', and other costly shows in the annual midsummer pageant regularly erupted in the years around 1600. At Norwich the Florists' Feast was held with great sumptuousness right down to the Civil War, and the St George's Day procession still featured 'Old Snap' the dragon and other popular characters until the victorious

Parliamentarians outlawed them in the 1640s.[12] Villages also had their processional rituals during their church ales and revel feasts: 'hardly a rural merry-making or wake', E. K. Chambers observes, 'is without its procession'. They were rarely as elaborate as the urban ones, though there were some exceptions, like the celebrated hobby-horse dance at Abbots Bromley in Staffordshire, which was as complex and colourful as anything in the towns.[13]

Another obvious way of classifying variations in popular culture is geographical, either by identifying large, imprecise regions such as the North, the West Country and East Anglia, or smaller, more precise ones such as the counties. In either case we can observe numerous signs of cultural variation. There were even greater differences between local dialects than there are today, and, in the remoter parts of Wales and Cornwall, completely different languages – though Richard Carew complained of English linguistic imperialism, which by Elizabethan times had driven the Cornish tongue 'into the uttermost skirts of the shire'. Yet some dialects were sufficiently recognisable to be easily caricatured, for example in printed ballads plentifully sprinkled with the *z*s that signalled Somersetshire dialect to the knowing.[14]

Local customs differed as much as language or pronunciation, and their strength was often affected by the region's religious loyalties; hence the survival of a distinctive Catholic culture in areas of Lancashire and other parts of the North. It was after observing the symptoms of cultural conflict in the county that James I issued his *Book of Sports* in 1617. Lancashire was not the only part of the North where ancient festive customs retained their vitality during the early seventeenth century. There is a charming example of this in the commonplace book of Richard Shanne, a yeoman from Methley, Yorkshire, who recorded rushbearings, Whitsun plays and other festive customs, and recalled the Rogationtide processions in which he and his neighbours sang psalms 'to the glory of God, in the sweet meadows and fields'.[15] Yet there were differences in the modes of organisation of popular festivities between the two ends of England: church ales were harder to organise in the large, scattered parishes of the North than in the more compact parishes that were common in the arable parts of the South.[16]

As for cultural forms associated with different counties, the huge proliferation of county folklore studies is sufficient evidence of their frequency. Songs and stories, myths and legends: the collection of information about such local customs has occupied successive generations of folklorists ever since they began the 'discovery of the people' in the eighteenth century.[17] Some of the county customs are of course connected with the economies of particular regions, like those of the Forest of Dean miners or the Cheshire marlers. The marlers used to elect a 'lord of the pit', whose job it was to solicit donations from neighbouring landlords, after which the marlers would form a ring, holding hands and chanting in chorus the names of the benefactors and the amounts given. The Cornish tinners, on Carew's showing, do not seem to have had any specific rituals of their own, but they had plenty of spare time, which they employed at 'quoits, kayles [skittles], or such idle exercises'. They were also famous for their wrestling.[18]

Another way of studying local cultural differences is to look for regions which are smaller than huge areas like the North or East Anglia, but which have an identifiable territorial unity, either because of topography or economic activity, or both: the sort of regional unit that in France is called the *pays*. The *pays* is not always easy to define, and often splits counties or spans county boundaries, but some historians regard it as the most useful unit for the study of localities.[19] Examples come quickly to mind: the Weald and the Fens are obvious ones. Both of these regions are easily recognisable as geographical units, and there are many other smaller regions that have a distinctive topographical and (possibly) cultural identity: ranges of hills like the Cotswolds and the Mendips, for example, or smaller areas of fenland like the Somerset levels. Some of these regions certainly had their own distinctive culture, though in others it may have been artificially constructed or reinvented – which was perhaps the case with the famous Cotswold Games, founded by Robert Dover in 1612.[20]

One offshoot of the *pays* as a unit of study is the familiar arable–pasture division, about which I have written a good deal elsewhere. The standard hypothesis derived from this is that the compact, densely settled parishes of the sheep–corn regions of southern England (one kind of *pays*), with their open-field agricultural systems, tight manorial structures and other traditions of communal action, were likely to generate a more collectivist culture than the scattered, individualistic parishes that were the rule in a different kind of *pays*, such as the pasturelands of north Wiltshire or west Dorset. These latter were still communities, and had strong traditions of social action, but such action was likely to take more structured forms than the corresponding culture of the arable villages. In the southwestern counties at any rate, cultural forms such as church ales and maypoles survived longer in the sheep–corn regions and in other culturally traditional regions such as Blackmoor Vale than they did in the wood–pasture areas of north Somerset and Wiltshire. These patterns of cultural survival alert us to important features of the contrasting cultures of the respective regions.[21]

This or any other such typology inevitably greatly oversimplifies some bafflingly complex realities, and anyone who tries to fit particular villages or regions into this scheme quickly discovers how many exceptions there are to even the simplest generalisation. Far too many regions or individual parishes insist on being neither arable nor pasture – or insist on being both – far too many have to be put into other categories such as fens or hill pasture. Yet for many parts of England the *pays*, particularly in the form of the arable–pasture polarity, remains a useful conceptual model.

Much of the localism of popular culture does not need such broad, general theories to explain it. Perambulations survived in places where economic and social circumstances made it especially important for people to keep on defining the territorial limits of their parishes (because of the absence of adequate written evidence), and possible to do so (because of the absence of manmade barriers such as hedges, ditches and walls). Places with particularly strong local myths and legends naturally tried to hold on to the relics connected with them, as happened at Glastonbury with the Holy Thorn, planted by Joseph of Arimathea after the crucifixion, so the story went, from which the townspeople cut slips when it was chopped down by soldiers during the Civil War. The veneration of such relics was probably even more common in remote areas such as rural Wales, if Protestant complaints of superstitious abuses in the early seventeenth century are to be believed.[22] Ancient victories, real or mythical, still provided pretexts for celebration, for example the midsummer procession at Burford featuring a dragon and giants, in honour of a nearby West Saxon success against the Mercians in the year 750. Other ancient happenings might suggest more practical reasons for an annual festival, as was the case with the garland ceremony at Long Newnton, near Malmesbury, which commemorated the Anglo-Saxon King Athelstan's grant of a common to the village.[23] And local customs celebrating more recent events such as civil war battles and sieges do not need much explaining. Taunton and Lyme Regis both held annual exercises commemorating the arrival of relieving armies during the Civil War: in the case of Taunton the 11 May celebrations provided a Puritan substitute for the ungodly May Day festivities, and they continued well into the eighteenth century. On the other side, for almost a century after 1660 royalist Bruton used to ring the church bells every St Mathias's Eve, to commemorate a 1642 skirmish in which the townsmen defeated their roundhead neighbours, the hated Batcombites.[24]

Pride in local victories is an obvious explanation for some local rituals. But many other customs, even ones that are quite regionally widespread, are much easier to describe than to explain. Keith Thomas's 'barring-out' ritual is not the only puzzling manifestation of the cultural divide between North and South. Why were unruly, verbally violent women – scolds – subjected to different forms of punishment in the northern counties? The brank, or scold's bridle, was certainly not unknown in the South, but it was far more common in the counties north of the Trent; correspondingly, although some northern parishes had ducking-stools, they were more characteristic of the South. Perhaps ducking was thought particularly inhumane in the frigid north, but we know enough about the English climate not to be too dewy-eyed about it in more southern parts. Even the censorious Puritan magistrates of Dorchester once postponed a 'plouncing' (to use their onomatopoeic local term) until the weather was warmer. And it is hard to see how anyone could regard the sadistic and humiliating scold's bridle as preferable to a ducking. There must be other reasons besides a supposed northern concern for the health of scolding women for this regional difference in forms of punishment.[25]

Historians have suggested a variety of reasons for the cultural differences between English regions. One possible explanation for some of them is religion. As we have already noted, traditional cultural forms – rushbearings, religious plays and processional rituals, for example – survived longest in the least Protestant areas of the country. This pattern of survival is evident in Catholic enclaves like that on the Wiltshire–Dorset border, and in parts of Yorkshire as well as Lancashire. Richard Shanne, the Methley yeoman who recorded the rich, ancient culture of his Yorkshire parish, was himself a papist. But to say this is simply to push the need for explanation one stage further, for we still have to ask *why* Catholicism was so resilient and so important an element in the culture of these districts. Suggestions that the cultural differences of north and south Wiltshire can be explained as the products of the stronger 'Puritan' presence in the North encounter the same difficulty: *why* was north Wiltshire more Puritan? Religion is part – a very important part – of culture; but differences in religious loyalties need to be explained just as much as any other aspect of the subject.

Another possible explanation of these local cultural contrasts is the survival of age-old national or ethnic traditions – Celtic in Wales and parts of western England, Jutish in Kent and Sussex, for example. Now there can be no doubt that language and nationality made Welsh culture very different from English, and some historians claim to have identified symptoms of alleged Celtic survival even in parts of England. Settlement patterns, which almost certainly affect culture, in some areas date back to Celtic times. Alan Everitt suggests that this may account for the strikingly dispersed pattern of settlement in parts of Kent, for example.[26] Such ethnic traditions, slowly mediated over time, may have had an impact on such things as inheritance customs, though whether the practice of gavelkind (equal division of estates among heirs) can be attributed to the fact that Kent was originally settled by Jutes or Frisians remains an open question. If so, how do we explain the existence of similar practices of partible inheritance in other places with no known Jutish influence? An alternative possibility, it has been suggested, is that partible inheritance was adopted naturally in sparsely populated areas, where subsistence was easy because of plentiful fish or other conveniently accessible natural resources.[27] The Isle of Portland had gavelkind, and also some rather unusual marriage customs: for example, couples never married until the woman was pregnant, this being a sign that God approved of their union.[28] The obvious question is why customs like this survived more tenaciously in one region than in another. There may well have been other forces at work besides local ethnic and historical traditions.

It is thus much easier to formulate questions about popular culture than to answer them. There are innumerable possible avenues for further exploration of the subject – far more than can be satisfactorily discussed in an essay of this length. Let us therefore choose one topic for a case study: the distribution of rural sports in the early modern period. We can take our pick from many different sports, some with familiar names, such as football and cricket (though we should not be misled into thinking that they were the same games as their modern counterparts), others with less familiar ones, such as fives and stoolball. What can we learn from their geographical distribution?

The most popular plebeian sport in early modern England was football. It was played in so many parts of England, and in so many different forms, that it is dangerous to generalise about it. Broadly speaking, two different kinds of football can be distinguished. The football played in much of the midlands and southern England was a communal, collectivist game, with little resemblance to the more formal codes that developed into soccer and rugby in the nineteenth century. Any number could play (the village team usually consisted of all the able-bodied young men who lived there), there were no identifiable positions, and the playing area was the entire open space between the two competing villages. This kind of football provided a particularly effective bonding mechanism for young males, a shared experience of violence, in which injuries were marks of honour, and either victory or defeat could leave the participants with inspiring memories of collective action. Its collaborative, communal structure reflected the social and economic organisation of the open-field arable villages in which cooperative, semi-collective agriculture was the norm, and people were not very inclined to play sharply distinguished individual roles or pursue their own economic self-interest at the expense of the community. We might therefore expect to find that football would be especially popular in areas such as the Wiltshire and Dorset downlands, with their nucleated villages and sheep–corn economies, and this is indeed what we do find. But it was played in town as well as country – Shrove Tuesday was a popular date for urban contests – in arable and pasture regions alike. This type of football well expressed the culture of the pre-industrial community, affirming local identity through legitimised expressive violence.[29]

The other kind of football was more structured. There were numerous local variants, of which camp-ball, played throughout East Anglia, is the best known. Camp-ball was played by limited (and equal) numbers of players on each side, and it had recognisable rules. It may well be that this formal character reflects the more developed economy and more structured society of the eastern counties, compared with the midland and western regions in which ordinary football was played. Some curious patterns are obvious. Football was apparently less popular in some of the northern pasturelands, in the vales at any rate, than in the Pennine hill country. It was less commonly played – and less violently – in lowland Cheshire than in the Lancashire hills where, the historian of Cheshire tells us, 'township plays against township, with irons fixed in front of their heavy clogs'. Lest we suppose that this kind of savagery was necessarily a feature of hill countries we might note that in the eastern plains there was a form of camp-ball known as 'savage camp' in which kicking and many other kinds of brutality were permitted. Fatalities in all kinds of football were frequent.[30]

The Cornish variant of football was called hurling, and it too had some interesting features. The antiquary Richard Carew distinguishes between two different forms of hurling, associating each with a different part of the duchy: 'throwing of the ball . . . to goals' in eastern Cornwall, and throwing 'to the country' in the western parts. The eastern form was a highly structured game, with well-defined and elaborate rules. As in camp-ball, there were equal numbers of players on each side; the game was played on a restricted field with carefully marked out goals; forward passing was not allowed; and each player had to mark a corresponding one on the other side. It sounds much like rugby, and may help to explain Cornwall's modern excellence in that sport – though we might also wonder if the equally strong local tradition of wrestling may have something to do with that. At all events, hurling in eastern Cornwall was an elaborately structured game, in which every player had his own individual role. The western variant, on the other hand, was much more like the folk football that was popular over so much of England. It was more 'diffuse' and violent, Carew tells us, with virtually no rules. Like football, it was a contest between whole parishes or even groups of parishes, the goals were houses or landmarks miles apart, and any number could play. Carew has a famous description of the players returning home 'as from a pitched battle, with bloody pates, bones broken and out of joint, and such bruises as serve to shorten their days'. Yet, says Carew, 'all is good play, and never attorney nor coroner troubled for the matter': the bonding mechanism worked, in other words. The more structured eastern game no doubt fulfilled some of the same functions, but its rules and prescribed limits were more appropriate to a community in which the inhabitants took on distinct social and economic roles, or were at least more conscious of doing so.[31]

Carew's description of the two kinds of hurling might suggest that perhaps western Cornwall had a different pattern of settlement, or still retained older forms of agricultural organisation compared with those in the eastern parishes of the county. But that does not seem to have been the case: there were few nucleated villages in either area, and the enclosure of the relatively few surviving common fields seems to have been going ahead in all the inland regions of Cornwall during the sixteenth century. The only obvious difference between the two regions is that the agriculture of eastern Cornwall was more advanced, more market-oriented, than was the case in the west. The differences between the two kinds of hurling might suggest, therefore, that in Cornwall it was the level of economic development, rather than the settlement pattern or the mode of land-use, that determined the two local cultures.[32]

The two kinds of football offer some help to us in our search for regional cultural patterns. There other sports whose localism at first sight seems suggestive, like the one traditionally played on Palm Sunday with a ball and sticks on Cley Hill near Warminster in Wiltshire, and which seems to have been accompanied by other kinds of childish fun. (According to a local antiquary, the villagers of Corsley used to climb the hill and 'divert themselves with tumbling and rolling from top to bottom'.) But the absence of detailed descriptions of these customs makes it impossible to generalise about them. Other regional sports, like the famous bull-runnings at Stamford and Tutbury, are better known, but limited to so few places that no regional conclusions can be drawn from them either.[33]

A more widespread sport, with a strongly regional flavour, was fives – a primitive version of squash. It was one of several games resembling tennis; since tennis was played mainly by members of the aristocracy it is the popular variant, fives, that naturally concerns us. The central feature of fives was the bouncing of a ball off a large stone wall, and since in this period the only walls that were large enough tended to be the walls of churches, fives-playing in churchyards was common. It seems to have been especially popular in the western counties in the early seventeenth century, but we usually hear about it only when the players get into trouble for desecrating the sabbath or breaking windows in the church.[34] Fives was particularly strong in southeast Somerset, which in later times was the heartland of the game and may already have been so before 1600. When Queen Elizabeth was entertained by the Earl of Hertford at Elvetham in Hampshire in 1591, ten of the Earl's servants demonstrated their skill at a game that sounds like an early variant of fives: all were from Somerset.[35]

By the eighteenth century numerous churches in southern and southeastern Somerset had been adapted to the fives-players' needs, or were being protected from the damage the game was causing. At Penselwood and North Brewham special shutters were made to prevent windows from being broken, and at Martock holes were gouged in the church walls to provide 'scoring boards or tallies'. Eventually, in 1758, after several earlier failures, the Martock churchwardens took strong action, paying workmen to dig a ditch across the 'fives place', and thus put an end to the constant 'swearing, quarrelling and fighting' that the game was causing in the churchyard. But it looks as if there was connivance in many places, as there had evidently been earlier at Martock. At Montacute some ornamental stonework at the base of the tower was deliberately cut away to provide a smooth surface for the players, which could hardly have been done without the approval of the minister or churchwardens. As late as 1813 one east Somerset parish (West Pennard) had a fives court built at the base of the church tower, but by now a combination of ecclesiastical distaste and the recognition by tavernkeepers that fives, like other sports, could be a source of profit to them, was moving the game out of the churchyards and into pub gardens. Publicans began to build fives walls (or 'towers' – the ecclesiastical influence is apparent both in the term and in the new structures' architecture) behind their hostelries. Virtually all the known examples are in southeast Somerset.[36]

Fives clearly had some connection with the culture of this area, though it is not easy to define that connection precisely. This was a region in which the old festive culture was especially resilient in the early seventeenth century, and in which the inhabitants showed a good deal of initiative in creating their own elaborate amusements. It was also pasture country, where people farmed as individuals rather than collectively, and this may explain the attraction of an individualistic sport of this kind. It is also arguable that fives was encouraged by the easy availability of the leather gloves that were used in the sport: there was a strong tanning industry in this area.[37]

Like tennis, fives was more of an individual than a team sport (the Elvetham reference is the only known one involving more than two people on a side), and it is harder to see social and cultural significance in individual sports than in team ones. Fortunately we have many different bat-and-ball games to choose from that were played by teams: stoolball and cricket, among others. They had different local rules, of varying complexity, but the crucial element was always the individual confrontation between batsman and bowler, hitter and pitcher. Let us start with the most popular variant in the early modern period, stoolball.

There were at least two kinds of stoolball, and most of the recorded references to the game are to the simpler form, in which the hand or a small paddle was used instead of the longer willow bat employed in the more serious Wiltshire mode. The simple form was little more than a children's game, played by boys and girls at village revels – Nicholas Breton nostalgically evokes a charming picture of young people 'playing at stoolball for a tansy and a banquet of curds and cream'. Like football, it was played all over the country. But the more serious kind of stoolball that John Aubrey describes, played by adults with a hard ball and known locally as 'stobball' or 'stopball', was confined to north Wiltshire and the adjoining counties. I have argued elsewhere that this kind of stoolball was an appropriate expression of the culture of the pastoral 'cheese country', reflecting as it did the individualism promoted by the relatively scattered rather than nucleated settlement pattern, the structure of agriculture – carried on in enclosed family farms rather than more collectively in the open fields – and the weak manorial control that accustomed the inhabitants to somewhat more self-government than was the rule in the more

firmly controlled arable parishes. Yet we should not exaggerate the
individualism. Stoolball players were still members of teams; their
parishes were still communities.[38]

Cricket originated in a different part of the country, but as a cultural phenomenon it was not essentially different. The game has
received an enormous amount of historical attention, much of it
antiquarian, statistical or sentimental.[39] But if we are careful about
chronology it is possible to get a reasonably clear idea of cricket's
geographical origins, and of the local culture which it expressed.
There are problems, of course. One is that by the later seventeenth century cricket was being taken up by members of the elite,
and once this happened its geographical distribution became
blurred, as the aristocracy participated in a national culture, not
one that was primarily local in scope. The Earl of Sussex attended
a match near Herstmonceux in 1677, the aristocratic Pelhams
were betting on cricket in Sussex at least by 1694, and the Duke of
Richmond – the first of a dynasty of enthusiastic cricketers – was
sponsoring a team in Sussex by 1702, rewarding them with brandy
after they had defeated Arundel in that year.[40] By the middle of the
eighteenth century Richmond, Dorset and other noblemen were
vigorously promoting the game, spreading it among their friends
and kinsmen, and professionalising it by employing many of the
best players from the lower classes.

All this aristocratic patronage notwithstanding, even in the second half of the eighteenth century cricket was still a people's
game, and its heartland was where it had always been: in the south-
eastern corner of England, in the 'forest counties' of Kent, Surrey
and Sussex – an area which needs to be expanded only a few miles
to the west to include the famous Hambledon club just over the
Hampshire–Sussex border. This is where most of the players came
from, and where before 1800 most of the matches took place,
though as the game became commercialised the better teams were
increasingly often lured to London. Can we be any more precise
than this about the geographical origins of the game? If we
refrain, as we ought, from etymological speculations and dubious
interpretations of Edward I's household accounts, medieval
stained glass windows or illuminated manuscripts, we find that the
first certain reference to cricket locates it at Guildford, Surrey,
around the middle of the sixteenth century. In 1598 John Derrick,
gentleman, aged 59, testified in a suit over a piece of land there

that when he was a boy at the Free School he and his schoolfellows
used to play cricket in the field in question, which was also used
for bear-baiting.[41]

In spite of this very early reference to cricket in Surrey, Kent and
Sussex probably have better claims to be the cradle of the sport.
Let us begin with Kent. A tithes case shows that it had been played
by teams near Chevening in 1610, and in 1629 the curate at Ruckinge, in the same county, was charged with playing on a Sunday
after evening prayer. Cricket was being played at Harbledown,
near Canterbury, before 1640, and in 1646 there was a game at
Coxheath (which long remained a popular venue for big matches)
on whose outcome a man from nearby Maidstone wagered six can-
dles. There had been cricket at Maidstone a few years earlier, a
local Puritan complained, along with morris dancing, cudgel playing, stoolball and other 'profane' behaviour on the sabbath day.[42]
As for Sussex, in 1622 a group of men at Boxgrove were prosecuted in the church courts for playing cricket on Sundays, for
breaking windows in the church (some big hitters, evidently) and
for nearly braining a small child with a bat. The players were all
local men, one of them the minister's servant, and two others
apparently sons of the churchwardens, who were accused of
'defending and maintaining them in it'. Cricket was being played
at Horsted Keynes in 1624 (a man was accidentally killed there),
and in 1647 a man at Selsey, a few miles south of Boxgrove, also
died from injuries inflicted by a cricket bat.[43] Most of this evidence
confirms that early cricket was a peasant game, though it also
shows that the local gentry (the gentry, it should be stressed, not
yet the aristocracy) often took part in their neighbours' recreations. The Ruckinge curate defended himself by saying that the
other players included 'persons of repute and fashion', while
among the participants in the Coxheath match were six local gentlemen, one of them a son of the Royalist political writer, Sir
Robert Filmer. But all these people were local gentry rooted in
their neighbourhoods, not remote aristocrats like Sussex and
Richmond later in the century.[44]

Almost all these early instances of cricket took place on the
boundary between the chalk downs and the adjacent wood–
pasture regions. Guildford, Chevening (just outside Sevenoaks,
which in the eighteenth century was to be another famous stronghold
of cricket) and Maidstone are scattered along the North Downs.

Boxgrove, a few miles northeast of Chichester, is on the edge of the South Downs. The next parish to the east is Eartham, birthplace of Richard Nyren, captain of the great Hambledon team of the 1760s and 1770s. Immediately east of Eartham is Slindon, which had an almost equally famous team in the generation before Hambledon's ascendency; its captain was John Newland, who was Nyren's uncle. Sussex historians who locate the cradle of cricket in the triangle of West Sussex bounded by Arundel, Chichester and Midhurst, are ignoring evidence for the equally early development of the game in Kent, but they are certainly right in claiming it as *one* of the cradles.[45]

Cricket, then, originated in the 'forest counties'. The area between the downs and the sea running west from Arundel to Chichester and beyond into Hampshire was originally one continuous tract of woodland. Much of it had been cleared by the seventeenth century, but Bere Forest in Hampshire survived, and Boxgrove was in the old forest of Arundel, of which traces remained. Herstmonceux, where cricket was played at least by the 1670s, is further east, in the valley between the hills of the Sussex Weald and the eastern end of the South Downs. 'The Dicker', another early cricketing site near Herstmonceux, was a surviving tract of woodland, part of Waldron Forest. Other early traces of cricket take us further into the Weald: to Horsted Keynes (1624), Cranbrook (1652) and Ruckinge at its eastern end. Harbledown is on the edge of Blean Forest, but also close to the downs. All this was still pasture country, and it was also a countryside with plentiful supplies of wood and skilled craftsmen to make the necessary implements of the game. So cricket appears to be a game that developed either in the Weald, or on the boundary between it or other wood–pasture and arable–downland regions. In the case of the Chevening match the evidence for this is more than speculative: the match is described as having been 'a cricketing between the Weald and the Upland'.[46]

The glorious days of the Hambledon club in the 1770s are too late to be used as absolutely conclusive evidence for the early history of cricket. But Hambledon's inhabitants seem to have been typical forest dwellers in their sturdy individualism and independence, and the village's geographical situation is almost paradigmatic. Hambledon stands in the shadow of the downs, just outside Bere Forest; but the matches took place up on the open downs, for

Broadhalfpenny was unenclosed sheep pasture.[47] More than ever it seems clear that cricket, like stoolball, was a sport that developed in wood–pasture regions; but it was played on the open chalk downlands, the most suitable terrain for a game that needed extensive open space, and for which the springy turf, closely cropped by the huge flocks of sheep, provided ideal playing conditions. The 'hard-ball' form of stoolball played in Wiltshire needed almost as much space as cricket, and equally well-cropped turf. John Aubrey tells us that on Colerne Down, a great site for stoolball contests, the turf was 'very fine, and the rock . . . within an inch and a half of the surface which gives the ball so quick a rebound'. This version of stoolball was played all along the south-eastern slopes of the Cotswolds; there is less evidence for it on the edge of the chalk country further south.[48]

The geographical distribution of cricket before it became a totally national sport confirms the game's forest–pasture roots. Besides the great teams at Slindon and Hambledon, with their aristocratic patrons and their matches at the Artillery Ground and White Conduit Fields in London, and their forays into Kent and Surrey, numerous other Kent and Sussex towns and villages had teams. In the first half of the eighteenth century there were matches in Sussex at Henfield, Steyning, Ifield Green, Newick and a score of such places; the game was part of the leisure scene for people of all classes, and matches provided convenient venues for electioneering and other kinds of social activity. In 1723 a passing nobleman watched a match in Kent between Tonbridge and Dartford, falling sufficiently for local propaganda to note that 'of all the people of England the Kentish folk are most renowned' for their cricket, adding that in Kent 'the men of Dartford lay claim to the greatest excellence'.[49]

The early history of cricket thus suggests some of the same conclusions as that of stoolball: bat-and-ball games do seem to express the individualism characteristic of the woodland or pasture community, even if cricketers often moved to the open downlands to find the best playing conditions. One qualification should be made, though; in Kent and Sussex the settlement pattern does not at first sight seem to have had much to do with it. Many of the villages in which early cricket was recorded, from Boxgrove to Slindon, appear to have been as nucleated as the downland villages of Wiltshire and Dorset in which football was more popular, though

Hambledon was a huge parish, in area one of the biggest in southern England.[50]

But why cricket in the southeast and stoolball (or 'stobball') in Wiltshire? Until the eighteenth century there may not, for all we know, have been much difference between the two sports,[51] but even if there was we have to allow something to chance. Once a game becomes popular it develops a momentum of its own, and I should be cautious about speculating as to whether there were other elements in the cultures of one area or the other that predisposed them to a particular form of the available bat-and-ball sports. It has been argued that cricket was originally a Celtic game, and that its early strength in counties such as Hampshire and Sussex can be attributed to some supposed Celtic survival there.[52] But this does not seem very plausible: if cricket was a Celtic sport, how do we explain its virtual invisibility in Wales in the early modern period? In the end cricket swamped all the other local variants, partly because the aristocracy took it up, thus giving it resources and national notoriety, but also because it was intrinsically a better game.

I suggested at the beginning of this essay that we should not stop at the forms, but should try to decode them to get at the culture they express. Having done so, I am inclined to a conclusion very similar to the one that I advanced in *Revel, Riot and Rebellion*, though I should now put less emphasis on settlement patterns as cultural determinants. Local culture is shaped in part by the nature of the economy, and the type of agriculture, as well as by tradition, custom and historical memory. The more individualistic the organisation of economic life, the more the culture is likely to reflect values emphasising individual, rather than collective, identity. We can go back to late medieval towns – to the Coventry so brilliantly described by Phythian-Adams, for example – to find elaborate plays and pageants expressing the corporate identity of distinct sections of the town such as guilds and confraternities, but even these offered great scope for the playing of individual roles. The Reformation wiped out the confraternities and their rich pageantry, and stressed instead the identity of the whole town on the one side, of the individual on the other.[53]

We should not dismiss the importance of chance in determining individual features of local culture: the influence of a minister or succession of ministers, as at Batcombe in Somerset, or of a powerful group of civic leaders, as at Dorchester. Why was the practice of giving children biblical-text christian names such as Joy-again and Turn-about so much more pronounced in some of the parishes of the Weald than elsewhere? Surely because of the influence of a handful of determined Puritan ministers.[54] Why were certain towns so resistant to Puritan cultural reformation? When Essex's army entered Thame in Oxfordshire in 1643, the soldiers smashed the cross, organ and popish images in the church and cut down the maypole, 'whereat the townsmen were extremely enraged', a Parliamentarian newsbook tell us, 'so well had the Cavaliers instructed them in popery'.[55] Why are these places so different? Why do certain complicated rituals survive in some places but not in others – the 'cuckoo king' at Mere in Wiltshire, the Haxey Hood ritual, with its team of twelve 'Boggons', in the Isle of Axholme?[56] The variegated details of the rituals can only be explained by the specific circumstances of their survival, in which chance and circumstance play a large, if indeterminate, part. But there may still have been general regional characteristics which predisposed people to transmit to their children and successors particular kinds of cultural traditions: in some areas ones emphasising collective communal action based on ancient custom and memory; in others more individualistic ones which reflect the nature of the region's economic development.

3. The Gendering of Popular Culture in Early Modern England

SUSAN DWYER AMUSSEN

Popular culture has been one of the most fruitful areas of study in social history. As readers of this volume are by now aware, the concept of popular culture is not without its problems: it is too easily reified, it easily becomes static and unified, and it suggests too sharp a divide between elite and popular. Historians have sometimes made popular culture seem more coherent than it really was. We need to restore the complications, by looking at the divisions and conflicts it expresses. One way to do this is to focus less on the exceptional – popular festivals, rituals and the like – and more on a broader conception of culture which emphasises the values and norms of ordinary people as expressed in the course of their lives.[1] Rather than being extraordinary, popular culture is everyday, and our task is to understand the 'webs of meaning' within which people lived and understood their lives.[2]

One of the central confusions of the use of 'popular culture' has been that its manifestations have become substitutes for the culture itself. At the same time, historians have often written about 'popular culture' as the exclusive domain of the common people, ignoring both what we know of elite engagement with it, and connections between popular and elite cultures. If instead of associating popular culture with its more dramatic manifestations we focus on the fabric and meanings of everyday life, we are no longer bound to a conception that ties it to one social group, though it will be shaped by social status. Furthermore, by its very nature, popular culture located within the everyday is plural, variable and multivalent. Although its general outlines will remain the same over much of England and over long stretches of time, aspects of popular culture will be specific to particular places, regions or times. It is vital that we use popular culture as an inclusive, not an exclusive, concept.

Popular culture is constructed at the intersection of ideology and experience. In popular culture, the theoretical pronouncements of theologians and statesmen about the nature of society and social relations confront the conditions of everyday life. Elite and popular cultures are not separate, and the theological, political and social ideas expressed in literate culture undoubtedly shaped the experience of all people. Yet the ideas of elite culture could not simply be applied to people's lives; they had to be shaped to fit local conditions. In this confrontation, not only is meaning given to events, but also theories are reshaped or refocused to reflect people's experience. If popular culture is created at the crossroads between theory and life, it becomes easier to understand not only the common themes in popular and elite culture, but also variations between them and – even more important – change in popular culture over time. This approach emphasises the multivalent and historical nature of popular culture.

To use this definition of popular culture for early modern England, we need to ask questions: how did people perceive the world? How did they perceive and judge each other? How were those perceptions and judgements expressed? To approach the study of popular culture through the study of the everyday is not to deny the importance of other aspects of or perspectives on popular culture: the popular rituals and festivities with which we are most familiar are often the points where the values of the everyday are most clearly expressed; popular literature helped communicate and shape ideological values. In the end, however, such dimensions of popular culture make no sense without the broader context of how the values and ideas they presented were lived out. This essay contributes to this much larger project by focusing on one aspect of popular culture – its relation to gender.

Popular culture played a critical role in sustaining and shaping gender relations in early modern society, just as it was in turn shaped by gender. While the treatises of learned commentators constructed a framework within which gender relations took place, that framework was modified and shifted in popular culture to conform more closely to people's perceived social needs. Not only are popular expectations enforced through informal means, but the violation of such expectations was a frequent cause of some of the best-known manifestations of popular culture (in the sense of festivities) – 'rough music'. Familiar as we are with the way women's subordination was sustained by popular rituals, we have a much fuzzier sense of how popular culture sustained the whole framework of gender relations – including but not exclusively patriarchy and women's subordination – in early modern England. Yet feminist scholarship has demonstrated that we cannot take gender for granted; we have come to see how both the conventional behaviour of women and men, and their experiences of sexuality are constructed in very different ways in different societies.[3] We must examine what people thought women and men in early modern England were like, how they expressed those ideas on a daily basis, and how they ensured that their neighbours and family did not transgress too far the boundaries of behaviour appropriate to their particular gender system.

It is not easy to provide answers to such questions; gender is such a basic category of human experience that people rarely articulate their ideas about it, and the formal statements by educated men provide only one side of the equation. Furthermore, cultural conceptions of gender are not fixed. Therefore, this essay will address the issue of the gendering of popular culture from two different and complementary perspectives. The first part will focus on concepts of gender expressed in ideas about women's relations with men, primarily in the context of sexuality and marriage. However, because gender affects all aspects of life, the second part will examine the ways in which the gendering of popular culture was reflected in one form of behaviour, violence. Violence is important not only for its ability to show the impact of gender on an apparently unrelated area of life, but also because of the role some feminist theorists have given to violence in sustaining the subordination of women. This dual approach will emphasise the pervasive impact of gender on popular culture in early modern England.

The core values of popular culture were profoundly misogynistic. This is manifest in the two central elements of gender ideology in early modern popular culture, both of which focused on women's behaviour in their relations with men. Women, and especially wives, should be subordinate to men; this was enforced by increasing legal disabilities for women. In addition, women were supposed to be chaste, engaging in sexual relationships only within marriage. However, it was also assumed that women – once initiated into sex – were sexually voracious, an idea that gained support from the prevalent belief that women had to have orgasms in order to conceive.[4] These ideas, with corresponding but less explicit ideas about men, form the scaffolding within which gender was constructed in early modern England. The gendering of other aspects of life drew on these core ideas.

Neither of these ideas was uncomplicated. For instance, what does subordination mean when the work of women was central to the household economy, as it was for most women? Or when the boundaries of women's and men's work were flexible, and a woman was expected to be able to do the work her husband did, and follow his business? Even the wealthiest men usually included their wife as one executor of their will, and most men made their wives sole executors. The ability of women to carry on their husbands' trades in the towns also reflects this sense of women's ability.[5] Women were expected to be able and intelligent co-managers of the household. Their abilities, like their bodies, were 'less' than those of men, but not profoundly different.[6] In this context, we need to talk about subordination in unfamiliar ways – as 'limited subordination'. Limited subordination creates tensions, tensions paralleling those created by the ways in which women's relationship to desire and sexuality was constructed. The combination of a demand for chastity and the assumption that women were incapable of it reinforced the need for subordination. By emphasising women's appetites, it also contributed to the image of women as witches, whose appetite – for love, goods or revenge – is out of control. Women were always difficult to control. While there was also considerable evidence that men were difficult to control, that was usually associated with drink, not gender.[7]

Subordination was the most commonly expressed of the ideas about the relation of women to men. It was constantly reiterated – in advice manuals, sermons and pamphlets, as well as in the speech and action of villagers themselves. Subordination, the pundits asserted, was necessary to ensure good order in the household; as Thomas Gataker remarked, someone in every relation had to be superior, and between women and men it was obvious that the man should hold authority.[8] Since the household in patriarchal political theory was compared to the state, order in it was of critical importance. But it was not only educated pundits who believed in the necessity and importance of women's subordination; most men and women agreed, though their interpretation of specific instances was not always the same.

The most explicit indication of popular attitudes towards the subordination of women to men is the ritual of the skimmington or other 'rough music' directed at women who beat their husbands. There was no similar ritual directed at men who beat their wives. These involved processions, of varying degrees of complexity, which re-enacted the original incident. The whole town might turn out, and women were certainly sometimes involved: in 1615 Alice Kemp told Faith Docking that 'If you beat cuckold your husband again about the horns, we will have a better riding than we had before.'[9] Yet some cases suggest ambivalence on the part of women about the need for a charivari. When Nicholas Rosyer was beaten by his wife, it was because he came home drunk – apparently not for the first time. The charivari which followed was planned entirely by men, and the evidence suggests that no women – or at least married women – were involved.[10]

Women's critical evaluation of whether behaviour deserved communal shaming is echoed in other evidence about the attitudes of women and men to subordination. Women and men attached very different meanings to the subordination of women to men. Men – not surprisingly – had a much broader sense of what was due to them from women than women did. Women, when asked in court about such things, used vague language: she never saw her 'commit or omit' anything due to her husband, or she gave him 'due care and respect', are the phrases employed by women to evade the definition of proper subordination. They were given as answers to questions, asked by men, which asserted that individual women had failed in their duty of obedience to their husbands. The vagueness of the language resists the definition of subordination, precisely where men wanted to define it more explicitly. Additionally, when women complained of defamation, the insults objected to were always sexual: they never focused on subordination. Women sought to avoid specifying the boundaries of subordination; they wanted it left open, though they always acknowledged its necessity.[11] At the same time, men – in court cases, theoretical writings and even popular literature – repeatedly tried to fix the nature of women's subordination.

If we understand that popular culture is constructed in the intersection of experience and ideology, this difference is not surprising. Women's lives gave them an appreciation of the complexities of their own subordination. Most production in early modern England was based on the household (including servants and apprentices) as the economic unit, and depended on the labour of wives as well as husbands. Remarriage rates provide a suggestion of the importance of women: widowers appear to have remarried as much as twice as often as did widows, and even those widows who did remarry took at least 50 per cent longer to do so. Furthermore, women remarried less and less often over the period.[12] The remarriage rates simultaneously acknowledge women's importance and suggest their interchangeability. Women appear to have been aware of the tensions and contradictions between subordination and their work. How was a woman supposed to be effective in ordering her servants around or bargaining at the market one moment, and a meek, obedient woman the next? As a result, women limited subordination as much as possible, although men had no reason to follow suit.

Women's role in the household as wives, and their frequent involvement in the overall economic production of the household, does not imply equality. While women's subordination was limited, they were far from equal to men. Women were expected to be – and were – as able as men in managing household affairs. But they had no access to formal political power, little access to the law and very few opportunities for formal occupational training. Women usually supported whatever occupation their husband had; pauper girls were frequently apprenticed in 'housewifery', 'husbandry' or other skilled, but unspecialised, female tasks.[13] They were trained for the domestic work all women did, and the rest they learned on the job. Their capabilities were respected, but they were not *equal* to those of men. And when they were paid for their work, it was always at a lower rate than men; our current pay differentials are nothing new.[14] Women's inequality was rooted in training and education, law, and structures of value.

Everything said so far applies primarily to married women, and especially women married to men who were householders. There were, of course, variations: women's subordination might be more limited in households involved with dairying, and the dynamics of subordination would also differ in labourers' households depending on whether husbands and wives worked at the same or different tasks; subordination might be more easily enforced for wealthy women who played a less active role in production. Yet the variations existed within the same framework, and – since most people thought about gender in terms of husbands and wives – it is a natural starting point. But what about other women? Single women were certainly important numerically, as our current estimates are that at least 10 per cent of all women never married.[15] But single women were rarely independent. Most had to work, and were expected to live in someone else's household as a servant. This was legally required of unmarried women and men between the ages of 15 and 45 who had no property, and it was enforced at least as often, if not more often, for women as for men. Single women living outside the boundaries of the household made early modern authorities (men) profoundly nervous. The lack of independence of single women was also shaped by inheritance practices: few women were left sufficient property, especially land, to live independently. Even women from gentry families often had to live in the households of their relatives.[16] As a result, single women were often more firmly subordinated than were married women – if not to a father, to a master and mistress. They had less of a public, recognised role than married women, and their contributions were seen as less significant. And like married women, single women were interchangeable.

If independence and autonomy were denied to single women, what about widows? After all, there are some truly extraordinary elite widows in the early modern period – Bess of Hardwick, Lady Anne Clifford (who is rarely referred to by her married name) and Lady Rachel Russell, among others. They managed their property with flair and success. But such widows were almost as rare as their social status. Although the widows of most men with land were given a life interest in it, they lacked the flexibility given by ownership. Many had very small amounts of property in any case. Their knowledge of the business of the household was not always enough. Widows of London tradesmen remarried more rapidly and more frequently than did other widows; not only did their shops make them desirable partners to men, but it was easier to run a shop with two adults.[17] In Abingdon, for similar reasons, widows of millers and innkeepers remarried more often than others: neither mills nor inns were designed to be run by one person.[18] Independence was not easy or necessarily desirable in an economy structured around the household. Some widows may have had the property, connections, desire and ability to construct an independent life for themselves, but for many independence meant poverty, not success: widows had to replace their husband's labour or wages. For labouring women, these problems were augmented by discriminatory wages. Wherever we look, widows constitute a disproportionate number of the neediest of the poor.[19] Widows were worthy recipients of charity because of both ideology (especially the biblical injunctions to care for widows and orphans) and real necessity.

As we examine subordination, we confront a series of paradoxes. Subordination was universally agreed to be crucial, but it was limited, so its terms and boundaries were contested. Though subordinate, women were generally assumed to be as capable as their husbands, and familiar with their husbands' work. At the same time, women were not equal: whatever their abilities, they had few political rights, limited rights at law and little access to formal education. Such formal disabilities reinforced ideas of subordination, and placed important limits on the ability of women to act independently.

The tension between subordination, work and the structure of inequality helps to explain how conceptions of gender in popular culture could change: women's freedom to contest the nature of their subordination was based on their role within the household. In 1724, Mary Hubard was criticised by other women for not following her husband to his 'country house', although her health would have permitted it. The country house suggests the degree of wealth, while other evidence suggests that Mary did not play an active role in running her household. As prosperous women like Mary Hubard played an increasingly limited (and less visible) role in the family economy in the eighteenth century, subordination was less readily resisted. Criticism like that of Mary Hubard, which accepts broad interpretations of subordination for other women, first appear in the early part of the eighteenth century, directed at women from prosperous families.[20] The interplay between subordination, work and inequality balanced in a very particular way in early modern England; as that balance changed, so necessarily did the cultural conception of gender.

If the subordination of women to men – or at least its extent – was sometimes contested, the importance of chastity, the second central pillar of the gender system, was not.[21] Chastity was a less flexible demand on women than was subordination, and it was at least assumed that the presence or absence of chastity was easy to determine. Unmarried women and men were closely observed by neighbours; if sexual activity was suspected, they could then be pressured to marry. If marriage was refused, at least neighbours would know who was responsible for any child that was born. Neighbours were critical observers, and did not always believe paternity accusations. When Agnes Haddon of Neatishead, Norfolk, was pregnant, her neighbours refused to believe that anyone other than John Brende, Gent., was the father of the child: his 'familiarity' with her had been 'very offensive unto the said neighbours ... and ministered cause of suspicion unto them of their incontinent living together.'[22]

Chastity was also expected within marriage, and the method of detection was the same – observation. Any unusual behaviour was questioned. If a woman was with a man other than her husband at unusual times or places, she was suspect: when Robert Armiger and Margaret Mollett of Thurton (both of whom were married) travelled together to Loddon on foot, and rode (with Margaret up behind Robert) to Norwich, neighbours were 'much grieved and offended', and assumed that their relationship was sexual.[23] Henry Chosell of Aylsham was suspected of 'living incontinently' with Henry Keymer's wife because she was seen 'many and sundry times as well in winter as in summer time late in the evening go to and come from the said Chosell his chamber ... when it had been more meet or fit for her to have been at home at her own house in her husband's company.'[24]

Accusations of adultery were evaluated by the context in which they were made and by the characters of accuser and accused. When Robert Vyneor of Denton was accused of adultery with Anne Plowman by his wife when they 'were at angry words together', he was duly presented to the ecclesiastical courts, but no one believed the accusation. Both Vyneor and Plowman were honest, among the best people in Denton, and the accusation had been made in anger. Had there been any truth to the accusation, there would have been other evidence.[25] Previous reputation was crucial in assessing accusations: Thomas Everett of Skeyton,

Norfolk, was 'a person well known to us to be of sober life and conversation, and a constant hearer of divine service and sermons
upon Sundays', so that when Sara Bate, who had already borne
two illegitimate children, accused him of adultery, she was not
believed.[26] Allegations of misconduct were carefully controlled.

Although all women were watched for signs of sexual misconduct, the chastity of widows was especially suspect. If women were
sexually voracious, widows, who had no man to meet their needs
legitimately, were particularly so. As a result, any intimacy was suspicious: when Edmund Rackulver remained as a servant with
Katherine Parker of Hellesdon, Norfolk, they were presented to
the church courts for incontinent living – though all the witnesses
agreed that Parker was 'a woman of good and honest report and
name', and that their relationship was that of mistress and servant.[27] The Woodalling clergyman Henry Atkyns lodged with
widow Mary Knowles; he told many people that she was 'familiar'
with Thomas Selfe, 'that he did fear the worst and that if any thing
happened otherwise than well it should be laid to him he being a
young man and lived in the house with her.' Such allegations
would, he hoped, avoid a paternity accusation should Knowles
become pregnant.[28] Some manors even had 'jocular' shaming rituals directed only at widows who were unchaste.[29] Because chastity
was thought to be impossible for widows, they had to prove their
chastity by conforming to standards of behaviour that were even
stricter than might have been expected. The tensions within cultural ideas of gender provided the framework for interpreting
behaviour.

Ideas about women's sexual appetites affected not only ideas
directly relevant to sexual behaviour, but also understandings of
witchcraft. Few of the witchcraft confessions in England include
the accounts of sexual orgies found in Continental sources: for the
purposes of English law, they were irrelevant. Yet – as on the Continent – most of those accused of witchcraft were women. Why? Historians have advanced a wide range of reasons, including the
theological belief in the sinfulness of Eve, the poverty of older
women, the psychodynamics of family life, the drive for ideological
conformity and conflicts about the nature of women's role.
Although each of these explains aspects of the witch hunts, none
of them adequately address why it was *witchcraft* that women were
accused of. The focus on witchcraft is less mysterious in the

context of the conceptions of women's sexuality and witchcraft in popular culture. If women's excessive sexual appetite is symptomatic of all appetites, their connection to witchcraft is logical. Witches were usually thought to be punishing those who had offended them by not giving them what they wanted: they had too great an appetite for money, food, love or even quarrels. It was an easy move from sexual to other forms of excess.[30] Witchcraft was imbedded in popular conceptions of gender.

Women's sexual appetite caused social problems. This affected the judgement of sexual misconduct, which was wrong for both women and men. Everyone used defamation suits to defend themselves against accusations of fornication or adultery. However, women who were guilty of fornication or adultery caused problems men did not – they might bear an illegitimate child, likely to be chargeable to the parish and an offence to good order. Those who were married simultaneously challenged the authority of their husbands and wreaked havoc with ideas of family property: one husband complained 'that he had paid for eleven church goings [the thanksgiving after childbirth], but God knew who was the father of his children.'[31] The concern with paternity was especially important with male children; when Nathaniel Stallworthy's wife had a child, a witness alleged that 'if it had been a boy it should have been Mr. Harman's man's, but being a girl the said Nathaniel Stallworthy was fain to father it.'[32] The cuckold was a two-fold figure of fun in popular culture: he could not control his wife, and he might be raising other men's children. Thus popular cultural attitudes are formed by the intersection of the ideological concerns with chastity and family property on the one hand, and the practical concerns of communities on the other.

Attitudes towards sexual misconduct by women and men reflected differences of degree, not kind. It was bad for the reputations of both women and men to be involved in fornication or adultery; men went to great lengths to avoid accusations of paternity for just this reason.[33] But such accusations were more important for women: women who bore bastards were probably less likely to get married than were other women; their social marginality might lead them into quasi-prostitution.[34] There is no evidence that fathering a bastard had a comparable effect on men. Women who cuckolded their husbands – and their cuckolded husbands – were the targets of charivari; there is no comparable ritual to shame men who were guilty of adultery. Desired behaviour was enforced by both practical consequences and community sanctions. Thus the meaning of chastity was gendered: popular culture was gendered as it enforced conceptions of gender.

The severity of popular penalties against women who were guilty of fornication and adultery were the result not only of the social consequences of these misdemeanours, but also of the difficulties of enforcing women's subordination to their husbands. The meaning of obedience and subordination was contested by women. The idea of chastity was not contested, and women willingly condemned infidelity in other women. As a result, attention that was displaced from obedience focused on chastity. Chastity was the female virtue that could be determined with some certainty, and its role in popular culture and popular conceptions of gender took on correspondingly greater weight.

Although the image of the sexually voracious woman was the dominant one in early modern popular culture, it had always coexisted with a popular vision of the pure, virtuous (and even naive) maiden. Romantic ballads of the period include both conceptions. Yet by the middle of the eighteenth century, the image of the lustful woman was losing much of its currency to her pure and chaste sister. Henry Fielding's *Joseph Andrews* offers an extended debate on the subject of women's sexuality, with Lady Booby representing the lustful woman and Fanny as her virtuous counterpart – and including a cameo appearance by Joseph's sister, the ultimate pure heroine of the period, Richardson's *Pamela*. For Fielding, Fanny is the true woman, Lady Booby the grotesque caricature.[35] In earlier times people had also wanted chastity in women, but they did not think it was easy or natural.

The reason for this change in attitudes is not clear. But it fits in with several other changes in attitudes to sexuality. The first is the increasing emphasis on sexuality as part of the private world of families – controlled, of course, by men. The separation of the public and the private increasingly deprived women's lives of political, public consequences – thus making sexual aggression on women's part seem less imaginable. At the same time, there were new developments in the technology of contraception. Before the late seventeenth century, the only widely available form of birth control (aside from *coitus interruptus)* was that provided by abortifacient herbs – knowledge that was shared by many women, and generally controlled by them. In the late seventeenth century, condoms began to be available, at least in London. Their use – first among the London prostitutes – made it much easier to deny women's power and control over sexuality and fertility.[36]

Aspects of gender identity which relate specifically to marriage, sexuality and relations between women and men are the obvious places to begin an examination of the gendering of popular culture. But they cannot be the end of the discussion. Because gender affects all aspects of life, we need to look at behaviour less directly tied to women's sexual nature. It is now time to turn to the other focus of this essay, how the study of violence illuminates cultural conceptions of gender. What is the relationship of women and men to violence? Were women and men violent in different situations? When were they victims of violence? And from whom?

Violence is particularly important because of the role many theorists have assigned to it in maintaining the subordination of women. They have seen the 'interconnection of sexuality, aggression and violence' as central to definitions of masculinity; such definitions of masculinity are complemented by conceptions of femininity which defined women as more vulnerable to attack and (paradoxically) unsafe except in the presence of men. Some versions of this theory suggest that aggression and weakness are natural attributes of male and female bodies, but it is increasingly evident that the character of violence is shaped by women's and men's socially constructed gender identity; thus violence needs to be historicised and contextualised. Violence is of crucial importance to our understanding of gender both inside and outside the family.[37]

Violence in English society was not wrong in and of itself. The legitimacy of violence was contingent, depending on the situation in which it took place and the relationship between those who engaged in it. Because of their subordination, women generally had less access to the legitimate use of violence than men; but men's access to violence as a legitimate tool in relations with other men was also dependent on social status. In theory, violence was legitimate from the state or its representatives against wrongdoers, by a husband against his erring wife, or from a master/mistress to servants, or from parents to wayward children. In other words, violence was legitimate as a form of correction in hierarchical social relations. As is so often the case in popular culture, the reality was more complicated; tacit legitimacy was accorded to a range of violent interactions that conformed to the model of correction and discipline.[38]

To begin with, we must get rid of any idea that women are naturally non-violent. Women used violence, although usually in different circumstances and ways than did men. Women might fall out with each other at the market, or on the way to church, or in other public settings; men most often fought on occasions involving drinking. When they fought, women were much less likely than men to be carrying weapons, so fights between women were much less likely than those between men to result in death. This means that records of women's violence are much sparser than those of men's: assault was less likely to get prosecuted (and much less likely to leave depositions) than was murder. Within the family, both women and men could use violence, against each other and, more often, against their children. While women accounted for only 7 per cent of the accused in non-familial murders, they made up 42 per cent of the accused in familial cases; about half of the victims were children, one-third spouses. Wives outnumbered husbands as victims by about two to one.[39]

Some sense of these differences can be gained from the petitions that communities offered to the justices of the peace complaining of the behaviour of unruly villagers. Sixty-two such petitions survive in the Norfolk Quarter Sessions records of the early modern period. Of these, six are directed against women, and a further five are directed against a husband and wife together.[40] The range of complaints against women is much the same as that of those against men: they abused their neighbours, were too willing to fight, disrupted economic relations, or ran unlicensed or disorderly alehouses. Catherine, wife of Symond Parsons of Sheringham, like many men, 'daily stir[red] up sedition and strife betwixt man and wife and betwixt neighbour and neighbour so that neighbours cannot live peaceably by her.' She beat an old man with a whip, and two boys so severely they were afraid to meet with her in the street, and she harboured suspicious people in her house.[41] Couples operated together to make life difficult for their neighbours: when Richard Cutter and his wife Frances were found cutting other people's wood, Frances would allege that she had been ravished in order to undermine the theft accusation.[42] Grace, the wife of Christopher Ward of Barton Bendish, assaulted Mr Lynghook with a pitchfork during a property dispute, while her husband stood by ready to stone him should his wife get hurt![43] The small number of complaints against women makes statistical analysis meaningless. Women might be in trouble for doing the same things men did, but women were more likely to offend as part of a disorderly couple or in ways that were particularly associated with women – such as witchcraft. Two petitions suggest witchcraft: Robert Greenfield alleged that since he had quarrelled with Joan Shilling, he had suffered a strange loss of cattle from diseases he had never seen before.[44] Amea, the wife of Richard Winter, and her daughters Edina and Margaret were obviously medically skilled, but some of their Grimston neighbours worried that illnesses followed quarrels with them, illnesses cured when a frog was burnt in a fire.[45] Women were never accused of abusing their official positions (they did not hold office) or of mistreating their families – a complaint which occurs in more than 20 per cent of the petitions against men. And only one woman was accused of offences relating to drink – as opposed to more than one-third (38.7 per cent) of the men.

Thus the large area of overlap between petitions against men and those against women hides significant differences. First, the comparative rarity of petitions against women suggests that their misconduct was less often a threat to social order.[46] Disorderly women were expected to be disciplined by their husbands, so that their neighbours rarely had to be involved. And what constituted trouble from women was significant; it was more serious when women attacked men than when they attacked other women. Only four of the petitions against women mention violent assaults, but three of those mention assaults on men with a weapon. Such assaults were 'insufferable', neighbours remarked of the behaviour of Mathye, wife of Robert Cambridge, who had 'such a mankind and furious disposition that she will challenge men to fight with them.' On one occasion she had rammed a pitchfork into Henry Harwick's body.[47] The focus was her inappropriate behaviour, not her opponent's shame in being attacked by a woman. Petitions are a very crude source for analysing behaviour, but they do point us to three areas of gender difference: witchcraft, drink and violence within the family. We will end with a brief look at each of these.

Witchcraft, I have argued, was associated with women in part because of the link made between women and uncontrollable desire. The relations of women and men to violence are also important in explaining the expectation that witches were women. Witchcraft is a crime of violence, but the violence is indirect: one person manipulates unseen powers to cause another person harm. That harm might take the form of the illness, laming or death of the victim or a member of the victim's family, or of the victim's livestock.[48] So there is violence. But women were thought more likely to use this form of violence than men; their association with such indirect methods suggests that they were expected to have less access to direct violence than men. The cursing and mumbling which were so often taken as signs of witchcraft were the responses of the impotent. Early modern England saw the abuse of language – both cursing and scolding – as peculiarly female behaviour.[49] As popular culture constructed and was shaped by conceptions of gender, women's weakness and their lack of access to other means – violent or not – of resolving problems or conflicts was embedded in it.

This difference in access to violence becomes even more evident when we look at brawls and drink. Men were much more likely to be involved in fights, particularly those involving drink. Although women frequented alehouses (though probably in declining numbers), it was among men that drink led to violence. Drinking played a role in the majority of brawls for which we have full descriptions. This is both because the alehouse was a central gathering place where many conversations, and therefore many quarrels between men, took place, and because of the effect of alcohol – however weak – on behaviour. One of the many reasons neighbours disliked alehouses was the frequency with which they were sites of brawls. However, brawls were not uncontrolled; onlookers sought to limit the impact of violence.[50]

The typical alehouse brawl followed a pattern that illuminates cultural attitudes to violence. When a quarrel began, some of the onlookers tried to make peace, but conflict eventually resurfaced and the combatants began to fight again. A typical brawl was one in a Leeds alehouse in 1642. Elizabeth Lovell, the alehousekeeper, reported that Nicholas Holmes was drinking with John Killingbeck when he asked Killingbeck for 2s. he owed him. Killingbeck did not object, but William Jackson did, and warned that Holmes might pick a fight. Lovell soon realised that Holmes was drunk, and asked him to go home, but Jackson took a cup and said 'If you will not come in and drink a cup I will not be friends with you', so Holmes returned. Within a quarter of an hour, Lovell heard a bench fall, and went to investigate; she found Holmes fallen on the floor and Killingbeck trying to pull Jackson off him. Jackson had already stabbed Holmes with his dagger, and Holmes soon died.[51] Here the double character of drink becomes clear: while it made Holmes and Jackson more combative, it was also the sign of friendship, and had Holmes left without drinking with Jackson, it would have been an insult, and might equally well have led to a quarrel. And, as was usually the case, the fight was dangerous because of the presence of weapons.

In this case, a woman was present as alehousekeeper; in many alehouse brawls women were present as spouses or companions of the combatants, as well as alehousekeepers. But the brawl itself was a male event; women were usually bystanders, not participants. Women were only occasionally involved in such fights: William Metcalf's wife hit an alehousekeeper's wife and boy when they refused to serve her more drink, and a general free-for-all followed, involving both Metcalfs and the alehousekeeper's entire household, until the Metcalfs were placed in the stocks.[52] John Hossell and Margaret Buck had an argument in the parlour of an alehouse in Ickleborough, but Buck left the room to be with her sister, Dey's wife, who was sick. Nothing more would have happened had Hossell not followed her into the sick-room, and they began to fight.[53] The absence of weapons in both these cases limited the damage that occurred.

Although there are exceptions, violence in the alehouse was a male activity. No one wanted such convivial gatherings to get out of hand, and it is striking how often a drinking companion intervened to try to stop violence. We do not know how often such intervention was successful, but the records of even those conflicts where it was unsuccessful suggest that there were rules and expectations for alehouse arguments.

If witchcraft involved women, and alehouse brawls men, domestic violence is the place where gendered expectations of both women and men are clear. On 5 November 1613, Richard

Hutchins of Stanton Bernard, Wiltshire, was 'somewhat out of order by reason of overmuch drink'. He and eight or nine of his friends wandered into the church of All Cannings, and he got into the minister's seat and began to speak:

> The twenty-first chapter of Maud Butcher and the seventh verse. Man love thy wife and thy wife will love thee, and if she will not do as thou wilt have her, take a staff and break her arms and her legs and she will forgive thee.[54]

Beyond its misogyny, Hutchins's impromptu scripture suggests a number of popular assumptions. First, that love between husband and wife was to be expected. Second, that it was perfectly legitimate for a husband to beat his wife. The third – and most surprising – is that violence is a way to make a wife love her husband.

The first two assumptions were commonplace; the third is not, and presumably represents a fantasy. Most evidence suggests that, more often than not, violence was destructive of love (or 'quiet') rather than constructive. Husbands were expected to 'correct' their wives, but the literature of the period – in both household manuals and legal treatises – was unclear as to the extent of the right of correction. Some commentators thought that husbands should never beat their wives, while others thought that in extreme cases (but not for 'those weaknesses which are incident even to virtuous women') it was allowable.[55] All observers and commentators put strict limits on the extent of the correction of a wife: it was not to threaten her health and safety; it was unacceptable if she were pregnant or in childbed; and it should not be unprovoked.

Such rules are, of course, somewhat vague; the woman who interrupted her neighbour saying that 'he was an ill man to beat his wife at that rate' certainly had an idea of what was appropriate, but it is impossible to understand precisely what it was. The servant who said that her mistress had no more reason to fear her husband than any other wife did also had a clear notion of the acceptable limits of violence, but again, the boundaries are imprecise.[56] Wives who complained of abuse often cite occasions when they were beaten when in childbed, expecting that to be considered more serious.[57] Neighbours frequently intervened in cases of domestic violence in order to protect women. They were most disturbed by unprovoked attacks on wives, but what constituted provocation could be open to debate.

Most of our accounts of violence are accounts of husbands who beat their wives, but there were also women who beat and even killed their husbands, although as we saw earlier, fewer wives killed husbands than husbands killed wives. Women who killed their husbands were guilty of petty treason, not murder.[58] Wives who beat their husbands were disturbing enough to merit a charivari to remind everyone that such behaviour was out of place. Thus domestic violence was engendered in popular culture: the more common form, men beating their wives, was less threatening than the rarer cases of women who beat their husbands; the disorder represented by such violence by women is connected to women's disorderly sexuality. Men's violence toward their wives could be legitimate; women's violence to their husbands never was. Whatever the act, it was more dangerous when done by women. People were more comfortable with women as victims than aggressors. Women could and did do the same things men did, but when they did, the actions carried different meanings.

As was the case with attitudes toward subordination and women's sexuality, there is some evidence of cultural change in the eighteenth century. The most visible change is that in the targets of English charivari from wives who beat their husbands to husbands who beat their wives.[59] Such a shift, which turns the focus to the dangers of women's victimisation rather than their threat to order, parallels the increasing focus on women as potential victims of predatory men, rather than as sexual predators on them. It also coincides with a greater separation – in ideological and to a lesser extent in practical terms – of the household from the neighbourhood, which made the intervention of neighbours in cases of domestic violence more difficult. Once again, we find popular culture changing as a result of changing conditions and ideas, and in ways that help explain the increasing emphasis on women's inferiority – not just their subordination – in society.

In some respects, the way popular culture constructed gender is unsurprising, and it offered no dramatic challenges to official doctrine. The focus on the place of popular culture at the intersection of ideology and material life enables us first to define a set of stresses – 'limited subordination' and chastity demanded of those with an insatiable sexual appetite. These tensions provided women with a limited freedom to move. By adding violence, we get a sharper sense of how subordination was enforced, and how (gradually) a notion of women's inferiority could develop in popular culture. Women used different kinds of violence, to different people, from that used by men. It was when women fought with men that they threatened order, not when they fought with other women. Women were more likely to use violence against other women, or indirectly, through witchcraft. They did not have access to the almost ritualised and quasi-legitimate combat of the alehouse brawl. When women used violence within the household, it was only legitimate when used as punishment of children or servants; there were no occasions when they could use violence against their husbands. The charivari evidence suggests that in the eighteenth century such women became unimaginable. And given the importance of violence as a form of power, women's more restricted access to it limited their access to power or even control over their own fate.

Ideas about gender were embedded throughout popular culture. The meanings attached to behaviour in popular culture are never fixed, and change with the tension between ideals and realities. We often forget how broadly the impact of ideas about gender is felt; we more often construe gender narrowly in terms of women's lives, or sexuality and relations between women and men. But it is evident that gender affected the meanings given to the behaviour of women and men in all contexts, and that their relation to every aspect of their daily lives – from family, to speech, to drink, to violence – was gendered. These meanings were in turn shaped by political, social and intellectual developments – from the nature of the state to medical conceptions of women's bodies.[60]

Popular culture as I have defined it is the locus in which ideas about gender are developed and transmitted within society. Ideas from literary culture are used, but they gain meaning as they are interpreted and redefined in everyday life. By looking at everyday behaviour, reactions and assumptions, we can begin to outline the gender system of early modern England. That system allowed women a certain degree of authority, and some respect. But though the extent of women's subordination was sharply

4. Literacy and Literature in Popular Culture: Reading and Writing in Historical Perspective

JONATHAN BARRY

Literacy and literature have been fundamental in discussions of popular culture in the early modern period. On the one hand, popular culture, defined negatively in contrast to elite culture, has often been seen as the culture of the illiterate, a culture transmitted orally by customs and practice, not through the printed word. It has been argued that the growing literacy of the middling sort, and the sharp social distinctions observed in the ability to sign, created a growing divide between a literate, respectable culture and the oral world of popular tradition. Yet, at the same time, historians have sought to uncover the values of popular culture through the growing mass of 'popular literature', notably ballads, chapbooks and other ephemeral publications but also the radical and other writings of the minority of working people who recorded their views and experiences in print. How can we reconcile these two apparently contradictory positions?

This essay will argue that we cannot reconcile them, if we persist in searching for a 'popular culture' that is clearly differentiated from an alternative culture. Instead, it is suggested, we should explore the ambiguities *within* the notions of literacy and literature, in order to gain a deeper sense of the issues involved in identifying 'popular' cultural practices in this period. Literacy and literature are themselves notions which, although they seem self-evident to us, have a distinct place in the history of how reading and writing developed and were debated as social practices. Like reading and writing, they lack simple meanings because, amongst other reasons, their significance depended on the social setting in which they were used. Given the changing issues involved in studying both literature and literacy in the nineteenth century, this essay will concentrate on the pre-1800 situation, though some reference will be made to nineteenth-century developments.[1]

When trying to capture the essence of popular culture and its distinction from elite culture, historians have often turned first to its non-literate nature. Keith Wrightson, for example, begins his chapter on cultural change between 1580 and 1680 with a contrast between the book-reading family of the young Richard Baxter and the 'communal merriment' of their neighbours. Wrightson portrays 'the profound alienation of [Baxter's] father's household from the customary culture of their neighbours, their withdrawal from that culture, that world of shared values, meanings and practices, and their seeking of an alternative guide to living in the word of scripture'. The 'cultural differentiation' involved is summarised in these terms: 'The spread of popular literacy and the progress of the Reformation had opened up new cultural horizons to a section of the common people. Yet they had also brought about a widening fissure between polite and plebeian culture, the informed and the ignorant, respectability and the profane multitude.' As the phrase 'popular literacy' suggests, Wrightson is well aware of the incorporation of literacy within popular culture, yet his overall emphasis is on a growing distinction and the formative role of literacy in this process: 'In 1580 illiteracy was a characteristic of the vast majority of the common people of England. By 1680 it was a special characteristic of the poor.'[2]

As the reference to the Reformation in Wrightson's account suggests, the opposition between a literate print culture and an oral communal culture was not just a matter of social behaviour. It can plausibly be identified with the wider cultural shift involved in the Reformation (and felt also in Catholic countries during the Counter-Reformation) whereby medieval Catholicism, which relied so heavily on rituals and images to convey its messages, was challenged by a new religion of 'the Word'. Thus, for many Protestants a religious as well as a cultural choice was involved in entering the culture of print; the relationship with the older culture could be one of self-conscious antagonism. If we add to this the repeated attacks, often led by Protestant evangelists, on oral, communal culture for its moral as well as religious vices, it is easy to see the makings of a highly polarised cultural confrontation between literate and oral cultures.[3] If, as Wrightson suggests, this was accompanied by a growing social polarisation, in which the 'haves' could afford the education and godliness of the literate culture and the 'have-nots' could not, then we have all the ingredients for a struggle between elite and popular culture. For many historians this conflict, whether it be styled patrician versus plebeian, respectable versus rough, or polite versus vulgar, characterised early modern England.[4]

'Popular culture', within this interpretative framework, is characterised by its 'survivalist' character, and in particular by its identification with customary or traditional ways of acting and thinking. Whilst historians using this approach have not neglected changes and adaptations within popular culture, they have emphasised the conservatism of its forms and values. These are seen as both reflecting and reinforcing its oral, non-literate nature. An oral culture passes down its knowledge and practices through tradition, above all by the repetition of practices on a calendrical basis, and uses ritual to ensure continuity. Whereas the world of print and literacy is widely supposed to foster a sense of the new and of the possibilities for change, an oral culture, it is argued, tends to conceal change by piecemeal adaptation. Whereas literate culture is often taken to be individualistic, the essence of oral culture is its communal nature, since it is the group and its practices which establish meaning.[5]

Studies of popular culture have therefore been based largely on communal events, such as crowd actions, seasonal or calendrical festivities or recreations. By understanding the practical and symbolic meanings of these activities, historians have produced a history 'from below', allowing the illiterate populace to speak.[6] Yet this attempt contains a number of ironies. As an approach to popular culture it reproduces the agenda of those contemporaries who sought to reform or attack ritual and communal practices and relies heavily on the evidence generated by their efforts, such as court cases or hostile accounts of popular customs. While the sophisticated historians who have used such materials have been well aware of their likely biases, they cannot entirely overcome them. We cannot be sure how far the 'traditionalism' constantly appealed to (by crowds, for example) accurately reflects their own perception of their activity, or represents a language adopted by people aware that, in putting their case, their best chance of legitimising their behaviour was to appeal to a sense of custom that still carried great authority in *elite* culture, especially where the law was concerned. But, if we reject contemporary accounts of the meanings of oral culture as too unreliable and rely instead on ethnographic description of popular cultural practices, ascribing meanings to these in accord with modern anthropological understanding, we run into further problems of interpretation. For such anthropological models offer the historian all too wide a choice, ranging from accounts which see oral traditional culture as a 'safety-valve', harmlessly expressing carnivalesque values, through to accounts which emphasise the potential for resistance to, and rejection of, elite values in popular practices. They thus reproduce the contemporary debate between the elite critics of communal culture (who viewed it as inherently subversive and unstable in its meanings) and those who defended festive rituals as safety-valves, through which popular belief could be channelled into support of the authorities in church and state.[7]

In attempting to judge between these rival models, historians have naturally sought to find contemporary sources which depend less heavily on elite mediation. Since we cannot recover the writings of the illiterate, we must turn instead to that minority of literate writers who are assumed, because of their social origins or position or because of the nature of what they wrote (many of the works of this kind are anonymous), to be part of popular culture despite their literacy. We can draw on writings by what Margaret Spufford has called 'humble autobiographers', taking this term broadly to include keepers of unpublished diaries, commonplace books or other memoranda of personal experience, as well as those who entered the public domain by writing and/or publishing. However, two problems arise with using this group as our interpreters of popular culture, if we take that to be primarily oral and communal. The first is that these literate people will necessarily be, at least to some extent, different from those without literacy, since they have access to, and are writing within, literate culture. If literacy structures thought, then they will think differently. Less portentously, they will be writing within genres which, whether published or private, contain their own traditions of expression which will shape what is recorded (and what is not). Secondly, those who committed their thoughts to writing usually belong to one of three types. Some, especially during the English Revolution and in the later eighteenth century, were self-conscious radicals, writing to challenge the existing social and cultural order. While some of these (such as Ranters and Diggers) might draw on aspects of communal culture in their critiques of their society, often they saw themselves as outsiders, enemies of a deferential popular culture. Others were self-made men who had risen from humble beginnings and wished to emphasise their distance from their cultural roots. A third group, which might overlap with either or both the previous categories, were religious writers describing their own spiritual experiences, for whom a narrative based on victory over worldly vices, whether their own in early life or those of the 'world' around them, was almost obligatory. All of these types had their own powerful reasons for constructing an image of a communal popular culture in need of reform, reasons just as powerful as those affecting elite commentators.[8]

Even greater problems of interpretation arise if we turn to the literature presumed to have been written 'for' the people and use this as evidence for popular attitudes. Strictly speaking, of course, if popular culture is non-literate, then there can be no genuine 'popular literature' of this kind. Yet, ever since the period itself, it has been common to regard the sentiments found in such genres as ballads, chapbooks, almanacs, jestbooks and other cheap and ephemeral literature as a guide to popular values and opinions. While earlier studies used these impressionistically, recent work has sought greater reliability by statistical analysis of their themes and contents.[9] Social historians interested in popular attitudes to subjects such as marriage, sexuality, old age and crime have assumed a correlation between the attitudes expressed in this literature and the opinions of its readers, because of its very 'popularity'.[10]

Yet, as many of these historians have been aware, such an assumption is highly dangerous. Some of the difficulties that arise are similar to those posed by study of rituals and customs. For example, how should we take the subjects for humour in ballads and jestbooks? Do jokes about dominant wives and hen-pecked husbands tell us about the realities of household life in an age when the ideal was husbandly authority, or are they a reinforcement of that male authority through mockery, or perhaps a challenge to that authority, offering an alternative view of society for women?[11] Other problems arise from the question of genres, as with the autobiographical accounts discussed above. Different

forms of popular literature offer us varying impressions of popular
tastes and values, since popular literature was already 'specialised'
into a series of recognised types, catering to varied audiences, or
perhaps the same audience in varied moods. The absence of serious religious themes in one genre may be misleading unless we
appreciate that such ideas played a leading role in another sort of
publication. As with humour, we face also the problem of how far
the ideas expressed in such genres were taken at face value, or
whether they were appreciated as fictional constructs. For example, the continued vogue for chivalric romances throughout the
early modern period has been seen as indicating either the continued dominance of an aristocratic ethos or the escapist tastes of the
popular audience (or both). As indicated later, we may see it
rather differently if we regard the chivalric romance as a publishing type, welcomed by both publisher and readers as a recognisable genre, but providing a theme which could then be used in
many different ways.[12]

Even more fundamental issues are raised if we consider more
seriously who exactly was writing for whom in such literature. If literate and popular culture were becoming increasingly dissociated,
then the capacity of the literate to capture popular tastes may have
been declining, while if the urge of the literate groups was to
reform popular culture through the press, then we should view
printed popular literature as an aspect of elite efforts at cultural
hegemony. Robert Mandrou, for example, has interpreted the
equivalent French literature of the 'bibliothèque bleu' in this
light.[13] The main argument against this is to point out that such literature was largely commercially produced and thus had to find a
public willing to buy it. But this depends on a rather naive view of
'consumer power', begging questions about the ability of the common people to produce any alternative form of printed material.

Furthermore, we may question how far this popular literature
was really intended for, or reached, the common people. If we
define such popular literature chiefly by its price and format,
rather than by direct evidence that it was read by common people
(and there is almost no evidence to test the latter), then we cannot
exclude the possibility that its main readership was amongst the
middling sort, or even the elite, who could easily afford such materials. Only if we can establish in advance that they would not have
wanted to read such materials can we interpret large sales as

indicating a genuinely popular market. For example, the 400,000 almanacs which it has been estimated were being produced annually in the mid- to late seventeenth century could have been purchased entirely by households in the top third of the social structure. And if we cannot be sure who is buying such material, then we cannot use the argument of its 'popularity' to obviate concern about the aims of those producing it. If, for example, ballads and cheap literature apparently aimed at domestic servants were actually being bought by householders, perhaps to give to their servants, then this puts a completely different construction on how we understand the 'success' of such items and the messages they contain.

Enough has been said, I hope, to indicate that any effort to recapture the nature of popular culture is required, if only from the nature of the evidence that remains, to consider at every stage the nature of the interaction between elite and popular, literate and illiterate. Rather than seeing literacy as a convenient dividing line between two cultures, we need rather to be aware of how far differential access to writing, and the forms of expression that writing encouraged, has structured our sources for popular culture. But we also need to look further, and reconsider our initial assumptions about the meaning of literacy.

The pioneering studies of literacy were concerned, naturally enough, to establish the quantitative dimensions of the subject and thus employed the only available measure for statistical analysis, namely whether people signed their names or put their marks to documents.[14] By this standard, you are either literate or not and the basic test is one of writing ability (a signature). In itself this has created problems of definition. For example, a clumsy signature may indicate less writing skill than a highly accomplished trade mark, and may even be the only piece of writing achieved by the individual, while some people appear to have alternated between signing and marking. Given a sufficiently broad statistical brush these issues may not seem critical and there is little evidence that there were many people who could *only* sign their name, without other literacy skills. More problematic is the relationship between signature literacy and the ability to read. A number of features, both of the educational system of the time and of the distribution of signature literacy, suggest that the correlation between these two skills, which we tend to take for granted, was then by no means automatic.

Studies of educational practice have established that reading and writing were taught as two separate skills, in sequence rather than together and often by different people. Whereas reading was seen as a skill that could be taught by anybody (within the family, at a dame school or by a neighbour), writing was a vocational skill identified with male writing-masters who also taught arithmetic and often other basic business or trade skills. Many children learnt to read by age seven or so, whereas writing appears to have been a rare accomplishment by that age, which was widely seen as the time at which children's labour might become valuable enough to put them to work. To continue past that age at an education including writing was thus a sign of parental prosperity (however humble) and was also gender-specific. Girls' education centred on reading, sewing and other accomplishments needed to gain a husband and then manage a household, with writing as an optional extra. As a consequence, there will be a much closer correlation between signing and reading ability among the sons of middling families than among the sons of the poor or the daughters of any class below the gentry.[15] Indirect confirmation of this is provided by the evidence that, once reading and writing began to be taught together and girls attended formal schools as much as boys in the nineteenth century, then the gap in signing ability steadily narrowed until, after 1850, women actually outstripped men in some regions.

The century between the Reformation and the Protestation Oath of 1642 appears to have seen a substantial, though not entirely steady, growth in male literacy, so that by 1642 between one-third and 40 per cent of adult males could sign. Female signing rates at this period were probably at less than half that level. The next occasion when we can get a reliable cross-section comes in the years after 1753, when the marriage register figures reveal about 60 per cent of grooms signing, compared to about 40 per cent of brides. However, the meaning of changes in literacy at a national level are far from obvious. There was no national educational network producing similar effects across the country. A changing national figure may not represent, say, a changing literacy level for farmworkers in Devon, but rather a changing balance of the overall population away from Devon farmworkers towards

London shopkeepers or Bristol sailors. As David Cressy has shown, the gradual increases in overall literacy levels conceal much more dramatic variations in literacy at any one time between different occupations, between town and country and between the sexes. The late medieval and Tudor period had already seen a steady growth in lay literacy amongst the gentry, mercantile and upper middling sort, whose adult males were almost all able to sign by 1600. Among the trading and farming classes we find growing adult male signature literacy in the late sixteenth and seventeenth centuries, particularly amongst the occupations that required writing skills for market transactions. Less skilled craftsmen and husbandmen were much less literate, while labourers and women formed the bottom of the literacy hierarchy. Broadly speaking the same pattern can be detected in the late eighteenth and early nineteenth centuries, by which time more plentiful sources allow us to establish a further range of variables.[16]

There is no scope here for detailed discussion of the ways in which historians have explained and interpreted these trends. While some have emphasised the supply of education, most have seen signature literacy as a result of the changing demand for writing skills, in turn determined by its utility, especially in economic terms. This emphasis has been given impetus by the use of literacy figures to measure educational skills during industrialisation. However statistical attempts to identify causal variables between literates and non-literates, whether at individual, family or community level, have generally proved inconclusive or contradictory. The clear urban advantage in literacy rates before 1800, for example, may be explained by superior schooling facilities (most writing-masters were urban) or by higher demand for writing skills in an urban environment. It may just reflect the higher concentration of literate occupations in towns, so explaining the decline in urban literacy advantage when new industrial towns developed with a large labouring rather than commercial population. But this process was itself tied up with increased poverty and rural immigration, overwhelming educational facilities provided by churches and charitable groups.[17]

Although ever more detailed quantitative work may throw further light on these issues, much of the problem lies with the undue weight being placed on the concept of 'literacy'. A substantial literature has now appeared that emphasises the varied forms and meanings of literacy, and the need to study this qualitatively as well as quantitatively. For example, Keith Thomas has pointed out that even the notion of 'writing', apparently straightforward to us, obscures the existence within early modern England of a variety of scripts, some printed and some handwritten, that were used for different purposes. Children's earliest reading lessons, from a hornbook, were conducted in a black-letter script distinct from any writing-hands then in regular use, but employed by governments on proclamations and by ballad-printers. Thomas suggests that this may have been a script specifically associated with those possessing only the most basic reading skills. In broader terms, he argues for the importance of identifying a range of types and levels of literacy, each potentially with a different significance and history.[18]

If this is true of writing, it may apply even more to reading. If we accept that sign literacy is associated largely with economic utility, and that this explains most, if not all, of its unequal distribution, then we are left with the likelihood that the history of reading ability may follow a quite independent course, itself involving many types of reading skill. This seems particularly likely of the pre-1700 period, when the linkage of the two skills in educational terms was very weak. Thereafter the growth of elementary education in charity and Sunday schools, some of whose teachers offered both reading and writing, may have strengthened the correlation, although even in the nineteenth century it was estimated that one-third more children could read than write. Earlier the gap was probably greater, and especially so for women.[19]

The likelihood of a separate history of reading ability is strengthened by evidence that the motivation for reading may have differed. Not only may reading have been taught cheaply to children as a way of keeping them busy, but it was widely viewed as a religious and cultural advantage, regardless of its economic value. The Reformation is clearly significant here, since it established knowledge of 'the Word' as central to Christianity. Admittedly, Protestant reformers were often lukewarm about the prospect of their flocks reading the Bible for themselves, preferring to offer it pre-digested in their preaching or in catechisms and other simplified (and perhaps sanitised) forms. But the vernacular Bible and other key Protestant texts (such as Foxe's *Book of Martyrs*) did gain very wide circulation. For many evangelists the advantages of promoting a reading public outweighed the possible dangers. Some found the Civil War a powerful counter-argument, but thereafter the existence of competing churches and of committed evangelical publishing and educational movements ensured that the religious motive for learning to read was always of great importance. But there were also many secular motives for learning to read, not least access to entertaining and useful literature.[20]

Here we return to the problem of judging the actual market for popular literature. If we assume that reading ability was much more widely distributed than sign literacy and may have reached some, at least, of the poor, then what measures can we have of the extent and significance of this popular audience? Contemporary comments on this are scattered and impressionistic and often come from those with a vested interest in either emphasising or downplaying the impact of print amongst the people. But there are no direct statistical tests of readership comparable to that for signature literacy. References to books in probate inventories cannot be relied upon as inventoried estates are heavily biased towards the better-off and though they may give us a rough guide to the ownership of substantial bound books, they offer little guide to the circulation of the more ephemeral items which would have formed the staple of popular reading.[21]

Faced with such problems, historians have increasingly turned to the press itself as a means of studying the market for its output. They have sought to identify those elements of publishing which, in terms of cost and style, appear aimed at the lower end of the market, and explored the changing techniques whereby the book trade sought to reach that potential market. They have also looked intensively at what publishers and authors were saying and assuming about their readers, both in their title-pages and prefaces and in the texts of their works. Both these approaches have involved a new interest in what we might call 'popularisation' – the attempt to mould the content, format and marketing of print to render it accessible to a wide public.

The renewed emphasis on accessibility is certainly timely, for, leaving aside questions of literacy, there were many obstacles to reading. These include lack of leisure and privacy, even the cost and efficiency of candlelight. The most obvious problem, however, concerned purchase price, and the implications of cost for the marketing of print. Hand-made paper and hand-controlled printing presses made printed material expensive and the bulkiness of paper made its transport costly, especially to those far from London, where, until the eighteenth century, the overwhelming majority of items were published. Add to this the perennial publishing problem that you are selling, not a small variety of standard items, but a bewildering range of different titles, and one can begin to appreciate the issues facing the early modern booktrader and, indeed, the potential reader. The most straightforward solution for the book trade was to concentrate its efforts on selling to the luxury end of the market, producing short print-runs of relatively costly items and making little effort to market them, relying instead on its buyers to come to the tight knot of booksellers found in various London streets, together with a number of bookshops in the larger towns of the provinces, dependent on London for supplies to satisfy customer orders. Such a pattern would establish a self-reinforcing link between reading and a minority of dedicated bookbuyers with good London (or at least urban) contacts and sufficiently educated to know what books they wanted. If we add to this the efforts of government to restrict the circulation and raise the price of books, in particular by the granting of monopolies, both on specific types of book and on printing in general, which was normally restricted to a select group of London printers before 1695, then we have a powerful case for believing that, whatever the theoretical reading capacity of the people, the world of print was indeed an elitist one, at least until the eighteenth century.[22]

What is striking, however, is that despite all these strong pressures towards exclusivity, the press always maintained an alternative strategy of broadening markets. The costs of paper and transport were minimised by producing brief and unbound items which could be carried by pedlars and sold in a range of shops, not just by specialist booksellers. The adoption of stereotypical formats and genres allowed each title to meet standard customer expectations, while claims to novelty, exclusivity and sensational relevance attracted the reader to that specific item. From the sixteenth century onwards simplified versions of elite texts were produced, as weighty tomes were translated, abridged, rewritten according to traditional formats and plundered for snippets in genres such as almanacs, jestbooks and school texts. The full

extent of this process of popularisation is only now becoming
clear, though the evidence will always be incomplete. Many such
publications have not survived, except as titles in the registers of
the Stationers' Company or, later, in catalogues and advertisements of items for sale, and even these sources will miss many
ephemeral works.[23]

Although the London press was already very active in these
areas before 1695, the spread of printing into the provinces during
the eighteenth century strengthened these tendencies. Together
with growing demand for stationery and improved transport links,
the availability of locally produced items encouraged the growth of
bookselling outlets in smaller towns. Furthermore a growing sector among the book trade specialised in catering to the popular
end of the market. In addition to producing more of the already
standard types of cheap literature, they took up 'serialisation', issu-
ing books in unbound parts which reduced the price paid at any
one time. This coincided with, and was promoted by, the proliferation of newspapers, magazines and other periodicals, which
assembled in convenient form material drawn from many less
accessible sources.[24]

The press thus became more accessible to non-elite groups,
especially in towns. As with many other items in the so-called 'consumer revolution' of this period, however, it is much harder to
judge the true extent of mass demand. An expanding and prosper-
ing middling sort were probably the chief beneficiaries and,
despite cost-cutting measures, even the cheapest of these items
would still have involved a substantial slice of the weekly income of
a labourer or craftsman. Hence the many devices adopted to
spread their purchase cost. Long before the reading clubs of nineteenth-century workers, groups had clubbed together to obtain
such literature or paid for it indirectly in the price of a drink in an
alehouse, tavern or coffee house. In such places all types of items
from ballads to newspapers would be available to read or hear read
(or sung) out loud. Equally important was the potential to hear or
see such items for free in the streets or on the village green, as
ballad-singers hawked their wares or items were shared around or
pinned up. Private lending was put onto a commercial footing in
the eighteenth century by subscription libraries, initially aimed at
a fashionable clientele but soon adapted to humbler purses. One
important feature of such libraries was that they had their stock on

display so readers could browse, and this was also a feature of the growing market in second-hand books, sold through fairs, market stalls and, in larger towns, old bookshops.[25]

We can interpret this evidence in several different ways. It points to a whole range of means whereby the constraints of access were being reduced, enabling print to play a larger role in popular culture. It also indicates, not only that cost remained a constant problem in 'popularisation', but that the nature of popular consumption of the press was deeply influenced by the very strategies adopted to get over these problems. Most notably, it suggests that the experience of print for many ordinary people may have been a public and communal one, in which any clear boundaries between oral and literate culture would have been blurred. This point has often been made about the earliest form of popular literature, the ballad, which as part-song, part-text, was intended to bridge the cultures. Printed ballads were soon playing a central part in traditional festivities and there was a constant interplay between 'folk-singing' and commercial ballad-writing, with many of the 'traditional' ballads later recorded by folklorists deriving from published sources.[26] It has sometimes been suggested that the later genres of popular literature, such as the chapbook, broke this connection between oral and written culture. While this may be true of some new genres (and of course the ballad remained a vital form), other new types, including the newspaper, continued to blur the boundaries of oral and literate reception.

A vital, if elusive, aspect of this question concerns gender. If women were less likely to be able to read than men (a big assumption, as we have seen), then access to people reading aloud would have been of greater importance to women. It is unclear how far women as a whole had equal access with men to the world of the street or the public house described above. Yet many ballads clearly envisage a female audience, perhaps gained during fairs or markets. Some women were bound to encounter such material, since they gained their living from hawking street literature or serving customers in public places, but others may have been excluded. For them the most plausible situation to encounter literature would have been within the household. There were well-established domestic traditions of reading aloud, ranging from family prayers and Bible readings to play-reading sessions. Domestic servants might also have had access to print purchased by the family. One of the most troubling features of the 'popularisation' of print in the eighteenth century to many commentators was its appeal to a female readership, whether it was fashionable novels or cheap romances.[27]

Historians (and literary critics) of print, no less than of literacy, have thus been drawn into the history of reading. How we understand the impact of print will depend on how it was read – in public or private, out loud or silently, as part of a defined group, voluntarily or not, at speed or slowly, memorising each word, understanding every point or just grasping certain themes. Within these possibilities it is possible to identify two alternative poles. One would be the public reader, accustomed to recitation and absorbing print slowly in communal settings where the text, often an authoritative one, such as the Bible, a proclamation or a traditional story already well-known in its essence, was to be pondered and remembered. The other would be the private reader, silently speeding through a novel for the immediate gratification of the story line or scanning a piece of non-fiction for some specific piece of news or useful information. Can we accept such a polarisation and if so can we then apply this to the categories of elite and popular culture? Does the distinction become, not one of literate or not, but of different types of reader?[28]

Let us reconsider the young Richard Baxter. The contrast between the pious reader of godly tracts and his ungodly neighbours, whose alehouse merriments doubtless included witty ballads, appears to fit the private/public distinction. But other aspects of the story are more troublesome. Surely it was the Baxter household, reading together with reverence the sacred text, which fits more closely the public model, while the neighbours enjoying a traditional story amidst their pleasures were the ones who were dipping into literature as a consumer good? A century later, where do we place the artisan scanning his newspaper over a cup of coffee, contrasted with the clergyman pondering a classical text or a women's reading group debating the moral message of Richardson's *Clarissa*? While the rising scale of publication, much of it topical, utilitarian or fictional, may well have led those who could afford it into new ways of consuming print, they also generated a counter-tendency which canonised parts of this new culture and the ability to respond to it with sensibility. By contrast, if we look at popular radicals and how they used print, we can see a strong contrast between mid-seventeenth and late eighteenth-century writers. The Levellers and others during the English Revolution drew very heavily on the Bible, Foxe and a limited range of other authoritative texts, while the later radicals, though still powerfully drawn to the languages, imagery and ideas of these texts, also had a much wider range of other genres available.[29]

At this point it is worth reconsidering the question of literacy, in the sense of how people learnt to read and the possible impact of this on reading practices. Reading was regarded as a passive skill, compared to the active art of writing, and it was associated with memorisation of authoritative, even sacred, texts. The small child, after learning letters from a hornbook, was taught to read with the aid of religious texts such as the psalter and then introduced to the Bible, working from the Old Testament to the New. Emphasis was on rote learning and recitation of words and passages. This made sense, of course, to a culture where the primary justification of reading was the study of 'the Word'. Not only must it have made reading very unattractive, but it also worked to associate reading closely with a public oral culture – such as the readings during church services. There was little here to encourage private reading and interpretation of the printed word.

Until the late seventeenth century there is little evidence that these methods of instruction varied noticeably between social groups. The elite were taught by the same techniques, which were also employed when they went on to study the classical texts at grammar schools, introducing them to yet another set of authorities. Indeed, even university education still involved a close association between reading and public recitation/argumentation. For the clergy and the lawyers, as for the gentry, the world of books was intended to furnish material for public conversation and eloquence – in pulpit, court and public life generally. For the upper classes, indeed, if there was a world of private reading, it may have been in large part that of 'popular literature'. Certainly ballads, romances and the like were treasured by elite children as an enthralling alternative world of print to the authoritative texts they endured at school. The same may have applied further down the social scale. Yet for all children the boundary between the myths of Greece, Rome and Israel on the one hand, and the stories of popular literature on the other, may have been a fluid one.[30]

During the later part of our period educational developments may have altered this picture. While the education of the poor apparently continued to stress rote memorisation, more 'liberal' methods became widespread in the education of the better-off. School books were published with schemes of graduated learning, more attractive texts for children were introduced and the scope of children's early learning was extended to incorporate subjects such as history, geography and English grammar and literature. One of the ostensible purposes of this was to generate in children a love of reading and an ability to read extensively. Here we seem to see the origins of our model private reader. Yet even here caution is necessary. Many of these new schemes were idealistic or just sales talk, ignoring the continued realities of schooling even for the better-off, where large classes, few texts and unprofessional teachers perpetuated old methods. Furthermore, even the new ideals were aimed as much at improving public reading as private. The emphasis was on correct elocution when reading aloud and on reading that would furnish topics for public conservation, not on personal enlightenment. There remained, moreover, a resolutely didactic approach, justifying reading in terms of morals learnt or examples set.[31]

A great deal more research will be needed before we can unravel these complex patterns, though it appears unlikely that the public and private reader will emerge as any more of a clear-cut distinction than literate and non-literate. What has already emerged, however, is a sense of the multiple meanings and uses of reading. It obviously matters how and why a text was read and in what contexts that reading was then, to use a fashionable and helpful term, 'appropriated' – that is, understood and acted upon by that reader. Rather than searching for a group of texts that are exclusively 'popular', or for a style of reading that distinguishes different social groups, we can focus instead on whether there are any distinctive ways in which reading is 'appropriated' into popular culture.[32]

Perhaps the most fruitful investigations into this subject over the last few years have been inspired by an interest in women readers. Here too the emphasis at first lay on women's exclusion from literature – written about rather than writing – with debate about the status of those women who did manage to write, even to publish, and whether they should be seen as representative or atypical.

Recently, however, there have been a number of sophisticated efforts to reexamine how women as readers might have read the literature – especially the literature aimed at wide audiences – available to them and how far their reactions might have shaped the development of such literature. The emphasis here has been very much on women's ability to read 'against the grain', finding meaning and inspiration for themselves even in apparently conventional 'patriarchal' writings, and on the pressure that women as potential consumers could put on writers to offer them material amenable to such readings. Here we return, of course, to the question of how far the producers of culture in this period could control their audiences.[33]

There is a danger that 'appropriation' can be carried too far, whether in the case of gender or popular culture, in ways that lead us to ignore the inequalities of power and resources involved between, say, a poorly educated woman reader and a well-established author or publisher. But the notion is valuable if it requires us to examine the issue in each case without pre-judgement. Not least, it has made us acutely aware of how far writers and publishers were constantly attempting to establish the nature of their audience and the terms of their relationship with it. As historians have interrogated literature (of all kinds) for evidence of its readership, they have realised that the results that emerge will indicate only very crudely the *actual* readers, but will tell us a great deal about the writers' and publishers' attitudes to their readers and attempts to educate their readers into fitting certain models. The aims and tensions involved in this process are themselves of great historical interest for our understanding of the relationship between elite and popular culture, suggesting a process of negotiation rather than domination, even if one side lacks a direct voice.

Indeed, it has become increasingly clear that the problem of 'the audience' – its definition and control – was of perennial concern to all those involved with print. As a medium, print was seen as lacking the safeguards involved in performance, where the nature of the audience and their responses could be, to some extent, managed. The 'public', anonymous character of print rendered it automatically subversive, at least in potential. To many contemporaries, one of the most powerful representations of this was the possibility that print power might get into the hands of the otherwise powerless; hence attacks on, and dissociation from, 'popular literature' were one of the standard ploys of writers and publishers. Popularisers always had to justify their work against complaints that they were disseminating knowledge too widely. But at the same time that such 'publicity' might be deplored, so the notion of 'the private reader' was also condemned, for much the same reason. A private reader, for example a woman, could also not be directed in their understanding and might 'appropriate' the texts *inappropriately*, by the standards of the establishment. This became a recurrent theme of the eighteenth-century debate over the novel and other new genres which had no authoritative public forum for their meaning to be established – at least until the literary critic emerged in the periodical press.[34]

The classic expression of such concerns was press censorship. Once the Reformation had made ideological pluralism dangerous, governments struggled to control press output. We have already noted the restriction of printing largely to London and the attempt to win the leading booktraders into compliance by monopolies. In addition an increasingly elaborate system of pre-publication licensing was established, first under royal prerogative through the church and then, after this collapsed in 1640, by parliamentary ordinance and act. When, due to party squabbles over details, this lapsed in 1695, successive governments attempted to manage print by threats of post-publication trial for seditious libel or blasphemy, by raising the costs of printing by stamp duties, and by bribing or sweetening the press through government patronage. One consequence of this is that, for most if not all of our period, writers and publishers could not express themselves freely. As Christopher Hill has long emphasised, we cannot take expressions of conservative and consensual values at their face value, but have to look out, as contemporaries were well capable of doing, for hidden meanings and subversive innuendoes, in writing of every type. In particular, the appropriation of standard genres and themes of writing for the expression of unwelcome messages, such as setting a plot in classical or chivalric times when commenting on contemporary politics, was a constant ploy. In this respect the statistical techniques of content analysis appear less suitable for studying the radical potentials of popular culture than the close literary analysis traditionally applied only to 'great writers'. Even here, our readings, necessarily restricted to the words, may miss the subversive meaning that could be supplied in performance,

for one of the objections to ballads and plays was that, when performed, lines that appear harmless could be rendered ironic, even
reversed in their meaning.

However, the history of censorship also appears to tell us
another story of relevance to popular culture. Until the Civil War
certainly, and arguably until 1695, the government's efforts to cen-
sor print appear to have been directed more at controlling the
reading of the elite than at popular reading. For governments concerned with contested interpretations of religious and political
legitimacy, it was upper-class access to controversial news or religious debates that created greatest concern. Admittedly, monarchs
such as Charles I saw such censorship in terms of a polarity –
knowledge and power flowing from above against that from below
– and justified controls by arguing that the rude multitude were
prying into secrets beyond their capacity, a language that elites
continued to use in opposing public access to ideas. But, in practice, it was not humble peasants that concerned Charles I, but
rather dissatisfied gentlemen and merchants. However, following
the Civil Wars, when collapse of censorship had seen a proliferation of radical writing and popular involvement, efforts to control the press became concentrated on keeping dangerous ideas
out of popular hands, rather than on preventing their circulation
among the elites. Such concerns were to reach their peak during
the French Revolutionary wars, when a whole series of restrictive
measures were enacted, from which the radical popular press was
gradually to free itself during the mid-nineteenth century.[35]

Such, at least, would be a plausible, if crude, reading of censorship history. It might be taken as implying that 'popular reading',
as a specific concern that can be differentiated from more general
fears of the impact of print, was a post-1640 development. This
would fit nicely with the evidence for the vigour of popularisation
during the later period. By contrast, those concerned with the
reform of popular culture in the earlier period concentrated their
efforts on attacking traditional customs. Interesting parallels could
be drawn here with broad changes in elite attitudes to popular literacy. Before the Civil War, despite paying lip-service to the notion
of a Protestant reading public, few measures were taken by the
elite to provide any schooling specifically for this group; reliance
was placed instead of training the clergy to educate the people. As
we have seen, this may have appeared the safer option. But the

religious pluralism of the 1640s and onwards threw this approach into doubt. While some reactionaries saw the revolution as proof of the dangers of any education for the people, others thought it proved the need for a fuller education. Although nothing immediate was done to implement the bold education schemes of the 1640s, the late seventeenth century saw an increased concern with primary education that surfaced most prominently in the charity school movement of the early eighteenth century. Although efforts at popular education then went through cycles of effort and stagnation, reflecting shifting elite concerns and strategies of control, the issue remained.[36]

It may be misleading, however, to relate such developments too closely to any real changes in the place of literature or literacy in popular culture. Not only are they distorted by changing elite concerns, but arguably they owe as much to changing relationships *within* elite culture as to any altered attitude to popular culture. Educational proposals owed much of their impetus to elite concerns about the correct form of their own education, for example the balance between classical and vocational or the type of religious training appropriate, as well as to competition between elite groups to indoctrinate the poor in their type of religion. The collapse of licensing reflected party rivalries, not any commitment to a free press. The upper classes, divided on party lines, could no longer speak too openly of restricting their own access to print. Instead the debate was redirected, with serious consequences for ordinary people, onto the control of others. Moreover, despite the measures taken to enforce such concerns, their success was never great. Both the commercial opportunities and the propaganda benefits of appealing to popular audiences proved too strong for government controls or elite self-control and, in competing for popular purses and minds, the press found itself bound to take account of popular styles and tastes.

For example, throughout our period governments and other elite groups found it expedient to adapt the styles and genres of popular literature in order to convey propaganda messages. During the Reformation Protestant writers used ballads, jests, plays and other genres to satirise Catholic practices (exploiting traditional anti-clerical prejudices). During the Civil War the defeated Royalists used bawdy, even pornographic, songs and stories to discredit the pretensions of the victorious army and Parliamentarians, who also found themselves assaulted from the left by the Levellers and Ranters. As Paul Monod has recently demonstrated, the Jacobite movement after 1688 found expression in many types of popular culture. Finally, during the Napoleonic wars, the conservative loyalists rivalled and in many ways out did radicals like Tom Paine in their appropriation of popular culture to their ends, for example in Hannah More's *Cheap Repository Tracts.* In all these cases, however, historians have shown the uneasy compromises required of the elite propagandists in adopting these techniques – concerns that surfaced at the time and led to doubts about their wisdom. For example, as Patrick Collinson has shown, Protestant evangelists, once established in power, shifted from the exploitation of popular culture to efforts at its repression, portraying as Catholic evils those very media such as plays they had at first been prepared to exploit. After the Civil War, such concerns were redoubled, but rarely prevented popularisation in practice, although they certainly affected the strategies adopted by writers and publishers to persuade themselves and others that they, not the readers, were in control.[37]

It was precisely in the context of such concerns that the terms literacy and literature were coined. Until the eighteenth century literature was a general term meaning anything that could be read by the literate. The word 'literate' was itself evolving from a medieval association with classical learning, in which the illiterate were those lacking Latin, towards a broader definition, just as literature, that available to be read, was broadening its own character. But, faced with the popularisation of print, authors and publishers from the sixteenth century onwards, but above all in the eighteenth century, sought to establish a superior sphere of writing, 'literature', that would, while taking advantage of the market for print, be able to avoid the democratisation and dependence on the reader that characterised mere publishing. A very similar process was, of course, occurring with the term 'culture'. Only once the social and cultural identities of both literature and culture as elite practices had been safely established could historians and others begin to look back into the past for an alternative 'popular' literature or culture. The ambiguity with which this essay began, as to whether popular culture must be oral or could have a literary form, reflects the uncertainties of this formative period when, on the one hand, popular culture was conceived as the pure residue of an earlier peasant world, untouched by modern developments such as print, yet, on the other hand, publishers and public alike were seeking to differentiate high from low culture within the ever-growing world of print.[38]

Our notions of literacy also reflect nineteenth-century concerns, above all about illiteracy. It was only then that educationalists and social commentators began to collect data on literacy as a measure of educational attainment because of growing social concern and debate about the effects of literacy on society. Faced with the massive social changes created by urbanisation and industrialisation – both assumed to be weakening the social fabric and bringing the threat of revolution – opinions were sharply divided over what effects these changes had actually had on educational levels. More fundamental, however, was the debate about whether being able to read and write would render ordinary people dangerous revolutionaries or respectable subjects. Opponents of mass literacy believed the literate masses would imbibe revolutionary ideas with their reading skills and use writing to organise themselves politically and industrially. Others argued that reading would mean learning the Bible and conservative texts, so breeding loyalty, and that writing skills would bring people better economic chances and a stake in society. At the same time, even in the mid-nineteenth century, Britons began to fear that their people's skills were falling behind those of economic and military rivals.

This nineteenth-century debate was not wholly new, as we have seen, but it did take a new form in the determination to measure numerically who could read and write. This was the product of an even more elusive history, namely the growth of numeracy: an ability with figures and a desire to apply these to understanding, not just personal business affairs, but social processes. This tendency emerged in the late seventeenth century as the commercial world grew more complex, expanded alongside such sectors as life insurance in the eighteenth century and matured into a statistical movement in the nineteenth.[39] It at once engendered a debate about the meaning of quantitative analysis, as opposed to qualitative, which is still with us today. Paradoxically, nowhere is this more clearly visible than in the historiography of literacy itself, with its contrasts between the statistical approach, concerned essentially to count signatures and marks and then infer causes and results from statistical trends, and the impressionistic methods of those who prefer to seek contemporary comments on what literacy meant and to elaborate the ambiguities in the very notion of measuring literacy. Historians, then, vary enormously in *their* literacy and numeracy and in the meanings that they assign to the notion of literacy.

Equally, it was only in the late nineteenth century that literacy became defined as ability in both reading *and* writing – and defined as a specific area of primary educational attainment. This notion of literacy is the product of the emergence of universal primary education in which children are taught reading and writing together, so that possession of the two skills – and indeed of basic arithmetic (the third R) – can generally be taken to go together. By the mid-nineteenth century most of the population had some primary training of this kind and educational concern and reform was targeted at reaching the minority who would not be educated unless extensive free, and finally compulsory, schooling was introduced. When this happened (in 1870 in England) illiteracy was already a minority phenomenon, affecting some 20–30 per cent of the population. Indeed the notion of *illiteracy* gained currency precisely because it identified a socially problematic minority in educational circumstances where the link between reading and writing was axiomatic.

Thus both the desire to measure illiteracy and the method of doing so through inability to sign reflect the conditions and assumptions of an urban, industrial and predominantly literate society. This does not mean, of course, that the question and method are invalid, but that, as for the notion of 'popular culture', we must be careful to distinguish the various, potentially contradictory, meanings which the term will have in pre-industrial England. Yet even the sources used by the statistical historians of literacy have their own, very significant messages to tell about the interrelationships of elite and people in the early modern period. As noted before, literacy studies rely on two key sources, which provide a national benchmark. The first is the Protestation Oath of 1641–2, a promise of loyalty to the Protestant national church ordered by Parliament in the run-up to the Civil War. This marked an unprecedented effort to enlist the support of the entire adult male population – which was assumed to incorporate women and children – at a moment of high national crisis. Although it was supported both by future Royalists and Parliamentarians, each eager to appear the loyal Protestant party, it was repugnant to the minority of Catholics, some of whom refused to participate. The decision to ask ordinary people to sign or mark is itself an important moment in English history – an indicator of the role popular opinion was to play over the ensuing decades. But contemporaries were not concerned to distinguish marks from signatures; it was the oath-taking that counted. Over the next century successive regimes were to demands oaths of loyalty from office-holders at frequent intervals, culminating in the anti-Jacobite oaths of the early 1720s, but although very minor office-holders were caught up, and the occasional zealous local official roped in the entire population, no such comprehensive effort was made again.[40]

The other crucial measure, the 1753 Marriage Act, owes nothing to elite interest in popular opinion or welfare. It was a highly controversial Act, pushed through by a government concerned with the threat to property posed by widescale marriage of young people without their parents' consent, when, for the elite at least, marriage was a vital property transaction. The requirement for both bride and groom to sign or mark was introduced to prevent clandestine marriages among the propertied, adopting the safeguard already employed for several centuries for marriages by licence outside the home parish. The measure reflected social changes, such as growing ease of travel and the impersonality of urban life, which had rendered the old oral means of controlling marriage – the reading of the banns to the local community who would all know the parties – insufficient as a check of authenticity.[41] Yet, as we all know, the old oral practice of reading the banns was retained, just as we still maintain the fiction of one party residing in the parish, even if only with a symbolic suitcase!

The future for studies of literature and literacy lies in exploring the varied meanings of reading and writing, both to individuals and society. As these last examples suggest, these involve, not just practical questions about educational practices, vocational needs and market conditions, but also fundamental notions of authenticity and cultural consensus. Historians, like contemporaries, have tended to polarise the choices involved, using distinctions of oral and literate, popular and elite and so on, to seek to capture a suppositional contrast between a traditional community and a modern society. If, as historians, we recognise that we are repeating the efforts of people at the time to bring order to a complex and

5. From Reformation to Toleration: Popular Religious Cultures in England, 1540–1690

MARTIN INGRAM

I

Popular religion, like other aspects of popular culture, is undoubtedly an elusive quarry. Plainly the focus of inquiry is the experiences of people below the ranks of the aristocracy and gentry and of other social and intellectual elites. But beyond this the issues are controversial, while the wide variety of existing approaches to 'popular culture' suggests that there can never be a single, authoritative definition. Certainly Peter Burke's influential model of 'elite' and 'popular' culture, and his related theory of a 'reform of popular culture' in the three centuries after 1500, are no longer regarded as satisfactory. Although Burke built into his arguments numerous caveats and qualifications, the model remains at base a stubbornly bi-polar one that makes it hard to do justice to the infinite gradations of the social hierarchy (and in particular to the middling social groups who straddled the world of the elites and of the common people), to the cultural variations to be found at any point on the social spectrum, to regional variations or to gender differences. It also tends to obscure areas of *shared* meanings – elements of common culture which persisted throughout the centuries of 'reform'. More fundamentally, the approach is vulnerable to criticisms that assume a different model of cultural diversity, for example that of the French historian Roger Chartier. Whereas Burke tends to view cultural artifacts (including symbols, rituals and performances) as specific to particular social levels, Chartier insists that what matters is how similar artifacts are understood, interpreted, employed, exploited, consumed – in Chartier's terms, *appropriated* – by diverse individuals and social groups. This approach has obvious relevance to the study of religion where, characteristically, a wide range of people share the same symbols, texts and rituals, yet may understand them in a multitude of different ways. More generally it offers a more plausible view of cultures not as rigid, monolithic entities, but as complex, dynamic exchanges and interactions which must be seen as much in terms of process as of structure.[1]

This leads directly to another approach to defining 'popular religion', or to thinking of religious aspects of 'popular culture': that is, in relation to official cults. Recent work is underpinned by the assumption that 'religion' as officially prescribed is invariably different from 'religion' as practised, and indeed may be only one element in a much wider pattern of cultural phenomena whereby people make sense of their experience and conceive of their relationship with the supernatural.[2] Yet this basic position can lead to widely differing interpretations. Some historians are inclined to see the mismatch between official prescription and popular practice in terms of potential or actual conflict, and hence to identify 'popular culture' with elements of opposition, resistance and difference. There are some persuasive reasons for this approach. In England as in other parts of Europe, the Christian church was an authoritarian institution which saw it as its duty to enforce an officially prescribed pattern of beliefs and observances. Popular religion thus evolved within a framework of coercion, and must be understood at least partly in terms of evasion and of passive or even active resistance. The approach has its dangers, however, in that it tends to exaggerate the oppositional element to the neglect of consensus. Compliance with official requirements is an equally important theme; and, more subtly, it is necessary to be sensitive to the ways in which ordinary lay people, while experiencing and understanding certain aspects of faith and practice differently from their clerical mentors, might nonetheless remain within the framework of orthodoxy and regard themselves as stolid conformists.[3]

An approach which emphasises interactions between official doctrine and popular culture is particularly apt for understanding religious experience in England in the century and a half between the Reformation and the Act of Toleration. Throughout this period the official church played such a central cultural, social and political role that 'popular religion' can hardly be understood except in relation to its influence. Christian doctrine as expounded by the church was not merely one among a number of available philosophies but defined the dominant framework for understanding the world and man's place within it. Likewise, the church as a legal, administrative and pastoral organisation – with its complex of spiritual courts and its network of local churches, its bench of bishops and its army of parish priests – had immense impact on society; through its sanctification of Sundays and holy days as times of special religious observance, through the rites of baptism, marriage and burial, through its close association with education and poor relief, and in a multitude of other ways it pervaded everyday life and impinged on the individual to an extent that is hard to grasp today. It is symptomatic of its dominance that many of the most informative sources for popular religion in Tudor and Stuart England – particularly the records of the ecclesiastical courts, which are used extensively in the following pages – were drawn up by the church hierarchy and are concerned with deviations from officially prescribed standards of religious belief and practice.[4]

Within this broad framework there were of course changes during the period, some of them of profound and far-reaching importance. The Reformation in its successive stages, extending into the reign of Elizabeth and beyond, represented a massive doctrinal and jurisdictional shift. It involved among other things the destruction of religious houses (whose *raison d'être* had been as powerhouses of prayer, charity and holy living); the abolition of prayers for souls in purgatory, thus effecting deep changes in parish religion and rupturing the bonds between the living and the dead; the restructuring of other aspects of worship, including changes in church services and the abolition of pilgrimages, processions and the veneration of the saints; a reduction in the numbers of the clergy and alterations (of which clerical marriage was one symptom) in their religious and social role. More generally it entailed the desacralisation on a large scale of places, times and objects that had hitherto been seen as holy. These changes may be summarised as a move to a primary emphasis on faith rather than works, to a religion of the Word (scriptures and sermon) rather than ritual practice, and towards increasing stress on the personal responsibility of the individual in religious faith and observance.

They represented a seismic shift not merely in 'popular' culture (however that may be conceived) but in English culture as a whole.[5]

A variety of consequential changes made the effects all the more far-reaching. The Reformation involved a strong element of iconoclasm – the destruction of images of God, Jesus Christ, the Virgin Mary and the saints in the form of sculpture, wall-paintings and even stained glass. The sequel was a downgrading of the visual image and arguably, the injection of an iconophobic element into English culture.[6] On the other hand the text of the Bible was exalted. Made officially available in vernacular translation for the first time by Henry VIII, its words and images seeped into, and eventually saturated, religious mentality in what was a period of rising literacy.[7] But it was not only the Bible that the people came to read: a feature of the seventeenth century was a proliferation of varieties of religious literature, written with diverse aims – catechetical, liturgical, devotional, and so forth – and often designed carefully to appeal to particular classes of readers.[8]

Another ramification was the increasingly close association of church and state. For centuries religious orthodoxy had been yoked with political loyalty, and the reliance of civil society on religious sanctions was reflected in the remarkable frequency of oath-taking both in the judicial system and in the processes of parish, borough, city and national government. But in the religiously divided realm that Elizabeth inherited, conformity with the established church was yet more firmly associated with political obedience. The matter became even more salient in the wake of civil war, regicide and interregnum: complicated by Charles II's ambivalence towards Catholicism, and James II's active support, the relationship between church and king became one of the most important political issues of the late seventeenth century.[9]

One of the key co-ordinates of debates about religion and loyalty was anti-Catholicism, which developed into a characteristic facet of English culture – popular and otherwise – in this period. Its origins lay in Elizabeth's reign, in the context of zealous Protestant evangelism, of hardening government action against Catholic recusants in England, of plots sanctioned by the papal bull of excommunication against the queen, and of war with Spain after 1585. Insistently the Papacy was identified with the Antichrist, and Roman Catholicism was associated with England's enemies. At the

same time Catholics at home were smeared as disloyal or potentially disloyal. This did not usually lead to hostility in day-to-day
relations with Catholic neighbours, but as a system Catholicism
was remorselessly linked with tyranny, oppression and persecution.
Such messages were reiterated not only in books (of which John
Foxe's *Actes and Monuments* or 'Book of Martyrs' is the most
famous) but also in sermons, pageants, plays and ballads, hence
reaching a mass audience including the illiterate. Anti-Catholic
sentiment became grafted onto traditional English xenophobia
and by the early seventeenth century appears to have been fully
absorbed into the national consciousness.[10] It was related to a pervasive (though often latent) millenarianism: the belief that this
was the 'last age' of the world, and that the hoped for defeat of
Antichrist would usher in the Second Coming of Christ. This in
turn was linked with the providential belief that God, far from
being a remote presence, intervened actively in the world to bless,
warn and chastise His people, and with the idea that in some sense
England had succeeded Israel as God's chosen nation.[11]

Yet even when the religious discourse of anti-Catholicism
seemed most rampant, around the time of the Exclusion Crisis
and the Glorious Revolution, alternative modes of viewing the
world were beginning to emerge. Religious divisions and religious
conflicts fostered reflection and discrimination that tried to establish limits to the state's right to coerce consciences. More profoundly the findings of the new natural philosophy (or 'scientific
revolution'), while remaining within a Christian frame of reference, cast doubt on old dogmatic certainties and began to explore
the limits of religious knowledge. Moreover for a variety of reasons, as much political and pragmatic as principled, a measure of
religious toleration was introduced by statute in 1689.[12] More generally the changes of the sixteenth and seventeenth centuries may
be seen as a process whereby people became increasingly self-
conscious about religion. Amid the debates over doctrine and
pious practice generated by the Reformation and its aftermath,
'religion' ceased to be something that could be taken for granted.
More and more it came to be identified as a matter of choice and
commitment, and hence diversity and potential conflict, in personal and social life. As a corollary religious *division* came to be
seen as a fact of life that had to be accommodated if it could not
be eliminated. It is not helpful to present these changes, as

LIBRARY
LRS

C. John Sommerville has done, in terms of 'secularisation', since religion remained so dominant a feature of English society long after 1700; but his idea of a shift from an all-embracing 'religious culture' to a more self-conscious 'religious faith' does capture an important transformation.[13]

Thus the results of the Reformation were complex and ambiguous. In some respects Protestantism was successfully established as the religion of the English people and the focus of national loyalties. The ecclesiastical authorities worked hard – by a variety of coercive, persuasive and educative means – both to inculcate the new patterns of belief and observance and to eradicate the old.[14] However, the cataclysmic changes of the Reformation profoundly disturbed existing patterns of popular belief and observance, inducing in the short term bewilderment, loss of confidence, even alienation; so also did the only slightly less dramatic changes of the civil wars and interregnum. New patterns took time to establish and were always in some respects fragile. More generally, at every stage the changes of the period demanded a renegotiation of the relationship between official prescription and lay practice, while within the broad framework of imposed uniformity there existed a variety of possibilities for oppositions, evasions and alternative understandings. The nature of lay responses was further complicated by the inconsistencies and ambiguities of official policy. During the periods of major change the parish clergy and ecclesiastical hierarchy were themselves divided. Even in normal circumstances the church was never a monolithic institution capable of speaking with a single voice, and the *variety* of official viewpoints – sometimes competing, sometimes merely diverse, and articulated at various levels in the ecclesiastical hierarchy – inevitably fed into the vagaries of popular religious behaviour.

Thus to explore popular religion in this period is a complex undertaking. It is first of all vital to recognise the immensely powerful field of force exerted by the official church, strong enough to keep in check (though not necessarily to eradicate) beliefs and practices of which it disapproved. But within that gravitational field there existed a *range* of *overlapping* and *interacting* religious cultures, not related in any clear-cut way to the divisions of the social hierarchy, and in complex interaction with official doctrines and precepts which were themselves by no means unitary or unchanging. Moreover there were shifts over time. The disruptions of the Reformation period eventually gave way to a more settled regime in the later years of Elizabeth and under James, but the pattern remained in some ways unstable and by the mid to late seventeenth century was in a renewed state of flux.

What follows is an attempt to explore the main features of the religious cultures of Elizabethan and Stuart England in the light of the foregoing discussion, concentrating chiefly on the period before the Civil Wars. The essay will examine in turn the most intense forms of Protestant piety, or 'Puritanism'; the evidence for popular ignorance and irreligion; the importance or otherwise of witchcraft and magical beliefs; and what may loosely be termed the 'parish Anglicanism' of the majority of the people. A brief coda will review some of the disruptions and changes of the mid to late seventeenth century, concluding with the suggestion that in important ways the Toleration Act of 1689 may be seen as the end of an era. Clearly, to cover so much ground in one brief essay requires a highly schematic approach. Thus only passing reference will be made to regional and local variations, though in reality these were both numerous and important. (Indeed detailed local studies, together with biographies of individuals and studies of particular groups, are the best means of getting close to the religious life of the period.) Moreover gender differences, which are only now beginning to attract the attention they deserve, will likewise receive short shrift in this chapter.[15]

II

In theory the post-Reformation Church of England embraced the entire population, but in practice its hold was never complete. Some Catholics resisted an increasingly elaborate body of penal laws to persist as a tiny, embattled but defiant minority of 'recusants'. However Elizabethan and early Stuart Catholicism was mainly a seigneurial religion. More humble Catholics did exist, as servants and other followers in the households of Catholic gentry or nobility, and as adherents of the old religion in their own right in pockets of Catholic survivalism in the north-west and elsewhere; but they represented only a tiny sub-section of opinion among the mass of the common people. Even less numerous, until the very eve of the Civil Wars, were Protestant sectaries who regarded the established church as ungodly and irredeemably corrupt, and on principle separated themselves from it – some emigrating to the Low Countries and later to New England.[16]

More crucial to understanding popular religion is to recognise that even within the bounds of the Church of England there was diversity. The most intense form of Protestant lay piety was that of the self-styled 'godly' or 'professors' of true religion, now commonly referred to as Puritans, who wished to carry the Reformation further than the Elizabethan Settlement allowed. Historians have conventionally thought of such people as enemies of popular culture rather than as elements of it; but on the perspective adopted here they can – within limits that will emerge from the discussion – fruitfully be seen in this light. Unquestionably they formed a highly distinctive religious culture. In a few areas they gave their children idiosyncratic names redolent of their hopes, fears and ideals – Fear-God, Flee-sin, Safe-on-high, and so forth.[17] More characteristic was addiction to sermons, lectures, Bible-reading, meetings for 'repetitions' of sermons, the self-examination of the personal diary and spiritual account-book. These features, grounded in a strong conviction of the sovereignty of God, the sinfulness of mankind, the assurance of election and the sanctity of the sabbath, were some of the more obvious manifestations of an intense religiosity which at its best linked a strenuous personal spiritual regime with a powerful sense of fellowship in Christ. Their activities were watched warily by the church authorities and by their neighbours and sometimes led to disciplinary action for attending private religious meetings or 'conventicles' (thought to be seditious), or for 'gadding' to hear preachers in neighbouring parishes. Some of the godly went as far as to deny the efficacy of the sacraments administered by a non-preaching minister or 'dumb dog'. Thus at Box (Wiltshire) on Easter Day 1603, a weaver and a roughmason, in church before morning prayer, 'denied' the Book of Common Prayer and the official Homilies, saying 'that there would be no edification for the people in them, and that the unpreaching minister could not rightly, and had not the power to administer the sacraments'.[18]

But to understand the culture of the godly it is necessary to supplement their public complaints and the statements of their detractors with their own personal utterances. One of the best documented individuals from the ranks below the gentry is Nehemiah

Wallington, a London wood-turner, who was born in the closing years of Elizabeth and died in the same year as Oliver Cromwell. Even for a Puritan his behaviour was eccentric. Intensely troubled in his youth by lustful thoughts – 'a sty of filthiness within me which did boil and bubble up' – his clumsy attempts at seduction alternated with fits of despair during which he tried repeatedly to poison himself with ratsbane. His stern but loving father married him off early in an attempt to steady him. Thereafter Nehemiah worked at his trade as an independent householder, but contrary to Weberian theory he never throve. The accounts that mattered to him were of another kind: volume after volume of notes on religious works that he had read, sermons he had heard, discourses with the local minister and with others; of comments on public affairs; of accounts of family matters and, above all, of records of personal examination, conscience-searching and spiritual endeavour. He was aware of political events, compiling a series of 'historical notices' vibrant with an intense providentialism. He was also profoundly concerned with the sins of his fellow men; much influenced by Thomas Beard's *The Theatre of Gods Iudgments* (1597), he compiled an elaborate 'Memorial of God's Judgments' and 'Ensamples of God's Wrath upon those that have broken his Commandments'. Yet he was most preoccupied with his own sinfulness and the state of his own soul, always seeking but never wholly securing a sure sense of God's grace.[19]

Godly lay piety, of which Nehemiah Wallington represents one extreme type, was an increasingly important phenomenon under James I and Charles I. In assessing its contribution to popular culture, however, it must be borne in mind that Puritanism was always heavily dependent on highly trained clerical leaders. It is probably also true that the attractions of Puritanism were culturally and socially selective. There are indications of ways in which the spiritual benefits of fluent literacy could be mediated to the unlettered or partly lettered, for example by the reading over of sermon notes.[20] However the fullest participation in Puritan piety undoubtedly demanded literacy; ideally it also required some leisure and a degree of privacy. Patrick Collinson, Margaret Spufford and others are right to challenge an unthinking assumption that Puritanism had no appeal to the poor; but what evidence is available does suggest that Puritans were mostly to be found in the middling to upper ranks of society, and that they were relatively few in number.[21]

On the ground the distribution of Puritans was likewise very uneven. Regionally they were more likely to be found in certain areas than in others – notably in London, parts of Essex and East Anglia, the Weald of Kent and East Sussex, some Midland counties, parts of Somerset and other western counties, and more patchily in Lancashire and other parts of the North. This pattern was conditioned by many factors, including early Protestant traditions, the patronage networks of sympathetic or convinced Puritan nobles and gentry, connections with Puritan colleges in the universities, and other influences which if not random are harder to pin down. David Underdown has argued for an affinity between Puritanism and wood–pasture regions in lowland England. To the extent that these overlapped with cloth-working areas, where the literacy and far-flung marketing networks of some of the inhabitants may have eased the reception of a Bible-centred religion, he is on familiar ground. Beyond this Underdown's 'ecological' argument remains unproven, admitting of too many obvious exceptions.[22] Even in regions where Puritans were most common there were numerous local variations. Absent from some parishes, a mere scattering in others, in the most favourable conditions the godly could constitute a sizeable group. A clique might even seize effective control of the machinery of local government and policing, as seems to have happened in the rural parish of Terling (Essex) and in a number of market towns such as Bury St Edmunds (Suffolk) and Dorchester (Dorset); in the latter it was 'fire from heaven', a conflagration which destroyed many of the buildings in 1613, that galvanised the inhabitants into converting the town into a godly citadel.[23]

Wherever they were found the godly tended to be involved in campaigns of moral activism. There was a positive side to this in commitment to education and the relief of 'God's poor' (the old, the sick, the orphaned child, and so on). On the other hand they waged an untiring war against idleness, drunkenness, swearing, sexual immorality and religious laxity. Puritan gentry and urban oligarchs were often able to exploit their position as magistrates to further such 'reformation of manners'; at the less elevated social levels with which this chapter is concerned, the godly did likewise through their exercise of local office as constables, churchwardens and overseers of the poor. Their targets included the dissolute and unruly among the poorer ranks of society; but youth of whatever social rank – whose irresponsibility and inclination towards 'liberty' were proverbial – were especially likely to attract their strictures, while the extremes of Puritan moralism often brought them into abrasive contact with neighbours of all sorts who thought that respectability was consistent with a degree of 'good fellowship'. It is hardly surprising that the godly were often bitterly attacked as 'precisians', 'hollow-hearted men', 'hypocrites and dissemblers'.[24]

III

The precisians were apt to view the rest of society as the ungodly multitude, and some historians (whether influenced by such judgments or not) have argued that there did exist substantial numbers of people whose ignorance, indifference or even scepticism alienated them from the church, made them susceptible to magical alternatives to Christian teachings, and could in some cases lead to a virtual rejection of all religion.[25] Two weavers of Lacock (Wiltshire) in 1656 provide what appears at first sight a striking example: the views that they expressed combined antinomian ideas with star worship, a denial that heaven and hell existed save in a man's own conscience, and a willingness to sell all religions for a jug of beer. That this case has been very widely quoted by historians reflects the fact that it was extremely unusual, and to draw wider conclusions about 'popular scepticism' from such a case is hazardous.[26] It is true that throughout the sixteenth and seventeenth centuries the ecclesiastical authorities occasionally trawled up accusations of atheism or scepticism, but few of these cases seem to have amounted to much. The more articulate expressions of irreligion seem mostly to have come from gentlemen with some formal education, though instances among somewhat humbler members of society are not entirely unknown. Thus Robert Blagden, a substantial yeoman of Keevil (Wiltshire), was accused by his enemies in 1619 of having 'made doubt ... whether the prophets' and apostles' writings were true or not'.[27] Probably much commoner than considered scepticism was the scoffing variety, sometimes triggered by drink, sometimes by the ebullience of 'wit' which contemporary writers particularly associated with 'atheism'. (Significantly enough, the meaning of this word was much wider than it is today, extending to behaviour which through immorality or lack of devotion implied indifference to the Almighty.) This humour was often verbal but sometimes took practical forms, such as baptisms of animals or the staging of mock sermons. In either case it drew on a stock repertory. When the rector of Holland Magna (Essex) preached in 1630 about Adam and Eve making themselves coats of fig-leaves, one of the congregation demanded to know where they got the thread to sew them with. A generation before, Nicholas Gibbens in *Questions and Disputations Concerning the Holy Scripture* (1601) had noted that 'there are of this our age, which ... will be so mad as to demand, where Adam had a thread to sew his fig leaves'.[28]

There is no doubt that the Christianity of the mass of the population was compatible with magical beliefs and recourse to magical practices of which the church disapproved. Yet it is doubtful if these can be considered a really serious rival to official religion; rather they should be seen as a syncretic blend of Christian and non-Christian elements held uneasily within the church's field of force. Belief in witches and their power to do harm was, of course, in itself orthodox doctrine, and various forms of witchcraft were proscribed by statute. The witches were supposed to have succumbed to the blandishments of the devil, and were sometimes charged not only with doing physical harm by witchcraft but also with anti-Christian practices or participation in the witches' sabbath. However, the accused often vehemently asserted their Christian faith, and such accusations can hardly be taken at face value.[29] The evidence of prosecutions for maleficent witchcraft in England presents many puzzles which deserve (and are beginning to receive) further study. It is already plain that cases were patchily distributed in space and time: from the evidence available it would seem that the county of Essex, in particular, witnessed an exceptional number of cases and that Elizabeth's reign was the period in which prosecutions were most intense.[30] Yet it would be a mistake to lay too much emphasis simply on the pattern of court cases, since it appears that there were persistent, perhaps powerful, undercurrents of fears and beliefs about witchcraft which did not necessarily lead to legal action. Over 500 of the patients that the astrological physician Richard Napier saw in his house at Great Linford (Buckinghamshire) thought they had been bewitched – though this was over many years (from 1597 to 1634) and they came from far afield. Even towards the end of the seventeenth century, when official concerns about witchcraft were rapidly receding, such anxieties occasionally surfaced in terrifying incidents of unofficial counter-action against suspected witches, such as 'pricking' (that is, thrusting) them with a long pin to see if they had any insensitive or 'dead' spots, searching them for witches' marks, or 'swimming' them in a pond or river. Nonetheless the indications are that fears of witchcraft, potent enough when they were aroused, were ordinarily marginal rather than central to most people's lives, and became more so as the period went on. Thus local studies generally yield only a few references to maleficent witchcraft over many decades; references to orthodox religious belief are by contrast legion.[31]

Perhaps slightly more central were practitioners of white magic – 'cunning men' and wise women (some of them were also supposed to be black witches) who undertook to cure humans and animals, 'discover' maleficent witches, find out lost goods, identify thieves, supply love charms, and so forth. Their characteristic methods were the sieve and shears, magic glasses, bowls of water in which images might be seen, written charms or mottoes to be fed to sick animals or hung in the mane or tail of an ailing horse, the burning of hair of bewitched animals or humans. The charms sometimes embodied religious invocations, and Agnes Pinberrye of Barnsley was even said to be 'allowed to charm by the Bishop of Gloucester' when one of her clients was brought in question in 1582.[32] Many of the other devices had no Christian significance, but should not necessarily be seen as pagan – except to the professional theologian there was no obvious reason to brand them as non- or anti-Christian. Certainly magical practitioners continued to operate throughout the sixteenth and seventeenth centuries, though not necessarily in great numbers: about forty have been identified from Essex records for the period 1560–1600, but only half that number were named in the following eighty years. It would seem that official hostility gradually made people self-conscious and possibly uneasy about resorting to them. Astrology, originating as a learned pursuit but increasingly accessible through the cheap almanacs which sold in huge numbers by the mid-seventeenth century, and given a great boost by the remarkable events of the Civil Wars and Interregnum, could claim greater authority and was viewed more equivocally by the church; its practitioners were thus able to retain their prestige longer.[33] And, of course, there existed a rich variety of magical and superstitious practices to deal with everyday frustrations, longings and dilemmas, and with the anxieties associated with what Sir Keith Thomas calls the 'hazards of an intensely insecure environment'. But when John Aubrey sought the 'remains of gentilism and judaism' in the post-Restoration world he found only fragments.[34]

IV

It seems incontrovertible that the Christianity which officially dominated Tudor and Stuart society was in some sense accepted by the mass of the people. But *precisely* what the religious beliefs of ordinary people amounted to is a moot point. Such evidence as exists is often highly suspect. The contemporary divine William Pemble told of an old man who, despite having been all his life 'a constant hearer as any might be, and ... forward in the love of the word', thought that God was 'a good old man', Christ was 'a towardly young youth', his soul was 'a great bone in his body', and that 'if he had done well', after he died 'he should be put into a pleasant green meadow'. This vivid anecdote became as famous in the seventeenth century as it now is among historians, but it was hearsay at best, Pemble having taken it 'from a reverend man out of the pulpit, a place where none should dare to tell a lie'.[35] Even more problematic are the sourer utterances of Puritans such as Richard Greenham, minister of Dry Drayton (Cambridgeshire) from 1570 to 1591, who despite preaching some six thousand sermons and otherwise endeavouring to be a 'painful' pastor, eventually threw up his ministry in the village and moved to London because of 'the intractableness and unteachableness of that people'. As a number of historians have recognised, men such as Greenham demanded impossibly high standards which jaundiced their view of their flocks. Moreover, seeing themselves as among an elect chosen out of the unregenerate multitude, yet at the same time convinced of their own personal unworthiness, they had expectations of failure that were reflected in their outlook and in some of their pronouncements. Nonetheless their tone varied and in a pastoral context they could be altogether less harsh, more optimistic and more discriminating about the varieties of religious belief and observance.[36]

Of contemporary writers perhaps Arthur Dent, despite his critical stance, came closest to the beliefs of the majority. He ascribed to the rustic characters in *The Plaine Mans Path-way to Heaven* (1601) a kind of jumbled and misty half-knowledge of all but the most basic doctrines, yet a firm conviction that religion had much to do with right living, charity, and 'peace' among neighbours. A similar emphasis on peace and quiet, and a strong dislike if not hostility towards contentious doctrines or 'brabbling' behaviour, emerges in numerous forms in contemporary sources and was one of the main reasons for hostility to precisians. Yet not all currents of popular belief were at odds with godly doctrines. In particular it is clear that a providential framework of thought, which could give meaning to both the pains and the satisfactions of life, was with varying degrees of intensity shared by all ranks of society. Thus wills conventionally voiced thanks for 'the worldly goods that it hath pleased God to bestow', and expressed a routine resignation to His will: 'if it happen that God call my child'; 'after it shall please God to call me'. But its most intense manifestations were evoked by local or national disasters, such as fire, famine and plague, and at a personal level by the accidents that could reduce their victims to abject dependence. The call of preachers and pamphleteers for prayer and humiliation evoked a response precisely because they offered some means of explanation and amelioration of calamity.[37] To think of the religion which combined these various elements as semi-pagan superstition, as some historians have done, seems wide of the mark. While not necessarily Protestant in a strict doctrinal sense, it was both plainly Christian and – to use Tessa Watt's useful term – distinctively post-Reformation, and was nourished by the religious ballads, chapbooks, and other forms of cheap literature (including illustrated material) that were widely available and consumed in this period.[38]

Despite these insights, we shall never know *in detail* what ordinary people believed because there was no systematic official attempt to find out. The stress in the English church was on outward conformity, and in these circumstances the best approach to popular religion is to study the pattern of observances that shaped most people's experience from the cradle to the grave. These reveal on the whole a fair degree of compliance with official requirements, though it was far from being unquestioning or total. Certainly it would seem that in the late sixteenth and early seventeenth centuries there was very little evasion of the rites of passage. Baptism or 'christening' was regarded as an important ritual to the extent that Puritan ministers who scrupled to sign the infant's forehead with a cross were likely to arouse fierce hostility from ordinary parishioners.[39] For obvious reasons death and burial had the greatest power to focus the minds of everyone involved on sin, heaven, and hell. Thus the late medieval tradition of *ars moriendi* was refashioned in Protestant England into an all but universal aspiration towards a 'good death'. The middling ranks and upwards could command the assistance of physicians and clergy (though the involvement of ministers at deathbeds seems to have declined during the period) and could expect to have their spiritual struggles commemorated in funeral sermons; they might also expect to be remembered in church or churchyard monuments, which from around the middle of the seventeenth century gradually became available to people below the rank of gentry. But even the poorer sort could (with or without the clergy) expect the assistance of fellow-parishioners in making a good death, and the 'ringing of the great bell' at their funeral. When a tailor of Wylye (Wiltshire) died in 1620, his neighbours testified that he 'christianly committed his soul into the hands of Almighty God, with comfortable hope of His everlasting mercy'.[40]

Naturally the hale and hearty often had a different order of priorities. In theory everyone was supposed to honour God by abstaining from work on Sundays and holy days; throughout the period practice failed to match up, especially on the lesser feasts. Some parishes customarily held fairs on certain festivals, so that in response to the authorities' inquiries about holiday work the churchwardens were constrained to admit that 'we are all guilty'. From the later years of Elizabeth's reign the church became increasingly strict in this matter, and by the 1620s and 1630s had secured compliance to the extent that work was firmly restrained in most parishes at least on Sundays and the major holy days.[41] A more contentious issue was games and sports, which were traditional on Sundays and festivals and were officially licensed (subject to the restriction that they should take place after evening prayer) by the royal Declarations of Sports of 1617–18 and 1633. Herein lay the substance of a real culture clash, but one that should be seen not in simple terms as an elite attack on popular culture but as the expression of differences of religious outlook that ran as a vertical fissure through the social structure. Among some committed Protestants an increasing stress on sabbatarian doctrine from the 1580s made Sunday sports anathema. In any case the godly were apt to see maypoles, hobby horses, morris dancing, rushbearings, well-dressings and the like as blasphemous idols or profane relics of paganism, and denounced dancing, pipes and tabors, church ales, wakes and feasts as evil provocations to drunkenness and sexual immorality. By the 1630s sports had become a national issue, and differing stances on the morality or otherwise of maypoles, cakes and ale became symbolic of wider doctrinal, ecclesiological and political positions. Even before this there were serious conflicts in some towns and villages, such as Banbury (Oxfordshire) in 1589 and Wells (Somerset) in 1607; in many other places there were occasional minor skirmishings. Disagreement was apt to flare up most bitterly where the local minister took a strong line in parishes which were not fully in the control of the godly. Thus in 1634 the curate of Bodicote (Oxfordshire) was taken to task by his parishioners for allegedly inveighing against the *Book of Sports* and preaching that 'the [May] garland was brought into the church under pretence of adorning the same therewith, but ... it did deflower the said church ... [and] that by keeping of Whitsun ales the people did make the church of God an alehouse'.[42]

Puritan attacks on sports may have been excessive, but the belief that piping, fiddling, dancing, a multitude of other games and pastimes and, of course, tippling drew people away from church undoubtedly had substance. There were moreover numerous other reasons why people stayed at home, including lack of decent apparel (which in the opinion of respectable neighbours and perhaps in their own eyes made them *unfit* to attend), the minding of children and fear of arrest for debt. But the most common reason was simply disinclination. Absenteeism was apparently particularly rife during the early to middle years of Elizabeth's reign, in the immediate aftermath of the mid-century disruptions. From about 1570 church courts, parish ministers and some magistrates strove more consistently to ensure that religious obligations were fulfilled, and their task probably became easier as the Protestant church gradually gained acceptance. Evidence from many parts of England suggests that by the 1620s and 1630s reasonable levels of church attendance and participation in the communion were taken for granted. Of course there were many regional and local variations, as well as fluctuations from month to month, year to year, and incumbency to incumbency in any given parish. But some places for which figures are available have revealed striking levels of observance. It might have been thought that religious rituals would have been particularly vulnerable in the expanding metropolis. But there is evidence that in St Saviour's parish in Southwark over 90 per cent of the inhabitants received communion annually during the Easter season. While it is clear that the churchwardens here were particularly meticulous in their efforts to secure compliance, and there is somewhat earlier evidence from certain other London parishes to suggest that the Southwark figures were unusually high, they nonetheless remain impressive. Much evidence from rural parishes likewise suggests good attendance: in Steeple Ashton (Wiltshire) in 1639, for example, the total wine bill came to £4 19s. 6d. for 100 quarts for seven celebrations of the communion.[43]

These facts cannot be understood simply in terms of coercion by the authorities, nor do they necessarily imply egregious piety. The aesthetic and emotional appeal of the Anglican liturgy, which by the early seventeenth century had attained the dignity of long continuance, should not be underestimated. Nor should the attractions of the communal singing of metrical psalms: sophisticated observers found the standard Sternhold and Hopkins version execrable, but at the same time testified to its popularity. Sermons, too, could have a popular appeal, if they were pitched at the right level and of sensible length.[44] More generally attendance figures must be seen in the context of the central role that ecclesiastical institutions played in social life. In the sixteenth and seventeenth centuries the parish became increasingly important as a unit of administration for secular as well as ecclesiastical administration, and it was actually in the church, churchyard and adjacent buildings that numerous forms of local business, such as the election of officers and the casting of accounts, were regularly transacted. Fire-fighting equipment and the parish armoury were often stored on church premises – a reflection of the church's role as a rallying-point in times of crisis. The church bells were rung to signal alarms and to celebrate joyful events (including the annual celebration of Queen Elizabeth's Accession Day and other royal occasions), and ordinarily one of them was rung 'for curfew and day'. There was often a school of some sort associated with the church or minister. Rhymes and lampoons against whoremasters, whores, cuckolds and other local ne'er-do-wells were sometimes pinned up on the church door – a reflection of the church's status as the moral centre of the community.[45] For individuals as for the parish as a whole, participation in the services of the church was intimately associated with local identity, respectability and status. This emerges most vividly from arrangements for seating in church. Households and individuals were assigned particular places, some of which were attached by right to certain holdings or properties. Broadly speaking the seats in the church were arranged in order of social importance. Better and more elaborate 'rooms' at the front were allotted to gentry and other leading parishioners (the best had high panels for protection against draughts, curtains, cushions and other conveniences); the poor were assigned to mean benches at the back; in the middle were a variety of intermediate sittings. Often there were other divisions – between 'men's seats' and 'women's seats', and between accommodation for the householders of the parish and subsidiary provision for servants, apprentices and other youngsters. Clearly such arrangements were designed to give symbolic expression to the parish hierarchy – a conservative vision of a well-ordered community, meeting in the presence of God, in which everyone knew his or her place. Of course no such entity existed, and even if it had it could not have been adequately represented in the static, physical layout of the seats. As a result there were sporadic scuffles as individuals contested particular seats or tried to claim 'better' ones; while sooner or later the effects of social mobility, movement in and out of the parish and other demographic changes would make necessary a total reallocation of seats – often presaged by general grumbling if not contention. But the very fierceness with which places were cherished indicates how important these matters of status were, and how far the aspirations of parishioners locked them into the system of corporate worship.[46]

The strength of such attachment may well have varied with social status. Probably it was the middling ranks of society upwards – those who monopolised such local offices as churchwarden and overseer of the poor, and who contributed most to the upkeep of the church and the well-being of the parish through the payment of church and poor rates and through contributions to local voluntary charities – for whom the forms of religion were of greatest social importance. However, a number of recent studies caution against supposing that the appeal of church membership was necessarily much weaker lower down the social scale. Many 'honest householders' of the poorer sort, who had a definite albeit modest stake in the community as payers of some local rates with a right to a place in church, may plausibly be supposed to have shared similar values. Moreover, within the framework of conformity there were presumably many variations in personal piety which were unrelated to social status in any simple way. Nor should one assume any kind of simple contrast between town and country. Local attachment to the church has been documented for rural parishes in Wiltshire, Norfolk and elsewhere. But it certainly existed also in urban parishes, in London, Bristol, Chester and other provincial towns.[47]

V

Yet the limits of parochial participation, and its ambiguous significance in relation to religious belief and commitment, must also be recognised. Contemporaries themselves knew that disputes over pews reflected badly on the piety of the participants, and in any case this was merely one of a variety of ways in which church services were likely to be disturbed. Actual complaints to the authorities about unruly parishioners were in most areas fairly infrequent, and it may well be an exaggeration to think of the average congregation as behaving, as some historians would have it, like 'a tiresome class of schoolboys'. But unquestionably there were some who instead of attending to the service slept (with or without their hats on), spat, broke wind, told jokes or indulged in other forms of irreverence. Parishioners who were bored by mercilessly long, dry sermons, or who had an axe to grind against the minister, could be deliberately and provocatively disruptive.[48] Bell-ringing, at first sight a healthy sign of lay participation in church activities and a kind of sport that encouraged rather than conflicted with church attendance, could also be contentious. The parishioners tended to regard the belfry and the bells as their province, and sometimes fell foul of clergymen who thought differently. Thus at Washington (Sussex) in 1614, when the minister tried to stop bell-ringing he was told 'Shall we be ruled by one peeled scurvy forward wran-

gling priest? We will ring!' On the other hand, some bell-ringers
were clearly addicts whose monopoly of the bells brought them
into conflict with other would-be ringers, or simply drove the rest
of the parish mad with 'unseasonable ringing'. At Cassington
(Oxfordshire) in 1594, nocturnal bell-ringing led to an
unseemly incident in which the church was locked and the door-
handle smeared with dung to keep out other parishioners.[49]

Parish religion was perhaps undermined also in more
insidious ways. The fact that certain religious duties were
compulsory and defined by canons and statutes, combined with
the law-mindedness characteristic of the period, encouraged a
minimalist approach to devotion. Demarcation between the
duties of rectors (clerical or lay) who had responsibility for the
upkeep of chancels, and those of the parishioners who were
charged with maintaining the rest of the church, was rigorously
insisted on. Church buildings and furnishings *were* generally
maintained, perhaps better than historians have commonly
supposed. But much of it was done by means of compulsory
rates which some paid grudgingly and others refused to pay at
all. Such communal customs as had survived the Reformation,
notably the Rogationtide procession of the parish boundaries
with the 'drinkings' that certain holdings along the way
were charged with providing, were hard to keep up; the subject
requires further research, but the general impression is one of
declining incidence in many areas. Wills, with their provisions
for funeral ceremonies, bequests for the poor, and (in some
areas) legacies to the local church or to the minister, in general
give a more positive impression of devotion, though the
degree of local and individual variation was immense. Some
studies, such as David Levine and Keith Wrightson's account of
the rapidly developing coal-mining parish of Whickham
(County Durham) reveal definite signs of evaporating local
commitment.[50]

The fact that the authorities had to keep up the pressure to
enforce even the basic duties of church attendance and participation in the communion likewise reflects a certain reluctance,
which some people erected into a virtual principle. 'Browne the
lighterman' of St Lawrence in Thanet (Kent), 'being willed to
come to church' one Sunday in 1581, retorted that 'it was never
merry England since we were impressed to come to the church';

Thomas Rigglesworth of Padbury (Buckinghamshire), apparently a husbandman of moderate substance, allegedly declared in 1635 that 'if he come to church but once a month it is enough and it is puritanism to press the needfulness of evening prayer'. More generally it would appear that servants, and perhaps other young people, were in many parishes neither expected nor encouraged to come to church frequently: John Taunton of Westbury (Wiltshire) was said to have declared in 1614 that if householders 'did send their people [i.e. servants] to prayers they were as good send their horses'.[51]

The catechism, which was designed to prepare the young for their religious duties, was another bone of contention. Charges of neglect were occasionally brought against individual clergy, but the latter generally pleaded that they had done their best but found the youngsters unwilling to come. Parents, masters and mistresses were supposed to compel them, but this assumed a control over the young that was not always apparent. Richard Chapman of Stoke Talmage (Oxfordshire), when upbraided by the rector for not sending his children to catechism in 1633, 'asked what he would have him do; for he had given them warning and without he should bring them upon his back he knew not how to bring them'. The pattern of prosecutions suggests that the clergy were generally conscientious in doing what they could, but over time their expectations were trimmed and some gave up in the face of apathy.[52]

As to participation in the sacrament itself, the high figures for Easter communion reported from Southwark and elsewhere are (as Ian Archer has pointed out) in fact somewhat double-edged: the *Book of Common Prayer* actually prescribed that parishioners should receive *three* times a year *at the least*. It seems that the authorities had to recognise that this level of observance was impossible to enforce. Even the annual drive at Easter regularly produced a crop of defaulters and of people who at first failed to receive and had to be coerced. And of course there were complaints about the cost of communion bread and wine, and occasionally unconventional attempts to circumvent it: thus in 1635 William Nash of Thornborough (Buckinghamshire) was in trouble 'for bringing his peculiar wine in a shepherd's leather bottle to the communion table and his own peculiar bread for himself and his own household ... to free himself from the ... charge of the communion.'[53]

One of the excuses that was often made for neglect is particularly revealing. The *Book of Common Prayer* prescribed that the minister should refuse the sacrament to 'evil livers' (such as notorious adulterers) and also 'those betwixt whom he perceiveth malice and hatred to reign; not suffering them to be partakers of the Lord's Table, until he know them to be reconciled'. Moreover the 'Exhortation before Communion' warned intending partakers of the sacrament to repent their sins, make reparation where possible, and reconcile themselves to their enemies before they received, 'lest ... the devil enter into you, as he entered into Judas, and fill you full of all iniquities, and bring you to destruction both of body and soul'. This vigorous language evidently impressed itself on many listeners, and was sometimes echoed in the discourse of ordinary parishioners. Thus in 1604 Roger Hill of Pewsey (Wiltshire), just before the celebration of communion, upbraided one of his neighbours with the words: 'Goodwife Monday, remember yourself how you have used me, do not you think to go ... to take the communion, and take God by the hand and forsake God and go to the devil' – a challenge which led the minister to advise Monday to abstain from the communion, and provoked her in turn to upbraid another woman (who was actually on her knees and about to receive the sacrament) with being the cause of her 'falling out' with Hill.[54]

Such an incident nicely reveals some of the complexities and ambiguities of popular religion. It reflects how closely devotion and disturbance could be intertwined. It suggests that church and sacrament held considerable emotional power for some parishioners, yet also reveals how doctrine could (from the point of view of the authorities) be misunderstood or even perverted. However it represents merely one of a variety of responses to the sacrament and of understandings of its meaning. It is known from other cases that some parishioners used the approach of communion as a genuine opportunity to settle their quarrels with neighbours, or to effect reconciliations between others, so that they could receive the sacrament in a spirit of Christian charity and fellowship. In this way the services of the church could reinforce the high value which contemporaries, as was noted earlier, placed on communal harmony – on 'peace', 'love', 'charity' and 'quietness'. Thus in a Kentish parish around 1564 the churchwardens and principal parishioners, 'minding to end all controversies between Warner's wife and Wootton's wife', brought the two women together and persuaded them to be 'at unity and concord and each to forgive [the] other': Wootton's wife shortly afterwards received communion 'as a Christian woman ought to do ... with divers other parishioners ... declaring thereby her reconciliation'. Similarly a Wiltshire man reported 'on Easter even last [1615] ... going to Richard Ambrose of Boyton to reconcile himself'. Yet on other occasions enmity far outweighed any impulse to reconciliation and the communion was powerless to resolve it. For some 'being at enmity' was used as a cynical excuse for not receiving the sacrament, and among Catholic recusants became a common stratagem for avoiding the law; others perhaps were fearful of the consequences of receiving in an unworthy frame of mind and preferred to play safe.[55]

VI

The relationship between the established church and the religious cultures of the people in early seventeenth-century England was thus complex and in certain respects fragile; it was to be disrupted, and eventually altered profoundly, by the successive religious changes which occurred during the Civil Wars, the Interregnum and the Restoration period. The lapsing of censorship, the abolition of episcopal government and church courts, and the catalytic experiences of the Civil Wars and their aftermath shattered the uneasy unity of the period before 1640 and led to a proliferation of religious groupings – from moderate Presbyterians, through less conservative Independent congregations (who did however accept infant baptism and were prepared in some sense to work within the structure of a state church), to the more radical Baptists (who decisively separated themselves), and the 'world turned upside down' of extreme sects such as Fifth Monarchists and Quakers. Whatever the social standing of pre-Civil War Puritans, the following of some of these newer religious groupings certainly included lower-class elements – thus further complicating the relationship between religious cultures and social status. The Prayer Book itself was proscribed and those who remained loyal to it were cast in the role of nonconformists; yet the Presbyterian 'Directory of Worship' that was designed to replace it was never fully accepted. The religious and political world turned again in 1660 when the revolutionary regime collapsed and Charles II came back in triumph. But although the Church of England was restored it was never able to recover its near-monopoly of religious allegiance: Protestant dissent in a variety of forms became – alongside Catholic recusancy – a permanent feature of English society.[56]

It would be wrong to exaggerate the numerical and social importance of these nonconformist groups, or to emphasise unduly their cultural distinctiveness. Although precise figures are elusive – not least because there were undoubtedly substantial numbers of 'floaters' who attended both Anglican churches and nonconformist meetings, sometimes on the same day – it does seem clear that outright dissenters formed only a small proportion of the population. Yet global figures can be misleading. Dissent was regionally and locally a very patchy phenomenon and nonconformists could constitute a formidable presence in certain places, notably in parts of London but also in some provincial towns and certain rural parishes.[57] How far dissenters were set apart from their neighbours is a question that yields ambiguous answers, in part depending on the kinds of sources that are consulted. Recent research indicates that they were more widely distributed in the social scale than has often been thought, and local records often indicate both their strong economic and social ties with other members of the community, and routine involvement in the structures of local office-holding. The outlook of Presbyterians and other of the more conservative dissenters was often close to that of conformists; indeed many of them would fain have belonged to a broader-based national church. Yet it is equally plain that some dissenting groups exhibited – even flaunted – a cultural identity that set them apart. The early Quakers, guided by a breathtakingly radical 'inner light' theology, deliberately and flagrantly drew attention to themselves. The rough northern dialects of the pioneer Quaker missionaries were themselves a source of culture shock in the southern areas that they penetrated; yet more alienating was the refusal to do 'hat honour' (to doff the cap to superiors), the 'plain speech' of theeing and thouing, the rejection of oaths, the deliberate disturbance of ministers and the disruption of services in what the Quakers contemptuously called 'steeple houses', and theatrical gestures – such as 'going naked as a sign' – that were designed to induce conversion through shock. Quakers became less confrontational, more quietist and accommodating as time went on, yet they did not necessarily become less separate. Their meeting books reveal a rigidly enforced endogamy, while an even more potent sign of otherness was burial outside the churchyard. By the same token the Baptists' rejection of infant baptism – an all but universal rite before the Civil Wars – could not fail to mark them off from their conformist neighbours.[58]

Relations between dissenters and Church of England folk could, moreover, be ruptured by actual conflict. In the immediate aftermath of the Restoration, nonconformists in some communities struggled with the legal incumbent for spiritual and social control of the parish. Sometimes occupation of the parish church was only yielded up by the dissenters after fierce resistance, and even then the nonconformists sometimes maintained a sustained campaign of legal and physical harassment. Adapting an old tradition of horseplay, some dissentients expressed their disgust by urinating from the belfry – pissing on the 'piscopal congregation below. It has been suggested that such tensions centred primarily on ministers and less often affected relations between dissenters and ordinary parishioners. Yet conflicts among lay people of differing religious opinions were certainly evident in post-Restoration London, where the prosecution of dissenters and the deliberate searching out of Quakers and other sectaries caused much bitterness. Such tensions can sometimes be glimpsed in country parishes under the surface of other disputes. Thus at Tilehurst (Berkshire) in 1692, the defendant in what appeared at first sight to be a routine slander suit was described as 'a dissenter from the Church of England, and of different persuasion from the plaintiff ... and also an ill-natured and cross neighbour'.[59]

Among the conforming majority, loyalty to the rites of the established church not only survived the disruptions of the mid-seventeenth century but was in some respects reinforced. The Puritan regimes of the 1640s and 1650s tried to abolish Christmas and other traditional festivals, wedding ceremonies in church (replaced by a civil contract before a magistrate), the rituals of infant baptism and of the burial service, regular communions open to all adult parishioners, and indeed the entire pattern of the Anglican liturgy. But in so doing they met widespread passive resistance and some overt opposition; the *Book of Common Prayer* continued to be used (more or less surreptitiously) in some places throughout the Interregnum, and was enthusiastically restored almost everywhere when the king came back in 1660.[60] Yet the substance of popular observance was not unaltered. There are strong indications that fear of the communion, already evident before the Civil Wars, intensified in the late seventeenth century. Part of the reason was the extreme emphasis that some Puritan clergy had placed on the danger of receiving the sacrament unworthily and the need for the most rigorous preparation. Thus at Berwick St John (Wiltshire) in 1662 it was complained that the minister had announced in a sermon 'that one unworthy receiver being admitted to the sacrament would draw down damnation on all the rest of the communicants'. Such messages proved hard to eradicate; indeed it would appear, from the evidence both of printed pastoral works and local references, that by the closing decades of the century there was a widespread belief that communion 'did nothing but damn people; it was impossible to receive it worthily and those that received it otherwise did damn themselves'. Some even thought that 'those were damned, that so much as laughed after they had received it'. To many ordinary people the solution seemed plain: to avoid communion as much as possible. It is true that in some parishes high rates of attendance could still be achieved: at Clayworth (Nottinghamshire) they reached a peak of 90 per cent in 1677. But beliefs about the sacrament help to explain why in many areas of Restoration England levels of communion reception were low and declining.[61]

How far had patterns of worship changed in other respects from the pre-civil war situation? The evidence at present available is unfortunately limited, but Donald Spaeth's findings for the county of Wiltshire are suggestive. In this area, it would seem, the church and Prayer Book continued to matter to villagers in Charles II's reign, but they were even less slavish in their conformity than they had been before 1640. Though they were reluctant to receive communion they did for the most part attend church once a week on Sunday; they generally abstained from non-essential work on the sabbath and major festivals, but ignored the church's ban on labour on other holy days; in church they generally listened attentively enough to the service and valued the sermon, but in some parishes which had developed an anti-ritualist tradition there was reluctance to kneel at prayers, stand at the Creed and Gospel, and make 'due reverence at the name of Jesus'. Late seventeenth-century parishioners could also be remarkably assertive in dealing with drunken, incompetent or over-zealous clergy. Sometimes an unpopular minister simply found himself without a congregation. Or parishioners might continue to attend church, but only to give the clergyman a foretaste of hell. At Marcham (Berkshire) around 1700 the congregation laughed and jeered openly at the minister in divine service, while out of church they abused him behind his back and broke his windows.[62]

The fact was that changing conditions were strengthening the position of congregations relative to their clergy. By now they had experienced generations of Protestant preaching and teaching, and they had acquired a sense of what they did not like as well as what they did. Moreover, unlike their pre-Civil War counterparts, parishioners were well aware of *alternatives*, including dissent; if they were dissatisfied with their ministers they were inclined to complain vociferously, sometimes threatening to join the noncon-formists. Another factor was the gradual growth of education among laymen that gave parishioners the cultural self-confidence and rhetorical skills necessary to make their protests. The wording of parochial petitions against unsatisfactory ministers neatly illus-trates the point. Clergymen had long had a tendency to denounce their parishioners as ignorant and ungodly; by the 1680s disgrun-tled parishioners were able to turn the tables by describing minis-ters as 'uncivil' and 'heathen'. Another, related, point is that by the late seventeenth century ordinary people were less dependent on their parish ministers for religious information. There was by this time a veritable *market* for religious instruction and advice – a market met by both conformist and nonconformist ministers who, along with other writers, penned a great variety of religious works, ranging from weighty tomes of theology and devotion down to the 'penny godlinesses' or small religious chapbooks hawked up and down the country by pedlars and chapmen. On the other hand, the church authorities had become less confident about their abil-ity to coerce religious belief and observance, or even of the utility of doing so. Even the church courts, which had been revived after the Restoration, were often halting and uncertain in their approach to the slack and to the recalcitrant; and even when the authorities were zealous they were not always able to secure the co-operation of churchwardens in detecting offenders. Church-men increasingly saw the need to *persuade* and *educate* rather than merely to dictate; yet that was tacitly to admit that the opinions of lay people were worth attention, and parishioners' stubborn persistence in these views sometimes drove clergy to despair.[63] As the rector of Hethe (Oxfordshire) commented sadly in 1682, 'men are so wedded to their dogmatical humours, though never so erroneous, that the clergy may time after time admonish and persuade in vain, and find little or no remedy or amendment'. Their resistance was sustained by a shrewd perception of the limits of the law. As another Oxfordshire curate recognised, 'they judge what they are not forced to, [to be] left to their liberty'.[64]

Clearly the times were changing, and it is against this background that the effects of the Toleration Act of 1689 must be understood. Originally designed to provide a limited degree of relief for Protestant dissenters, as popularly interpreted it effectively destroyed the legal basis for the enforcement of religious discipline.[65] This set the seal on earlier, *de facto* developments towards religious voluntarism. Just what this meant in terms of church attendance and other indices of religious observance is a complex matter that requires further research. Many observers did note a falling away, which can sometimes be corroborated by other records: thus at Clayworth in Nottinghamshire, the Rector's Book records a steady decline in numbers of people attending communion during the 1690s.[66] However, as usual the pattern was regionally and locally diverse, and in certain circumstances losses could be made good. Nonetheless in an important sense it was in fact the end of an era. What had gone was a set of conditions which had through all the vicissitudes of the sixteenth and seventeenth centuries succeeded in maintaining a close if ambiguous relationship between popular and official religion. In destroying the coercive framework in which the Church of England had hitherto operated, the Toleration Act had created a distinctively different context in which popular religious cultures would henceforth be shaped, and hence a different matrix for our understanding of 'popular culture'.

6. The People's Health in Georgian England

ROY PORTER

POPULAR, POLITE AND PROFESSIONAL MEDICINE

Historians have argued that the divides between 'high' and 'low' cultures in England were becoming more acute during the eighteenth century and were being more sharply policed. Patrick Curry, for instance, has convincingly argued that, whereas 'everybody' subscribed to astrology in 1650, a century later, such beliefs had been relegated to the 'vulgar'.[1] This model, however, applies only very partially to medicine. A glance at any surviving manuscript remedy book compiled by a gentry family between the Restoration and the Regency will reveal the vast range of sources from which medical truths continued to be culled.[2] The hotch-potch of so-called 'receipts' recorded in such collections – deriving from family secrets and eminent physicians, from lords and ladies, from kitchen maids and stable lads, from learned texts, newspapers, or such time-tried works – epitomises the entrenched and enduring pluralism of pre-modern medical care.[3] At the same time, an oral lore continued to circulate above and below stairs, imparting such proverbial gems as:

> Prevention is better than cure.
> Ague in the spring is physic for a king.
> Agues come on horseback, but go away on foot.
> A bit in the morning is better than nothing all day.
> You eat and eat, but you do not drink to fill you.
> At forty a man is either a fool or a physician.[4]

This eclectic openness to all manner of medical knowledges – what else made sense in an age before sure-fire scientific medicine? – was reflected in, and reinforced by, medical practice itself. Contemporary letters and diaries attest the continuing willingness of the educated to resort to popular healers and remedies – at least when all else failed.[5] Candid regular practitioners, too, admitted that key breakthroughs – inoculation against smallpox, and the use of digitalis to treat dropsy and heart conditions – owed much to folk beliefs and practices. The discoverer of vaccination, Edward Jenner, drew upon village talk that those who, like milkmaids, suffered cowpox, escaped smallpox.[6] The Midlands practitioner William Withering picked up the properties of digitalis from countryfolk. 'In the year 1775', he wrote:

> my opinion was asked concerning a family receipt for the cure of dropsy. I was told that it had been kept a secret by an old woman from Shropshire who had sometimes made cures after the more regular practitioners had failed ... This medicine was composed of 20 or more different herbs; but it was not very difficult for one conversant in these matters to perceive that the active herb could be no other than foxglove.[7]

The picture is thus one of pluralism and fluid interchange of ideas and information. Vital necessity meant that healing practices transcended educational and class barriers.

It was a two-way process. The quality still drew upon popular medical beliefs; and the poor, for their part, were being increasingly exposed, as we shall see below, to the ministrations of regular practitioners, thanks to the opening of scores of charitable hospitals and dispensaries, the philanthropic activities of well-to-do physicians, and the growth of medical aid under the old Poor Law.[8]

Some scholars have interpreted these developments as a 'medicalising' invasion by the professionals, or in other words, as the hegemonic imposition of elite medicine within a wider programme of the neutralisation or suppression of 'low culture'.[9] Certainly, occult powers were losing their intellectual credit, witch beliefs were being ridiculed, and popular customs put down. Not surprisingly: for the elite felt uneasy at certain elements of 'folk medicine'. Village wise-women and nurses were often suspected of collusion with abortion, contraception and even infanticide. Enlightenment propaganda encouraged genteel mothers to suckle their own babies (lest ignorance and superstition prove catching), and urged the replacement of 'granny midwives' with smart new university-trained *accoucheurs*

– suggesting the wish to ensure not merely that 'high' should dominate 'low' culture, but that male knowledges should supplant female.[10]

The polite deplored the medical follies of their inferiors. When smallpox broke out in Eliza Pierce's household, one of her maids had to be confined to bed. The other, fortunately, had been inoculated, so the mistress felt confident the outbreak would spread no further. Not so the stupid abigail – for 'she has taken it into her Head that she should have the disorder, tho' she was inoculated about three years ago, and had them very thick'. Miss Pierce was mad:

> this has provoked me & done me more harm then anything else, as she wou'd sit like a dead thing, and no reasons had any effect on her. [I] am convinced that had she had the least real complaint, or any feverish disorder that the College of Physicians could not have saved her Life, so strongly was she prepossessed she would have the small Pox.[11]

Relations between the medical beliefs of the learned and vulgar were not, in other words, tension-free. Yet it would be too extreme to imply that there was any concerted, still less successful, drive to eradicate popular medicine. To understand medicine in the 'world we have lost', we must think away anachronistic assumptions. Medicine today is dominated by professional elites and technico-scientific authority. In Georgian times the medical map was differently drawn. Many types of healing coexisted, overlapping and clamouring for the public ear. No single, privileged medicine – hypothetically, medical science, as endorsed, say, by the Royal Colleges – was driving other types of medical beliefs (popular, folk, oral, female, etc.) out of circulation and out of business. No united front of magistrates, media men and the medical top brass, backed by Parliamentary statute, was silencing popular healing by imposing monopoly medicine from above.

If anything, the reverse was true. Georgian medical provision shared in an effervescent, demand-led and increasingly *laissez-faire* economy. The medical market was expanding, and healing remained open, in practice at least, to anyone seeking to ply his or her own trade.[12] Medicine formed an active part of the marketplace. Healers – regular, irregular and amateur – touted rival services before clients confident of their ability to make informed choices. Hence, those selling services in what was cynically styled the 'sick trade' had to bow and scrape before their more affluent customers.[13] Qualified practitioners possessed few of the choice professional privileges guaranteed them by the mid-Victorian state; they were forced to operate in open competition against itinerants, vendors and quacks, brazenly exploiting the new opportunities afforded by advertising, mass production and speedier communications. Regulars were thus in no position to dictate to their affluent clients, or even perhaps to the humbler. All needed to turn a penny and make their services marketable.[14]

It would, in sum, be anachronistic to suppose a concerted alliance in the Georgian century of elite opinion and the medical profession to suppress vulgar errors and demotic healers. Commercial conditions precluded it. Given the diversity of medical services on offer, prevailing relations would better be characterised by the term 'exchange'. And exchange relations in turn encouraged 'commodification'. Even reputable practitioners – to say nothing of empirics – promoted patent medicines and proprietary nostrums, bulk-produced and available, gaudily-packaged, by post, through newspapers, or over the counter from myriad retail outlets.[15] Others, as we shall see, published 'do-it-yourself' books of kitchen physic, offering easy-to-use diagnostic guides for a range of readers from graduates to the barely literate.[16] Pamphlets, magazines and ephemera also broadcast popular medical knowledge: almanacs such as the *British Merlin* carried advice about seasonal disorders, precautions and cures, while also, like newspapers, carrying patent medicine advertisements.[17] Such self-medication texts, it goes without saying, far from neutralising popular medicine, tended to flatter lay capabilities.

We can occasionally document grassroots medicine in practice. Joseph Gutteridge, an artisan born at the close of the Georgian era, began by studying herbals and ended up a lay healer. 'My father gave me an old edition of Culpeper, with coloured plates', he explained: 'By the aid of this book I soon found out not only the common names of plants but their uses and medical properties.' He started to making drawings of medicinal leaves, and 'I experienced great delight in delineating the forms and colours of plants and flowers. The ability to do this proved to me in after times a ready means of fixing in my mind the peculiar characteristics of plants that otherwise might slip my memory.' Gutteridge's first step towards abandoning doctors altogether was taken when his eldest son fell sick, and he could not afford a practitioner.[18]

> We were obliged to fall back upon our own resources. To succeed in this I procured by loan or purchase all the medical and physiological works I possibly could, especially books treating on the eyes, including Fyfe's 'Anatomy', Grainger's 'Elements of Anatomy', Southwood Smith's 'Philosophy of Health', and two or three Dictionaries of Medicine, but the work most suited to my wants was Gray's 'Supplement to the Pharmacopoea.'

Gutteridge was a confident medical autodidact: 'It is said that "A little knowledge is a dangerous thing"', he noted, but 'the sentiment would perhaps be more accurate if it read "Too little knowledge, or knowledge mis-applied, is a dangerous thing."'[19]

Georgian medicine thus comprised complex networks of commercial and cognitive exchanges, wheels within wheels. Amongst medicos, individual skill, ambition, know-how, contacts and cash-in-hand counted for more than professional qualifications and career ladders. Amongst patients, in an age of lethal infections, 'try anything' made sense.[20] Such conditions inhibited the emergence of medical 'separate spheres' compartmentalising high and low healing, professional and lay, male and female. Space limitations preclude full exploration of the criss-crossing circuits operating within this system. I shall therefore attempt to depict a few aspects of this complex picture, before venturing some broader conclusions.

MEDICINE AND THE DECLINE OF MAGIC

Twenty years ago, Keith Thomas traced the decline of magic in early modern England.[21] As part of that process, the decline of medical magic is especially hard to plot, since for healing there was, of course, no equivalent to the repeal of the Witchcraft Laws (1736), legally and symbolically drawing down the curtains on the supernatural. It is never easy to judge when 'magic' was thought to be at work. Thus, when Parson Woodforde had a stye on his eye, he heeded a 'common saying' and rubbed it with a black cat's tail.

Result: 'After dinner I found my Eye-lid much abated of the swelling.' Though an Oxford graduate, Woodforde clearly felt no out-and-out antipathy to folk remedies. But was he aware of the colour magic in the 'black'? Possibly, for he added, 'any other Cats Tail may have the above effect in all probability – but I did my Eye-lid with my own black Tom Cats Tail'. Yet when he bought eighteen yards of ribbon to wrap round his household's throats to prevent sore throats, it was specifically *black* material he purchased, just as the recipe he followed for throat troubles also specified blackcurrants (if unobtainable, redcurrants could be used instead). But in this case, Woodforde gives no sign of acknowledging the white magic latent in the black symbols. Or take another case: in 1771, Richard Brookes, a regular practitioner, advised readers of his health care book, 'when there is a Pain in the Head with a Delirium, cut open a live Chicken or Pigeon, and apply it to the Head'. Such a practice surely took its original meaning from a sacrifice, but Brookes showed no sign of endorsing its magical factor.[22] It is, thus, often difficult to gauge how far supernatural elements were acknowledged. But it is beyond dispute that a huge corpus of medical magic was in circulation through the Tudor and Stuart eras. Much was explicitly religious, consisting in commandeering the sacred symbols of Christianity for therapeutic ends. Bread baked on Good Friday would never go mouldy; if stored, it would treat all manner of disease. Rings made out of silver collected at Communion would cure convulsions. Confirmation would ward off sickness (for this reason, people sometimes sought repeated confirmations, rather like vaccine boosters). Gospel texts and Bible stories were often written out as charms. Such beliefs had been authorised within the proliferating healing rites of medieval Catholicism. With the Protestant anathematisation of pilgrimages, relics, holy waters and the invocation of saints, similar 'superstitions' continued, though now with popular, not ecclesiastical, sanction.[23]

But, independently of Christian healing, charms, amulets, girdles and rings were widely worn as specifics against maladies and maleficium. To prevent ague, observed John Aubrey, inscribe ABRACADABRA in a triangle and wear it about the neck. Aubrey also promoted a bulletproof vest. 'To make a man Gunne-proofe', he recorded, 'write these characters + Zada + Zadash + Zadthan + Abira + in virgin paper (I believe on parchment), carry it always with you, and no gun-shot can hurt you.' Alternatively, the way of health might be to eat your words. 'A spell to cure the Biting of a mad Dog', Aubrey transcribed: 'Rebus Rubus Epitepscum. Write these words in paper, and give it to the party, or beast bitten, to eat in bread: Mr Dennys of Poole in Dorsetshire sayeth this Receipt never failes.'[24]

Medical magic worked in other modes too. Disease could be transferred, transplanted or transformed. A sick person should boil eggs in his own urine and then bury them; as the ants ate them, the disease would also be eaten up. Similarly whooping cough sufferers should stand on the beach at high tide: the ebbing tide would carry the cough with it.

Above all, disease could be transferred to the dead. A sick person should clutch hold of a limb of a corpse awaiting burial; the disease would quit his body and enter the corpse. This mode of magic explains why mothers crowded around the scaffold, struggling to thrust their sickly infants into contact with a felon's lifeless body.[25]

Alongside transference or substitution, magic could equally work by similars. Many plants carried signatures, keys to the disease for which they would prove specifics. Wood sorrel was a cordial, because it was shaped like a heart, celandine was yellow to show it would cure jaundice, walnuts were good for brain disease – all such beliefs were common in seventeenth-century herbals. And diseases were supposed to carry their own cures. For a mad-dog bite, the remedy was the hair of the dog that bit you. Likewise viper fat cured viper bites, honey soothed bee stings, and moss growing on human skulls soothed headache.[26]

The doctrine of signatures was of course coterminous with astrology. Plants governed by Venus, Culpeper had explained, would aid fertility, those under Mars would prove strengtheners. The Moon itself loomed large in medical magic: rubbing hands in the moonlight cured warts. And such object magic went far beyond astrology's system of meanings. The cauls of newborn babies, the hangman's rope, the sloughed skins of snakes – all were repositories of magical powers. A law of opposites governed much object magic: vile things like candle snuffings, cobwebs, dung and so forth being credited with precious virtues. Toads applied to tumours would cure cancers, and spiders became the grand panacea: 'I took early in the morning good dose of elixer and hung three spiders about my neck, and they drove my ague away', wrote Elias Ashmole in 1681, adding, perhaps prudently, 'Deo Gratias'.[27]

Medical magic had taken many forms. Certain individuals had special powers. With much hand-me-down magic, on the other hand, what counted was literal adherence to the healing ritual. A child might be cured of rupture if passed *thrice* through a cleft ash sapling. If the tree subsequently grew whole again, the child would recover completely. No single explanatory system governed it. Indeed, its popular mystique probably lay in its very lack of explanation; the peremptoriness with which it commanded: 'Take this, follow that' was of the essence, if magic was to meet a vulnerable society's need for confidence-boosters.

Widely accredited, medical magic was practised across the social spectrum through the Stuart age. 'Sorcerers are too common', remarked Robert Burton, 'cunning men, wizards and white witches as they call them, in every village, which, if they be sought unto, will help almost all infirmities of body and mind.'[28] Aubrey recorded a wizard in Wells who had cured over a hundred people of the ague by giving them a paper with abracadabra written on it as an acrostic. The young Dr Edward Browne, FRS, communicated to his father, Sir Thomas, 'a magical cure for the jaundice which hath greater effects than is credible to any one that shall barely read this receipt without experiencing' – a not uncommon linking of magic and experimentalism. Christopher Wren, future President of the Royal Society, cured his wife of thrush by 'hanging a bag of live boglice around her neck'; and Robert Boyle, pioneer mechanical chemist, informed Aubrey 'that he alwayes weares a peice of gold about his neck: as Magnetique to mercuriall humours that are in the body and he very well sayes that there are no doubt many other occult qualities not yet discovered'.[29] Nevertheless, though medical folklore continued to thrive, medical magic, in the strict sense, suffered long-term decline. Doubtless, Victorian antiquarians could still find practices similar to those recorded by Aubrey, but only amongst the yokelry, and in the dark corners of the kingdom. Even the 'peasant poet', John Clare, was remarkably disdainful of gypsy healers ('they had pretentions to a knowledge of medicine, but their receipts turned more on mystic charms and spells').[30]

Though the demise of medical magic in the Georgian era comes as no surprise, exactly how, when and why this process occurred still await precise investigation. Yet the symptoms are unmistakable. Take, for instance, the *Gentleman's Magazine*. Founded in 1731, this became the leading quality miscellaneous magazine of the century. Thousands of items in the *Magazine* covered the gamut of matters medical: readers, for instance, sent in local and family cures – goose grass as a strengthener, salt-water bathing to heal wens. But in all this, there is not the slightest indication of magical healing, even for fatal conditions such as cancers where 'try-anything' might have been expected. Commercial quacks got a mixed but not wholly unfavourable reception, but the occasional mention of cunning women or white witches triggered disbelief and hostility. Thus a report upon Bridget Bostock, the Cheshire healer who claimed to cure by prayer and spittle, condemned her as a throwback to popery.

I have similarly examined a score of family recipe books kept between the late seventeenth century and the Regency. What do we find of medical magic? Almost nothing. One eighteenth-century volume contained a recipe for Sir Kenelm Digby's powder of sympathy; to heal the wound, it noted, soak the soiled bandage in the preparation. Another urged throwing a sick person's urine on the fire as a jaundice cure. A further offered a cancer cure with the following appendix: 'Perhaps Abaracadabra would do as well, but there is a great virtue in mysteries and we admire a thing often because we do not understand it.' Aside, however, from these brief glimpses, the hundreds of recipes I have examined, many testifying to flourishing domestic arts and herb lore, proved secular and pragmatic.[31]

Georgian letters and diaries tell similar tales. Such records of the better-off testify to a lively lay medical culture: kitchen skills, family cures and a vibrant curiosity in disease aetiology, diagnosis and therapy. Providence and prayers are prominent. But there is a notable absence of magic or recourse to magical healers. The Georgian cultural elite had evidently broken with magical medicine – seemingly confirming parallel changes in the public domain, such as the abandonment of touching for the 'King's Evil' (scrofula) by the Hanoverian line.[32] The pieces of evidence all point in the same direction: a genuine demise of medical magic, especially amongst the literate. What caused this?

Thomas points to shifts in cultural psychology. Amongst the educated, the Enlightenment 'recovery of nerve' dismissed 'magic' as a mark of ignorance and superstition.[33] And, noting that people embrace magic when their capacity to cope with dangers is precarious, Thomas points to real medical improvements: the growing availability of new drugs from America and the Indies, and the Georgian wave of hospital foundations.[34] Yet one must not push these factors too far – after all, the hospital movement gathered national momentum only from mid-century and affected only a small sector of the population.

Nevertheless, key shifts in material culture were afoot, upstaging magic. In the Georgian commercial boom-time, medicine became increasingly commodified, as part of the remarkable expansion of the service economy historians have recently emphasised.[35] Certain preparations became popular whose ingredients and formulae were common knowledge: one might buy Daffy's Elixir from the local apothecary or druggist as today one would buy linctus or aspirin. But a nationwide market mushroomed for brand-name proprietary potions, patent medicines and nostrums, distributed from London warehouses to retail outlets, through newspapers which both advertised and distributed such wares. Some of these were respectable, such as the eighteenth century's main fever-reducer, Dr James's Powders. Others were arrant frauds – Solomon's Balm of Gilead, Brodum's Cordial and so forth, meant to restore youth or compensate for venereal indiscretions. Some were sinister, such as Hooper's Female Pills, essentially an abortifacient. A score of big-selling medicines helped change the nation's dosing habits. In thousands of households, the automatic response when falling sick was now to swallow something from a shelf of medicaments stored at home, perhaps even held in a proprietary medicine chest. Thus commercialised and routinised, sickness and healing were shorn of some of their mystery. Taking shop-bought medicines was now presented as the natural thing to do. When, in the best-selling children's story, *Little Goody Two Shoes*, little Margery's father falls sick, no good fairy comes to save him. Instead, we are told, 'He was ... seized with a violent Fever in a place where Dr. James's powder was not to be had, and where he died miserably'.[36]

No room seemed left for magic. Or, more precisely, magic was sublimated within the medicine business. For certain commercial medicines offered themselves as charms, as for example the famous 'Anodyne Coral Necklace', to be worn by babies against the pains of teething. Likewise many 'quack' nostrums flooding the market – gaily packaged, mass advertised, available anonymously by mail order – claimed the infallible properties traditionally associated with magic: Rose's Balsamic Elixir would cure 'the English Frenchify'd beyond all the other medicines upon the face of the Earth. It removes all pains in 3 or 4 doses and makes any man, tho' rotten as a Pear, to be sound as a sucking lamb' – it would, in other words, work like magic.[37] Or medical magic survived, transmogrified into the person of the up-market mountebank, who sanitised wizardry by turning it into spectacle. Performers like John ('Chevalier') Taylor, the itinerant eye specialist whose patter was a spellbinding mix of Latin and Johnsonian English; James Graham, who disappeared into mud baths while singing the praise of his medicines; Gustavus Ketterfelto, flu-remedy pedlar accompanied by a bevy of talking black cats, whose advertisements ran 'WONDERS! WONDERS! WONDERS!' – those were names to conjure with, for they 'conjured' in that sense of the word which became standard in the Georgian popular theatre, performing by sleight of hand. Just as the traditional figure of the Fool turned into the stage comedian, so the medical magic of the wizard found his new incarnation in the up-market quack performer.[38]

And making magic obsolete at a more mundane level was the growing presence of everyday medical practitioners: apothecaries, druggists, and so forth. This was the century in which surgeon-apothecaries and general practitioners set themselves up in every market town and large village. And for the indigent, by contrast, traditional medical magic sometimes yielded to medicine under the Poor Law, first through *ad hoc* arrangements, and then via regular parish contracts with surgeons. The everyday medicines and ministrations of ordinary practitioners did not often 'work'. But their growing routine presence steadily created expectations of medical normality and rationality which gradually squeezed medical magic to the sidelines.[39]

POPULARISED MEDICINE

Traditional oral lore was also elbowed aside by the remarkable growth of 'popularised' medical knowledge – regular medicine diluted and made palatable for the common reader in works of domestic physic. The genre was far from new; it was, in fact, almost as old as printing.[40] But it was only after the Restoration that such works as *Physick for Families, Every Man his own Physician* or *The Female Physician* circulated in vast numbers. John Wesley's *Primitive Physick*[41] and William Buchan's *Domestic Medicine* ran perhaps to hundreds of editions, and evidence from diaries proves they were useful rather than ornamental. None of these bestselling Georgian works of popular medicine had any room for magic. Wesley put his trust in cleanliness, godliness and a small armamentarium, in which cold water, honey, brimstone and onions were prominent. Buchan repudiated the 'mystical jargon' of old wives and traditional learned medicine alike, and offered a health regime built upon moderation and common sense. Immensely popular, such works imparted medical outlooks that fostered self-help, gave their readers some leverage against the medical profession, but also – most important – set them a cut above the arts of the cunning women and the oral lore of the barnyard. Through them healing became medicalised, not in the sense of lay practice bowing before an intrusive medical presence, but because the language and concepts of regular physic, with its vision of natural body function and the regular pattern of disease, was rendered in the language of educated lay people.

'Popularised medicine' is a multifaceted genre, that defies simplistic interpretation. It often carried a populist radicalism, an Enlightenment faith in the diffusion of knowledge. But there was also an agenda of 'reforming' popular beliefs. Instructional texts would denounce folk cures as superstitious, and seek to inculcate moral ideals such as cleanliness. And in any case, the growth of popular medical texts should be read as an expression of economics no less than ideology: popular texts were money-spinners. In the emergent consumer society, more people were consuming more knowledge, not least medical knowledge, alongside a diet of drugs and medications.[42]

Such texts reveal disagreements about popular healing. It was axiomatic that ignorance and error must be combated, and progressive attitudes propagated towards health, disease, treatments and doctors. But how far was it desirable that the common man be encouraged to be his own physician? A brief examination of three doctors, prominent for their contributions to this didactic genre,

may be illuminating: William Buchan, Thomas Beddoes and James
Parkinson – late eighteenth-century doctors who shared a common
political radicalism, railing against Old Corruption, denouncing
despotism and parading their contempt for grandee corruption.
Each embraced the cause of the people, and propounded an
Enlightenment faith in human betterment, to be achieved by the
defeat of vested interests, the progress of science and the diffusion
of useful knowledge. Each diagnosed ill-health as symptomatic of
the evils of the *ancien régime* body politic, tolerated by the nepo-
tism, toadyism and incompetence of a medical profession moved
by love, not of health, but of wealth. All believed the rights of man
included the right to health, indeed, the right to its self-manage-
ment. Beyond such consensus, however, their views notably
diverged, in ways suggestive for the future politics of health.[43]

William Buchan, a Scots-born Edinburgh graduate, was the
author of the evergreen *Domestic Medicine* (1769), reprinted well
into the nineteenth century, and also of *Observations Concerning
the Prevention and Cure of the Venereal Disease* (1796).[44] Sympathetic to both the American and the French Revolutions,
Buchan became a bitter critic of the medical establishment.
Domestic Medicine went beyond the bare recipes of Wesley's
work, expounding a broad philosophy of health to be achieved
through temperance, hygiene and obedience to Nature's laws.
Especially in his *Observations Concerning ... Venereal Disease*,
Buchan embraced a democratic late Enlightenment populism,
aimed at 'rendering medicine more extensively beneficial to
mankind'.[45] The people were medically benighted, the root
cause of which was that 'Physic is still engrossed by the faculty';
medicine must stop being a closed shop whose shop-talk was a
dead tongue.[46] 'While men are kept in the dark, and told that
they are not to use their own understanding, in matters that
concern their health', Buchan explained, *à propos* of venereal
disorders:[47]

they will be the dupes of designing knaves; and a disease the
most tractable in its nature, and almost the only one for
which we possess a specific remedy [i.e. mercury], will be suffered to commit its ravages on the human race, and to embit-
ter the most delicious draught that Heaven has bestowed for
the solace of human life.

An age of revolution thus demanded the democratisation of medicine, and that meant openness and education. 'It is no more necessary', he argued, 'that a patient should be ignorant of the medicine he takes to be cured by it, than that the business of government should be conducted with secrecy in order to insure obedience to just laws.' The goal? 'To bring medicine out of the schools, to lay open its hidden treasures'. The means? 'A code of laws for the preservation of health'. 'Medicine will be little better than a piece of mummery', he believed, till its 'doctrines are laid open, and candidly submitted to the examination of all men.'[48] Once medicine was taught to all, most disorders could be self-treated. A reader of *Domestic Medicine* would conclude that few clinical problems lay beyond the capacities of a sensible layman or woman. In Buchan, the Enlightenment ideal of 'committing the care of ... diseases to the people' – medicine for the people, by the people – appears in its most triumphant form.

Thomas Beddoes was an ardent libertarian and arch-enemy of Pitt the Younger;[49] yet he felt less confident than Buchan about democratic medicine. Beddoes insisted that the profession was mercenary and that the people ought to be caretakers of their own health. But the knowledge which they ought then to acquire was emphatically *not* the principles and practice of medicine. In lay hands, Beddoes never tired of insisting, medicine was a menace. Clinical treatment was an art so intricate, requiring vast experience and refined judgement, that only the trained physician should tackle it. Lay physic was bad physic.

Here Beddoes departed from Buchan's Jacobin aim to impart 'all the information in my power, both with regard to the prevention and cure of diseases'.[50] The desideratum must be to teach the people, not the arts of self-medication – physic must be left to experts! – but skills in cultivating and preserving health. Above all, he wished to promote the application of 'physiological knowledge to domestic use' – it would be desirable, he argued, if 'physiology will come to be considered as the domestic science *par excellence*'.[51]

Crucial to Beddoes's strategy was health education by public lectures, instruction in anatomy and physiology, and homely advice, as in *Good Advice for the Husbandman in Harvest* (1808). Beddoes looked to enlightened doctors to instruct the people, as is plain from his most popular tract for the times, *The History of Isaac Jenkins, and of the Sickness of Sarah his Wife, and Their Three Children*

(1792), a moral tale of a lower-class household that fell into destitution and sickness once the husband had taken to drink. Fortunately, the intervention of a wise and worthy surgeon helped to restore both the morale and the health of the family. The homily ends with a heartwarming vignette of the simple but honest Jenkins household, toiling hard to maintain its dignity, but, thanks to its freedom from fashionable vices, well on the road to recovery.

James Parkinson, a talented scientific polymath, general practitioner and parish doctor in London's East End, was a political radical of real stature, in the 1790s being active in the pro-Jacobin London Corresponding Society.[52] He too wrote numerous health advice books, including *The Budget of the People* (1793), *The Town and Country Friend and Physician* (1803), and *The Villagers's Friend and Physician* (1802) – this last also being condensed into a handbill, entitled *The Way to Health* (1802). Like Beddoes, he was given to a rather sentimental ideal of paternalist doctors tending honest swains. Self-medication was hazardous; expert help was best. Hence *The Villager's Friend and Physician* instructed readers when sick to 'apply directly to the man of judgment and experience'.[53] If a regular could not be afforded, try a hospital, Parkinson advised, but never a quack or the neighbourly amateur who 'possesses a medicine chest and the small share of skill which is derived from the perusal of some treatise on domestic medicine'.[54] Yet Parkinson was a realist, who knew people would inevitably undertake self-medication. Hence his *Medical Admonitions to Families Respecting the Preservation of Health and the Treatment of the Sick* (1801) was designed to enable readers to judge, from self-scanning of symptoms, which disorders required professional aid and which could safely be handled by domestic first aid. His most popular appeal, *The Way to Health,* was a body maintenance guide for manual labourers. Work and plain fare were healthy; liquor and idleness brought diseases.[55] Medicine thus afforded Parkinson an idiom for imparting to the poor a homespun moralism that valued personal responsibility. If the unlettered poor were presently the authors of their own misfortunes, with instruction they could become guardians of their own health. Responsibility for health rested ultimately in the individual's own hands.

My rapid survey of this triumvirate of radicals has thus revealed certain ambiguities in the enterprise of the popularisation of medicine. There was something inherently radical about spreading medical knowledge. Yet Beddoes and, to a lesser degree, Parkinson were convinced that the population would cease to be sick only when it ceased to medicate itself, and trusted instead in the enlightened, expert practitioner. Doctors were needed to protect the people from their own folly. Herein lies the classic radical doctor's dilemma: might not the people, to echo Rousseau, also need to be forced to be healthy?

ACCIDENTS

What did all these teachings amount to in reality? Finally and briefly, I wish to glance at one area of intensely practical medical concern: accidents. Pre-industrial society was certainly no less accident-ridden than ours. Roads were abominations, work animals were unruly, and there were the hazards of open fires, naked lights, universal darkness and ubiquitous infants ('What a many such scrapes from death doth a boys headless [*sic*] life meet with', remembered John Clare).[56] Newspapers tell endless tales of tragic falls, fires, drownings, firearms explosions, mishaps with tools and knives, potions and poisons, and traffic spills ('I shall begin to think from my frequent overturns', rued Elizabeth Montagu, 'a bone-setter a necessary part of my equipage for country visiting').[57] From its opening issue in 1731, the *Gentleman's Magazine* carried a column headed 'Casualties', a term still carrying providential implications to the Protestant mind.

Faith in personal providence was universal in early modern times, a way of coping with a menacing environment. But Enlightenment minds came to match providence with probability, precautions and prudence. The insurance industry grew, and the Enlightenment spirit of pragmatic improvement devised self-help against disaster. Fire-fighting became better organised. Amateur fire brigades were set up, spurred in America by Benjamin Franklin. Alas, neither providence nor prudence always prevented personal injury. In the days before ambulances, hi-tech casualty wards, X-rays and operating theatres, the medical profession was rarely able to make a decisive contribution.

Struck by everyday accidents, people applied first aid. 'Cut off the top of my thumb', lamented Robert Hooke, 'but cured it in 4 days by Balsamum Peruvianum.'[58] They aided others. 'In shearing

Wheat this Afternoon', reported Parson Woodforde, 'Briton cut of part of his left hand Thumb with the Sickle, owing in a great measure to his making too free with Liquor at Norwich to day ... It bled very much. I put some Friar's Balsam to it and had it bound up, he almost fainted.'[59] Enlightenment practicality and consumerism got first aid organised, not least through the sale of ready-made medicine chests (Richard Rees marketed three sorts, one for gentlemen, one for ladies, one for horses).[60] All such crisis self-help left doctors ambivalent. They fretted about silly folk-saws which could prove fatal; but increasingly gave practical advice for village self-help. Thus in his *Domestic Medicine*, Buchan condemned the 'horrid custom immediately to consign over to death every person who has the misfortune by a fall, or the like, to be deprived of the appearance of life'. But he countered apathy with advice. 'The unhappy person [should be] carried into a warm house, and laid by the fire, or put in a warm bed.'[61]

Buchan set great store by lay first aid. Careful folk could handle most accidents, even serious-sounding conditions such as fractures or dislocated necks ('I have known instances of its being happily performed even by women, and often by men of no medical education'). At bottom, Buchan argued, 'every man is in some measure a surgeon whether he will or not'.[62] Of vital importance, however, was proper instruction in accident management, for the desire to help was rarely matched by adequate skills. With wounds, cuts and bruises, it was best to let be, and take plenty of rest: 'It is Nature alone that cures wounds.'[63] No mysterious expertise was needed, no miracle cures to be expected. He would give no elaborate details about bandaging, he told readers, because 'common sense will generally suggest the most commodious method of applying a bandage'.[64] James Parkinson's *The Villager's Friend and Physician* similarly taught labourers how to cope with high-risk environments, and his *Dangerous Sports: A Tale Addressed to Children* (1808) warned naughty boys not to climb trees or play in toolsheds.[65]

Enlightenment optimism held that hazards lay within human power. Accidents could be avoided, or damage limitation put in hand. Sometimes collective action followed. In particular, the Humane Society was founded, seeking to spread skill in rescue techniques, especially in drownings, though in other sorts of apparent sudden death too.[66] The Society supplied equipment, awarded prizes, and published pamphlets and promoted its views in periodicals such as the *Gentleman's Magazine*, advocating mouth-to-mouth resuscitation, tobacco clysters, and the importance of rubbing and keeping warm. And public activism went beyond the drowned: the *Gentleman's Magazine* is full of practical tips, contributed by medical men and layman alike, for countering domestic emergencies – crises caused by eating toadstools, swallowing arsenic, snake bites, farm injuries, mad-dog bites and the like.[67] And, from mid-century, in London and most provincial cities, the new charity hospital movement provided a further site for dealing with emergencies: the casualty ward. Increasingly, as Mary Fissell has shown, sick people seeking admission would present themselves as casualty patients. In time, the public came to view hospital as the standard site for casualties to go to.[68]

This last discussion has, I hope, been illuminating. It has sought to show the gradual but pervasive emergence of an apparatus of civilisation: practical, utilitarian attitudes, the spread of literary information and technical skills, the work of charitable organisation, the growing presence of the profession. These factors did not decisively create a division between professional and popular medicine (still less did they decisively improve health or slice the death-rate). There is always an argument for continuity over change. At the very beginning of the Victorian era, Fenwick Skrimshire published *The Village Pastor's Surgical and Medical Guide,* in which, having condemned the 'old crone' still to be found in many villages, who acted as its 'oracle in all matters of surgery and medicine', and the 'uneducated pretending quack', he mused whether 'medical works, written for unprofessional readers, were not calculated to do as much mischief as good'. He therefore urged that, in view of the great development of 'professional works written by surgeons and physicians of eminence' (presumably he would have included himself), the parson should assume care of the medical needs of villages – obviously a little like James Woodforde did, sixty years before.[69] Nevertheless, things were indeed changing. By the end of the Georgian era, a broad, better-educated public had emerged, far more familiar with medical book-knowledge than had been the case a century earlier. If that may have had only a marginal effect in actually improving the people's health and changing morbidity and mortality rates, it had had an important impact in transforming attitudes towards nature and the body. The involvement of a larger sector of the population in

7. Women, Work and Cultural Change in Eighteenth- and Early Nineteenth-Century London

PATTY SELESKI

In the month of July, 1842, as I was passing the site of the Royal Exchange, then in course of re-erection after being burnt down, my attention was caught by one of the very numerous bills with which the boards, at the time surrounding it, were covered: It ran thus – 'Susan Hopley, or the Life of a Maid Servant.' This book, I thought to myself, must be a novelty; for although female servants form a large class of Her Majesty's subjects, I have seen but little of them, or their affairs in print: sometimes indeed, a few stray delinquents, from their vast numbers, find their way into the police reports of the newspapers; and in penny tracts, now and then, a 'Mary Smith,' or 'Susan Jones', is introduced, in the last stages of consumption, or some other lingering disease, of which they die, in a heavenly frame of mind, and are duly interred.[1]

Thus intrigued by the possibility that a domestic servant's life might be realistically portrayed in the story of Susan Hopley, Mary Ann Ashford, herself a former domestic servant who worked in the first two decades of the nineteenth century, bought a copy of the book. To her dismay, however, it turned out to be a work of fiction. Ashford's response was to write the story of her own life, the 'real truth', and in it to avoid the errors she viewed as common to middle-class authors: these writers, she complained, either fed their audiences sensationalised tales of 'a few stray delinquents' or they sentimentalised and idealised servants as pious and frail creatures.[2] To Ashford, domestic servants were neither social predators nor otherworldly, grateful employees. Instead, she saw servants in a 'matter-of-fact' way, merely as women who worked in order to maintain themselves.[3] Ashford's insistence on defining domestic servants as ordinary working women challenged dominant assumptions about the home and those who worked within it. Middle-class culture, its systems of meanings and forms of behaviour, attached great significance to the home as a woman's natural domain. Yet such an investment of meaning had little resonance either in the experience of Mary Ann Ashford or in the experience of the countless female servants who worked in the homes of the middle class. These women attached different meanings both to their own domestic lives and to the work which made possible the domestic lives of middle-class women.

Ashford's resistance to the definitions of her life in service signified by the middle-class home is surprising given our prevailing assumptions about domestic service. Indeed, domestic service has long been seen as a type of employment that acted as a cultural bridge between the labouring poor and their betters. Because domestic servants both worked and lived in the homes of their employers, historians frequently have viewed domestic servants as cultural amphibians who lived in the cultural worlds both of the people and of the elite, but who did not quite belong to either. Variously characterised as mediators between cultures or as transmitters of elite culture to the people, the supposed efforts of domestic servants to better themselves by adopting the manners of their employers have been credited with (and blamed for) diffusing elite behaviour and values into popular culture. In what is essentially a 'trickle-down' model of culture, historians use domestic servants' status as cultural amphibians to give the multitude of domestic servants employed in the eighteenth-century city the role of important actors in the process of cultural change and transmission.[4]

Less explicitly acknowledged is the fact that most domestic servants were women. Domestic service was the employer of women, especially those between the ages of 15 and 24, *sine qua non*. In London, over 50 per cent of employed women in the metropolis, representing perhaps as many as 80,000 women, may have been in service at the end of the eighteenth century.[5] According to some estimates, women made up the vast majority of those employed as servants in the early eighteenth century and by the end of the century had further increased their hold on the occupation.[6] Very little, however, is known about the experience of women servants: their lives in service are as hidden to historians as their presence was unavoidable in the eighteenth-century city. By and large, assumptions about domestic service, including those about betterment or about the 'trickle-down' model of cultural transmission, rest on arguments about the behaviour of male servants and their masters. The difference that the gender of the servant or of the employer might make to conclusions about domestic service has gone largely unexplored.[7]

This essay considers the positioning of women as cultural mediators through an investigation of domestic service as an occupation that had a history and that underwent significant changes in its organisation and practice throughout the eighteenth century. Although women no longer inhabit the margins of popular culture studies, neither women nor their experiences, especially their work experiences, have as yet found their way to the centre of such studies. Both the sheer numbers of women employed at some point in their lives as servants and the large numbers of women who employed servants suggest that the employer/employee relationship constituted an important point of contact between cultures. But what was the nature of this contact? How was it structured and experienced by women? Does it make a difference that most women servants worked in the homes of the middling sort, often as the only servant, while male servants were concentrated in much wealthier households, usually as one among many male and female servants?[8] Can the experience of women in service tell us anything about the relationship between popular and elite culture?

In his classic study of popular culture, Peter Burke briefly cited the mistress/servant relationship as a relationship important to the process of cultural transmission, suggesting that because households mitigated hierarchical social relationships with personal ones, elite women acted in concert with women servants as mediators between cultures. He put forward the relationship of the noblewoman with her nursemaid as a way of suggesting that women shared experiences that blurred the boundaries between elite and popular cultures.[9] But as employers, the middle-class masters and mistresses of women servants were distinguished from their maidservants as well as from the gentry: if, unlike their maidservants, they were not among the people who made up the lower orders, neither were they members of the elite. Recent interpretations of eighteenth-century social structure tell us that these middle-class employers were distinguished economically from both the people and the elites, but also that their conscious and aggressive articulation of distinctive middle-class modes of behaviour and systems of meaning distinguished them *culturally* from the rest of society as well.[10] Positioned as witnesses to the 'making' of the English middle classes by virtue of their occupation, women servants also found their occupation colliding with a domestic ideology at odds with their own experiences and expectations.

At the heart of this domestic ideology lay new interpretations of gender and of the differences between men and women: middle-class domestic ideology designated women as the 'natural' managers of family life.[11] Although recent research concerning the middle-class project of dividing the world by gender largely neglects class relations, the creation of a middle-class domestic ideology and the re-creation of the household as the natural and exclusive domain of women involved domestic servants from the very beginning.[12] Thus the question of gender and domestic service takes on a double-edged character: not only were most domestic servants and their mistresses women, but in their work lives they came into contact with new articulations and definitions of womanhood. Women servants' experience of the making of the middle class lay precisely in this confrontation. For servants, the formation of a middle-class gender system was more than just ideology; rather, it shaped their work lives. As the day-to-day management of the home became a central part of a middle-class woman's education, among her lessons were those about how to control and to manage servants. The mistress's position in the home became analogous to that of a man's role in business. Whether in the shop or at home, formal rules in and regulation of the workplace increased. The transformation of the household meant the transformation of the workplace: in consequence, service underwent a reorganisation.[13]

Middle-class domestic ideology implicated middle-class women as cultural missionaries whose vocation lay in improving and reforming their servants along the lines of that ideology, thus complicating Burke's image of mistresses and maidservants as cultural collaborators by introducing an element of conflict to their relationship. Households were undoubtedly homes for women servants; certainly the personal element inherent in service persisted, and some mistresses did take seriously their quasi-parental role. But households remained workplaces, too. Though both servants and their mistresses might face, as we have read elsewhere in this volume, a misogynistic patriarchy in their daily lives, and though there were ways in which both maidservants and their mistresses might be 'mastered for life' in significantly similar ways, servants might have more likely complained of being 'mistressed', if not for life, then at least on a daily basis.[14] That the domestic ideology of the middle class which overlay maidservants' experience of their workplace emphasised the personal relationship and shared gender experience between maids and mistresses should not obscure either the fact that the *domestic economy* of the middle-class household was also a form of *political economy* or that the mistress/servant relationship was at its core a labour relationship. Efforts to control both the workplace and the behaviour of maidservants saw women servants' lives located at the intersection of middle-class ideology and their own expectations about work and domestic life. These efforts shaped the experiences of women servants on a daily basis. By the end of the eighteenth century, the household was a contested space where cultures met and often clashed, especially about issues related to work rules and rhythms and to gender identity. The history of domestic service suggests that the role of the household in cultural exchange and transmission is more problematic than historians have assumed.

Despite its seemingly unchanging nature, domestic service was never a static occupation. In both its theory and its practice, service had its origins in agricultural society where parents routinely sent their adolescent children into their neighbours' households. Service balanced the labour requirements of the nuclear family with the resources available to it: families with too many surviving children to maintain sent their children to families with labour needs. In exchange for their labour, adolescent servants received maintenance and training from the households which took them in and they became an integral part of the productive family unit. Cash wages, while not uncommon, were less important than the provision of room and board. Service was almost entirely contiguous with adolescence and young adulthood and it played an important role as a stage in women's lives during which they had the opportunity to learn the secrets of housewifery from their mistresses before they themselves became mistresses. Indeed, domestic service, along with apprenticeship, functioned as the major ways in which children were educated to their adult responsibilities. Servants left their places as a matter of course to marry and to establish their own productive households. Only a very few lingered on past their late twenties in what was primarily an occupation based on individuals' life-cycles.[15] In this sense, service *was* a bridge occupation that marked the transition between adolescence and adulthood.

By the early eighteenth century, however, domestic service had already undergone important changes in its traditional structure and organisation. Though most servants in the eighteenth century were still in their teens and twenties, service was less a life-cycle occupation that held in it an implicit promise of establishing one's own independent household and more of a form of waged labour. This was especially so in the cities, most of all London.[16] Unlike earlier forms of service, urban domestic service emphasised the social distance between servants and their employers. Keeping servants announced one's middling status or one's aspirations in that direction.[17] That urban servants primarily performed menial and not productive labour within the household re-emphasised their social distance from their employers: the domestic drudgery which dominated maid-servants' days could not be confused with the duties of a mistress in training.[18]

The litany of complaints about servants' behaviour that started to appear in the early years of the eighteenth century and continued until well into the nineteenth century suggests that both the transformation of service into a menial form of wage labour and the retreat from service as both an occupational and a social stage in a woman's life-cycle cemented a link between maid-servants and the rest of the labouring poor. Daniel Defoe decried the rapacity of female servants when he detailed 'the inconveniences daily arising from the insolence and intrigues of our servant wenches, who by their caballing together, have made their party so considerable that every-body cries out against 'em'.[19]

Those who saw the metropolis as a breeding place of crime, disorder and poverty and who sought to reform the labouring poor often pinpointed servants, male and female, as particularly egregious offenders against the public order. John Beattie notes that there were at least twelve attempts in the reigns of William and Anne to pass legislation regulating the behaviour of servants. He speculates that the anxiety servants' behaviour and their potential criminality occasioned in employers was heightened by the high levels of property crime after 1710, as well as by a general sense of disorder in the metropolis.[20]

Some, like Henry Fielding, placed the blame for disorder squarely at the feet of workmen and the freedom they had over the work process and Fielding was himself an advocate for labour that was regulated, restricted and supervised.[21] But though he deplored the independence of working men, working women, especially women servants, also enjoyed such independence. Maidservants' independence rested primarily on the ease with which they could change jobs, but it was increased by the assumptions that governed the workplace and servants' behaviour within it.

Women servants were, in fact, notorious for their habitual changes of employment. The belief that 'there are more places than parish churches' and the charge that servants 'on the least occasion presently give warning' became commonplaces among employers and found their way into housekeeping manuals throughout the whole of the eighteenth century.[22] Using settlement examinations from St Martin-in-the-Fields, D. A. Kent has found that less than 30 per cent of servants at mid-century stayed three or more years at the same service, while slighly over 50 per cent stayed in place only one year.[23] The median period of service for all domestic servants at the London Foundling Hospital between 1759 and 1772 was a mere twenty weeks: the median for scullery maids was only ten weeks, while as many kitchen maids lasted fewer than thirty-four weeks as stayed in their places at the Foundling Hospital beyond that period of time.[24]

Even more telling than the frequency with which servants changed places were the reasons servants left one place for another: after all, a servant might be dismissed as easily as leaving a situation of her own accord. Middle-class commentators such as the anonymous author of *Satan's Harvest Home*, who found servants' independence both annoying and inconvenient, put servants' restlessness down to their viciousness and licentiousness, as well as to their resistance to discipline:

> Many of them are as restless as a new equipage, running from Place to Place, from Service to Bawdy House again; for, if the Matron uses them ill, away they trip to Service, and if their Mistress but gives them a wry Word, whip, they are as ready to be gone, *as a relieved Guard, or a discharged Jury* [original emphasis].[25]

Others criticised their 'roving disposition' and lamented that maidservants were 'indifferent about retaining or quitting their place of service; they apprehend no ill consequence from a change of situation'.[26] In fact, it does appear as if servants' eagerness to change their situations was at least as common a reason to leave a place as were employers' decisions to discharge their servants: somewhat more than half of the Foundling Hospital's servants left their situations at the hospital voluntarily, with the notation, 'own desire', entered in the column which cited the reason for leaving the Foundling Hospital's service. As was the case outside the walls of the hospital, other servants left when they were dismissed for poor performance or bad behaviour, became ill or because there was no work for them to do.[27] Places were plentiful and many servants appear to have used this fact to their best advantage.

The ease with which servants could exchange one situation for another did nothing to aid efforts to reform the workplace. Restraints on behaviour proved ineffective when a maidservant could give warning and depart the house confident of obtaining another position. In regard to work rules, however much pundits might complain, the household was relatively relaxed and unstructured, in some instances verging on the chaotic.[28] Such was the case in the Miller household, where Martha Miller employed Hannah Binney as her only servant for over three months without knowing 'her right names'.[29] In fact, Martha Miller knew very little about Hannah Binney including, at most times of the day, her whereabouts. The extent of the disorganisation in Miller's household surfaced when Hannah Binney delivered herself of an illegitimate child whose death was investigated by the Westminster coroner. At the inquest, Miller deposed that she often was unaware of what her servant was doing and that on the day Binney gave birth, Miller had 'asked her husband where Pat [Martha] was, he said he did not know anything of her'.[30]

The irregularity of domestic service, both in regard to the duration of any one situation and in its day-to-day rhythms, contributed to keeping women servants closely connected to the labouring classes. Servants frequently left one place without immediate prospect of another and in these circumstances took advantage of lodging houses or relatives until they entered service again. Jane Gladville consistently returned to Mrs Phillers' lodging house in Broad Street, Bloomsbury, during the course of her four years in London. When she left a place in Tottenham Court Road where she had been for about a year, she stayed at Mrs Phillers' for a month before taking a place in Spa Field. During this time she met and was courted by a young carpenter who also lodged at Mrs Phillers'.[31] Jane Egerton appears to have worked primarily to support a non-marital relationship with Thomas Cotter: when Jane earned enough in one place to keep them for a while, she gave warning, withdrew from service and the two of them cohabited until their money ran out. At that point, Jane would take a new situation and start the cycle over again.[32]

Maidservants did more than tend to their intimate relationships when out of place. Before unemployment strained their savings and while they could still afford to do so, they frequented the haunts of the labouring poor in search of company and amusement as well as romance. While out of place, Mary Warnett and Mary Curtain spent a good deal of time at a public house near the Honey Lane Market, Cheapside. As they drank, they took part in the singing and other forms of conviviality going on there. Their flirtatious behaviour led some newcomers to the pub to suspect them of being prostitutes, but the pub's regular customers defended their high-spirits and good-humour as innocent fun. Temporarily out of service, they looked and behaved like others among the labouring poor. That they did so was not always a comforting thought to writers such as Defoe, who equated unemployment with criminality: 'Is it not time to prevent the increase of harlots, by making it penal for servants to be harbor'd in idleness, and tempted to theft, whoredom, murder, etc., by living too long out of place?'[33]

Opportunities for mixing with the rest of the lower orders were not limited to periods of unemployment. The drudgery of service was undeniable: servants rose early, often before dawn, to begin the ritual of lighting fires, cleaning house and preparing meals. But servants, especially when they were the only servant kept in a household, spent a good deal of their time running errands outside of the house for their employers. At these times, servants escaped the supervision of their mistresses. They frequently used the opportunity to see friends, to meet lovers, to stop and rest, or even to look after new places. Both Sarah Lister and Sarah Blake began and maintained sexual connections while on the job: Lister did so while she walked out with her mistress's children, while Blake was a frequent customer for her mistress at the shop where her lover, Thomas Grattan, worked.[34]

What free time servants had was also given over to these ends. This free time, typically consisting of Sunday afternoon plus one entire Sunday each month and perhaps one evening a week, employers intended for servants to spend at church or visiting their families. Servants, to the despair of the middle class, saw things a different way. With some obvious exasperation, Eliza Haywood posed the question to which many employers might have wished to know the answer: 'how many of you had rather walk in the Fields, go to drink Tea with an acquaintance or even lie down to sleep' rather than attend church services?[35] In fact, some servants did all of these things in lieu of attendance at worship. Sarah Pooriman, Mary Baxter and Isabella Brown met at the Duke of Gloucester in Park Street where they drank 'five pints of ale and a Pot of beer. . . all in perfect humour and merriment', and then paired off with some young men they had met.[36] Sarah Wise frequented Mr Bird's Pork Shop in Hammersmith, while Mary Miller and Mary Holliday used their time off to go walking in the parks and fields in and around the metropolis.[37] Those with family in town, like Amey Trinder who regularly took tea with her brother and sister-in-law, used their free time to visit them. In fact, the frequent changes of service, with time spent in and out of place, might mean that a servant knew people all over London and that she was firmly embedded in local networks of working people, as well as in networks of previous co-workers, former servants and their families.

The strong connections of servants to the lower orders, as well as the ease and frequency with which they mixed with them, occasioned no little discomfort among the middle classes. Their frustration with the situation and their inability to break those connections or to control the nature of their servants' contacts with the working classes found its way into print, in the countless pamphlets and manuals directed at serving maids which were published throughout the eighteenth and into the nineteenth century. Whether the complaint was 'gadding abroad', tarrying when on an errand or nibbling at leftover food, the targets were the customary behaviours clustered around the workplace that expressed popular expectations about work.[38] Servants saw stopping to talk with friends while on an errand or nibbling the odd crumb of food as their right or as customary forms of compensation.[39] Employers saw their behaviour as theft. Tarrying while running errands wasted time: 'for while you are in the condition of a servant, your time belongs to those who pay you for it; and all you waste from the employment they set you about, is a Robbery from them'.[40] Equally reprehensible was unauthorised eating: 'to pick the fruit out of a tart, to break off the edge of pastry. . . is an act of positive dishonesty. . . It is a crime, for the commission of which a mistress would be perfectly justified in instantly discharging her servant'.[41]

The clash between cultures extended beyond issues of work rhythms and perquisites to the issue of the character of the people itself. If one believed, as did many middle-class pundits, that 'London is so much the sink of vice, that the lower class of people are very much corrupted', then employers 'cannot be too particular' about the maids they hired.[42] The fear, that London women knew the town too well, that they alternated between service and prostitution, that their acquaintances encouraged them in bad habits, in short, that they were no different from the common people, was a constant source of anxiety to employers. A 1752 *Proposal for the Amendment and Encouragement of Servants* made the link explicit:

Complaints have frequently been made, and with great Justice of the behaviour of servants. The numberless disorders from thence have proved very inconvenient, and sometimes destructive, to private persons and families; and the publick has severely felt the mischievous effects of it, from that idleness and immorality, which have of late spread themselves so wide among the common people.[43]

Controlling the experiences of their servants seemed the only way to ensure the employment of women not infected by the multitude. Thus, the middle class became obsessed with the question of 'character' and how to guarantee it. In addition, they proposed ways of encouraging servants to adopt middle-class values and to stop acting like the rest of the people.

To this end, not only did the century see the publication of numerous tracts, pamphlets and manuals directed at servants which aimed to reform their behaviour and to reinforce their reformation with biblical authority, but projects of a more material nature were proposed to address the problem of servants.[44] Because employers saw the continual movement in and out of service as increasing servants' contact with a suspect popular culture, they put a premium on long service. Under a scheme put forward in 1752, servants would be rewarded for staying in place by cash awards that could be used as an annuity. The author of the plan hoped that 'though it would not cure the common people of their vices (and what scheme is there that would?) yet it would greatly contribute to such cure, and would strengthen the foundations already laid, for the promoting of sobriety and good manners'. Still, he admitted that 'this proposal is not calculated for the benefit of servants in particular, so much as for that of the publick'.[45]

Another project inaugurated in the 1750s was the establishment of register offices. Envisaged as employment agencies where qualified and exemplary servants could find good situations, register offices adopted strict guidelines to regulate their procedures: 'the publick may be assured, that the utmost care will be taken to prevent any imposition; and that none will be registered in this office who give the least suspicious account of themselves, and who have lived in any disreputable places'.[46] Though the intentions were good ones, no sooner had the office opened than it gained a largely undeserved reputation for encouraging fraud and deceit. Pamphlet writers and even playwrights portrayed register offices as manufacturing good characters for dishonest servants and as selling characters 'from five shillings to five guineas'. Middle-class employers were urged to seek servants through tradesmen, through friends or to bring them from the country themselves. In short, they were directed to look everywhere, except register offices, for help.[47]

A more extreme strategy lay in legislation. Like their counterparts after the Restoration, middling Londoners at the end of the
eighteenth century looked to Parliament to inoculate both their
household and their servants against the supposed viciousness of
the people. In the 1790s, the British Society for the Encouragement of Servants circulated a petition among the householders of
Westminster and the City of London to punish both servants for
using false characters and employers who gave inaccurate or false
characters. With almost three hundred petitions in hand, the leaders of the society testified that a 'Bill to Prevent the forging and
counterfeiting certificates of servants' characters' would 'have a
strong tendency to reform the morals and behaviours of servants
throughout the kingdom'.[48]

Although the King gave his assent to the measure in 1792,
employers had little success in solving the servant problem with
projects, prosecutions or parliamentary measures. As long as the
demand for servants was growing, few incentives offered by
employers could keep them in place. Likewise, though prosecu-
tors could apprehend a few servants with false or counterfeit characters in hand, in a city with a population close to one million in
1800, little could be done to enforce the law in any consistent
way.[49]

For all the formal measures taken to solve the servant problem,
the most important efforts to control servants and to regulate
their behaviour came from inside the home as a result of articulat-
ing a separate middle-class culture. The project of gendering the
middle-class home to make it the exclusive domain of women gave
over to mistresses the primary responsibility for supervising, controlling and reforming servants. Thus it was the development of a
gender system within the middle class and the consequent feminisation of the middle-class home that had the greatest impact on
the structure and organisation of service, as well on the experiences of maidservants.

Middle-class culture reconstructed the world, dividing it into a
series of opposing ideas: public and private; masculine and feminine; rational and emotional; intellectual and moral. Gender differences were reinterpreted as natural differences between men

and women.[50] Women's natural domain was seen to be the home and as the concept of household management evolved in the course of the eighteenth century, the duties of a mistress also became part of women's natural role. As the author of one influential guide to housekeeping noted:

> that important branch of study which regards their domestick concerns; by which I understand those cares that more immediately relate to the interior government of a house; to expenses for clothes, equipages, and furniture; for the education and rearing of children, and for the wages and maintenance of servants. All this is, properly speaking, the science of the female sex. This is the peculiar employment which Providence has assigned them, by way of inheritance; and for the execution whereof they are naturally better qualified than men are. 'Tis this makes them truly worthy of our highest esteem and applause, when they are so happy as to accomplish all these duties.[51]

Women expended their energies as household managers for the benefit of their husbands. Ultimately, though, their efforts were expended on behalf of the nation: 'to promote domestic virtue, and preserve the happiness of the fireside, is an effectual, as well as a simple means of increasing national prosperity'.[52] Because 'the situation and prospects of a country may be justly estimated by the character of its women', the feminine, which embraced women's role within the home, became a pillar of middle-class culture on which rested their claim to moral, economic and political power.[53]

Although ostensibly a natural talent, the large numbers of manuals and guides to household management testify to the fact that running a household did not come easily or so naturally to many middle-class women.[54] The authors of housekeeping manuals, authors who quite often were men, made a well-regulated and orderly home the end of women's efforts. In order to create such a household, authors gave women advice about how to keep and to organise accounts; about how to arrange their day by the hour; and about marketing and cookery. A good deal of ink was expended on the issue of hiring and controlling servants. Manuals offered advice about how to search for good servants; about wages;

and about the limits that should be set on servants' behaviour. Advice givers acknowledged that 'the art of governing servants is not so easy as it is necessary'.[55] But, they nonetheless insisted that the effect of their advice would be to give women the means by which to take control of the workplace.

Commentators urged middle-class women to institute new rules in the workplace. Hiring, for example, should never depend exclusively on written 'characters' or recommendations from tradespeople; rather in an effort to be 'minute' in inspecting the characters of potential employees, women were directed to seek interviews with former mistresses so that 'from her appearance, and the state of her house, you may draw some inference to assist your decision'.[56] A good deal of Mrs Elizabeth Tyrrell's time was spent in this way, making enquiries about potential servants. The entries in her diary suggest that she found the process useful and vastly preferable to relying on written testimonials or oral referrals. She spent the entire month of May 1809 trying to find a cook, 'going after' the characters of applicants by visiting their current or former employers only to find that most 'would not answer', until she finally found one who would suit her family.[57]

Mistresses' responsibilities did not end with hiring suitable servants. Although the wealthiest of middle-class women might employ a housekeeper to oversee things around the house, maintaining a household in most middle-class homes required constant effort and personal supervision by the mistress. Every manual or guidebook directed mistresses to get up early, for 'early rising, and a proper disposing of time, are essential to economy. The necessary orders, and an examination into household affairs, should be dispatched early in the day'. Indeed, the morning was the time for the mistress to give orders for 'the whole day'. The rest of the day was to be spent supervising the completion of her orders. All manner of benefits resulted from her vigilance, while only disaster befell those mistresses who shirked their duties: 'where the mistress is an early riser, we may take it for granted that her house is orderly and well-managed, but when the heads of families are too lazy to leave their beds, the servants will follow their example and neglect be the consequence.' Getting up early had a preventive aspect too. Constant supervision kept the servants on task, but it also kept them under surveillance in order to prevent against misbehaviour: 'early rising, where the health will permit, produces more advantages then the mere lengthening of the day . . . where servants are ill-disposed, and their employers are known to be safe in their chambers till a late hour, depredations to no inconsiderable amount may easily be carried on.'[58]

A good mistress's labours never ended. She created and maintained the household's routine, 'apportioning various parts of the day to particular purposes' and 'as nearly as possible, at the same hour every day', in order to get 'your servants into a regular system, and they will regulate their work accordingly'. A mistress must never forget that 'in all cases, the welfare and good character of her household depends on her own active superintendence', or that 'the welfare and good management of the house depends on the eye of the superior; and consequently that no thing is too trifling for her notice'.[59] If all of these conditions were met, the household would run smoothly:

> that house only is well conducted, where there is a strict attention paid to order and regularity. To do every thing in its proper time, to keep every thing in its right place, and to every thing for its proper use, is the very essence of good management, and is well expressed in ... 'to have a place for every thing, and every thing in its place'. While some think they have no time to put things away, others assert that they have no time to misplace them; no half hours to spare in searching for lost good. The time of every individual ought to be precious; with the mistress of a family it is peculiarly so; and a proper adjustment of this cannot be too forcibly inculcated. Meals should always be ready at the stated time; and servants, if possible, obliged to be punctual; but to effect this, and prevent confusion, they must receive clear and early orders.[60]

As mistresses superintended the work days of their servants, so too were they instructed to superintend their leisure and their moral development. In order to prevent against the countervailing influence of the lower orders, mistresses attempted to cut off the access of their servants to persons outside the household. Since mistresses both imagined and were instructed by domestic manuals to imagine that the most dangerous contacts women servants had outside the home were with potential suitors, they imposed 'no followers' rules to restrict these relationships. They also reduced the amount of leisure time given to servants, so that time servants had previously spent with family and friends became unavailable to them.[61] Enjoined to provide religious instruction, 'to make all that are hers to God's servants also', mistresses were urged to preside over family prayers. They were expected to be patient with servants, to temper strictness with kindness and to provide correction with 'soft words' so as to encourage improvement.[62]

All of the measures which mistresses were urged to take in defence of their homes and families were but manifestations of their own character. The mistress of the house had to be well-ordered and predictable before her house could be so. Household regulations could only come from self-regulation: 'she who has the best regulated mind will, other things being equal, have the best-regulated family.'[63] The ultimate ability to run a household was contingent on a mistress's character. Good or bad management was a function of a good or a bad mistress; indeed, within middle-class domestic culture, being a good mistress was in the end a question of being a good woman. As household manuals told women, good mistresses could control the household and the servants within it because they were in control of themselves:

A mistress should understand how to do every thing with propri-ety and in season, to employ her servants with so much ease and order, as may make their labour pleasant, and their duty desir-able; but above all, she must be sure to command that only, which may, and ought to be performed; other wise it will be impossible to preserve in them that respect which is due to her person. If she be addicted to passion, or be too conceited, she will dangerously expose herself on every occasion, will require such things to be done as are impracticable and absurd; and will never be able to get either the good will, or the good word of those that are about her. If she prove humoursome towards them, or too flexible, and given lightly to change her mind, and contradict what the minute before she had order'd to be done, her authority will soon be at an end; she will infallibly make her-self despised, and indeed, it will be no more than what she actually deserves.[64]

The domestic ideology of the middle class put middle-class mistresses into an impossible situation. To be a bad mistress, to fail at running a home, meant failure at a woman's natural role. To fail in this regard put home, family and nation at risk. Servants could ruin mistresses' attempts at successful home management, and although servants were recognised to be troublesome and often vicious, if servants did undermine a woman's attempt at managing her home, the fault would be laid to her.

For example, consider the criticism directed at Mrs Connally by the London magistrates. When Elizabeth Tarrier, one of Connally's servants, was raped in the Connally's home one morning, Mrs Connally was still asleep. The court heard from Tarrier that the servants were expected to rise at six, but that Mrs Connally customarily did not wake until nine. The court expressed its outrage that Connally could have been so remiss in her duties as mistress, asking Tarrier: 'then you was in the house...and nobody to control you?'[65] Good mistresses, of course, were early risers. By failing in this, Mrs Connally put both her servant and her family at risk.

Because they were expected to control servants, good mistresses protected their families from the lower orders. Bad mistresses, like Charlotte Turner, a stationer's wife, left their husbands and families at risk. Turner hired a servant, Eliza Fenning, who was later accused of attempting to poison the Turner family with some arsenic-laced dumplings. On the basis of Mrs Turner's testimony and some dubious circumstantial evidence, a jury convicted Eliza Fenning and sentenced her to death. Fenning's story did not end with her death, however. After mobs rioted to protest against her execution, the authorities reopened the case. During their reinvestigation, Mrs Turner came in for special criticism. The real problem in the Turner household was not that Fenning was a bad servant, but that Mrs Turner was a bad mistress: in fact, Fenning was a bad servant *because* Turner was a bad mistress. Critics focused on the lack of control that Mrs Turner exercised over herself and her household. They concluded that because of Turner's lack of vigilance in supervising her staff, anyone could have attempted the poisoning. Their vilification of Mrs Turner did not end there but continued: she had put her husband's life at risk; she was an indifferent housekeeper, who though severe in matters of discipline, was unwilling to work hard herself; she was to blame for not correcting Fenning's behaviour effectively and for not setting the right moral tone in the household.[66]

The populace rioted to defend Eliza Fenning as one of their own who had been unjustly accused and executed. But Mrs Turner was not so lucky. Rather than receiving sympathy for the ordeal she and her family had suffered at the hands of an evil servant, she found herself the target of middle-class attacks. The Fenning case illustrates the pressure under which middle-class domestic ideology placed middle-class women. They were expected to take control of the household and to guarantee its smooth and efficient management. To be able to do so was natural, a sign of a woman's worth and good character. But middle-class homes were also maidservants' workplaces. Replacing the lax, somewhat chaotic, household of the earlier eighteenth century with the strictly regulated home expected of middle-class mistresses proved difficult as a matter of day-to-day practice and it put maidservants into direct conflict with their mistresses.

Both maids and mistresses lived out their lives in a daily engagement with middle-class domestic ideology. What was 'natural' to mistresses, however, involved a drastic restructuring of the workplace and a new set of work rules for servants. Mistresses' success in their new cultural role required them either to elicit the cooperation of servants or to find ways of coercing them. Models of domestic service as a bridge occupation in which the goal of the servant lay in her adoption of the household's values as a path to betterment see mistresses as being largely successful in their efforts to transform the household and its members. Indeed, the success of mistresses in controlling their female domestic servants has been identified as one source of working-class conservatism. While that claim is perhaps overstated, the link which historians make between a servant's receptivity to middle-class cultural values and her (or her parents') desire for social advancement does suggest that domestic service did work as a bridge over which middle-class values passed into the working class.[67]

Ideally, cooperation between servant and employer flowed from the positive influence of mistresses. Servants responded to this positive influence by absorbing the values of the feminised household that controlled and routinised their existence: 'by the happiness and comfort resulting from our conduct towards our domestics, should they be made sensible of virtue and piety... The regulations you will think proper for the preservation of order and morality among your domestics must be enforced by your own example, or they will have little or no effect.'[68]

Lest sheer influence fail to elicit cooperation in real life, mistresses could rely on certain types of coercion to improve their servants. For example, requiring a 'character' in order to get a new situation emphasised a servant's personal attributes, and thus highlighted her behaviour in addition to her work abilities: maintaining her character in ways that pleased her mistress and would be reflected in subsequent references left a servant susceptible to her mistress's influence and control.[69] Indeed, not only could mistresses favour those servants who exhibited proper behaviour, but the issues surrounding 'character', most particularly its non-specific personal quality, provided mistresses with an opportunity to improve their servants by instilling in them the values, systems of meaning and behaviours of the gendered household. Thus mistresses sought to reform their servants' characters by increasing servants' dependence on them as a way of increasing their receptivity to middle-class influence.

In order to encourage further their servants' sense of dependence on them, some mistresses actively sought servants from the country who had no family connections in London. The absence of local social or familial networks, combined with long distances from their homes and their families, bred tractability and submissiveness in young girls who were isolated within middle-class households. There is some indication that mistresses succeeded at this. As the nineteenth century approached, fewer of the servants who gave their work histories to the London Foundling Hospital either came from London or had relatives or friends living there. Indeed, these servants were three times likelier to be orphans than similarly circumstanced servants in previous decades had been. In addition, there is some hint that isolated circumstances did work to foster loyalty and commitment to mistresses among these servants: compared to other servants who sought the Foundling Hospital's help in this period, especially those with strong London or Home County connections, those servants without London networks seem to have changed situations less frequently and to have stayed longer in place when they were employed.[70]

Yet most middle-class mistresses could not afford to bring a girl out of the country. For these women eliciting the cooperation of servants either by assuming a quasi-maternal concern or by more coercive means could prove difficult. Margaret Marsh, the wife of a china dealer in St Martin-in-the-Fields, found this to be true in her dealings with her servant, Rebecca Cowley. Cowley rebuffed every overture Marsh made and rejected all Marsh's offers to assist her, declaring 'that she [Cowley] wished people would trouble themselves with their own business': she even turned aside Mrs Marsh's threats to bring the local constable into their disputes. Likewise, Mrs Tyrrell's nurserymaid, Lucy, not only resisted all instruction, advice and encouragement in her duties, but she also ignored Mrs Tyrrell's most pointed corrections. After one incident in which she had left the Tyrrell children alone while she went to eat, Lucy announced to Mrs Tyrrell that 'we had better part'. All Mrs Tyrrell could do was to acquiesce meekly and to sputter (after the fact), that 'I certainly was dissatisfied when ever my children were left and therefore we would part.'[71]

Were Rebecca Cowley and Lucy particularly uncooperative young women? Or, was their resistance to their mistresses the norm? Their behaviour does little to advance the argument that mistresses had much success in their mission to transform either the workplace or its inhabitants. Nor do their examples suggest motivations centred on ideas about betterment or self-improvement. In fact, their behaviour supports the contention that servants contested middle-class culture on a daily basis as they looked to retain some independence in the workplace.

Certainly, however, the experiences of women servants were different. Service was a hierarchy and the work experiences of upper servants – ladies' maids, companions, housekeepers and cooks in large households – differed quite significantly from those of lower servants – cooks in small households, chambermaids, housemaids, kitchen maids, scullery maids and maids-of-all-work – who formed the bulk of servants in middle-class households. John Gillis suggests that upper servants imbibed the values of middle-class culture and, as a result, expected to marry into the lower-middle or upper-working class on their exit from service. Gillis documents the willingness of upper servants to risk pregnancy and disgrace in order to catch eligible men who would enhance their social status and whose income would allow them to replicate the gendered middle-class home for themselves.[72]

But lower servants, those who performed the most menial of household tasks, may have had different expectations from service and their notions about things such as betterment or domestic happiness also may have differed from those of upper servants. That lower servants adopted certain middle-class habits, such as tea drinking, or aspired to ape, in so far as their limited finances permitted them to, ladies' fashions in their own dress, speaks less to the question of cultural transmission as it affected the fundamental values and the systems of meaning available to maidservants than it does to the participation of these women as wage earners in a consumer-oriented society that involved persons from every class.[73] What such purchases represented as markers of aspiration to middle-class status is problematic, but there is some evidence that women servants' values about the meaning of work and family life remained centred on those of the labouring classes: in fact, rather than endure the restrictive and ideologically charged middle-class household, however ineffective it might be at times, urban servants chose to leave service whenever any other sort of work presented itself.[74]

When Mary Ann Ashford criticised middle-class writers for their inaccurate portraits of female servants, she, in effect, confronted the question of service's role as a bridge occupation that transformed women workers into poorer versions of their mistresses. In her *Life*, she addresses the question of betterment as well as issues related to the residual effect of the gendered middle-class household on servants who left service in order to marry. Indeed, Ashford's *Life* demonstrates how problematic a question cultural tranmission is: her autobiography provides evidence that the meanings which Ashford and her fellow servants attached to work and to the household largely resisted the middle-class project of gendering the world.

Mary Ann Ashford entered service in 1803. She was 13 and had recently lost both her parents. She entered service, not to better herself, but because it provided steady work. In fact, she entered service against the advice of her relatives who wished to place her 'genteelly' as an apprentice to a milliner. She recorded that her decision to become a servant meant that rather than improving her social position, she had 'lost caste' by becoming a servant.[75]

Like the servants about whom Defoe and other commentators had complained throughout the eighteenth century, Ashford seemed to believe that there were indeed as many places as parish churches. She was unafraid of unemployment, often leaving one position before securing another, even in times of scarcity. In her sixteen years of service between 1801 and 1817, Ashford changed places fourteen times. Her reasons for leaving her situations were various, but they frequently revolved around her relationship with her mistress. In one place her mistress was a scold; in another her mistress half-starved her in order to save money and she charged Ashford with theft when she discovered her servant paring slices of cheese to stave off hunger; in a third place, Ashford recorded leaving a situation precisely because the house was over-regulated: 'There was to be many fresh regulations, I said I would leave.'[76] Though a bad mistress would encourage her swift exit from a situation, a good mistress could not induce her to stay merely by being an 'excellent manager': given the opportunity to leave Mrs Pearce, whom she records as being 'very kind indeed', for a rise in salary from seven pounds to ten guineas a year, Ashford departs Mrs Pearce's service with little regret.[77] Despite continual reminders from moralists that 'long service shows worth' and that 'the servant that often changes his place, works only to be poor; for the rolling stone gathers no moss', Ashford showed no concern about the frequency with which she changed jobs.[78] Instead, her portrayal of her life in service is characterised by constant negotiations to allow her some degree of independence and to escape the restrictions of the middle-class home:

> I went into many shops and heard of many cook's places, and, I think, went after nine or ten, but did not engage with any: there was either something I did not suit them, or they did not suit me.[79]

In each of her situations, Mary placed prime importance on her own response to the immediate work situation and to its ability to meet her needs. It is also clear that motives of social mobility or betterment did not define her needs. Higher wages did not invariably attract her; neither did the social status of her employers. She took jobs with a kept woman, a Jew, a clerk, a clergyman's family and a waiter, as well as with merchants and bankers.[80] Plotting the locations of her successive situations reveals no particular pattern of directed social aspiration: she worked all over the metropolis, seeming to prefer City places, but also on occasion working in the East End and Lambeth. She ended her career at a place in Chelsea, chosen not for its social cachet, but because of a desire to be near an aged aunt.[81] The lack of direction of any sort in her employment pattern suggests that questions of working conditions and the question of her independence were paramount to Mary Ann Ashford.[82] In this, she sought to resist middle-class notions of female submissiveness and to escape the ministrations of mistresses in their attempts to transform her way of perceiving her situation.

Ashford's *Life* also reveals how limited was mistresses's success in persuading servants to accept ideas about femininity and about the naturalness of the gendered household. Married (almost by chance) when she was about thirty, Ashford rejected a model of marriage that saw her as dependent, preferring instead to remain 'among the "hewers of wood and drawers of water", and keeping myself'.[83] In fact, the circumstances of her life did not allow for any acceptance of a private sphere that was natural to women. She and her husband managed their money jointly, and though married, she assisted her second husband in his tailor's shop.[84] Her husband's growing infirmities forced her to take an active public role as she made the rounds of charitable institutions and parish officers to provide for herself and her children. Indeed it is her resourcefulness in contrast to her husband's passivity that rescued her family from eviction and poverty.[85] Ashford never sought to replicate the gender relations she saw in the middle-class households where she served; instead, she relied on a different meaning of domesticity and on an alternative model of woman's nature that more accurately reflected her marital circumstances.

Given Mary Ann Ashford's experience it seems unlikely that domestic service acted as a bridge across which cultures were transmitted in any systematic or predictable way; rather domestic service appears to have been more of a battlefield where different cultures, different systems of meanings, were contested. The evolution of middle-class domestic ideology and the tangible ways in which it changed customary work patterns and organisation presented a powerful challenge to serving women. Middle-class women did not just 'do things differently' around the house; their behaviours and domestic style carried with them meanings central to the origination of domestic life, to the meaning of femininity as well as to the middle-class's claim to political power. If the values that organised the middle-class household did not transform maidservants' behaviour in any automatic way, they did circumscribe it. By and large, servants were more restricted in the workplace as middle-class mistresses did institute stricter work rules and new forms of work discipline. Working women's independence was asserted less frequently in the workplace, and more often by leaving it.

As maidservants attempted to assert some control over their work lives and situations, they challenged the fundamental definitions of femininity that existed within middle-class culture. Indeed, the idea that women's relationships were based on a supposedly shared women's nature and that these relationships were harmonious ones that bridged social differences does not survive the contest that women servants waged with middle-class ideology throughout the eighteenth century: women servants resisted middle-class definitions of femininity in order to retain some control over their work situations, but they also did so because the circumstances of their lives did not support the behavioural implications that clustered around the ideas of domesticity, private spheres and natural roles.[86] The history of domestic service and of domestic servants as an occupational group suggests that relations between women of different classes were shaped by class-specific constructions of gender and that historians must look beyond the walls of the household for the sources of cultural transformation.

8. Against Innovation? Custom and Resistance in the Workplace, 1700–1850

JOHN RULE

Few male workers spent less than twelve hours of most weekdays at work, whether this period of time was determined by the task in hand; by the number of pieces needed to be made to maintain a living; by custom or agreement; or even by Act of Parliament. For some work was not separated from home and individuals aggregated not so much into distinct workforces as into occupational communities. Even for those whose work was separated from home, the associations of the workplace could continue in out-of-work hours, centred for example, on particular public houses and manifested from time to time in public ceremony. Episodes such as riots or strikes can sometimes provide fissures revealing levels of working life otherwise submerged, but work was inevitably central to working-class experience, and the historian must try to go deeper in search of the everyday. High days and holidays too reveal the occasional: it is often harder to discover the 'usual'. 'Outsiders' to particular worlds of work were simply that, while 'insiders' concealed as much as they revealed. Sometimes they did so deliberately (see below, p. 178); sometimes because they expected no interest in the ordinary, as in the case of working-class autobiographers who preferred to relate extraordinary moments such as a religious conversion or a political awakening.

This essay will begin with an examination of customary work practices and the way in which they provided a degree of control over the labour process. It will proceed to assess how, increasingly, conflict developed as employers sought to break through traditional practices and impose new ways of working and new forms of hiring or paying. Finally it will be suggested that in the context of the workplace, customary culture cannot be simply represented as the antithesis of 'market culture'.

'Custom' was central in the culture of work in the eighteenth and early nineteenth centuries. Over the later nineteenth century customary evaluations and practices were increasingly marginalised. In public discourse they lost out to the printed regulations of organised trade unions. Agreements with employers became formal and 'working to rule' became in itself a tactic of collective bargaining. Custom, though, has never completely disappeared from the workplace where there still exists, albeit shrinking, an inner world whose norms and expectations have been no less hegemonic for being known only to those who belong.[1] In an earlier period custom pre-scribed, proscribed and legitimated the ways of work, especially those of skilled work. Although the association of custom with the 'trade' or 'craft' may simply reflect our greater knowledge of artisans, the evidence which does survive from other worlds of labour suggests that wherever people worked together for any length of time, then customary practices tended to emerge. Custom determined expectations from work. It conditioned attitudes and practices in performing it and framed relations with fellow workers and with employers. At times it even defined relations with the state.

In areas of cottage manufacturing organised under the putting-out system and based on the family as a unit of labour, customs of the trade merged into customs of the wider community. Here women as well as men participated in it, although perhaps, as Sally Alexander has suggested, with different roles: with that of the women less public than that of the male artisans who dominated organised protest forms like trade unions. In the occupational communities of weavers and framework knitters, for instance, the family was the unit of labour and the cottage its site. In such a social system kinship and neighbourhood interactions naturally interacted in a particular matrix of popular culture. Within it women not only performed reciprocal services in childbirth, ill-ness and child-minding, but from their special role in the food market were led to play a leading role in the most common form of popular protest, the food riot, as well as in other forms. As Berg has put it: 'It was the women who led the food riots, organised the gleaning, mobbed the poor law officials'.[2] So far as forms of pro-test such as industrial action and food rioting were concerned, there was bound to have been an overlap, not only in participation (although the form may have varied) but in the 'moral' values which legitimated them. The customary expectations being defended, whether those of a 'just price' for grain or of a fair reward for labour, or even of the right to work at home rather than in the factory or weaving shed, were not in such communities separate, but part of a holistic perception of the legitimate nature of traditional social and economic relations. As Charlesworth and Randall have recently suggested, 'It was among these industrial workers that the plebeian culture of the eighteenth century was forged', where 'the defence of customary definitions and expectations reinforced and underlined the moral economy of the crowd'.[3]

Women, however, were increasingly excluded by the late eighteenth century from even those artisan organisations which had previously included them: e.g. from silkweavers' societies in 1769, from bookbinders in 1779. Trades such as hat-making and tailoring no less than the building trades saw the exclusion of women as critical if the frontier of skill was to be held against the swamping of the labour supply. Not suprisingly, not only organisations, but their language and even the perception of skill itself became increasingly masculine. The worlds of workshop, shipyard or mine with which this chapter is mainly concerned were gender exclusive. This was not simply a characteristic. It was a perceived condition for survival.

CUSTOMARY PRACTICES AND THE LABOUR PROCESS

Where men worked away from home, they usually did so along with others in labour which, even if individually remunerated, was commonly collectively performed to some degree. This was the context for the customary popular culture of the manufacturing, building or mining workplace. Accounts of customary work practices survive for many trades. For printing they go back into the seventeenth century. The origin of calling a printshop 'the chapel' is unknown, but a senior compositor taking of the title 'father of the chapel' was a pivotal figure well before 1700 in ensuring the observance of good, mutual work habits. Within each chapel in a larger works the compositors were organised into 'companionships' of three to six journeymen. These were led by the 'clicker', who apportioned the work among the men, who usually earned a lump sum collectively on the basis of the number of lines set. The 'fat' – that is, work consisting of the half-printed pages bearing titles etc., which were paid as full pages – was by custom shared equally among the companions. Discipline was based upon the chapel. When a member had a complaint against a fellow, the father held a 'chapel' – a trial – before the 'imposing stone' and, if convicted, the offender was fined – a 'solace'. A long list of rules existed, which for the most part were intended to ensure harmonious relations among the journeymen and encourage working habits which were for the collective good. Thus fines were imposed for swearing, fighting or defaming; drunkenness or gambling at work; dropping or leaving tools or type dirty or in the wrong place and for leaving a candle burning at night. Fines were usually paid, for refusal could bring eleven strokes across the buttocks with a board.[4]

Similar procedures were invoked among the hatters. A detailed account from the 1850s indicates their persistence. On the occasion of an offence such as 'calling a workmate by an opprobrious name', the 'constable of the shop' called a court known as a 'garrett', made up of the workers in that particular shop, and levied a fine. More serious offences called for a 'dozening', when the court was made up of men selected from twelve shops. Better known is the experience of the Chartist leader William Lovett in a carpenter's shop in the 1820s. Lovett had not been apprenticed to that trade. He was a ropemaker and his fellows regarded him as an interloper and 'set Mother Shorney' at him. That is, they hid his tools and damaged his work in an attempt to drive him out. He, however, was able to invoke another custom of the trade and call a shop meeting. This involved first sending out for a quantity of ale, and then striking his hammer and holdfast together, to assemble the workforce around his bench. A chairman was appointed and Lovett succeeded in presenting a case to continue working. That first ale purchase was not the only treating that fell to his cost:

> But the demands made upon me for drink by individuals among them, for being shown the manner of doing any particular kind

of work, together with fines and shop scores, often amounted to seven or eight shillings a week out of my guinea.

Drinking played a large part in the customary culture of the workplace. It was much more than a simple excuse for indulgence. Treating symbolically confirmed the wish to belong. As a means of spending fines it allowed a point to be made about norms of behaviour, while at the same time re-emphasising the harmony and fellowship which the deviant had disrupted. It also marked the rites of passage enacted when the ending of an apprenticeship brought a new member to the trade. A young printer had to become a 'deacon' before being admitted as a full member of the chapel. Holding a wooden sword he headed a processioning of the workplace before kneeling before the father of the chapel. He was exhorted to be observant of his business and not to betray the secrets of the workmen. Beer was poured over his head and he was given a mock title. While he was on his knees, the chapellonians worked around him singing an anthem, 'which is done by adding all the vowels to the consonants in [this] manner. Ba-ba; Be-be; Bi-bi; Bo-bo; Bu-bu; Ba-be-bi-bo-bu – and so on through the rest of the consonants'. Finally coming out of his time, the apprentice had to endure 'banging-out'. He was smeared with printers' ink and led through the workplace, promising beer-money to all the workers. Among coopers the equivalent rite was known as 'trussing'. The young man had to stand in a barrel of his own making which was then heated. He then got down into the barrel and was covered with soot, shavings, feathers, treacle and beer. He was rolled three times around the workplace and then taken out and tossed three times in the air.

Newcomers to established shops, even if they had served their full time elsewhere, were expected to buy their new colleagues drinks: a 'maiden garnish'. A hatter in the mid-nineteenth century recalled that it had cost him 9s. 8d. (48p) to treat thirty-two fellows. Treating in this trade also took place when a hatter moved to a new 'plank' and when he put on his first silk 'under'. In the print trade the maiden garnish was known as a *bien venue* and fixed in amount. When the young Benjamin Franklin came to work in a London printshop in the 1720s and, putting temperance before custom, refused his garnish, he was subjected to the 'Chapel Ghost', who mixed his type and transposed his lines. After three weeks he gave in, 'convinced of the folly of being on ill terms with those one is to live with continually'. A century later, the compositor Manby Smith, whose autobiography records his strong distaste for the custom of the trade, was so unpopular with his fellows that they goaded him into fights, so that he might be fined amounts which could then be spent on drink.

Fines and treating were special, if frequent, occasions of drinking in the workplace, but beer-drinking was an everyday feature of work as well as of leisure time. Outside of work, its tendency to take place in particular public houses associated with individual trades, both reinforced the sense of the trade as a community, and provided a headquarters for a range of collective organisations including the early trade unions.[5] In the tailoring trade the 'House of Call' acted as a labour exchange, while in many London trades, including coachmakers, carpenters, smiths, plasterers, plumbers and builders, wages were paid in public houses on Saturday nights. This was linked with drunkenness, and in 1789 William Wilberforce's Proclamation Society proposed that not allowing pay tables to be set up be made a condition for licensing. However, Francis Place, writing in 1825, thought that the custom had only recently died out.[6]

Franklin found to his dismay that London print works employed a boy full time to fetch and carry their ale. Typically a pressman drank six pints in the working day at a cost of four or five shillings from a weekly wage of a pound or less. Coopers were among the trades where beer was not paid for but expected as a customary allowance. 'They will have as much beer as they please; if we only happen to be out of beer for ten minutes all the yard is in a ferment', an employer complained in 1825, after describing the expectation as having existed 'for years'. West Country shipwrights, resisting cuts in wages and changes in hours in 1766, also insisted upon the 'usual allowance for liquor'.[7]

Sometimes the degree of co-operative working was such that wages were paid to the group or gang, rather than to individuals, while in many cases personal safety depended upon the skill and care of others. Whether the make-up of gangs was determined by employers or their agents, by middlemen, or were formed by the workers themselves, mutuality ensured that one member should not advantage himself at the expense of the others. Typically groups were made up of equal adult partners assisted by less skilled supplementary labour, often supplied by family members or apprentices. Where custom influenced the composition of the group it was usually to some purpose. In the royal dockyards 'shoalling' mixed good and bad workmen in impermanent gangs. This ensured that the wages of those getting on in years would not suffer and reasonably level earnings persist through a shipwright's working life. Even where wages were individual and age not a limiting factor, fair sharing of available work was an important aspect of mutuality. Compositors in the London print trade had long practised it. When a provincial journeyman came to work there in the early nineteenth century, he was, as he later put it, 'a stranger to the custom of the trade'. Thinking that he could earn as much as he was able, he found himself frustrated by those customs. An agreement had been made that none should touch the type except between 8 a.m. and 8 p.m. Even within those hours, he complained, work done by one man was 'limited to the capacity of the meanest ability'. No printer was to be paid for more than sixty hours a week. He was told that he would not be paid for twenty-two of them, which would be 'put on the shelf' until the end of the following week, during which he should work only thirty-eight hours: 'you must take what comes and mike [idle] a bit now and then if you are such a fast man'.[8]

By this time in some cases the customs of the trade had already become incorporated into trade union rules. This had happened as early as 1801 among the printers, when the journeyman compositors established a 'society' to correct 'irregularities' and to bring 'the modes of change from custom and precedent into one point of view, in order to their being better understood by all concerned'. Yet four years later they were complaining that some employers were taking advantage of ignorance on the part of newer journeymen, 'by disputing or denying custom, and by refusing to acknowledge precedents, which have hitherto been the only reference'.[9] The hat-makers of the Stockport area issued a printed set of rules and regulations when they were in dispute with their employers in 1809. It included reference to the custom of the trade that men take work in turn and share it equally: 'if either maker or finisher accuses any man of his time, and cannot make his accusation good, to be under a fine of one guinea'.[10] The leader of the London shipwrights, John Gast, justified the formation of a union on the Thames at the end of the eighteenth century by the need to control a situation in which:

> it was nothing uncommon for men to take such a quantity of work that many men were left destitute; that I am sure many men died a premature death for want of sustenance, because the greater part of this employ was engrossed by a few hands. The union provides against it ... that no man is to engross or take to himself a greater quantity of work than what he can accomplish. The result is, it throws it open for other people to come in. By that means many a man gets a job who would not get a job, supposing the old system of working was adopted.[11]

It may have taken the organising of a union to achieve this on the Thames, but from other shipyards the evidence suggests that unions simply added their authority to existing customary practice. At Liverpool shipbuilding workers who took more than their share of work were 'drilled' for three weeks. Drilling meant that none would work with them for a period, thus effectively keeping them from working. By 1823 this sanction was imposed by the union, but the fact that shorter periods of drilling were imposed for offences such as drunkenness or bad language and that the practice did not appear as a formal entry in the rule book, suggests it was a long-established way of disciplining unpopular workmates. As a shipwright put it: 'They do not like to work with him, because he is a very droll character, a proper idle character; then people refuse to work with him; that is the meaning of it.' There were strong feelings about fair work-sharing at Liverpool. In 1817 the young and fit workers agreed to give up a piece-rate scheme which would have brought them higher earnings, in favour of a return to traditional day rates with all getting the same:

> It was proposed on account of the old men; when piece work was brought in, they were mostly put off work, and the members

thought it very hard to see the old men walking about, without being able to get a day's work.[12]

In coal mines the particular place of work in a mine could significantly affect earnings when pitmen were paid by quantity. Custom ensured that management could not use this as a means of favouring some over others, by insisting that place of work was allocated by 'cavilling' – that is, by casting lots. In the Cornish copper mines, teams of miners known as 'tributers' worked defined places underground for an agreed share in the value of the ore raised from them. According to the system the places were offered at periodic intervals as 'bargains' to the whole workforce, the group of tributers who offered to work for the lowest proportion of raised ore securing the right to work there. However, a strong custom limited the effect of this. There was to be no 'bidding against the old pare' – that is, the tributers already working a place were in effect given an opportunity to agree terms and continue there if they so wished and a constraint was placed on the competitive bidding down of wages.[13]

Behagg has suggested that in Birmingham, with its huge range of discrete crafts and accordingly relatively small trade societies, few attempts were made by the workforce to systematise workplace customs fully into formal agreements and regulations. The brass-cock founders were organised from the late 1820s, even if they exerted collective pressure on their employers only spasmodically. An observer noted in 1851 that 'by a rule of the union' no journeymen could take more than one boy to work under him. Yet no rulebook as such existed before 1885. The Britannia metal workers operated a tightly closed shop by the late 1830s, yet one member admitted that there was 'no rule of the union' forbidding employers from taking on non-members, but unionists 'do not and will not associate with others except members of their own body which is pretty much the same as forbidding them to work in that establishment'. In 1838 a button-burnisher was disciplined for breaking a regulation of the trade. Despite his protest that 'we have no written regulations', he was expelled for infringing 'long established laws and practice'.[14] Yet other trades seem to have followed the pattern of the printworkers and taken care by the early nineteenth century that their custom and practices were properly recorded. The woolcombers prefaced a printed list of forty-four articles in 1812 with the claim that

> There never was to our knowledge, any well regulated articles which took into their cognizance so many particulars ... in which, we have endeavoured, to consider every general circumstance and particular usage in the trade.[15]

Twenty-five years before that the journeyman brushmakers, finding that their customary control over apprenticeship was breaking down, met at Manchester, formed a society and 'established rules for the better regulation of this business', which were accepted by journeymen 'throughout the whole Kingdom'. They placed notices advising employers and customers of this in newspapers as far afield as Exeter.[16] By the closing years of the eighteenth century having printed rules could in itself be part of the presentation of a more respectable image. The United Society of Cordwainers included this passage in the preface to the second edition of their *Articles* in 1794:

> Many are the advantages and good effects of our Constitution, that barbarism, with which the trade has been but too justly branded for centuries past, is now totally dispelled. There is no more working on Sundays, nor sotting and swearing in public houses on Mondays like vagabonds as usual; this attainment must give infinite pleasure to every sober thinking man. Our rules if strictly adhered to, have a tendency to improve the morals and cultivate the manners.[17]

Obviously in some circumstances journeymen's societies took a risk when they printed regulations of identifying themselves as trade unions and thus risking prosecution. The fact that at times of disputes employers considered such publications as evidence of illegal combination and sent them to the Home Office confirms that this was not an unfounded fear. Some journeymen's societies therefore continued to rely on the oral transmission of customary practices and the demonstration effect of occasional unofficial sanctions on those who broke them. There were, however, some public actions, including ceremonies, which amounted to street theatre. Other customs served best when they were retained as part of a private world. Ceremonial forms of initiation or other rites of passage, with their awesome oaths against betrayal, were part of this world, as were the traditional sanctions employed against members who broke the 'customs of the trade'. Secrecy was essential. Outsiders found it hard to penetrate the inner practices of the workplace. That was intended. For as well as seeking to establish mutuality rather than self-interest among the work force, insisting on customary work practices was an attempt to keep a considerable degree of control over the labour process. It defined the rights of skilled craftsmen over the nature and pace of their work, while allowing to the employer the separate sphere of initiating the process of production and of marketing the product. The old usage which gave a journeyman who had served his time a right to exercise the 'mystery' of his trade continued to carry important meanings both of rightful possession and of justified exclusiveness.

Even when the 'rules' remained secret and unprinted, there was still a public dimension. The ceremonial and processioning which accompanied funerals and those which were performed on the particular feast and saints' days of the trades were street theatre: an outward show of the solidarity of the brotherhood of the craft. At the bitter heights of industrial disputes ritual humiliations were no less public, whether the victim was strike-breaking fellow, rate-cutting master or brought-in blackleg. The form was usually related to the long-established traditions of 'rough music' or 'charivari' employed against those who offended the moral code of the community, from wife-beaters, through young espousers of old rich women to long-standing cuckolds.[18] In 1793 around 300 Banbury woollen weavers, who took in work from the same master, refused to work when one of their number took an apprentice in a manner which 'transgressed their laws'. Learning that a weaver had broken ranks and 'contrary' to their order, had 'betook himself to work', 200 of them, after parading the streets to 'martial music', marched, two by two, the two miles to the offender's home. They seized the cloth from his loom, and marched back bearing it upon the back of an ass. They finished by laying it at the door of the master who had put it out to the weaver. In the dispute of 1725/6 which ranged fiercely over the serge-weaving district around Exeter and Taunton, weavers carried a piece of serge cut from a loom around the towns, 'declaring they would do the like' to masters who refused to increase wages. Witnesses reported seeing masters 'carried about on a coolstaff' by angry crowds. During the strike of seamen at South Shields in 1792, three who broke ranks 'were stripped naked and made to walk in that situation up the street of South Shields and round the Market Place'. Custom is not always 'nice', still less quaint, but it is often about solidarity over collective interests which could not otherwise have been defined and defended.[19]

CUSTOM AND CONFLICT

In 1718 West Country woollen workers protested that the clothiers were seeking to reduce their earnings by methods which were 'contrary to law, usage and custom from time immemorial'.[20] In a better-known conflict almost a century later, the Nottinghamshire Luddites declared that they would continue to smash the stocking-frames of hosiers who were employing cheap, unapprenticed labour ('colting') to make inferior stockings ('cut-ups') until 'full-fashioned work at the old-fashioned price is established by Custom and Law'.[21] The defence of the 'rights' of skilled labour, which underpinned so much of the industrial protest of the time, did not view custom and law as alternative legitimations. Rather, in the artisan's expectation they were congruent. When custom came into conflict with law it was because new enactments, fresh interpretations or wilful disuse destroyed or threatened this congruity. The clauses of the Elizabethan Statute of Artificers of 1563 which required all those who worked in trades to have served an apprenticeship had been widely disregarded for more than a century before the statute was finally repealed in 1814 – one year after the wage-fixing clauses of that same statute had been removed. Its reach had also been narrowed in case law, notably, for example, when it was ruled not to apply to trades which had not been in being at the time of its passing. This had the particular effect of excluding the late eighteenth century's fastest-growing manufacture: cotton.[22] The case of statutory apprenticeship provides examples of exclusion, disuse, reinterpretation and finally repeal, but other customary usages and expectations were sometimes denied by fresh legislation. Artisans in many trades traditionally made use of some of the 'scrap' materials which occurred when they manufactured from put-out or workplace materials. Hatters took expensive materials to make up on the side and called it 'bugging'. Tailors over-measured their bespoke customers and did likewise with the resulting 'cabbage'. Weavers felt themselves entitled to the 'thrums', the ends left on the loom after the piece had been removed. Shipwrights in the royal dockyards carried out substantial amounts of timber off-cuts and called them 'chips'. All of these were considered legitimate and justified contributions to earnings. However, such appropriations were increasingly contested by employers, who secured from the legislature from the mid-eighteenth century a series of statutes relating to their particular trades which criminalised as theft the customary taking of perquisite materials in a range of trades from woollen weaving, through hat-making to metal-working.[23]

Even more contentious were conflicting views over time and work discipline. Among the Cornish tinners the first Friday in March had been observed in a peculiar manner. A young lad was sent to the highest point of the works to sleep there as long as he could. The length of his siesta was then taken as the measure of the tinners' afternoon nap for the following twelve months. Underground tin and copper miners too then worked at a pace which was hardly relentless. A treatise of 1778 remarked:

> When a pair of men went underground formerly, they made it a rule to sleep out a candle, before they set about their work ... then rise up and work briskly; after that, have a touch pipe, that is rest themselves half an hour to smoke a pipe of tobacco; and so play and sleep away half their time: but mining being more expensive than it formerly was, those idle customs are superseded by more labour than industry.[24]

Similar practices were described in many other trades and occupations. Most symbolic of customary irregular working was the observance of 'Saint Monday' – that is, keeping Monday as a holiday and hardly beginning the week's work until Tuesday. The first verse of

'The Jovial Cutlers', a song from Sheffield at the end of the eighteenth century, runs:

> Brother workmen, cease your labour,
> Lay your files and hammers by;
> Listen while a brother neighbour
> Sings a cutler's destiny:
> How upon a good Saint Monday,
> Sitting by the smithy fire,
> Telling what's been done o't Sunday,
> And in cheerful mirth conspire.[25]

It has been suggested that among urban workers, Saint Monday was so generally observed by the later eighteenth century that a 'regular' week of which Tuesday was the first full working day was already in existence. However, it seems clear that irregular time-keeping remained a source of running conflict between employers and some groups of workers well into the nineteenth century.[26]

Edward Thompson pointed out that many groups of journeymen inherited their conception of rights not only from custom and statute law but also from those rights which government had conferred on the craft guilds. He has drawn attention to an iconography of display which 'emphasises an appeal by the early trade unionists to tradition, and an attempt by the journeyman's club or union to take over from the masters' guild or company the representation of the interests of the "the Trade"'.[27] Such characteristics were considerably more marked in the case of some other countries where the guild tradition had been stronger: in France until the Revolution of 1789 and in Germany until 1848, although in both they were under constant attack from 'enlightened' liberal economic thought. Even institutions such as the 'tramping system', whereby unemployed journeymen went on the road seeking work and experience, being supported en route by the local societies of their respective trades, were more universal, more ritualised and more of an expected period in the life-cycle of the artisan.[28] The sense of a community of 'the Trade', residing, now, more in labour than in capital, was nevertheless still strong in Britain. The Nottinghamshire Luddites twice referred to themselves as 'the

Trade' in their best-known protest song, 'General Ludd's Triumph':

> These engines of mischief were sentenced to die
> By unanimous vote of the Trade;
> And Ludd who can all opposition defy
> Was the grand Executioner made.
>
> ......
>
> Then the Trade when this ardorous contest is o'er
> Shall raise in full splendour its head,
> And colting and cutting and squaring no more
> Shall deprive honest workmen of bread.[29]

It was similar usurpation which had caused the masters in the serge-manufacturing districts around Exeter to complain in 1725 that the weavers had their clubs, 'where none but weavers are admitted, and they have their ensigns and flags hung out at the door of their meetings'. Here they made 'bye-laws' over matters such as apprenticeship and piece-rates.[30]

Thompson also argued that in the early nineteenth century a culture of tradition and persistence became a culture of resistance; custom became rebellious. When 'innovating' employers were increasingly seeking to impose changed methods of working and of organising labour over a range of manufactures, then skilled men, seeing in this an attack on their living standards or even fearing displacement by cheaper labour, organised to oppose change. He placed the Luddism of 1811–16 at the 'crisis point in the abrogation of paternalist legislation and in the imposition of the political economy of laissez-faire upon and against the will and conscience of the working people'.[31] By then only the bare bones of paternalist regulation remained, but even the Statute of Artificers retained much symbolic as well as some actual importance. Randall has shown how the woollen workers of the West Country organised themselves in 1755/6 to secure legislation requiring the justices of the peace to fix wages annually and enforce their payment by the clothiers. This had been done between 1728 and 1732, then, despite the fact that the Act was still on the statute book, the practicehad lapsed. Briefly they triumphed. An Act was secured in 1756, but following counter-petitioning by the clothiers was repealed in the following year. Success was shortlived, but long remembered.[32]

The Essex woolcombers put memory in verse in the late seventeenth century:

> From such as would our rights invade,
> Or would intrude into our trade,
> Or break the law Queen Betty made
> Libera nos Domine.

So did the London saddlers in 1811, when the struggle over statutory apprenticeship was getting underway:

> Her memory still is dear to journeymen,
> For sheltered by her laws, now they resist
> Infringements, which would else persist:
> Tyrannic masters, innovating fools
> Are check'd and bounded by her glorious rules.
> Of workmen's rights, she's still a guarantee.
> And rights of artisans, to fence and guard,
> While we, poor helpless wretches, oft must go,
> And range this liberal nation to and fro.[33]

The disregard of manufacturers for laws which had not been repealed and the connivance of government at this disregard do not remove the fact that 'V Elizabeth' retained a special meaning for skilled workers in symbolising the regulated economy. They did not readily cease to act as if legislative remedy for their grievances was obtainable. At the crisis points in the relationships between labour and capital over a range of manufactures, workers petitioned for government regulation of their trades. They retained a powerful vision of a time when well-being had been preserved by custom and protected by law. The cherished Elizabethan statute had a reality in the notion of what *ought* to be, to which artisans appealed. In a sense the repeal in 1813 of its wage-fixing clauses and, even more so, in 1814 of those which enforced apprenticeship, were a delayed, but critical and symbolic, ending to the era of paternalist regulation: an official announcement of the triumph of political economy in the state as well as in the operating economy. But the state already had been abdicating its role with a speed which bewildered petitioning artisans. The calico printers were among those trades which, not having been in existence in 1563, were not, according to the lawyers, protected by the Act. In 1804 they were facing a severe overstocking of their trade by employers who were taking on large numbers of boys in the guise of apprentices. Sitting on their petition for a regulation law, a parliamentary committee recognised 'that the dispropor-tion of apprentices to journeymen exists to a degree far beyond that understood to prevail in any other mechanical profession ... [it was] extraordinary [to] anyone in the least degree acquainted with the custom of trade'. The committee, however, declared itself 'not friendly to the idea of imposing any restric-tions upon trade'. The petitioners gained only sympathy.[34] The several Acts dating from the sixteenth and seventeenth centu-ries regulating woollen manufacture, which had restricted employer's freedom to introduce machinery and implement the factory system, were repealed in 1809 after weavers and shearmen had made them the basis of their struggle against innovating clothiers.[35] When the cotton workers failed to secure a minimum wage in 1811, they were 'utterly at a loss to conceive on what fair ground legislative interference can be improper under circumstances so necessitous'.[36]

By the early nineteenth century a change in rhetoric on the part of some skilled workers can be discerned, although it had no greater effect on the legislature. They began to justify 'protection' of their exclusive right to their trades, less in terms of a 'timeless' right and more in terms of a 'property of skill':

> The weaver's qualifications may be considered as his property and support. It is as real property to him as Buildings and Lands are to others . . . [1823]

or, from the watchmakers in 1817:

> apprenticed artisans have, collectively and individually, an unquestionable right to expect the most extended protection from the Legislature, in the quiet and exclusive use and enjoy-ment of their several and respective arts and trades, which the law has already conferred upon them as a property, as much as it

has secured the property of the stockholder in the public funds.[37]

CUSTOM, WAGES AND THE LABOUR MARKET

Custom and tradition were not invoked in a desperate struggle with 'capitalism' in an historically unspecific sense. Indeed, as Randall has pointed out, what gave solidarity and identification to protesting occupational groups such as rural weavers and knitters working under the putting-out system, coal miners and the growing class of permanent urban journeymen, and what defined and shaped their forms of protest was precisely that they had developed the traditions of wage-earners employed by capitalists.[38] They depended on the capitalist for work, but could still stress 'independence': the right to work in their own time, in some cases in their own home, and for whomsoever they chose. The struggle between labour and capital often took the form of conflict between capitalist attempts at subordination and labour's cherished independence.

Emphasis on 'custom' and 'tradition' has led to a concentration on the defensive aspects of artisan culture. Strikes, for example to resist cuts in wages, increases in hours or the de-skilling effects of changing forms of hire, have received more attention than those which Adam Smith characterised as 'offensive' – that is, attempts to advance wages or improve conditions.[39] Customary culture is not the simple antithesis of 'market culture'. The culture of the wage-dependent artisan was in itself the product of a capitalist market economy, yet it presumed that the forces of the labour market and the distribution of power within it should be restrained by custom and the claimed rights of labour. On the northern coalfield in 1765, the pitmen fought the attempt of the coalowners to change the time of their annual bonding and through a 'certificate of leave' prevent them from moving from one employer to another. The miners resisted because they correctly perceived that an attempt was being made to reduce their bargaining power at the point of hire. They fought to preserve what had in fact become a customary system of hiring which allowed some power to the suppliers of labour. Free movement and annual negotiation were the essentials of what the pitmen deemed to be a fair labour market. By the beginning of the

nineteenth century the industrial culture of the northeastern pitmen embraced an acceptance of market relations and of the
importance of what has been called by Jaffe 'the struggle for
market power' – that is, the struggle against disadvantage in their
particular labour market.[40]

Manufacturing artisans also largely accepted the idea that
bargaining was one of the processes which determined the
price they got for selling their skilled labour power, but they too
thought in terms of a 'fair' labour market, not an 'open' self-
regulating one in which employers could employ whom they
chose at the lowest price.[41] A fair labour market was one in
which the respective powers of capital and labour were not
hugely unequal. In such a system of exchange, the exclusive
rights to a trade were recognised and machines did not displace
labour simply to enhance the profits of capital. Machinery in
itself was not necessarily an issue. The Nottinghamshire Luddites did not oppose knitting-frames, they opposed adaptations
which enable some hosiers to employ cheap labour in the production of inferior stockings.[42] Woollen weavers in many districts readily accepted the spring loom ('flying shuttle') into
their cottages when employers allowed them to retain some of
the extra productivity by not cutting piece-rates. The early spin-
ning jennies in cotton manufacture were also small enough to
be worked in the cottage, and until this situation changed, were
readily taken up by the women whose earnings they enhanced.
As Randall has pointed out, a critical determinant of the
response to machinery was 'the way in which the innovation in
question might or might not be integrated into the organisation of production without detriment to employment or
custom'.[43]

So far as wage expectations are concerned there is substance to
the suggestion by some historians, that conservative acceptance by
skilled workers of 'customary' living standards may have meant
that they settled for less than the market price for their labour.[44]
However, there is much that points to the employment of calculated strategies to maximise the advantages of collective bargaining. This is indicated not only by the building up of strike funds in
advance, but also in the timing of strikes. The weavers and comb-
ers of the southwest were said in 1726 to strike in the spring when
there was 'the greatest demand for goods, and most plenty of

work'. Shipwrights and coopers knew their strength when the fleet was fitting out for war. Fellmongers in the leather trade chose Michaelmas, when the pre-winter killing of livestock placed large numbers of deteriorating hides on their employers' hands. Tailors and black-ribbon weavers were well aware that a death in the royal family worked to their advantage. By the end of the eighteenth century several groups had begun to employ the 'rolling strike' – that is, turning out one shop or works at a time, so that those remaining in employ could more easily sustain those chosen to strike.[45]

Perhaps the final point is that the language of custom does not necessarily indicate an unchanging reality. In 1766 the ship-wrights at Topsham, on the Exe, complained that their masters were seeking to reduce wages from the level that had been 'from time immemorially paid' and to pay those for more hours than had been 'usual and customary for journeymen shipwrights to work and labour'. The wage the journeymen were seeking to defend was 2s. 6d. a day: very good wages indeed for provincial artisans in 1766 and hardly likely to have been normal before the outbreak of the Seven Years War in 1756 had increased the demand for skilled shipyard labour in south Devon.[46] Hobsbawm has put it that:

> the custom of the trade or the shop may represent not ancient tradition, but whatever right the workers have established in practice, however recently, and which they now attempt to extend or defend by giving it the sanction of perpetuity. 'Custom' cannot afford to be invariant because even in 'traditional' societies life is not so.[47]

Even so, the tendency to sanctify usages and expectations as customary when they may be of recent origin, while it belongs in part to the process of 'inventing' pasts, which has recently been stressed by historians, nevertheless indicates the import-ance of custom as a legitimating device, ascribing continuity to what may in fact be nearer to innovation. As Behagg has shown in detail for the Birmingham trades, 'custom' and 'tradition' were necessarily omnibus terms which could be used either to cover agreements and forms of working that were of actual longevity, or to legitimate more flexible strategies designed to meet the changing needs of labour: 'To systematise too formally what "customary practice" actually was could only serve to weaken its force as a universal argument and severely hinder its adaptability.' Thus custom could be a means of incorporating and consolidating what was seen to be of advantage, as well as one of resisting the unwanted as unwonted. Randall has argued similarly that the West Country shearmen in their conflicts with the clothiers over the eighteenth century were 'more than willing to force new regulations and practices on their employers. Once accepted, these too became enshrined as part of the customs of the trade'.[48]

9. 'Tacit, Unsuspected, but still Implicit Faith': Alternative Belief in Nineteenth-Century Rural England

BOB BUSHAWAY

I

Part of the title of this essay is taken from the writings of a late nineteenth-century clergyman whose parish lay in the northern part of the Yorkshire dales. As an indication of the familiarity with which he knew his parish, the Reverend J. C. Atkinson calculated that he had walked more than 70,000 miles, in pursuance of his clerical business, across forty years of residence. Despite noting the modernisation of local farming practice, a decline in 'rowdyism', the decay of local dialect and the advance of education, he could still record the widespread acceptance of alternative belief in the late nineteenth century as 'a living faith'.[1] His informants were often reluctant to converse with him on this subject, through fear of being thought 'credulous or superstitious',[2] but, despite this reluctance, he was able to describe a holistic structure of folk beliefs. These were not rooted in ignorance but were at odds with orthodox belief; yet they often sat comfortably alongside formal knowledge or religious belief. One of his informants was

> the worthiest of my many worthy parishioners, a man sensible, clear-headed, intelligent, one of my best helpers in all good and useful things ... a man with the instinctive feelings of the truest gentility, but who always seemed averse to entering on any folklore talk or inquiry, and was, even

admittedly, on his guard lest he should be led on to speak of them inadvertently.[3]

This reluctance is not surprising as the enquirer was in this case a representative of the official authority on supernatural belief. Neither was Atkinson's an isolated example of alternative belief. In many places in nineteenth-century rural England the labouring poor maintained a framework of local beliefs, legend, knowledge, remedy and explanation, which lay outside the experience of the representatives of official knowledge and belief but which coexisted with the formal agencies of church and education. This framework was consistent. Atkinson's many parishioner-informants 'all spoke of the matters they talked to me about as things that had been, and were real, and not as creations of the fancy, or old-wives' tales and babble'.[4] Despite varying social and economic backgrounds and a persistent notion among folklorists that 'popular superstition' only lingered in relatively remote and backward regions, evidence can be found throughout the nineteenth century and from widely differing rural communities for a coherent and alternative set of beliefs and practices.

Recent historians have characterised English rural society in the nineteenth century as in process of transformation.[5] A chronology for this process of transformation has become orthodox. The impact of capital-intensive farming, enclosure, evangelicalism, communications, education and popular literacy, changed rural England irrevocably from a customary world to one in which relationships were contractual.[6] The process of transformation was accelerated by mechanisation and the application of new techniques to the farming process which, in turn, was followed in mid-century by rural depopulation to the towns and overseas. Towards the end of the nineteenth century rural society was characterised by the rise of agricultural trade unionism and the spread of literacy through education. In this chronology, non-orthodox beliefs and practices are ignored or marginalised and are generally cast as 'popular superstitions' – a phrase also popular with contemporary clergymen, folk collectors and educationalists. Their 'decline' is welcomed as generally beneficial. Such beliefs were regarded by working-class radicals and middle-class reformers alike as harmful, indicative of ignorance and unenlightenment and conservative.

Alternative belief is not usually discussed in the context of a specific customary culture. Not to do so ignores its variety, vitality and longevity for the labouring poor in many rural areas. Some historians have acknowledged the importance of alternative beliefs in nineteenth-century rural culture.[7] Yet one historian writes: 'However colourful and diverting they ["superstitions"] might be, the orally transmitted folk traditions embodied a fundamental failure of comprehension.'[8] To consider alternative belief in nineteenth-century rural England from a rational and scientific viewpoint is to adopt the critical perspective, held by many contemporary commentators on rural life, that the rural poor were stupid and held firmly to popular delusions which could only be eradicated by the judicious application of education. An early twentieth-century rural commentator, Alfred Williams, attacked contemporary versions of this attitude as misguided. 'There is', he wrote in 1912, 'a great deal said concerning the ignorance and stupidity of rustic people, their slavishness, and clownishness, and the rest of it. I have even heard that we lead an "animal kind of existence" ... the fact of a man's being deeply attached to the soil, and careless of the world's strife and tumult, does not make him an animal.'[9] Thus, the historiography of rural England before the First World War gives little attention to or is merely critical of alternative belief.

Part of the reason for the reluctance of social historians to consider this aspect of rural culture lies in the nature of the sources. For the most part, evidence for alternative knowledge and belief is to be found in the papers of nineteenth-century folklorists, antiquaries, county societies and field clubs. Much of the material is interpreted within the framework of a prevailing contemporary analysis which placed most emphasis on notions of survival and ethnocentricity. Victorian society, for such people, represented a zenith of achievement whose distant ethnic origins were worthy of study. Rural culture seemed to them already a part of a quaint past which could be picked over in support of contesting theories of England's pre-history and whose surviving representatives were akin to living artefacts in touch with a precursive rural simplicity. To accept the views of the critics and collectors of rural culture is to misrepresent both the form and context of collective belief and its function for the rural labouring poor as a sustaining value system distinct from the dominant culture.

Some Victorian mediators of rural culture, such as Thomas Hardy, regarded by many of his contemporaries as an accurate rural commentator, were convinced that the transformation of rural England had been largely brought about by a fundamental and irreversible change in its social structure. 'The change at the root of this', he wrote,

> has been the recent supplanting of the class of stationary cottagers, who carried on the local traditions and humours, by a population of more or less migratory labourers, which has led to a break of continuity in local history, more fatal than any other thing to the preservation of legend, folk-lore, close inter-social relations and eccentric individualities. For these the indispensable conditions of existence are attachment to the soil of one particular spot by generation after generation.[10]

This was a characteristic view. Hardy believed himself to have sprung from such stock and his difficulty in comprehending the rise of a rural proletariat in nineteenth-century England together with his unfamiliarity with its representatives means that his readership was presented with alternative belief as something antique, gothic and sensational, or confined only to a few colourful and eccentric individuals rather than as a general part of local culture. This is particularly so of Hardy's short stories.

Alternative belief was a nexus between the families of the rural labouring poor which provided cultural self-awareness and was underpinned by custom. It was not a quaint set of picturesque practices and comprehensions which gave colour to drab lives and which could be used as sources of literary titillation for an urban readership facing *fin-de-siècle* ennui. Alternative belief was an holistic structure in which the labouring poor sought to reinforce their view of the external world and which provided a means of dealing with the chance incidence of personal loss, illness, economic hardship and the uncertainties of life. This was particularly important at a time when the structurally superior elements of rural life (farmers, landowners, clergymen, doctors, teachers) sought to impose new standards of behaviour, work practices, and neoteric value systems. Rather than taking the form of a mishmash of disconnected, benighted and potentially destructive practices, persisted in from ignorance, alternative belief in rural England in the nineteenth century provided a form of cultural and social independence for many labouring families.

II

What is alternative belief? In general, it is a way of looking at external phenomena which does not conform to prevailing orthodoxies. Nineteenth-century English folklorists used a variety of terms to describe those examples of what earlier collectors had referred to as 'popular antiquities'.[11] The most usual form was the all-embracing term 'popular superstition'.[12] As much of the source material for alternative belief is drawn from the collections of folklorists it is important to consider their understanding of their material. Nineteenth-century folklorists were usually concerned to search for examples of 'popular superstition' in rural England rather than the working-class communities of Victorian towns and cities because of the general assumption that 'popular superstition' was the survival of an older, more systematic, pattern of pre-christian, or, at least, pre-Reformation, religious belief largely associated with a predominantly oral culture. Edwin Hartland wrote of Gloucestershire in 1892 that

> everywhere there has lingered, and lingers still among the uneducated classes, a number of traditions – songs, tales, proverbs, riddles, games, customs, institutions, leechcraft, superstitions – distinct from and only partially sanctioned by the religion, the literature, the science and arts, which together sum up what we understand by civilisation. These traditions constitute our Folk-lore.[13]

The classification used by Hartland was a common one. Leechcraft refers to alternative medical knowledge. He was clear that those who lived among the poor were the best placed to collect folk materials. 'There must be many educated persons', he continued,

> who are familiar with the beliefs and practices of the uneducated and who would find it a source of pleasure to record and discuss their beliefs and practices if they were assured of the importance attached to them. Already the science of Folk-lore is

indebted for some of its most valuable material to clergymen, medical men, elementary schoolmasters, and to ladies in various stations of life – material gathered all over the country, often amidst onerous avocations, from which it has been a relief to the collectors to turn to subjects not merely of scientific value, but subjects fruitful of human sympathy with their lowlier neighbours.[14]

A dichotomy is established by the collector between the 'uneducated' and their 'popular superstitions' and the 'educated' and their 'civilisation'.[15] Nineteenth-century English folklorists, even where a sympathetic view was adopted, considered folklore to be the lingering survival of past patterns of social life. Systematic study was urged to illuminate understanding not of the cultural activity of contemporaries but of society in its infancy or of an earlier geography of racial distribution in Britain. The folklorist Sabine Baring-Gould wrote:

Here, in Great Britain, we form an amalgam of several races, and each race has contributed something towards the common stock of folk-lore. In my own neighbourhood we have two distinct types of humanity: one with high cheekbones, dusky skin, dark hair, full of energy, unscrupulous as to the *meum* and *tuum*, money-making, by every conceivable means. The other is fair-haired, clear-skinned, slow, steady, honourable, with none of the alertness of the other ... Through intermarriage there is an importation of the superstitious beliefs of the lower type into the higher.[16]

Alternative belief was not thought to have relevance in Victorian England except as a middle-class leisure pursuit which might provide evidence of the past. One of the main developments of English folklore studies in the nineteenth century was its rapid fragmentation into a series of separate areas of study – folk-dance, folk-song, calendar customs, folk-narrative, etc. The folklorist's desire to establish a scientific approach to the collection and classification of material actually destroyed its holistic and locally specific structure.

Alternative belief in nineteenth-century rural England was based upon the relationship of the individual to place, the natural world, the working environment, human life and the supernatural. Belief was largely phenomenological and observation and experience were its principal components. Events which occurred during an individual's life were interpreted against a consistent structure whilst magic itself was left to key specialists in the rural community. Figure 9.1 shows the structure of unofficial knowledge and belief in nineteenth-century rural England. Alternative belief was essentially anthropocentric and interconnected rather than merely fatalistic. It was based upon a direct and interconnected relationship between the events of human life and those of the natural and supernatural worlds. Thus, local lore and language, folk-narratives and tales, weather lore, popular religious beliefs, divination rituals, belief in ominous occurrences, charms and remedies, life crises rites of passage, calendar and work customs, and formal magic were an integral part of its structure.

Folklorists and antiquaries prior to the Victorian period had simply referred to unorthodox beliefs as 'vulgar errors', or 'credulities'.[17] In 1831 a correspondent of William Hone referred to 'popular superstitions of the present day, at which the rising generation may smile when the credulous are dead and only remembered for their fond belief'.[18] He went on to record in detail and from personal observation many contemporary examples of 'popular superstition' which were still extant at the end of the nineteenth century. He included a description of the process of divination derived from the use of a key with the Bible. He had

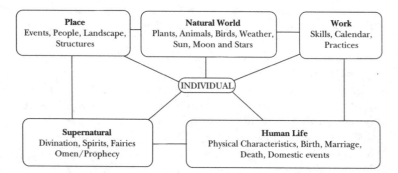

Figure 9.1 *The structure of alternative belief in nineteenth-century rural England*

become involved because a neighbour's child came to borrow his Bible for the purpose as 'neither a Bible nor a key belonging to any person living in the house would do'.[19] The neighbour was attempting to discover the identity of the thief who had stolen her husband's shirt. The key was placed in the Bible against the seventeenth verse of the first chapter of the Book of Ruth, 'the Lord do so to me and more also', the verse was incanted with a list of names, the notion being that when the correct name had been mentioned an indication would be given by the falling of the Bible to the ground from the child's hand. In fact the shirt had been misplaced but the defender of the practice proclaimed that 'it never failed before, nor would it have failed then, but that the man in the corner, meaning me, laughed; and, she added, with malicious solemnity, that the Bible would not be laughed at'.[20] Late nineteenth-century attempts at objectivity could not disguise the interest of many of the members of local folklore societies and field clubs in 'popular superstition' as a collection of curious and exotic perceptions and practices found in small and isolated rural communities and which, in their view, could be traced to the various ethnic strands in Britain's past history.

Partly because of the influence of the value system of nineteenth-century collectors and partly because of an over-concentration on radical elements in the transformation of rural England, social historians have not directed much attention to alternative beliefs in this period but have usually dismissed them as irrelevant or regressive.[21] Yet alternative beliefs and practices were widespread and received general tacit support throughout the nineteenth century and even into the twentieth. The historian of the New Forest could write in 1863,

> I do not mean, however, to say that these beliefs are openly avowed, or will even be acknowledged by the first labourer who may be seen. The English peasant is at all times exceedingly chary – no one perhaps more so – of expressing his full mind; and a long time is required before a stranger can, if ever, get his confidence. But I do say that these superstitions are all, with more or less credit, held in different parts of the Forest, although even many who believe them the firmest would shrink, from fear of ridicule, to confess the fact. Education has done something to remove them; but they have

too firm a hold to be easily uprooted. They may not be openly expressed, but they are, for all that, to my certain knowledge, still latent.[22]

By the end of the nineteenth century, some folk collectors did accept that a study of popular beliefs and practices could provide insights into a previously closed world but they increasingly recorded reluctance on the part of rural labourers to reveal information on their beliefs. Hartland recognised that 'popular superstitions' were either ignored by the professional and middle-class inhabitants of rural communities as 'trivial matters unworthy of serious attention'[23] or were actively opposed by official agencies such as the church and the law. By the early twentieth century, he had formed a view that the study of 'popular superstitions' could reveal the inner lives of the rural labouring poor. 'If we want to gauge', he wrote,

> aright the mind of the community, the social relations, the pleasures, the pains, the hopes and sorrows and all the thousand details that fill and colour its life – in short, to know the people as it has been and as it is – we must turn to the oral traditions, the institutions and practices of the peasant and labourer. These are things the law barely recognises. The Church frowns on them, ignores them or tolerates them ... political and even ecclesiastical revolutions sweep over them, and leave them – not the same, but changing so slowly that, if not roughly interfered with by external authority, the alteration is only perceptible by comparison at rare intervals.[24]

This was written only two years before the outbreak of the First World War and reveals a new awareness, drawn from the work of social anthropologists, that contemporary relevance could be found in the study of 'popular superstition'. It also shows how folklorists were moving away from the emphasis on the search for origins in past history. This was in marked contrast to earlier collectors who thought that

> The prime origin of the superstitious notions and ceremonies of the people is absolutely unattainable. We must despair of ever being able to reach the fountain-head of streams which have

been running and increasing from the beginning of time. All that we can aspire to do, is only to trace their courses backward, as far as possible, on those charts that now remain of the distant countries whence they were first perceived to flow.[25]

In working with their source materials, social anthropologists have not viewed 'popular superstition' in a pejorative way. Ioan Lewis writes:

> I certainly do not believe in witchcraft. I make this declaration ... to show that we do not need to share other people's beliefs in order to understand them sympathetically: we can see the sense in beliefs even when we are convinced they are based upon false premises ... we can appreciate that the most erroneous of assumptions may yet serve as a perfectly sound basis for a coherent and logically satisfying system of beliefs.[26]

Alternative beliefs in nineteenth-century rural England should be regarded as a consistent and comprehensive frame of reference by which the labouring poor could view their lives, external agencies and the supernatural. These beliefs were not an irrational response to their experiences but a shared understanding of the world around them. This could take a locally specific form but often provided a general purpose response to universal problems. For example, the incidence of aborted or prematurely born calves in pasture areas was frequent and was regarded as an act of chance. In most rural areas in nineteenth-century England, actions were prescribed to meet the occurrence. In North Yorkshire, the required response was to bury the aborted calf at the threshold of the cowhouse 'on its back, with its four legs all stretching vertically in the rigidity of death'. One informant, when questioned on the practice, said 'Ay ... there's many as do dis it yet. My au'd father did it. But it's sae money years syne, it must be about wore out by now, and I shall have to dee it again.'[27] In Dorset, local culture provided a different response for the same occurrence. The dead calf was placed high up in the branches of a maiden ash tree as a preventive measure.[28] These different responses, separated by great distance, represented a common approach by smallholders to a universal problem in dairying areas.

It is also misguided to hold the view that alternative belief 'declines' across time. Theoretical and empirical studies of contemporary society do not support the theory of decline. Antonio Gramsci argued that folklore should be regarded as a coherent belief system and a valid perception of reality. 'It must first be shown', he wrote,

> that all men are 'philosophers', by defining the limits and characteristics of the 'spontaneous philosophy' which is proper to everybody. This philosophy is contained in: 1. Language itself, which is a totality of determined notions and concepts and not just of words grammatically devoid of content. 2. 'Common sense' and 'good sense'. 3. Popular religion and, therefore, also in the entire system of beliefs, superstitions, opinions, ways of seeing things and of acting which are collectively bundled together under the name of 'folklore'.[29]

It is in this sense that alternative beliefs and knowledge in nineteenth-century rural England operated as a value system, providing options and responses to the needs and imperatives of labouring lives, rather than as a set of confused, erroneous but picturesque practices and views rooted in some earlier religious system which had survived into the nineteenth century as degraded and deformed reminders of past beliefs.

Recent work has suggested that contemporary society still sees little contradiction between alternative beliefs and orthodox knowledge. A recent study of British society has suggested that 'not only does magic persist as a formal tradition of belief and activity, but also in various forms and social contexts it continues to provide a symbolic universe in which the individuals and groups may locate and interact their experience of social reality'.[30] The same study concludes that 'By observing superstition and magic in their social and symbolic context, it is possible to see how, far from being an anomolous eccentricity, they reflect and to an extent may control experience in significant areas of life. It is clear that individuals do not approach all experience "rationally" in all contexts'.[31] Another recent study of contemporary belief concludes that

> superstitious sayings and practices are widespread phenomena of considerable significance. The reasons why this should be so,

in this comparatively enlightened age, are obscure and may never be fully understood, but, on the available evidence, the idea ... that 'everyday' superstitious sayings and habits may well constitute an established and well-used 'coping mechanism' against 'anxiety' cannot lightly be discounted.[32]

One social psychologist has taken the view that 'It is tempting to infer that superstition is a mere survival in our kind of society. Working-class people, being less educated, cling to them longer, but sooner or later they will die out altogether. This is a rather common notion among people who regard themselves as enlightened.'[33] A recent definitional article, 'Folk Lore', points out that 'The latin word *superstitio* which lives on in the vocabulary of the educated, bears witness to the antiquity of interest in folklore of a religious kind. *Superstition* still conveys a negative attitude that sought to eradicate beliefs and practices not in keeping with the official religion; the pejorative connotation confirms this interpretation.'[34] Judgemental language should be avoided when dealing with alternative beliefs in rural England in the nineteenth century.

III

What, then, were the specific characteristics of the alternative view of the external world and social reality held by the rural labouring poor and rural smallholders and producers in many different parts of England? First, although the form of response was often local, actions and beliefs were commonly applied to universal situations. Second, responses provided a knowable mechanism by which people could approach and have apparent control over the ungovernable aspects of life and counter its difficulties. Third, wisdom, often residing in individuals, but available collectively, was accessed by the community as need arose. Fourth, most rural communities had specific and identifiable individuals who could be approached for explanations, remedies, information, formulas and solutions. These 'wise women' or 'cunning men' are familiar to readers of nineteenth-century rural literature.[35] Usually approached with respect and awe, and only on infrequent occasions, these individuals transferred their knowledge, often without payment. These approaches could coexist with more formal sources of knowledge such as doctors and clergymen. Nineteenth-century folklorists occasionally referred to these people as 'witches' and their knowledge as 'witchcraft'. In many cases, these individuals were seen to live on the margins of the local community, part of but apart from ordinary experience. A Hampshire source refers to a man called Lankester who was also known as 'The King of Thieves'. When objects or animals were lost or strayed, local people went to him to have them 'found'.[36] Another example, from Ropley in Hampshire, in the middle decades of the century, was a man called Thorpe. Two accounts of his power give two views of local belief. The first related to a misfortune which befell some men attending a shearing supper who were attacked by a pack of beagles from behind a wall thought able to constrain them. This was seen as 'entirely the work of Thorpe the Wizard'. The second was to do with theft of property. Some money had been stolen from a cottage and Thorpe was consulted. 'He at once pointed to a certain house saying "There lives the man who took your money – but do nothing it will be returned to you." And sure enough, soon afterwards, the thief was seen stealthily to enter the cottage and replace the money from where it had been taken, in fear (as was supposed) of being discovered.'[37] In this latter account no supernatural powers appear to have been invoked except the ability to prophesy future events. As to the agency which caused the thief to regret his action no comment is made. Local deeds of this kind were part of local legend. The power of witchcraft was not disputed by many of the labouring poor even when educated opinion was on hand to contradict the belief. One Somerset clergyman in 1830 found it impossible to dissuade a sick man that the cause of his illness did not lie in witchcraft and that he should believe only in God. 'I ... endeavoured', he recorded in his diary, 'as much as possible to do away with those unfortunate fancies he labours under about being bewitched, but I fear I shall not succeed. I explained to him the nature and full meaning of the Sacrament, which he never yet has received. He says he means to come to Church on Good Friday.'[38] The difficulty for a clergyman in this situation was to dissuade a parishioner from belief in the supernatural power of witchcraft whilst, at the same time, persuading him to accept a belief in divine power which involved the notion of Satan and extolled the spiritual power of the sacrament. A similar problem was faced by the rural medical practioner, the efficacy of whose own prescriptions could rarely by explained to or be understood by the patient. As Lucy Mair has pointed out, 'although some people in the technically sophisticated world really understand the natural sciences, the majority do not; all most of us know is where to go for explanations'.[39]

Some knowledge was available from specialists who were little more than herbalists, able to produce treatments and cures from a variety of plants, grown or collected, and applied in time-honoured fashion or in accordance with the many commercially available books of herbal remedies.[40] Such unofficial experts were just as likely to receive professional censure as local 'conjurors' and 'wise women'.

Other, more grandiose, reputations were earned by local 'conjurors', some of almost legendary character. The prominent figure at Danby in Yorkshire in the early years of the nineteenth century was John Wrightson, the wise man of Stokesley. 'To this fellow', Atkinson recounted,

> people whose education, it might have been expected, would have raised them above such weakness, flocked; many came to ascertain the thief, when they had lost any property; others for him to cure themselves or their cattle of some indescribable complaint. Another class visited him to know their future fortunes; and some to get him to save them from being balloted into the militia, – all of which he professed himself able to accomplish. All the diseases which he was sought to remedy he invariably imputed to witchcraft, and although he gave drugs which have been known to do good, yet he always enjoined some incantation to be observed, without which he declared they could never be cured.[41]

Interestingly, he described himself as a 'cow-leech' and the investment of skill within a series of 'mysteries' to accompany his trade would not have been unfamiliar in other callings such as that of blacksmith or horseman in the same period.[42]

In Dorset, the practice of consultation was widespread, especially in cases of being 'overlooked' – that is, where an individual's misfortune was attributed to the power of witchcraft. One collector recalled that 'These "wise women" and "cunning men" have at times attained considerable notoriety for their imaginary powers and the supposed efficacy of their spells or charms; and superstitious persons from far and near were drawn to them for the purchase of their charms or the benefit of their advice.[43] In Somerset, white witches were still prevalent in the present century. At Alcombe, in 1939 it was believed that the local blacksmith had special power.[44] Brought up in the Warwickshire Village of Tysoe, Joseph Ashby could recall incidents of witch beliefs. He once saw a man 'on horseback spurring and whipping his nag that refused to go on through a narrow section of a path. A garden thrust out into the path at that point and an old man was working on it. "Years ago" said someone, "they'd ha' said it was because old Job Welton's a wizard."'[45] The rise of the professional doctor and veterinarian in the village during the nineteenth century did not extinguish the role of the wise man or woman as far as remedies for illness was concerned. At the end of the century, one folklorist remarked that 'so long as medical advice must be paid for, while the village blacksmith or old man at the woodland cottage refuses even to accept thanks for the remedies he gives, so long will the minor ailments to which flesh is heir to be liable to be treated by the charmer rather than by the qualified practioner'.[46]

The role of cunning man or woman was open to ambivalence and, in some cases, legal action for 'pretended witchcraft' might be brought by dissatisfied clients. The consensus of support depended solely upon the outcome and not upon a broader acceptance or understanding of belief, which was reinforced by the occasions when a remedy or other form was seen to work rather than those when it was seen to fail. In other cases, local agencies sought to expose or prosecute wise men and women themselves. One clergyman wrote in 1874, 'Nor let anyone suppose that the office of the cunning man or woman has died out in Wiltshire. There is generally one such to be found in most neighbourhoods.' He referred to the conjuror's built-in guarantee of infallibility. 'Should the charm by any accident not succeed', he continued, 'of course the failure is to be attributed, not at all to its fallibility, but to some accidental omission or error in working it out on the part of the patient and his friends.'[47] He had personally intervened in the practices of one cunning woman in his area whom he threatened to prosecute for obtaining money under false pretences.[48]

The availability of official sources of knowledge did not deter people from seeking other advice. Indeed, the contest between official and unofficial knowledge was characteristic of the development of the medical profession in the nineteenth century. Both sources proved attractive to the labouring poor but both were approached with some trepidation. It was not seen by them as a dichotomy between orthodox and unorthodox knowledge. Some of the remedies proposed by the local doctor in the nineteenth century might have seemed equally as mysterious or bizarre as those of the local conjuror. Nor did resort to a local conjuror imply acceptance of an organised religious system in opposition to orthodox Christian belief. Ambivalence was the most likely attitude. The use of proprietary divination texts was commonplace.[49]

Despite the passing of statute law in the previous century (1736 9. Geo.II.c.5) which ended the capital offence of witchcraft and established the much less severe crime of pretence,[50] conjurors prevailed in many rural areas throughout the nineteenth century. In some places, however, popular retribution, resulting from circumstances of witch belief, was more akin to the harsh penalties for witchcraft inflicted by the state prior to the national repeal of 1736. Most examples of popular collective action occurred mainly in the eighteenth century, for example, at Tring in 1751 and Seend in 1773.[51] At Seend in Wiltshire in 1773 a dying woman's illness was attributed to witchcraft. The villagers

> went instantly to the supposed witch's house, procured a rope, tied it about her middle and carried her to the mill pond where they cruelly gave the accustomed discipline of ducking. On throwing her twice or three times headlong into the water, and being unable on account of her clothes to keep her under, they were perfectly convinced of her power of witchcraft, and supposing this discipline might deter her from exercising any further cruelties to the poor woman, they allowed her to go home.

The punishment was to be repeated, however, when the sick woman's fever did not abate but the intervention of the local magistrate prevented the villagers from carrying out their intention. In this case, a local schoolmaster in the district drew up a 'curious receipt for the cure of witchcraft' which was widely distributed to allay anxiety arising from witch beliefs.[52] However, similar incidents were not unknown in the nineteenth century. In September 1875, for example, a most notorious and tragic case resulted in the murder of an old woman called Ann Tennant by a labourer, James Heywood, in the South Warwickshire village of Long Compton.[53]As late as 1905, in Worcestershire, a woman was charged with pretended witchcraft by a man who thought his pigs were 'overlooked'. Having visited her, the man himself fell sick and he not only doubted her powers but felt himself to have been swindled. The ambivalence of the relationship between client and conjuror is highlighted by one contemporary who knew the events and wrote, 'The widow stoutly denied that she used or promised to use witchcraft, and said she only gave her advice upon the treatment of the pig, and in the end the case against her was dismissed.'[54] Nonetheless the same contemporary, writing in 1911, was quite confident that in Worcestershire 'White witchcraft, by means of charms and spells, is still practised, and there are persons who are credited with the "lucky hand" for curing warts by their mere touch'.[55] This was also known in Wiltshire in the middle of the nineteenth century. 'I remember when I was quite small', wrote one collector,

> seven or eight, my brother was much troubled with warts on his hands; so he was taken to an old lady, a Miss Yockney, who was to charm these warts away. I made fun of my brother's misfortune and she told me if I laughed the same mischance might overtake me. A few days after I had a wart on my index finger, and a very long time it stayed there – for punishment, I was told. This good body was famed for wart charming and other doctoring.[56]

In 1874 another Wiltshire commentator could relate an anecdote which indicated that the client saw the treatments prescribed by a local doctor and those of a cunning man as of equal value in their likely efficacy.[57] Some beliefs were universal and, although subject to local variation, were held in many parts of rural England. The same Wiltshire informant cited an incident connected with the very widespread belief that bread baked on Good Friday determined the success of domestic baking throughout the rest of the year. 'On my enquiry', he wrote, 'as to the result she said "her bread had been light and good ever since...but then to be sure my bread has been so before".'[58] The ritual baking of Good Friday bread was also common in Dorsetshire.[59] This particular practice was held to provide, not a cast-iron guarantee, but a safeguard against misfortune.

Positive opposition was a decisive factor and in part explains the reluctance of some informants to discuss their beliefs with folklorists. The attitude of the local clergyman was usually hostile. At Scopwick in Lincolnshire in the 1830s the local clergyman campaigned actively against 'popular superstition'. 'I have never waived', he wrote, 'an opportunity of combating a prejudice, or endeavouring to eradicate a superstition which tended to weaken the influence of Christianity in an uninstructed mind.'[60] Despite opposition, his experience of Lincolnshire indicated how fully developed and sustained was alternative belief in the nineteenth century. 'Amongst the inhabitants of Lincolnshire', he continued, 'these hateful corroders of happiness are far from being extirpated. Credulity and superstition still reign with tyrannic sway in many hearts, how reluctant soever they may be to acknowledge it.'[61]

George Sturt attributed the fierce Christian belief of his grandmother as the reason his own youth was free of the supernatural in the 1860s in a way that was not true for many of his contemporaries. 'We had no country "charms"', he recalled,

> no rural lore at all, though my mother had been born and brought up in a farm-house... I got from nowhere any of the local country superstitions, and the reason was almost certainly that my mother's own mother had a strong religious disapproval of such ideas. I never heard of fairies as if they were anything real; or of ghosts, or spirits, or omens. So a religious sentiment came passing down the generations in our family; and, reaching me, saved me, for one (others in my family were not so fortunate) a good deal of real anguish.[62]

He could, however, recall folk treatments such as the application of dock to nettle stings or the thrashing of chilblains with holly until they bled.[63] He does not add whether he used the protective incantation 'Nettle out, dock in, dock remove the nettle sting' which was very common.[64] Stock rhymes may have performed the function of mnemonic rather than charm. The reason why such domestic remedies were common, in Sturt's view, was the expense of orthodox medicine. 'You took risks for it cost too much to go to a doctor.'[65]

More than mere lip service was often paid to witch beliefs even by more socially elevated elements of village society. The local hunt, in one West Country village, always made certain that a particular old woman was visited before the day's hunting began. 'In a certain village', it was recorded,

> resided a woman who was supposed to be gifted with a knowledge of the future, or with 'second sight'– if the hounds passed through the village and by her door, it was always considered a good 'omen' if she stood outside and said 'Good mornin, gentlemen, I wish 'ee good luck to-day', when away they all went happy in the sure knowledge that good fortune awaited them.[66]

IV

Alternative beliefs prevailed which connected the locality, the landscape, the natural world, domestic pursuits, work practices, the church, the weather, the seasons and time, local antiquities, personal knowledge, life crises rituals, legend and history and the future, not as an oppressive structure, but in order to provide mechanisms for coping with anxiety against the chance aspects of life. Figure 9.2 illustrates the relationship between official and unofficial belief. The right-hand section of the graph represents knowledge which was formally sanctioned by orthodoxy or the representatives of authority – orthodox religious beliefs and practices, for example, and professional medical or other knowledge. The left-hand section represents knowledge which had popular sanction but which was not part of formal systems of knowledge. This area covers most examples of alternative belief – proverbial wisdom, weather lore, herbal remedies, popular religious practices, ritual practices not sanctioned by the church, domestic or workplace beliefs and local lore and legend. The area of intersection indicates the beliefs common to both.

During the nineteenth century, in many parts of rural England, a clash could be discerned between official and unofficial knowledge and between formal and informal practices. Increasingly, the area of intersection was extended as alternative knowledge

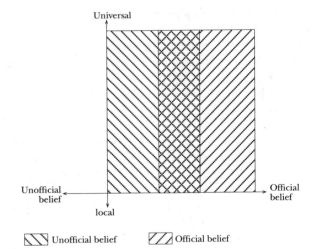

Figure 9.2   *Alternative belief in nineteenth-century rural England and its relationship to official belief*

and beliefs were marginalised and self-help was denied the rural poor in preference to the professional sources of assistance made available by the dominant culture.

One function of alternative belief for the labouring poor was the provision of a record of the local community in which its present position was related to time past. The collective memory of the structurally inferior (wage labourers, smallholders, cottagers, squatters) could be maintained within a framework of local lore and legend, sometimes to the disadvantage of the structurally superior who wished, for example, to see the record of pre-enclosure boundaries or customary rights erased from memory. Much of this knowledge was empirical and related to seasonal time, farming practice, weather and herbal lore, and proverbial wisdom, formula or incantation. Empirical knowledge was communicated either by special agents (cunning men, wise women) or within kinship groups or work environments. Some of this knowledge was gender distinctive or operated only within the context of a rural youth culture.

Belief in supernatural agencies and forces was also widespread. At Bentley a foreman gave the reason for the hanging of a stone with a hole through it behind the horses in the stables as 'to keep the fairies from riding the horses at night'.[67] This was a common practice in buildings in many parts of Cambridgeshire[68] and at Abbotsbury in Dorset, when the device was used to protect fishing boats from magical interference.[69] Whilst the foreman's more rational and enlightened employer, who recorded the story in the 1850s, was more prepared to accept that overnight sweating in horses was caused by indigestion or an overheated stable, he would still, from habit, follow the practice of some farm valuers he had known who only 'go round the farm...by following the sun and will only measure a rick by the same rule'.[70]

The practice of hanging a bullock's heart in the hearth to prevent fairies and witches entering the house via the chimney was a common one in Dorset[71] and incidences can be found which date from the 1820s, 1884 and 1901.[72] Protective rites of this kind were common throughout the nineteenth century. In 1904 in Wiltshire it was noted that

> an old woman in a neighbouring village [to Stourton] believed herself to have been 'overlooked'. She cast about for means of deliverance from the black magic, and revenge on the perpetrator of the outrage. A bullock's heart was procured, and thickly stuck with pins; then, as night drew on, the fire was made up, and the heart set to roast. All night long the witch-ridden victim sat watching, and as each pin dropped from its place she rejoiced that a pin pierced the heart of the evil eye.[73]

Divination beliefs and practices, together with ominous events, formed part of daily life. Observation of the natural world provided empirical data on coming events. Weather lore was the most common form but the attitudes and behaviour of animals and birds were thought to betoken individual fate. One of the most common forms which this took was the interpretative rhymes concerning magpies. Versions of this rhyme were recorded from Northumberland to Dorset during the nineteenth century. It was also commonly believed that to spit three times or to hail the birds politely would avert the ill luck associated with seeing a single magpie.[74]

The most common forms of ominous events were those associated with impending death. Taking only examples collected in Dorsetshire in the late nineteenth century, death omens were attributable to the behaviour of birds, dogs, bees, church bells, noises at night and other deaths. Taking birds alone, it was recorded that a robin entering a house was ominous, as was any bird tapping at the window. The cuckoo's song after old Midsummer Day or in a churchyard foretold death, as did cock crow at night.[75] It is perhaps not surprising that observation of the natural world should produce such morbid interest amongst the labouring poor when, for most of the nineteenth century, their life-spans were usually so uncertain and often attended with daily hardship. The loss of family members not only led to social but also to economic dysfunction. The rites of passage associated with death were adhered to with equal tenacity[76] and have only, in recent times, been modified by what one social anthropologist has referred to as the 'professionalisation of death'.[77] In the nineteenth century, death usually occurred in the domestic environment, except in cases of accident, and funeral procedures usually fell to family members or unofficial village specialists without the intervention of professional agents. This was equally the case for birth.

For many rural labourers alternative belief gave a view of the natural world which was a sustaining one, providing both a world order, local and specific, but also a set of universal principles for both controlling chance and detecting coming misfortune. Effectiveness was rarely questioned and the occasions when coincidental reinforcement of belief occurred were remembered with more force than those occasions when they failed. In any case, should failure occur, reasons for fallibility were readily detected.

A resident of North Staffordshire gave an instance of such reinforcement in the late nineteenth century despite, in this case, middle-class denial of any connection. A maid became agitated by the fluttering of a bird against the fanlight over the front door of the informant's house.

It had been there some time, she said, and was a sure sign of death in the family. She was told not to believe such a foolish notion, but to occupy her mind with her household duties. The next morning her agitation returned, for the bird was there again. Her distress was quite genuine, and her mistress found it useless to allay her anxiety. Within a fortnight we had lost two of our nearest relatives and two of our dearest friends who were not relatives. The young woman was too well-behaved to say 'I told you so,' but she could not quite conceal her elation at having been proved, as she supposed, to be right.[78]

The contest between the official and unofficial sources of knowledge developed throughout the nineteenth century with the increasing impact of official agents and intermediaries. In one sense, a form of cultural hegemony was taking place which first required the dismantling of the pre-existing rural culture, based on its customary framework and location within a local world, or, at least, its marginalisation and modification. That the labouring poor could draw on these coexisting resources without any apparent contradiction was a source of irritation to the new professional class. This was especially so for the medical profession in rural areas. In one Dartmoor case,

A doctor, visiting a sick man, was told by the wife that her husband had been 'overlooked'. When asked her reason for such a belief the woman replied, 'Because yesterday he was covered with varmin and now there be none'. She actually expressed her intention of sending for 'the white witch' – a *man* named Snow, now dead – but the doctor very properly declined to meet the witch, or rather wizard, in consultation.

This particular informant had become used to the involvement of his patients with alternative purveyors of treatment and stated that 'an unlimited supply of similar anecdotes could be furnished'.[79]

This was also the case with the contest between veterinary medicine and the cures and remedies applied by small farmers to their beasts. The Norfolk 'King of the Poachers' recalled in 1933 that

Then there was a lot of charms the farmers used to believe in for the Animiles. Wen cows calved, the after berth had to be hung on a white thorn bush, as it was said to prevent Milk fever and other ills. Do not think that we used to hear so much of that kind of thing as at the present day. No doubt the feeding of cows on artifichell food is responseble for some of it, as I believe most of the truble is over flush of milk that force the blood to the cow's brain, as I have seen them die nearly mad. The Old People beleved in their charms but the Vetinary of today have put all those things away.[80]

The contest between knowledge systems is an illusion as it is the circumstances of life which guarantee the need for alternative beliefs. Charlotte Burne recognised that 'though customs decay, superstition still lives. It may be weakened by the spread of education and the increased facilities for travel of modern days, but it has its roots deep down in human nature – in fear, affection, greed, curiosity, credulity – and it can only change as human nature changes.'[81] For the rural labouring poor and some of their smallholding neighbours in nineteenth-century England, coping with the destruction of their customary world provided urgent reasons for the maintenance of alternative beliefs and knowledge. Indeed, it could be argued that the nineteenth century saw a resurgence of those beliefs at a time of upheaval and uncertainty when the external threats to the labourer's livelihood were increasing. Fear might be of unemployment, the Poor Law workhouse, injury and incapacity, illness and death, and the lack of any form of safety net save the mutuality of the poor to protect the rural labourer and his family and, in those circumstances, alternative beliefs flourished. What Thomas de Quincy referred to as 'Modern Superstition' was not something rooted in past religious beliefs but that which retained a contemporary function in the lives of the rural poor. When writing of the foretelling of events, he commented:

Birds are even more familiarly associated with such ominous warnings. This chapter in the great volume of superstition was indeed cultivated with unusual solicitude amongst the pagans – ornithomancy grew into an elaborate science. But if every rule and distinction upon the number and the position of birds, whether to the right or the left, had been collected from our own village matrons amongst ourselves, it would appear that no more of this pagan science had gone to wreck than must naturally follow the difference between a believing and a disbelieving government. Magpies are still of awful authority in village life, according to their number.[82]

Radical writers in the late nineteenth and early twentieth centuries regarded such practices as fatalism – an acceptance of destiny – but for many families non-orthodox customary beliefs and views of the world provided an underpinning for their lives which, at moments of crisis, could allay anxiety, reinforce their view of social reality, provide self-help approaches for the difficulties of illness, injury, work and labour and could deal generally and specifically with the intrusion of misfortune.

V

The notion that the march of rationalism, scientific knowledge and education swept away this customary framework has been propounded at many different times in the history of rural England from the seventeenth century onwards. Early collectors of popular antiquities such as John Aubrey thought that the decline of 'popular superstition' was attributable to the rise of Protestantism and the Civil War. 'When the wars came', he wrote, 'and with them liberty of conscience and liberty of inquisition, the phantoms vanished.'[83] Later collectors blamed their decline on the disappearance of a pre-enclosure social structure. J. Harvey Bloom collected his materials in the villages and hamlets of the Cotswolds. 'Enclosure acts', he wrote, 'have played havoc with the past, but in one of these hamlets, Crimscott, the act has never been put into operation, and the strips and ridges of the common field remain today as they have ever been.' His informants, in Bloom's view, remained in rustic simplicity untouched by 'the passing of the ancient ways of hand workmanship, the personal relation of master and man, before the paid agitator had his way'.[84]

Much earlier, William Howitt also thought that the world of superstitious beliefs was in the past. 'Modern ambition', he thought, 'modern wealth, modern notions of social proprieties, modern education, are all hewing at the root of the poetical and picturesque, the simple and candid in rural life'.[85] This was written in 1841.

Unorthodox practices and beliefs are part of our psychological outlook. Soldiers – many of them volunteers from rural districts – were quite prepared to believe in a form of supernatural salvation by angelic host at Mons in 1914; that a statue of the Virgin hanging precariously from a church spire in Albert in 1916 could determine the outcome of the war; that a variety of personal talismans and good-luck charms might prevent their deaths; and that a third light from a single match was not propitious. The common factor between the lives of these men during the First World War and those of their forebears in nineteenth-century rural England was their powerlessness to control the events which befell them and their urgent need for a sustaining philosophy which would enable them to cope with their situation.

What alternative beliefs and knowledge also gave the rural labourer was a sense of cultural self-respect and self-awareness in which his culture was not devalued. Dad Eldridge, a carter from the region of the White Horse in Berkshire, and his retired shepherd neighbour could converse in 1912 in detail and with certainty about the locality's lore and legend.

> Sometimes the talk is of the wonderful golden coffin, full of treasure, buried on the downs between the White Horse and Wayland Smith's Cave; at another time it is of the famous Horn of Pusey, or the phantom coach and horses on the highway; the haunted well at Kingstone Warren, that utters a roar like thunder, or again it is of old Molly Jones, the cripple, who drove plough, hopping on one toe; honest Farmer Brooks of Stanford-in-the-Vale, who always felt miserable and ill when one of his men was about to leave him; the White Horse Revels of 1857, when it took all the horses in Woolstone to draw the wild beasts up the hill; the old-time ballad-singers, ducking the pickpockets in the pond at Wadley Fair: the jolly harvest-homes, sowing, reaping, threshing and many other matters. 'Tha' tells I as we be ignerant, an nat much good fer anything, but just let thaay come an' listen to I an' my owl' shepherd, we'll soon let thaay know whether we be ignerant or nat; we'll show thaay as 'tis thaay as be ignerant, an' not we, right anuf.'[86]

It is in this sense that the culture of the rural labouring poor in nineteenth-century England should be considered. Not as deformed or degraded survivals of ignorance and credulity but as a dynamic, vital and vibrant view of life and the external world. Some of this knowledge, far from being irrational, was empirical and based on personal experience and observation. Where this was not the case, where there was no logical relationship between ends and means, alternative beliefs made up a frame of reference which offered a perception of reality, of being and of social relationships which enabled the rural labourer to confront the external forces in his world. Self-reliant and self-aware, alternative knowledge and belief was a coping mechanism which could deal with the aspect of chance but was also a source of dignity, self respect and self-help. This is the texture of rural culture for the labouring poor in nineteenth-century England.

Notes and References

1. PROBLEMATISING POPULAR CULTURE *Tim Harris*

1. I would like to thank Peter Burke, Martin Ingram and John Rule for their comments and criticisms on an earlier draft of this essay.

2. Peter Burke, *Popular Culture in Early Modern Europe* (London: Temple Smith, 1978). The quote is on p. 270.

3. Keith Wrightson and David Levine, *Poverty and Piety in an English Village: Terling, 1525–1700* (London: Academic Press, 1979), quotes on pp. 172, 177, 181.

4. Keith Wrightson, *English Society 1580–1680* (London: Hutchinson, 1980), pp. 220–1.

5. Robert W. Malcolmson, *Popular Recreations in English Society 1700–1850* (Cambridge: Cambridge University Press, 1973). Cf. Robert D. Storch (ed.), *Popular Culture and Custom in Nineteenth-Century England* (London: Croom Helm, 1982), pp. 5, 72, 102, 116, 130–1, 136; Bob Bushaway, *By Rite: Custom, Ceremony and Community in England 1700–1880* (London: Junction Books, 1982), Ch. 7.

6. Douglas A. Reid, 'The Decline of Saint Monday, 1766–1876', *Past and Present*, LXXI (1976), pp. 76–101; A. P. Donajgrodzki (ed.), *Social Control in Nineteenth-Century Britain* (London: Croom Helm, 1977); Eileen and Stephen Yeo (eds), *Popular Culture and Class Conflict 1590–1914: Explorations in the History of Labour and Leisure* (Brighton: Harvester Press, 1981); E. P. Thompson 'Time, Work Discipline and Industrial Capitalism', in his *Customs in Common* (London: Merlin, 1991), pp. 352–403.

7. Anthony Fletcher and John Stevenson, 'Introduction', in Anthony Fletcher and John Stevenson (eds), *Order and Disorder in Early Modern England* (Cambridge: Cambridge University Press, 1985), pp. 3, 10.

8. Peter Borsay, *The English Urban Renaissance: Culture and Society in the Provincial Town 1660–1770* (Oxford: Clarendon Press, 1989), p. 285.

9. Peter Burke, 'From Pioneers to Settlers: Recent Studies of the History of Popular Culture', *Comparative Studies in Society and History*, XXV (1983), pp. 181–7.

10. Important studies in this regard are: Bob Scribner, 'Is a History of Popular Culture Possible?', *History of European Ideas*, X (1989), pp. 175–91; Steven L. Kaplan (ed.), *Understanding Popular Culture: Europe from the Middle Ages to the Nineteenth Century* (Berlin: Mouton, 1984); Barry Reay (ed.), *Popular Culture in Seventeenth-Century England* (London: Croom Helm, 1985); Tessa Watt, *Cheap Print and Popular Piety, 15xs50–1640* (Cambridge: Cambridge University Press, 1991); Roger Chartier, *The Cultural Uses of Print in Early Modern France*, trans. by Lydia G. Cochrane (Princeton: Princeton University Press, 1987); Tim Harris, 'The Problem of "Popular Political Culture" in Seventeenth-Century London', *History of European Ideas*, X (1989), pp. 43–58; J. M. Golby and A. W. Purdue, *The Civilisation of*

the Crowd: Popular Culture in England 1750–1900 (London: B. T. Batsford, 1985); Hugh Cunningham, *Leisure in the Industrial Revolution c. 1780– c.1880* (London: Croom Helm, 1980).

11. Burke, *Popular Culture*, p. 49.

12. J. S. Morrill and J. Walter, 'Order and Disorder in the English Revolution', in Fletcher and Stevenson (eds), *Order and Disorder*, pp. 139–40.

13. J. F. McGregor, 'Seekers and Ranters', in J. F. McGregor and B. Reay (eds), *Radical Religion in the English Revolution* (Oxford: Oxford University Press, 1984), pp. 121–39; J. C. Davis, *Fear, Myth and History: The Ranters and the Historians* (Cambridge: Cambridge University Press, 1986); Christopher Hill, 'Abolishing the Ranters', in his *A Nation of Change and Novelty: Radical Politics, Religion and Literature in Seventeenth-Century England* (London: Routledge, 1990), pp. 152–94.

14. Watt, *Cheap Print*, pp. 3–5; Roger Chartier, 'Culture as Appropriation: Popular Cultural Uses in Early Modern France', in Kaplan (ed.), *Understanding Popular Culture*, pp. 231–2; Scribner, 'Is a History of Popular Culture Possible?', p. 176.

15. Tim Harris, *London Crowds in the Reign of Charles II: Propaganda and Politics from the Restoration until the Exclusion Crisis* (Cambridge: Cambridge University Press, 1987), Chs 5–7; Tim Harris, *Politics under the Later Stuarts: Party Conflict in a Divided Society 1660–1715* (London: Longman, 1993), Ch. 4.

16. Robert S. Thomson, 'The Development of the Broadside Balled Trade and its Influence upon the Transmission of English Folksong', unpublished Ph.D. thesis, Cambridge University (1974); Margaret Spufford, *Small Books and Pleasant Histories: Popular Fiction and its Readership in Seventeenth-Century England* (London: Methuen, 1981), p. 9; Watt, *Cheap Print*, Chs 1, 2; David Vincent, 'The Decline of the Oral Tradition in Popular Culture', in Storch (ed.), *Popular Culture*, pp. 26–7.

17. Scribner, 'Is a History of Popular Culture Possible?', p. 179; R. W. Scribner, 'Luther Myth: a Popular Historiography of the Reformer', in his *Popular Culture and Popular Movements in Reformation Germany* (London: Hambledon Press, 1987), pp. 321–2.

18. These remarks are based on my own extensive research into judicial records, including allegations of seditious words. See Harris, *London Crowds* and *Politics under the Later Stuarts*.

19. Clive Holmes, 'Popular Culture? Witches, Magistrates, and Divines in Early Modern England', in Kaplan (ed.), *Understanding Popular Culture*, pp. 89, 105.

20. Thomas Hobbes, *Leviathan*, ed. Richard Tuck (Cambridge: Cambridge University Press, 1991), p. 248; *Oxford English Dictionary*; Kevin Sharpe and Steven N. Zwicker, *Politics of Discourse: The Literature and History of Seventeenth-Century England* (Berkeley: University of California Press, 1987), pp. 4–5.

21. A. L. Kroeber and Clyde Kluckhohn, *Culture: A Critical Review of Concepts and Definitions* (Cambridge, Mass.: Papers of the Peabody Museum of American Archaeology and Ethnology, Harvard University, XLVII, no. 1, 1952). For the enumeration, see p. 149, footnote 49.

22. Ludmilla Jordanova, 'The Representation of the Family in the Eighteenth Century: A Challenge for Cultural History', in Joan H. Pittock and Andrew Wear, *Interpretation and Cultural History* (London: Macmillan, 1991), p. 118. Cf. Peter Burke (ed.), *New Perspectives on Historical Writing* (Cambridge: Polity Press, 1991), pp. 10–11.

23. B. Malinowski, *A Scientific Theory of Culture and Other Essays* (Chapel Hill: University of North Carolina Press, 1944), p. 38; Mary Douglas, *Purity and Danger: An Analysis of Concepts of Pollution and Taboo* (London: Routledge & Kegan Paul, 1966), p. 69. Discussed in Margaret S. Archer, *Culture and Agency: The Place of Culture in Social Theory* (Cambridge: Cambridge University Press, 1988), pp. 2–4.

24. Robert Muchembeld, *Popular Culture and Elite Culture in France 1400–1750*, trans. by Lydia Cochrane (Baton Rouge: Louisiana State University Press, 1985).

25. Thompson, *Customs in Common*, p. 6; Renato Rosaldo, 'Celebrating Thompson's Heroes: Social Analysis in History and Anthropology', in Harvey J. Kaye and Keith McClelland (eds), *E. P. Thompson: Critical Perspectives* (Philadelphia: Temple University Press, 1990), Ch. 4; Archer, *Culture and Agency*.

26. Meric Casaubon, *A Treatise Proving Spirits, Witches and Supernatural Operations* (London, 1672), p. 231; Newton E. Key, 'Politics beyond Parliament: Unity and Party in the Herefordshire Region during the Restoration Period', unpublished Ph.D. thesis, Cornell University (1989), pp. 30–1.

27. Joan H. Pittock and Andrew Wear, 'Introduction' to their *Interpretation and Cultural History*, p. 3; Jonathan Barry, 'Provincial Town Culture, 1640–80: Urbane or Civic?', in ibid., pp. 198–234; David Underdown, *Revel, Riot and Rebellion: Popular Politics and Culture in England 1603–1660* (Oxford: Clarendon Press, 1985).

28. Kroeber and Kluckhohn, *Culture*, p. 157.

29. Keith Thomas, 'The Double Standard', *Journal of the History of Ideas*, xx (1959), pp. 195–216.

30. Catherine Hall, 'The Tale of Samuel and Jemima: Gender and Working-Class Culture in Nineteenth-Century England', in Kaye and McClelland (eds), *Thompson: Critical Perspectives*, pp. 78–102.

31. Peter Burke, 'Popular Culture in Seventeenth-Century London', in Reay (ed.), *Popular Culture*, p. 32; Harris 'Popular Political Culture', p. 45.

32. Charles Leslie, *Rehearsal*, I, no. 44, 26 May–2 June 1705.

33. F[rancis] A[tterbury], *The Voice of the People, No Voice of God*, (London, 1710), pp. 6, 13.

34. David Cressy, 'Describing the Social Order of Elizabethan England', *Literature and History*, III (1976), pp. 29–44.

35. F. J. Furnivall (ed.), *Harrison's Description of England* (London: New Shakespeare Society, 6th series, no. 1, 1877), Part I, Ch. 5 (quote on p. 105); Wrightson, *English Society*, pp. 17, 19. Cf. Sir Thomas Smith, *De Republica Anglorum*, ed. Mary Dewar (Cambridge: Cambridge University Press, 1982), pp. 65–77.

36. Peter Laslett, *The World We Have Lost Further Explored* (London: Methuen, 1984), pp. 32–3; W. A. Speck, *Stability and Strife: England, 1714–1760* (London: Edward Arnold, 1977), pp. 31–3; G. S. Holmes, 'Gregory King and the Social Structure of Pre-Industrial England', *Transactions of the Royal Historical Society, 5th series,* XXVII (1977), pp. 41–68.

37. George Foster, *The Sounding of the Last Trumpet* (London, 1650), p. 17; Christopher Hill, *The World Turned Upside Down: Radical Ideas during the English Revolution* (Harmondsworth: Penguin, 1975), p. 223.

38. George Rudé, 'The London "Mob" of the Eighteenth Century', in his *Paris and London in the Eighteenth Century: Studies in Popular Protest* (London: Collins, 1970), p. 293; Lucy S. Sutherland, 'The City of London in Eighteenth-Century Politics', in Richard Pares and A. J. P. Taylor (eds), *Essays Presented to Sir Lewis Namier* (London: Macmillan, 1956), p. 66.

39. Wrightson and Levine, *Poverty and Piety,* pp. 34–5.

40. Morrill and Walter, 'Order and Disorder', p. 152; Geoffrey Holmes, *Augustan England; Professions, State and Society 1680–1730* (London: George Allen & Unwin, 1982); Borsay, *English Urban Renaissance,* pp. 204–11; Peter Earle, *The Making of the English Middle Class: Business, Society and Family Life in London, 1660–1730* (London: Methuen, 1989); John Rule, *Albion's People: English Society 1714–1815* (London: Longman, 1992), Ch. 3.

41. Harold Perkin, *The Origins of Modern English Society 1780–1880* (London: Routledge, 1969), p. 21.

42. James Sharpe, *Crime in Early Modern England 1550–1750* (London: Longman, 1984), p. 76; Joan R. Kent, *The English Village Constable 1580–1642: A Social and Administrative Study* (Oxford: Clarendon Press, 1986), Ch. 4; Keith Wrightson, 'Two Concepts of Order: Justices, Constables and Jurymen in Seventeenth-Century England', in John Brewer and John Styles (eds), *An Ungovernable People: The English and their Law in the Seventeenth and Eighteenth Centuries* (London: Hutchinson, 1980), pp. 26–9; Harris, *London Crowds,* pp. 17–21; James Sharpe, 'The People and the Law', in Reay (ed.), *Popular Culture,* p. 254; J. S. Cockburn and T. A. Green (eds), *Twelve Good Men and True: The Criminal Trial Jury in England, 1200–1800* (Princeton: Princeton University Press, 1988); Cynthia Herrup, *The Common Peace: Participation and the Criminal Law in Seventeenth-Century England* (Cambridge: Cambridge University Press, 1987), pp. 98–109, 136–41; Michael MacDonald and Terence R. Murphy, *Sleepless Souls: Suicide in Early Modern England* (Oxford: Clarendon Press, 1990), pp. 111–12

43. Nathaniel Johnston, *The Excellency of Monarchical Government, Especially of the English Monarchy* (London, 1686), p. 410.

44. More recently, however, Wrightson has stressed the 'ambivalent position' occupied by the middling sort, 'who formed a social-structural buffer between the ruling gentry and the mass of the common people'. See Keith Wrightson, 'The Social Order of Early Modern England: Three Approaches', in Lloyd Bonfield, Richard M. Smith and Keith

Wrightson (eds), *The World We Have Gained: Histories of Population and Social Structure* (Oxford: Basil Blackwell, 1986), pp. 200–1.

45. Morrill and Walter, 'Order and Disorder', p. 152.

46. Thompson, *Customs in Common*, p. 56.

47. Quoted in Roy Porter, *English Society in the Eighteenth Century* (Harmondsworth: Penguin, revised edn, 1990), p. 73.

48. Reay (ed.), *Popular Culture.* See esp. pp. 1–2.

49. C. Holmes, 'Drainers and Fenmen: The Problem of Popular Political Consciousness in the Seventeenth Century', in Fletcher and Stevenson (eds), *Order and Disorder,* pp. 166–95.

50. Peter King, 'Decision-Makers and Decision-Making in the English Criminal Law, 1750–1800', *Historical Journal,* XXVII (1984), pp. 25–58 (the point about the game laws is on p. 54); Douglas Hay, 'Property, Authority and the Criminal Law', in Douglas Hay, Peter Linebaugh, John G. Rule, E. P. Thompson and Cal Winslow, *Albion's Fatal Tree* (Harmondsworth: Penguin, 1975), p. 39, footnote 1; P. B. Munsche, *Gentlemen and Poachers: The English Game Laws of 1671–1831* (Cambridge: Cambridge University Press, 1981), Ch. 4.

51. Rule, *Albion's People*, p. 87. See also: Earle, *Making of the English Middle Class*; Leonore Davidoff and Catherine Hall, *Family Fortunes: Men and Women of the English Middle Class, 1780–1850* (London: Hutchinson, 1987).

52. John Brewer, 'English Radicalism in the Age of George III', in J. G. A. Pocock (ed.), *Three British Revolutions: 1641, 1688, 1776* (Princeton: Princeton University Press, 1980), pp. 323–67.

53. Cf. David Cressy, 'Literacy in Context: Meaning and Measurement in Early Modern England', in John Brewer and Roy Porter (eds), *Consumption and the World of Goods* (London: Routlegde, 1993), pp. 310–11.

54. Wrightson, *English Society,* pp. 194–5; Barry Reay, 'The Context and Meaning of Popular Literacy: Some Evidence from Nineteenth-Century Rural England', *Past and Present,* CXXXI (1991), p. 118.

55. Underdown, *Revel, Riot and Rebellion*; Margaret Spufford, *Contrasting Communities: English Villagers in the Sixteenth and Seventeenth Centuries* (Cambridge: Cambridge University Press, 1974), pp. 300–6; Margaret Spufford, 'Puritanism and Social Control?', in Fletcher and Stevenson (eds), *Order and Disorder,* pp. 41–57; William Stevenson, 'The Economic and Social Status of Protestant Sectarians in Huntingdonshire, Cambridgeshire and Bedfordshire (1660–1725)', unpublished Ph.D. thesis, Cambridge University (1990); Watt, *Cheap Print*; D. A. Spaeth, 'Parsons and Parishioners: Lay-Clerical Conflict and Popular Piety in Wiltshire Villages, 1660–1740', unpublished Ph.D. thesis, Brown University (1985); Barry Reay, 'Popular Religion', in Reay (ed.), *Popular Culture,* pp. 91–128; Tim Harris, 'Introduction: Revising the Restoration', in Harris, Paul Seaward and Mark Goldie (eds), *The Politics of Religion in Restoration England* (Oxford: Basil Blackwell, 1990), pp. 20–3; Harris, *London Crowds*; Harris, *Politics under the Later Stuarts*; J. J. Hurwich, 'Dissent and Catholicism in English Society: A Study of Warwickshire 1660–1720', *Journal of British Studies,* XVI (1976), pp. 244–58; Susan Wright (ed.), *Parish, Church and People: Local Studies in Lay*

Religion 1350–1750 (London: Hutchinson, 1988); J. D. Walsh, 'Elie Halévy and the Birth of Methodism', *Transactions of the Royal Historical Society*, XXV (1975), pp. 1–20; J. D. Walsh, 'Methodism and the Mob', in G. J. Cuming and D. Baker (eds), *Studies in Church History*, vol. 8: *Popular Belief and Practice* (Cambridge: Cambridge University Press, 1972), pp. 213–37.

56. Malcolmson, *Popular Recreations*; Underdown, *Revel, Riot and Rebellion*, Ch. 10; Dudley W. R. Bahlman, *The Moral Revolution of 1688* (New Haven: Yale University Press, 1957); Robert B. Shoemaker, 'Reforming the City: The Reformation of Manners Campaign in London, 1690–1738', in Lee Davison, Tim Hitchcock, Tim Keirn and Robert B. Shoemaker (eds), *Stilling the Grumbling Hive: The Response to Social and Economic Problems in England, 1689–1750* (New York: St Martin's Press, 1992), pp. 99–120.

57. Underdown, *Revel, Riot and Rebellion,*, pp. 65–8; Malcolmson, *Popular Recreations*, pp. 11–12.

58. John K. Walton and Robert Poole, 'The Lancashire Wakes in the Nineteenth Century', in Storch (ed.), *Popular Culture*, p. 102.

59. Cunningham, *Leisure in the Industrial Revolution*, pp. 46–51.

60. Golby and Purdue, *Civilisation of the Crowd*, pp. 51–60, 84–5.

61. Martin Ingram, 'Ridings, Rough Music and Mocking Rhymes in Early Modern England', in Reay (ed.), *Popular Culture*, pp. 166–97; E. P. Thompson, 'Rough Music', in his *Customs in Common*, pp. 467–538.

62. Lilian Lewis Shiman, *Crusade against Drink in Victorian England* (London: Macmillan, 1988), pp. 29–34; Brian Harrison, *Drink and the Victorians: The Temperance Question in England 1815–1872* (London: Faber & Faber, 1971), pp. 137–9, 366–7; Brian Harrison, 'Religion and Recreation in Nineteenth-Century England', *Past and Present*, XXXVIII (1967), pp. 98–125; John Rule, 'Methodism, Popular Beliefs and Village Culture in Cornwall, 1800–50', in Storch (ed.), *Popular Culture*, Ch. 3.

63. Walton and Poole, 'Lancashire Wakes', p. 116; Storch, 'Introduction: Persistence and Change in Nineteenth-Century Popular Culture', in his *Popular Culture*, pp. 5–8; Golby and Purdue, *Civilisation of the Crowd*, pp. 86–7, 184–5; Cunningham, *Leisure in the Industrial Revolution*, pp. 38–41.

64. Walton and Poole, 'Lancashire Wakes', p. 104.

65. Cunningham, *Leisure in the Industrial Revolution*, pp. 194–5; Scribner, 'Is a History of Popular Culture Possible?', pp. 180–1.

66. Gareth Stedman Jones, 'Class Expression versus Social Control? A Critique of Recent Trends in the Social History of "Leisure"', in his *Languages of Class: Studies in English Working-Class History 1832–1982* (Cambridge: Cambridge University Press, 1983), pp. 88–9; Storch, 'Persistence and Change', pp. 11–12; Douglas A. Reid, 'Interpreting the Festival Calendar: Wakes and Fairs as Carnivals', in Storch (ed.), *Popular Culture*, p. 136; Bushaway, *By Rite.*

67. J. H. Plumb, 'The Commercialization of Leisure in Eighteenth-Century England', in Neil McKendrick, John Brewer and J. H. Plumb

(eds), *The Birth of a Consumer Society: The Commercialization of Eighteenth-Century England* (Bloomington: Indiana University Press, 1982), pp. 265–85; Borsay, *English Urban Renaissance*, Ch. 11; Cunningham, *Leisure in the Industrial Revolution*, Ch. 1; Golby and Purdue, *Civilisation of the Crowd*, pp. 32–40, 63–87; Porter, *English Society*, pp. 229–42.

68. Cf. Linda Colley, *Britons: Forging the Nation 1707–1837* (New Haven: Yale University Press, 1992). I remain less convinced by Colley's argument that a *British* national identity had emerged by the early nineteenth century. However, I believe a strong case could be made for arguing that a strong sense of *English* national identity had been forged by the end of the seventeenth century.

2. REGIONAL CULTURES? *David Underdown*

1. An earlier version of this paper was given at the conference on 'Agrarian Regions' organised by the centre for South-Western Historical Studies, at the University of Exeter, in June 1992.

2. Keith Thomas, *Rule and Misrule in the Schools of Early Modern England* ([Reading]: University of Reading, 1976), pp. 30–1. Schoolboys were particularly keen on preserving ancient customs: 'Remaines', in John Aubrey, *Three Prose Works*, ed. John Buchanan-Brown (Fontwell: Centaur Press, 1972), pp. 137–8.

3. My definition of culture is derived from anthropologists such as Clifford Geertz; see especially his *The Interpretation of Cultures* (New York: Basic Books, 1973), p. 89.

4. Bob Scribner, 'Is a History of Popular Culture Possible?', *History of European Ideas*, x (1989), pp. 173–91. See also Peter Burke, 'Popular Culture in Seventeenth-century London', in Barry Reay (ed.), *Popular Culture in Seventeenth-century England* (London: Croom Helm, 1985), pp. 31–2; Tim Harris, *London Crowds in the Reign of Charles II* (Cambridge: Cambridge University Press, 1987), pp. 15–16; and Tessa Watt, *Cheap Print and Popular Piety 1550–1640* (Cambridge: Cambridge University Press, 1991), pp. 2–6.

5. These issues are well discussed by Burke, *Popular Culture in Early Modern Europe* (London: Temple Smith, 1978), pp. 30–6, 50–6.

6. For the problem of mediators, see Burke, *Popular Culture in Early Modern Europe*, Ch. 3.

7. David Underdown, *Fire from Heaven: Life in an English Town in the Seventeenth Century* (London: HarperCollins, 1992), pp. 155–60; Richard Carew, *Carew's Survey of Cornwall* (London: Bentley, 1811), pp. 218–19.

8. Richard Gough, *The History of Myddle*, ed. David Hey (Harmondsworth: Penguin, 1981), pp. 84–96.

9. John Stow, *The Survey of London*, ed. H. B. Wheatley (London: Dent, 1987), pp. 84–96.

10. David Underdown, *Revel, Riot and Rebellion: Popular Politics and Culture in England 1603–1660* (Oxford: Clarendon Press, 1985), pp. 80–1, 90–1; Robert W. Malcolmson, *Popular Recreations in English Society*

1700–1850 (Cambridge: Cambridge University Press, 1973), p. 37; Lawrence Clopper (ed.), *Records of Early English Drama: Chester* (Toronto: University of Toronto Press, 1979), pp. 198, 331–2.

11. C. H. Mayo (ed.), *Municipal Records of the Borough of Shaftesbury* (Sherborne: J. C. Sawtell, 1889), pp. 31–2; Paul S. Seaver, *Wallington's World: A Puritan Artisan in Seventeenth-Century London* (Stanford: Stanford University Press, 1985), p. 53; George Ormerod, *History of the County Palatine and City of Chester* (London: Lackington, etc., 1819), III, pp. 229–30; Aubrey, 'Remaines', p. 189.

12. Underdown, *Revel, Riot and Rebellion*, pp. 45–6, 69, 259; Clopper (ed.), *Chester Drama*, pp. 197–8, 206, 268, 304; R. W. Ketton-Cremer, *Forty Norfolk Essays* (Norwich: Jarrold, 1961), pp. 14–16.

13. E. K. Chambers, *The Mediaeval Stage* (Oxford: Oxford University Press, 1903), I, pp. 118–19; Robert Plot, *Natural History of Staffordshire* (Oxford, 1686), p. 434.

14. Carew, *Cornwall*, p. 151. For an example of Zummerzetshire dialect, see 'The Somersetshire Man's Complaint', in F. T. Elworthy (ed.), *Specimens of English Dialects* (English Dialect Society, XXXV, 1879), pp. 7–9.

15. BL, Add. MS 38, 599, esp. fols 71, 78. For James I's *Book of Sports*, see James Tait, 'The Declaration of Sports for Lancashire (1617)', *English Historical Review*, XXXII (1917), pp. 561–5. The vitality of festive culture in Lancashire is also very obvious in T. E. Gibson (ed.), *A Cavalier's Notebook: Being Notes ... of William Blundell, of Crosby, Lancashire* (London: Longman, 1880), esp. pp. 233–40.

16. Judith Bennett, 'Conviviality and Charity in Medieval and Early Modern England', *Past and Present*, CXXXIV (Feb. 1992), p. 34 and n.; Sedley L. Ware, 'The Elizabethan Parish in its Ecclesiastical and Financial Aspects', *Johns Hopkins University Studies in Historical and Political Science*, series 26, nos 7–8 (Baltimore, 1908), p. 75.

17. The phrase is Peter Burke's: *Popular Culture in Early Modern Europe*, title of Ch. 1.

18. Ormerod, *Chester*, I, Introduction, p. liii; Carew, *Cornwall*, p. 35. Wrestling was also popular in neighbouring Devon: Dennis Brailsford, *Sport and Society: Elizabeth to Anne* (London: Routledge, 1969), p. 114.

19. For example, Alan Everitt, *Continuity and Colonization: The Evolution of Kentish Settlement* (Leicester: Leicester University Press, 1986), pp. 3–6.

20. For which see Brailsford, *Sport and Society*, pp. 103–4, 107–8, 113–14.

21. Underdown, *Revel, Riot and Rebellion*, passim; Underdown, 'The Chalk and the Cheese: Contrasts among the English Clubmen', *Past and Present*, LXXXV (Nov. 1979), 25–48. For a good discussion of the independence generated by the scattered settlement type (in this case in the Kent downlands as well as in the Weald), see Everitt, *Continuity and Colonization*, pp. 178–9.

22. Underdown, *Revel, Riot and Rebellion*, p. 259. Aubrey gives a different version: 'Observations', in *Three Prose Works*, p. 330. For complaints of Welsh superstition, see Maija Jansson and William B. Bidwell (eds), *Proceedings in Parliament 1625* (New Haven: Yale University Press, 1987), p. 86;

Christopher Hill, *Change and Continuity in Seventeenth-Century England* (London: Weidenfeld & Nicolson, 1974), p. 7.

23. Robert Plot, *Natural History of Oxfordshire* (Oxford, 1677), p. 349; Aubrey, 'Remaines', pp. 192–3. See also Underdown, *Revel, Riot and Rebellion*, pp. 96, 280, for the violence that sometimes marred the Long Newnton festivities.

24. For Lyme Regis, see C. Wanklyn, *Lyme Regis: A Retrospect* (London: Humphreys, 1922), p. 23. For Taunton, see Robin Clifton, *The Last Popular Rebellion: The Western Rising of 1685* (London: Temple Smith, 1984), pp. 45–6, 55; and Underdown, *Revel, Riot and Rebellion*, pp. 289–90. For Bruton, see Douglas L. Hayward (ed.), *The Registers of Bruton, Co. Somerset*, vol. I: *1554–1680* (Parish Registers Society, LX), p. 81.

25. David Underdown, 'The Taming of the Scold: The Enforcement of Patriarchal Authority in Early Modern England', in Anthony Fletcher and John Stevenson (eds), *Order and Disorder in Early Modern England* (Cambridge: Cambridge University Press, 1985), pp. 123–5; Lynda E. Boose, 'Scolding Brides and Bridling Scolds: Taming the Woman's Unruly Member', *Shakespeare Quarterly*, XLII (1991), pp. 179–213; Underdown, *Fire from Heaven*, p. 98.

26. Everitt, *Continuity and Colonization*, pp. 7, 41–2.

27. Cicely Howell, 'Peasant Inheritance Customs in the Midlands, 1280–1700', in Jack Goody, Joan Thirsk and E. P. Thompson (eds), *Family and Inheritance: Rural Society in Western Europe, 1200–1800* (Cambridge: Cambridge University Press, 1976), pp. 112, 117. And cf. Lutz K. Berkner in the same volume, p. 99. Everitt provides a brief, sensible discussion of the Kent situation in *Continuity and Colonization*, p. 179.

28. James A. Casada, 'Dorset Social History, 1540–1640', *Dorset Natural History and Archaeological Society Proceedings*, XCII (1970), p. 240.

29. For this paragraph see Underdown, *Revel, Riot and Rebellion*, pp. 75–6; and Malcolmson, *Popular Recreations*, pp. 83–4.

30. Edwin O. James, *Seasonal Feasts and Festivals* (New York: Barnes & Noble, 1961), pp. 298–304; Christina Hole, *English Sports and Pastimes* (London: B. T. Batsford, 1949), pp. 50–5, 57; Clopper, *Chester Drama*, pp. 234–5; Chambers *Mediaeval Stage*, I, p. 150; Alice B. Gomme, *The Traditional Games of England, Scotland, and Ireland* (London: David Nutt, 1894–8), I, pp. 56–8; Enid Porter, *Cambridgeshire Customs and Folklore* (New York: Barnes & Noble, 1969), pp. 230–1; F. G. Emmison, *Elizabethan Life: Disorder* (Chelmsford: Essex County Council, 1970), pp. 225–6; Ormerod, *Chester*, I, Introduction, p. liii.

31. Carew, *Cornwall*, pp. 195–7.

32. A. L. Rowse, *Tudor Cornwall: Portrait of a Society* (London: Jonathan Cape, 1941), pp. 32–40; Joan Thirsk (ed.), *The Agrarian History of England and Wales*, vol. IV: *1500–1640* (Cambridge: Cambridge University Press, 1967), p. 75; John Hatcher, *Rural Economy and Society in the Duchy of Cornwall* (Cambridge: Cambridge University Press, 1970), pp. 17–29.

33. Maude F. Davies, *Life in an English Village: An Economic and Historical Survey of the Parish of Corsley in Wiltshire* (London: Unwin, 1909), p. 96; BL, Add. MS 22, 836 (Maton Collection), fol. 20; Malcolmson, *Popular Recreations*, p. 47.

34. For examples, see BL, Add. MS 35, 331 (Yonge's diary, 1627–42), fol. 62v (Tiverton); Somerset RO, D/D/Ca 194 (Othery, 28 Sept. 1615); Wiltshire RO, Dean's Peculiar, Presentments 1625, no. 59 (Bere Regis); Wiltshire RO, AS/ABO 15 (1636–40), fol. 6v (Norton Bavant). See also Hole, *English Sports and Pastimes*, pp. 39–43.

35. Joseph Strutt, *Glig-Gemena Angel-Deod: or, The Sports and Pastimes of the People of England* (London: T. Bensley, 1801), pp. 75–6.

36. G. W. Saunders, 'Fives playing against Church Towers', *Somerset and Dorset Notes and Queries*, XVII (1921–3), pp. 75–7. I am indebted to Dennis Brailsford for this reference, and for much other information about the regional distribution of fives, which remained strong in Somerset until well into the nineteenth century. There is a particularly fine fives 'tower' in the garden of the Fleur de Lys at Stoke-sub-Hamdon. For pubs and the promotion of sports, see Malcolmson, *Popular Recreations*, p. 73; also Peter Clark, *The English Alehouse: A Social History 1200–1830* (London: Longman, 1983), pp. 154, 233–4.

37. I am indebted to Dennis Brailsford for this suggestion. For the cultural peculiarities of southeast Somerset, see Underdown, *Revel, Riot and Rebellion*, pp. 96–9.

38. Underdown, *Revel, Riot and Rebellion*, pp. 76–7, 111; Breton, 'The Court and the Country', p. 7, in A. B. Grosart (ed.), *The Works in Verse and Prose of Nicholas Breton* (Edinburgh: Constable, 1879), II; W. Carew Hazlitt, *Faiths and Folklore of the British Isles: A Descriptive and Historical Dictionary* (New York: B. Blom, 1965), II, p. 569. See also Hole, *English Sports and Pastimes*, pp. 59–60.

There are various spellings in references to the game in this region, includind 'stobball', 'stowball', 'staffball' and 'stopball'. See [John Goulstone], 'Stob-ball as a 17th Century Form of Cricket', *Sports History*, I (1982), pp. 19–21; *Calendar of State Papers, Domestic, 1631–33*, p. 312; Gloucestershire RO, GDR 108 (Office cases, 1609–10), fols 5v, 19v, 33; G. P. Scrope, *History of the Manor and Ancient Barony of Castle Combe* ([London], 1852), p. 331; *VCH, Wiltshire*, III (1956), p. 38; Wiltshire RO, B/ABO (Act Book, 1622–33), fol. 115v.

39. The 1984 edition of the standard bibliography contains over 8,000 entries, many of them historical, and there has been at least one supplement since then: E. W. Padwick, *A Bibliography of Cricket* (2nd edn, London: Library Association, 1984). I am grateful to Gerald Howat for lending me his copy, and for much additional help with cricket history.

40. John Marshall, *Sussex Cricket: A History* (London: Heinemann, 1959), pp. 2–3; Timothy McCann, 'Cricket and the Sussex County By-Election of 1741', *Sussex Archaeological Collections*, CXIV (1976), p. 122. For the role of the aristocracy in general, see Christopher Brookes, *English Cricket: The Game and its Players through the Ages* (London: Weidenfeld & Nicolson, 1978), Ch. 3–5.

41. *VCH, Surrey*, II, 526–7 (the deposition has been often quoted). For what follows, see Stephen Green, 'Some Cricket Records', *Archives*, XVIII, no. 80 (Oct. 1988), p. 187; see also Green, 'References to Cricket Pre-1700', *Journal of the Cricket Society*, X, no. 3 (autumn 1981), pp. 54–6.

I am grateful to Mr Green for bringing these articles to my attention, and for his generous help and advice during a visit to the MCC Library at Lord's.

42. Green, 'Some Cricket Records', p. 190; L. R. A. Grove, 'A Note on Early Kent Cricket', *Archaeologia Cantiana,* LXIII (1950), pp. 154–5; Edmund Calamy, *An Abridgement of Mr. Baxter's History ...: With an Account of the Ministers, Who Were Ejected after the Restoration* (2nd edn, London: J. Lawrence, 1713), II, 389; [K. S. Martin] (ed.), *Records of Maidstone* (Maidstone: W. Hobbs, 1926), p. 270. Filmer was from East Sutton, a few miles east of Boughton Monchelsey. Several of the other players appear to have been Royalists: ibid., pp. 118, 145, 158–63. For a later, eighteenth-century, match at Coxheath, see G. B. Buckley, 'Cricket Notices 1744–1845' (typescript at MCC Library), p. 3.

43. T. J. McCann and P. M. Wilkinson, 'The Cricket Match at Box-grove in 1622', *Sussex Archaeological Collections,* CX (1972), pp. 118–22; Marshall, *Sussex Cricket,* p. 2; *Sussex Notes and Queries,* XVI, no. 7 (May 1966), pp. 217–21.

44. For the gentry's involvement in popular sports, see Malcolmson, *Popular Recreations,* pp. 67–9; also Brailsford, *Sport and Society,* passim.

45. Timothy J. McCann, 'The Duke of Richmond, Slindon, and the 1741 Cricket Season in Sussex', *Journal of the Cricket Society,* XI, no. 1 (autumn 1982), pp. 29–31. See also Marshall, *Sussex Cricket,* p. 4.

46. Grove, 'Note on Early Kent Cricket', p. 154. Rowland Bowen, *Cricket: A History of its Growth and Development throughout the World* (London: Eyre & Spottiswoode, 1970), p. 29, argues strongly for the Weal-den origins. For the Sussex wood–pasture region, see *VCH, Sussex,* II, pp. 297, 313–14. I am indebted to Gerald Howat for the point about the implements.

47. R. D. Knight, 'F. S. Ashley-Cooper's *The Hambledon Cricket Chroni-cle:* A Re-Appraisal', Part I, *Journal of the Cricket Society,* X, No. 4 (spring 1982), p. 63. There is much evidence about Hambledon residents' lack of deference to authority in the early eighteenth century in E. P. Thompson, *Whigs and Hunters: The Origin of the Black Act* (New York: Pantheon Books, 1975), pp. 122, 136, 165–8, 228, 229n. Note also the references to the Aburrow family on pp. 229–30: another 'Curry' Abur-row was to be a noted Hambledon cricketer a generation later.

48. Aubrey, quoted in Hole, *English Sports and Pastimes,* p. 50. H. F. and A. P. Squire, *Pre-Victorian Sussex Cricket* (Henfield, 1951), p. 3, and Bowen, *Cricket,* pp. 33–5, disagree about the turf.

49. Dennis Brailsford, 'The Geography of Eighteenth-Century English Spectator Sports', *Sport Place,* I, no. 1 (winter 1987), p. 47; Mar-shall, *Sussex Cricket,* p. 3; McCann, 'The Duke of Richmond, Slindon, and the 1741 Cricket Season', p. 29; Historical Manuscript Commis-sion, *Portland,* VI, p. 76. See also John Bale, *Sport and Place: A Geography of Sport in England and Wales* (London: Hurst, 1982), pp. 70–1.

50. Hambledon encompassed 9,446 acres: *VCH, Hampshire,* III, p. 238. Herstmonceux was another large parish, though not as big as Hambledon: *VCH, Sussex,* IX, p. 131. Cf. Bishops Cannings (8,871 acres),

described as the second biggest parish in Wiltshire: *VCH, Wiltshire*, VII, p. 187.

51. A suggestion made by Bowen, *Cricket*, p. 46; and see also [Goulstone], 'Stob-ball as a 17th Century Form of Cricket'.

52. Bowen, *Cricket*, pp. 28–9.

53. Charles Phythian-Adams, 'Ceremony and the Citizen: The Communal Year at Coventry 1450–1550', in Peter Clark and Paul Slack (eds), *Crisis and Order in English Towns 1500–1700* (London: Routledge & Kegan Paul, 1972), pp. 57–85.

54. Nicholas Tyacke, 'Popular Puritan Mentality in Late Elizabethan England', in Peter Clark, A. G. T. Smith and N. Tyacke (eds), *The English Commonwealth 1547–1640: Essays in Politics and Society* (Leicester: Leicester University Press, 1979), pp. 77–92; Patrick Collinson, 'Cranbrook and the Fletchers: Popular and Unpopular Religion in the Kentish Weald', in Collinson, *Godly People: Essays on English Protestantism and Puritanism* (London: Hambledon Press, 1983), pp. 423–4.

55. BL, TT, E 56 (2): *Certaine Informations*, no. 23 (19–26 June 1643).

56. For which see Brailsford, *Sport and Society*, pp. 55–6.

3. THE GENDERING OF POPULAR CULTURE IN EARLY MODERN ENGLAND *Susan Dwyer Amussen.*

1. For some of these issues, see Bob Scribner, 'Is a History of Popular Culture Possible?', *History of European Ideas*, x (1989), pp. 175–91.

2. Clifford Geertz, *The Interpretation of Cultures* (New York: Basic Books, 1973), p. 5.

3. In addition to the works on women listed in the Bibliography, see, for instance, the classics: Anne Oakley, *Sex, Gender, and Society* (New York: Harper & Row, 1972); Michelle Zimbalist Rosaldo and Louise Lamphere (eds), *Woman, Culture and Society* (Stanford: Stanford University Press, 1974); for a summary of research, Cynthia Fuchs Epstein, *Deceptive Distinctions: Sex, Gender, and the Social Order* (New Haven and London: Yale University Press, 1988); for a survey of the biological evidence, see Anne Fausto-Sterling, *Myths of Gender: Biological Theories about Women and Men* (New York: Basic Books, 1985).

4. Keith Thomas, *Religion and the Decline of Magic* (London: Weidenfeld & Nicolson, 1971), pp. 568–9; for a popular seventeenth-century version, see Joseph Swetnam, *The Arraignment of Lewd, Idle, froward, and unconstant Women* (London, 1615), reprinted in Katherine Usher Henderson and Barbara McManus (eds), *Half-Humankind: Texts and Contexts of the Controversy about Women in England, 1540–1640* (Urbana: University of Illinois Press, 1985), pp. 189–216, esp. pp. 214–6; Thomas Laqueur, *Making Sex: The Body and Sexuality from the Greeks to Freud* (Cambridge, Mass.: Harvard University Press, 1990), Chs 2, 3, passim.

5. Susan Dwyer Amussen, *An Ordered Society: Gender and Class in Early Modern England* (Oxford: Basil Blackwell, 1988), Ch. 3, passim, esp.

pp. 81–5; Mary Prior, 'Women in the Urban Economy: Oxford 1500–1800', in Mary Prior (ed.), *Women in English Society, 1500–1800* (London: Methuen, 1985), pp. 93–117; but cf. Vivien Brodsky, 'Widows in Late Elizabethan London: Remarriage, Economic Opportunity and Family Orientations', in Lloyd Bonfield, Richard Smith and Keith Wrightson (eds), *The World We Have Gained: Histories of Population and Social Structure* (Oxford: Oxford University Press, 1986), pp. 122–54.

6. Laqueur, *Making Sex*, pp. 108–9.

7. See Swetnam, *Arraignment*, in Henderson and McManus (eds), *Half-Humankind*, pp. 205, 207, for the association of men with drinking; Keith Wrightson, *English Society, 1580–1680* (London: Hutchinson, 1982), pp. 167–70; Peter Clark, *The English Alehouse: A Social History, 1200–1830* (London: Longman, 1983), esp. Ch. 7.

8. Thomas Gataker, *Marriage Duties Briefely Couched Togither* (London, 1620), p. 8; cf. Amussen, *An Ordered Society*, pp. 41–7.

9. Norfolk RO, ANW 7/3, 1615, Faith Docking con Alice Kemp. For skimmingtons, see Bibliography.

10. Public Record Office, London (hereafter PRO), STAC 8/249/19, Nicholas Rosyer against James Quarry *et al.*; for further discussion of this case, see Amussen, *An Ordered Society*, p. 118, and Karen Newman, *Fashioning Femininity and English Renaissance Drama* (Chicago: University of Chicago Press, 1991), pp. 35–40, passim.

11. Amussen, *An Ordered Society*, pp. 117–20.

12. Brodsky, 'Widows in Late Elizabethan London', shows one exception, equally rooted in the family economy; Barbara J. Todd, 'The Remarrying Widow: A Stereotype Reconsidered', in Prior (ed.), *Women in English Society*, pp. 54–92: Todd does not give comparative figures for male remarriage rates; one can estimate remarriage rates from Peter Laslett, *Family Life and Illicit Love in Earlier Generations* (Cambridge: Cambridge University Press, 1977), 'Clayworth and Cogenhoe' (pp. 50–101) and 'Parental Deprivation in the Past: A Note on Orphans and Step-Parenthood in English History' (pp. 160–73): based on Tables 2.19 and 4.1, and information on p. 58, it appears that *c.* 65.2 per cent of the widowers in Laslett's sample remarried, while only *c.* 35.3 per cent of the widows did.

13. Natalie Zemon Davis, 'Women in the Crafts in Sixteenth-Century Lyon', *Feminist Studies*, VIII (1982), pp. 46–80; Norfolk RO, PD 193/92: of the five girls apprenticed between 1618 and 1716, two were in housewifery, one in husbandry and one in 'dairy affairs', while one was unspecified; seven of the eight of the poor boys bound over were bound in husbandry as well. Cf. K. D. M. Snell, *Annals of the Labouring Poor: Social Change and Agrarian England, 1660 -1900* (Cambridge: Cambridge University Press, 1985), pp. 279–82: in the seventeenth century, 68 per cent of the girls in his sample parishes were placed in either 'husbandry' or 'housewifery', while in the eighteenth century the comparable figure is 58 per cent.

14. Norfolk RO AYL/1 (Wages Assessment, 1613) is typical of these; Alice Clark, *Working Life of Women in the Seventeenth Century* (London, 1919, reprinted London: Routledge & Kegan Paul, 1982), pp. 60–3.

15. J. Hajnal, 'European Marriage Patterns in Perspective', in D. V. Glass and D.E.C. Eversley (eds), *Population in History: Essays in Historical Demography* (London: Edward Arnold, 1965), pp. 101–43.

16. A. L. Beier, *Masterless Men: The Vagrancy Problem in England, 1560–1640* (London: Methuen, 1985), p. 9; Susan Dwyer Amussen, 'Governors and Governed: Class and Gender Relations in English Villages, 1590–1725', Unpublished Ph. D. thesis, Brown University (1982), pp. 319–20; Amussen, *An Ordered Society*, pp. 86–92. Southampton regularly prosecuted suspected charwomen – single women who lived independently and worked by the day: seven were presented in 1606–8, nine in 1615–16; there do not appear to be similar prosecutions of men: W. J. Connor (ed.), *The Southampton Mayor's Book of 1606–1608*, in *Southampton Record Series*, XXI (Southampton: University Press 1978), and J. W. Horrocks (ed.), *The Assembly Books of Southampton*, vol. IV: *1615–1616*, in *Southampton Record Society*, XXV (Southampton: University Press, 1925). In Dorchester, Dorset, more men than women were prosecuted but women were more likely to be prosecuted more than once: I am grateful to David Underdown for this information. On gentry women, see Dorothy Osborne, *Letters to Sir William Temple*, ed. Kenneth Parker (London: Penguin, 1987), letters 62 ff., where she is passed among her family after her father's death.

17. Brodsky, 'Widows in Late Elizabethan London', pp. 17–22.

18. Barbara Todd, 'Widowhood in a Market Town: Abingdon 1540–1720', unpublished D.Phil. thesis, Oxford University (1983), pp. 190–2.

19. Paul Slack, *Poverty and Policy in Tudor and Stuart England* (London: Longman, 1988), pp. 75–6.

20. Amussen, *An Ordered Society*, pp. 120–2.

21. There were a few radical religious groups which rejected chastity, but as Christopher Hill has pointed out, without reliable contraception sexual freedom is for men only: Christopher Hill, *The World Turned Upside Down: Radical Ideas during the Puritan Revolution* (Harmondsworth: Penguin, 1975), pp. 314–23, esp. p. 319.

22. Norfolk RO, DEP/31, Ex Offic. con Thomas Haddon and Agnes Haddon, fols 433–41v; for the role of observation, see Susan Dwyer Amussen, 'Feminin/masculin: le genre dans l'Angleterre de l'époque moderne', *Annales ESC*, XL, 2 (1985), 269–87.

23. Norfolk RO, DEP/38, Offic. dmi con Robert Armiger and Margaret Mollett, fols 202–6.

24. Norfolk RO, DEP/28, Heasell con Chosell, fols 436–7.

25. Norfolk RO, DEP/29, Offic. dmni con Vyneor, fol. 107v; cf. Norfolk RO, DEP/33, Offic. dmni. con Thomas Shaxton, where Shaxton's defence against a charge of adultery was that the only report came from his alleged partner, Margaret Robinson, 'and did not labour amongst persons of good credit or estimation', while Margaret was 'a dishonest woman of her body ... a very poor and needy woman': fols 6r–7v.

26. Norfolk RO, TES/8, 1714/15, Testimonial from Skeyton.

27. Norfolk RO, DEP/27, Bk 29A, 1593, Allegations con Rackulver and Parker.

28. Norfolk RO, DEP/38, 1629/30, Mary Knowles, wid. con Henry Atkyns, Cler., fols 412r, 413v–15v.

29. E. P. Thompson, 'The Grid of Inheritance: A Comment', in Jack Goody, Joan Thirsk and E. P. Thompson (eds), *Family and Inheritance: Rural Society in Western Europe, 1200–1800* (Cambridge: Cambridge University Press, 1976), pp. 328–60, esp. pp. 349–51.

30. See the Bibliography for a sampling of the extensive work on witchcraft.

31. Norfolk RO, DEP/38, Offic. dmi. con Robert Armiger and Margaret Mollett, fol. 203.

32. Norfolk RO, DEP/42, Stallworthy con Rodman, fol. 526v.

33. Amussen, *An Ordered Society*, pp. 111–13.

34. Amussen, *An Ordered Society*, pp. 116–17; Martin Ingram, *Church Courts, Sex and Marriage in England, 1570–1640* (Cambridge: Cambridge University Press, 1987), pp. 161–3, 310–11.

35. For a discussion of the intellectual structure of this transformation, see Edmund Leites, *The Puritan Conscience and Modern Sexuality* (New Haven: Yale University Press, 1986). The idea of the lustful woman certainly survived in popular culture into the nineteenth century: James Obelkevich, *Religion and Rural Society: South Lindsey, 1825–1875* (Oxford: Oxford University Press, 1976), p. 96.

36. Angus McLaren, *A History of Contraception from Antiquity to the Present Day* (Oxford: Basil Blackwell, 1990), pp. 157–8; Amussen, *An Ordered Society*, pp. 114–15; cf. Cornelia Hughes Dayton, 'Taking the Trade: Abortion and Gender Relations in an Eighteenth-Century New England Village', *William and Mary Quarterly*, 3rd series, XLVIII (1991), 19–49.

37. For the theoretical issues, see Anne Edwards, 'Male Violence in Feminist Theory: An Analysis of the Changing Conceptions of Sex/ Gender Violence and Male Dominance', in Jalna Hanmer and Mary Maynard (eds), *Women, Violence, and Social Control* (Basingstoke: Macmillan, 1987), pp. 13–29, esp. pp. 18–19. For historical treatments, see Anna Clark, *Women's Silence, Men's Violence: Sexual Assault in England, 1770–1845* (London: Pandora Press, 1987). For the 'blame the victim' approach, see Roy Porter, 'Rape – does it have a Historical Meaning?', in Sylvana Tomaselli and Roy Porter (eds) *Rape* (Oxford: Basil Blackwell, 1986), pp. 216–36.

38. Susan D. Amussen, 'Running the Country, Running the Household, and Running Amok: Violence, Power, and the state in Early Modern England', Davis Center Paper, Department of History, Princeton University (May 1989); Joy Wiltenburg, *Disorderly Women and Female Power in Early Modern England and Germany* (Charlottesville: University of Virginia Press, 1992), Ch. 8, esp. p. 183.

39. J. A. Sharpe, 'Domestic Homicide in Early Modern England', *Historical Journal*, XXIV (1981), 29–48, esp. p. 37.

40. For this sample, see Amussen, *An Ordered Society*, esp. p. 166, n. 88. An analysis of the printed Staffordshire Sessions records shows a similar breakdown, though more petitions survived there in a shorter period of time. Between 1590 and 1609, communities offered fifty-nine

petitions against individuals, of which fifty were against men, eight against a man and woman, and only one against a woman: *The Staffordshire Quarter Sessions Rolls*, II–VI, ed. S. A. H. Bourne (vols II: *1590–1593*; III: *1594–1597*; IV: *1598–1602*; and V: *1603–1606*) and D. H. G. Salt (vol. VI: *1608–1609*); William Salt Archeological Society (later The Staffordshire Record Society) (ed.), *Collections for a History of Staffordshire*, 2nd series XXXI, XXXII, XXXIV, XXXVII and XLII and 3rd series VI (1929, 1930, 1932, 1935, 1940, 1949).

41. Norfolk RO, C/S3/17, 1611, Articles against Catherine the wife of Symond Parson of Sheringham, preferred by the inhabitants of Sheringham, Beeston and Renton.

42. Norfolk RO, C/S3/35, Barningham petition against Richard Cutter and wife Frances.

43. Norfolk RO, C/S3/17, Articles against Grace Ward, wife of Christopher Ward of Barton Bendish, and Articles against Christopher Ward, alehousekeeper. Lynghook is behind both these petitions, which are obviously related.

44. Norfolk RO, C/S3/17, 1610, Articles against Joan Shilling of Foulden by Robert Greenfield of Gooderstone.

45. Norfolk RO, C/S3/26, 1627, Articles against Amea, wife of Richard Winter, and her daughters Edina and Margaret, in Grimston.

46. In Staffordshire, the one petition directed only against a woman focuses on her sexual offences and disorderliness – though her husband was an alehousekeeper: *Staffordshire Quarter Sessions Rolls*, II, p. 53.

47. Norfolk RO, C/S3/26, 1627, Petition against Mathye, wife of Robert Cambridge.

48. Elisabeth Copet-Rougier, '"Le Mal Court": Visible and Invisible Violence in an Acephalous Society–Mkako of Cameroon', in David Riches (ed.), *The Anthropology of Violence* (Oxford: Basil Blackwell, 1986), pp. 50–69.

49. David Underdown, 'The Taming of the Scold: The Enforcement of Patriarchal Authority in Early Modern England', in Anthony Fletcher and John Stevenson (eds), *Order and Disorder in Early Modern England* (Cambridge: Cambridge University Press, 1985), pp. 116–36, esp. pp. 120–1.

50. See the sources in n. 7 above on drinking and alehouses. Alehouse brawls are similar to football in some ways: both were violent but structured activities that could lead to death – though in the case of football the death was more likely to be described as manslaughter: F. G. Emmison, *Elizabethan Life: Disorder* (Chelmsford: Essex County Council, 1970), pp. 225–6; Robert W. Malcolmson, *Popular Recreations in English Society, 1700–1850* (Cambridge: Cambridge University Press, 1973), pp. 82–4.

51. PRO, ASSI 45 1/4/23–7; cf. Corporation of London RO, Sessions Papers, May 1678, Inquest into death of Herbert Parrott, Esq., for a similar pattern.

52. Bod. Lib., Ms. Top. Norfolk c.2, fol. 80, 24 December 1638, Information of John Reve of Catton.

53. Norfolk RO, C/S3/20, 1615, Information of Barnaby Wyer of Foulden.

54. Wiltshire RO, Diocese of Salisbury, Bishops Acct. Book, Office 7, fol. 57: I am grateful to David Underdown for this reference.

55. William Whately, *A Bride-Bush, or A Direction for Married Persons Plainely Describing the duties common to both, and peculiar to each of them* (London, 1623), pp. 106–7; Amussen, *An Ordered Society*, pp. 42–3; T. E., *The Lawes Resolution of Women's Rights* (London, 1631), pp. 128–9. Wlliam Heale, *An Apologie for Women* (Oxford, 1609) argues that it is never permissible for a husband to beat his wife, while Mones A. Vauts, *The Husband's Authority Unvaile'd: wherein it is moderately discussed whether it be fit or lawful for a good man to beat his bad wife* (London, 1650) concludes that occasionally (but under very limited circumstances) it was permissible.

56. Norfolk RO, DEP/53, 28 Jan. 1696/7, Hannah Robinson con John Robinson, testimony of Rebecca Mallowes; and DEP/10, BK 10, 1565, Marie Beck con William Beck, esp. testimony of Margaret Goodwin.

57. Norfolk RO, DEP/34, Constance Boston con John Boston, fols 101–7v, esp. fol 101v; Northumberland RO, QSB Vol. 5, Morpeth Christmas Sessions, Information of Margaret Story, pp. 14–15: I am grateful to Miranda Chaytor for this reference.

58. Frances Dolan, '"Home-rebels and house-traitors": Murderous Wives in Early Modern England', *Yale Journal of Law and the Humanities*, IV, (1992), pp. 1–31: Dolan also notes notes that in literary popular culture, women who killed their husband were far more often the subject of pamphlets and other literary forms than the more common men who killed their wives.

59. E. P. Thompson, '"Rough Music": Le Charivari Anglais', *Annales E. S.C.*, XXVII (1972), pp. 285–312, esp. pp. 300–4.

60. Amussen, *An Ordered Society*, esp. Ch. 2; Laqueur, *Making Sex*, passim, for a full discussion of these issues.

4. LITERACY AND LITERATURE IN POPULAR CULTURE *Jonathan Barry*

1. D. Vincent, *Literacy and Popular Culture: England 1750–1914* (Cambridge: Cambridge University Press, 1989), is the fundamental study for this later period. For a review of recent work on British literacy see W. B. Stephens, 'Literacy in England, Scotland and Wales, 1500–1900', *History of Education Quarterly*, XXX (1990), pp. 545–71, and for Europe see R. A. Houston, 'Literacy and Society in the West 1500–1850', *Social History*, VIII (1983), pp. 269–93, and Houston, *Literacy in Early Modern Europe* (Harlow: Longman, 1988). For Ulster see J. Adams, *The Printed Word and the Common Man: Popular Culture in Ulster 1700–1900* (Belfast: Queen's University, Institue of Irish Studies, 1987). Studies of literacy in colonial and early North America raise many important issues for British history. See, for example, K. A. Lockridge, *Literacy in Colonial*

New England (New York: W. W. Norton, 1974); W. J. Gilmore, *Reading Becomes a Necessity of Life: Material and Cultural Life in Rural New England 1780–1835* (Knoxville: University of Tennessee Press, 1989); D. D. Hall, *Worlds of Wonder, Days of Judgement: Popular Religious Belief in Early New England* (New York: Alfred A. Knopf, 1989); R. B. Brown, *Knowledge is Power: The Diffusion of Information in Early America 1700–1865* (New York: Oxford University Press, 1989); C. N. Davidson (ed.), *Reading in America* (Baltimore: Johns Hopkins University Press, 1989).

2. K. Wrightson, *English Society 1580–1680* (London: Hutchinson, 1982), pp. 183–4, 220.

3. The key text for the cultural effects of the Reformation remains K. V. Thomas, *Religion and the Decline of Magic* (London: Weidenfeld & Nicolson, 1971), usefully summarised in I. Luxton, 'The Reformation and Popular Culture', in F. Heal and R. O'Day (eds), *Church and Society in England, Henry VIII to James I* (London: Macmillan, 1977), pp. 57–77, but for later historigraphy see P. Collinson, *The Birthpangs of Protestant England* (London: Macmillan, 1988) and M. Aston, *England's Iconoclasts* (Oxford: Oxford University Press, 1988). The wider European setting is provided by P. Burke, *Popular Culture in Early Modern Europe* (London: Temple Smith, 1978). There is insufficient space in this essay to do justice to the issue of visual materials, but for the growing scholarship on the widespread use of visual images by Protestants see T. Watt, *Cheap Print and Popular Piety 1550–1640* (Cambridge: Cambridge University Press, 1991) and, for its role after 1640, see M. Duffy (gen. ed.) *The English Satirical Print 1600–1832* (Cambridge: Chadwyck Healey) 1986), reviewed by R. Porter, 'Seeing the Past', *Past and Present*, CXVIII (1988), pp. 186–205; P. Anderson, *The Printed Image and the Transformation of Popular Culture 1790–1860* (Oxford: Clarendon Press, 1991).

4. E. P. Thompson, 'Patrician Society, Plebeian Culture', *Journal of Social History*, VII (1973–4), pp. 382–405; Thompson, 'The Patricians and the Plebs', in his *Customs in Common* (London: Merlin, 1991, Penguin edn 1993), pp. 16–96; E. and S. Yeo (eds), *Popular Culture and Class Conflict 1590–1914* (Brighton: Harvester Press, 1981); H. Medick, 'Plebeian Culture in the Transition to Capitalism', in R. Samuel and G. Stedman Jones (eds), *Culture, Ideology and Politics* (London: Routledge & Kegan Paul, 1982), pp. 84–113; B. Reay (ed.), *Popular Culture in Seventeenth-Century England* (London: Croom Helm, 1985).

5. J. Goody (ed.), *Literacy in Traditional Societies* (Cambridge: Cambridge University Press, 1968), W. Ong, *The Presence of the Word* (New Haven: Yale University Press, 1967) and Ong, *Orality and Literacy* (London: Methuen, 1982) offer the classic expressions of the argument for the revolutionary effects of literacy. For the developing debate on this see H. J. Graff, *Literacy and Social Development in the West: A Reader* (Cambridge: Cambridge University Press, 1981) and B. V. Street, *Literacy in Theory and Practice* (Cambridge: Cambridge University Press, 1984).

6. R. W. Malcolmson, *Popular Recreations in English Society 1700–1850* (Cambridge: Cambridge University Press, 1973); B. Bushaway, *By Rite: Custom, Ceremony and Community in England 1700–1880* (London: Junction Books, 1982); R. D. Storch (ed.), *Popular Culture and Customs in Nineteenth-*

Century England (London: Croom Helm, 1982); J. M. Golby and A. W. Purdue, *The Civilisation of the Crowd: Popular Culture in England 1750–1900* (London: B. T. Batsford, 1984); D. Underdown, *Revel, Riot and Rebellion: Popular Politics and Culture in England 1603–60* (Oxford: Clarendon Press, 1985); Thompson, *Customs in Common*.

7. Many of the methodological problems are lucidly described in S. Clark, 'French Historians and Early Modern Popular Culture', *Past and Present*, c (1983), pp. 62–99, in issue no. 10 of *History of European Ideas* (1989) devoted to popular culture and above all in M. Shiach, *Discourse on Popular Culture: Class, Gender and History in Cultural Analysis, 1730 to the Present* (Cambridge: Polity Press, 1989). Some helpful recent comments on problems of interpretation can be found in M. Bristol, *Carnival and Theater: Plebeian Culture and the Structure of Authority in Renaissance England* (New York: Methuen, 1985); L. Marcus, *The Policties of Mirth: Jonson, Herrick, Milton, Marvell and the Defence of Old Holiday Pastimes* (Chicago: University of Chigago Press, 1986); M. Harrison, *Crowds and History: Mass Phenomena in English Towns 1790–1830* (Cambridge: Cambridge University Press, 1988); and F. O'Gorman, 'Campaign Rituals and Ceremonies: The Social Meaning of Elections in England 1780–1860', *Past and Present*, cxxv (1992), pp. 79–115. The literature on crowds and riots is vast, but for a recent critique of Thompson's classic view of the 'moral economy' of the crowd, see J. Bohstedt, 'The Moral Economy and the Discipline of Historical Context', *Journal of Social History*, xxvi (1992–3), pp. 65–84.

8. P. Delany, *British Autobiography in the Seventeenth Century* (London: Routledge & Kegan Paul, 1969); O. C. Watkins, *The Puritan Experience* (London: Routledge & Kegan Paul, 1972); M. Vicinus, *The Industrial Muse: A Study of Nineteenth-Century British Working-Class Literature* (London: Croom Helm, 1974); M. Spufford, 'First Steps in Literacy: The Reading and Writing Experiences of the Humblest Seventeenth-Century Autobiographers', *Social History*, iv (1979), pp. 407–35; D. Vincent, *Bread, Knowledge and Freedom* (London: Europa, 1981); B. Maidment, 'Essayists and Artizans: The Making of Nineteenth-Century Self-Taught Poets', *Literature and History*, ix (1983), pp. 74–91. Recent studies of women's writings have developed these approaches most sensitively: E. Hobby, *Virtue of Necessity: English Women's Writing 1649–88* (London: Virago, 1988); E. Graham (ed.), *Her Own Life: Autobiographical Writings by Seventeenth-Century Englishwomen* (London: Routledge, 1989); D. Landry, *The Muses of Resistance: Labouring-Class Women's Poetry in Britain, 1737–96* (Cambridge: Cambridge University Press, 1990).

9. For the pioneering studies see L. Shepard, *The Broadside Ballad* (London: Jenkins, 1962); Shepard, *The History of Street Literature* (Newton Abbot: David & Charles, 1972); C. M. Simpson, *The British Broadside Ballad and its Music* (New Brunswick: Rutgers University Press, 1966); V. Neuburg, *The Penny Histories* (London: Oxford University Press, 1968); Neugurg, *Chapbooks* (London: Woburn Press, 1972); Neuburg, *Popular Literature: A History and a Guide* (Harmondsworth: Penguin, 1977); C. J. Sommerville, *Popular Religion in Restoration England* (Gainesville: University of Florida Presses, 1979); B. Capp, *Astrology and the Popular Press: English Almanacs 1500–1800* (London: Faber & Faber, 1979); M. Spufford, *Small*

Books and Pleasant Histories: Popular Fiction ˙ and its Readership in Seventeenth-Century England (London: Methuen, 1981). An excellent introduction to this work for the seventeenth century is provided by B. Capp, 'Popular Literature', in Reay (ed.), *Popular Culture*, pp. 198–243.

10. F. O. Waage, 'Social Themes in Urban Broadsides of Renaissance England', *Journal of Popular Culture*, XI (1977), pp. 731–41; V. Gammon, 'Song, Sex and Society in England 1600–1850', *Folk Music Journal*, IV (1982), pp. 208–15; J. A. Sharpe, '"Last Dying Speeches"; Religion, Ideology and Public Executions in Seventeenth-Century England', *Past and Present*, CVII (1985), pp. 144–67; Sharpe, 'Plebeian Marriage in Stuart England: Some Evidence from Popular Literature', *Transactions of The Royal Historical Society*, 5th series, XXXVI (1986), pp. 69–90; A. Tobriner, 'Old Age in Tudor and Stuart Ballads', *Folklore*, CII (1991), pp. 149–74; P. Linebaugh, *The London Hanged* (Harmondsworth: Penguin, 1991).

11. On these issues see: R. Thompson, 'Popular Reading and Humour in Restoration England', *Journal of Popular Culture*, IX (1975), pp. 653–71; K. V. Thomas, 'The Place of Laughter in Tudor and Stuart England', TLS, 21 Jan. 1977, pp. 77–81; D. Dugaw, *Warrior Women and Popular Balladry 1650–1850* (Cambridge: Cambridge University Press, 1989); J. Wiltenburg, *Disorderly Women and Female Power in the Street Literature of Early Modern England and Germany* (Charlottesville: University Press of Virginia, 1992); E. Foyster, 'A Laughing Matter? Marital Discord and Gender Control in Seventeenth-Century England', *Rural History*, IV (1993), pp. 5–21.

12. L. S. O'Connell, 'The Elizabethan Bourgeois Hero-Tale', in B. C. Malament (ed.), *After the Reformation* (Manchester: Manchester University Press, 1980), pp. 267–90; L. Stevenson, *Praise and Paradox: Merchants and Craftsmen in Elizabethan Popular Literature* (Cambridge: Cambridge University Press, 1984); D. Dugaw, 'The Popular Marketing of Old Ballads', *Eighteenth-Century Studies*, XXI (1987–8), pp. 71–90; N. Wurzbach, *The Rise of the English Street Balled 1550–1650* (Cambridge: Cambridge University Press, 1990).

13. R. Mandrou, *De la culture populaire au XVIIe et XVIIIe siècles* (Paris: Stock, 1964). On nineteenth-century England see L. James, *Fiction for the Working Man 1830–50: A Study of the Literature Produced for the Working Classes in Early Victorian England* (London: Oxford University Press, 1963).

14. L. Stone, 'Literacy and Education in England 1640–1900', *Past and Present*, XLII (1969), pp. 69–139; R. S. Schofield, 'The Dimensions of Illiteracy 1750–1850', *Explorations in Economic History*, X (1973), pp. 437–54; D. Cressy, *Literacy and the Social Order: Reading and Writing in Tudor and Stuart England* (Cambridge: Cambridge University Press, 1980); D. P. Resnick (ed.), *Literacy in Historical Perspective* (Washington, DC: Library of Congress, 1983); W. B. Stephens (ed.), *Studies in the History of Literacy: England and North America* (Leeds: Museum of the History of Education, University of Leeds, 1983); Stephens, *Education, Literacy and Society 1830–1870* (Manchester: Manchester University Press, 1987); Vincent, *Literacy*; W. Ford, 'The Problem of Literacy in

Early Modern England', *History*, LXXVIII (1993), pp. 22–37. A convenient summary of this work is provided by Cressy, 'Literacy in Context: Meaning and Measurement in Early Modern England', in J. Brewer and R. Porter (eds), *Consumption and the World of Goods* (London: Routledge, 1993), pp. 305–19.

15. J. Simon, *Education and Society in Tudor England* (Cambridge: Cambridge University Press, 1966); M. Spufford, 'The Schooling of the Peasantry in Cambridgeshire 1570–1700', in J. Thirsk (ed.), *Land, Church and People* (Reading: British Agricultural History Society, 1970), pp. 112–47; Spufford, 'First Steps in Literacy'; R. O' Day, *Education and Society 1500–1800* (London: Longman, 1982). These points are very well explained in E. J. Monaghan, 'Literacy, Instruction and Gender in Colonial New England', in Davidson (ed.), *Reading in America*, pp. 53–80, esp. p. 70. On the question of child employment see also H. Cunningham, 'The Employment and Unemployment of Children in England c. 1680–1851', *Past and Present*, CXXVI (1990), pp. 115–50.

16. In addition to the works already cited, see R. T. Vann, 'Literacy in Seventeenth-Century England', *Journal of Interdisciplinary History*, V (1974), pp. 287–93; J. A. H. Moran, 'Literacy and Education in Northern England 1350–1550', *Northern History*, XVII (1981), pp. 1–23; Moran, *The Growth of English Schooling 1340–1548* (Princeton: Princeton University Press, 1985); R. A. Houston, 'Development of Literacy in Northern England, 1640–1750', *Economic History Review*, XXXV (1982), pp. 199–216; Houston, 'Illiteracy in the Diocese of Durham, 1663–89 and 1750–62', *Northern History*, XVIII (1982), pp. 239–51; Houston, 'The Literacy Myth: Illiteracy in Scotland, 1630–1760', *Past and Present*, XCVI (1982), pp. 81–102; Houston, *Scottish Literacy and Scottish Identity: Illiteracy and Society in Scotland and Northern England 1600–1800* (Cambridge: Cambridge University Press, 1985).

17. M. Sanderson, 'Literacy and Social Mobility in the Industrial Revolution in England', *Past and Present*, LVI (1972), pp. 75–104; Sanderson, *Educational Opportunity and Social Change in England* (London: Faber & Faber, 1987); W. B. Stephens, 'Illiteracy and Schooling in Provincial Towns 1640–1870', in D. Reeder (ed.), *Urban Education in the Nineteenth Century* (London: Taylor & Francis, 1977), pp. 27–48; E. G. West, 'Literacy and the Industrial Revolution', *Economic History Review*, XXXI (1978), pp. 369–83; D. Levine, 'Education and Family Life in Early Industrial England', *Journal of Family History*, IX (1979), pp. 368–80; Levine, 'Illiteracy and Family Life during the First Industrial Revolution', *Journal of Social History*, XIV (1980–1), pp. 25–44; D. W. Galenson, 'Literacy and Age in Pre-Industrial England', *Economic Development and Cultural Change*, XXIX (1981), pp. 813–29; S. A. Harrop, 'Adult Education and Literacy: The Importance of Post-School Education for Literacy Levels in the Eighteenth and Nineteenth Centuries', *History of Education*, XIII (1984), pp. 191–205; S. J. and J. M. Nicholas, 'Male Literacy, "De-skilling" and the Industrial Revolution', *Journal of Interdisciplinary History*, XXIII (1992–3), pp. 1–18.

18. K. Thomas, 'The Meaning of Literacy in Early Modern England', in G. Baumann (ed.), *The Written Word: Literacy in Transition* (Oxford:

Clarendon Press, 1986), pp. 97–131. This is the approach to literacy advocated in Street, *Literacy*; for applications to nineteenth-century England see Vincent, *Literacy* and B. Reay, 'The Context and Meaning of Popular Literacy: Some Evidence from Nineteenth-Century Rural England', *Past and Present*, CXXXI (1991), pp. 89–129.

19. M. G. Jones, *The Charity School Movement* (London: Cambridge University Press, 1938); D. Robson, *Some Aspects of Education in Cheshire in the Eighteenth Century* (Manchester: Chetham Society, 1966); J. Simon, 'Was there a Charity School Movement?', in B. Simon (ed.), *Education in Leicestershire* (Leicester: Leicester University Press, 1968), pp. 54–100; T. W. Laqueur, *Religion and Respectability: Sunday Schools and Working-Class Culture 1780–1850* (New Haven: Yale University Press, 1976); Laqueur, 'Working-Class Demand and the Growth of English Elementary Education 1750–1850', in L. Stone (ed.), *Schooling and Society* (Baltimore: Johns Hopkins University Press, 1976); R. Hume, 'Educational Provision for the Kentish Poor 1660–1811', *Southern History*, IV (1982), pp. 123–44; C. Rose, 'Evangelical Phihanthropy and Anglican Revival: the Charity Schools of Augustan London 1698–1740', *London Journal*, XVI (1991), pp. 35–65.

20. V. Neuburg, *Popular Education in Eighteenth-Century England* (London: Woburn Press, 1971); T. W. Laqueur, 'The Cultural Origins of Popular Literacy in England 1500–1850', *Oxford Review of Education*, XI (1976), pp. 255–75; I. Green, '"For Children in Yeeres and Children in Understanding": The Emergence of the English Catechism under Elizabeth and the Early Stuarts', *Journal of Ecclesiastical History*, XXXVII (1986), pp. 397–425; E. Duffy, 'The Godly and the Multitude in Stuart England', *The Seventeenth Century*, I (1986), pp. 31–55; C. Hill, *The English Bible and the Seventeenth-Century Revolution* (Harmondsworth: Penguin, 1993).

21. P. Clark, 'Ownership of Books in England 1500–1640', in Stone (ed.), *Schooling and Society*, pp. 95–114, is the only extended discussion of the probate evidence, but see J. Barry, 'Popular Culture in Seventeenth-Century Bristol', in Reay (ed.), *Popular Culture*, pp. 59–90 at pp. 66–7. For an overview of inventories as a source see L. Weatherill, *Consumer Behaviour and Material Culture in Britain 1660–1760* (London: Routledge, 1988) (but her tables on book ownership cannot be compared with others, as she excludes Bibles!).

22. There is no good overview of the press as a whole througout this period, G. A. Cranfield, *The Press and Society* (London: Longman, 1978) being a rather superficial account largely of newspapers. The best guides are offered by G. Pollard, 'The English Market for Printed Books', *Publishing History*, IV (1978), pp. 8–48; J. Feather, 'Cross-Channel Currents', *The Library*, 6th series, II (1980), pp. 1–15; Feather, *A History of British Publishing* (London: Routledge, 1988) plus, for the pre-1640 period, the trilogy by H. S. Bennett, *English Books and Readers 1475–1557*, *English Books and Readers 1558–1603* and *English Books and Readers 1603–1640* (Cambridge: Cambridge University Press, 1952), 1965 and 1970). For the eighteenth century see Feather, *The Provincial Book Trade in Eighteenth-Century England* (Cambridge: Cambridge University Press, 1986), together with I. Rivers

(ed.), *Books and their Readers in Eighteenth-Century England* (Leicester: Leicester University Press, 1982) and, in particular, J. Raven, *Judging New Wealth: Popular Publishing and Responses to Commerce in England 1750–1800* (Oxford: Clarendon Press, 1992).

23. L. B. Wright, *Middle-Class Culture in Elizabethan England* (new edn, Cornell: Cornell University Press, 1958); Spufford, *Small Books*; Spufford, *The Great Reclothing of Rural England* (London: Hambledon Press, 1984); R. Myers and M. Harris (eds), *Spreading the Word: The Distribution Networks of Print 1550–1850* (Winchester: St Paul's Bibliographies, 1990); Watt, *Cheap Print*. For illuminating discussions of popularisation in two key areas, medicine and agriculture, see P. Slack, 'Mirrors of Health and Treasures of Poor Men: The Uses of the Vernacular Medical Literature of Tudor England', in C. Webster (ed.), *Health, Medicine and Mortality in the Sixteenth Century* (Cambridge: Cambridge University Press, 1979), pp. 237–73; R. Porter (ed.), *The Popularization of Medicine 1650–1850* (London: Routledge, 1992); A. McRae, 'Husbandry Manuals and the Language of Agrarian Improvement', in M. Leslie and T. Raylor (eds), *Culture and Cultivation in Early Modern England* (Leicester: Leicester University Press, 1992), pp. 35–62.

24. R. M. Wiles, *Serial Publications in England before 1750* (Cambridge: Cambridge University Press, 1957); J. Brewer, 'The Commercialization of Politics', in N. McKendrick, J. Brewer and J. H. Plumb (eds). *Birth of a Consumer Society* (London: Europa, 1982), pp. 197–262; M. Crump and M. Harris (eds), *Searching the Eighteenth Century* (London: British Library, 1984); J. Feather, 'British Publishing in the Eighteenth Century', *The Library*, 6th series, VIII (1986), pp. 32–46; C. J. Mitchell, 'Provincial Printing in Eighteenth-Century Britain', *Publishing History*, XXI (1987), pp. 5–24; Raven, *Judging New Wealth*. For the early nineteenth century see L. James, *Print and the People 1819–51* (London: Allen Lane, 1976).

25. For alehouses see P. Clark, *The English Alehouse* (London: Longman, 1983) and for libraries P. Kaufman, *Libraries and their Users* (London: Library Association, 1969); D. P. Varma, *The Evergreen Tree of Diabolical Knowledge* (Washington, DC: Consortium Press, 1972).

26. See above, nn. 10–13, together with A. L. Lloyd, *Folk Song in England* (London: Lawrence & Wishart, 1967); D. Buchan, *The Ballad and the Folk* (London: Routledge & Kegan Paul, 1972); D. Harker, *Fakesong* (Milton Keynes: Open University Press, 1985); A. Hawkins and C. I. Dyck, 'The Time's Alteration : Popular Ballads, Revolutionary Radicalism and William Cobett', *History Workshop Journal*, XXIII (1988), pp. 20–38. For a valuable discussion of these matters see D. R. Woolf, 'The "Common Voice": History, Folklore and Oral Tradition in Early Modern England', *Past and Present*, CXX (1988), pp. 26–52.

27. K. Shevelow, *Women and Print Culture: The Construction of Femininity in the Early Periodicals* (London: Routledge, 1989); P. H. Michaelson, 'Women in the Reading Circle', *Eighteenth-Century Life*, IV (1990), pp. 59–69.

28. R. K. Webb, *The British Working-Class Reader 1790–1848: Literacy and Social Tension* (London: George Allen & Unwin, 1955); R. D. Altick, *The*

English Common Reader: A Social History of the Mass Reading Public 1800–1900 (Chicago: University of Chicago Press, 1957); P. Saenger, 'Silent Reading: Its Impact on Late Medieval Script and Society ', *Viator*, XIII (1982), pp. 367–414; D. Vincent, 'Reading in the Working-Class Home', in J. Walton and J. Walvin (eds), *Leisure in Britain 1780–1939* (Manchester: Manchester University Press, 1983), pp. 207–26; R. Chartier, *The Cultural Uses of Print in Early Modern France* (Princeton: Princeton University Press, 1987); Chartier (ed.), *The Culture of Print* (Cambridge: Polity Press, 1989); J. Rose, 'Re-Reading the English Common Reader: A Preface to the History of Audiences', *Journal of the History of Ideas*, LIII (1992), pp. 47–70.

29. Compare, for example, the brief accounts of radical thought provided by F. D. Dow, *Radicalism in the English Revolution 1640–1660* (Oxford: Blackwell, 1985) and H. T. Dickinson, *British Radicalism and French Revolution 1789–1815* (Oxford: Blackwell, 1985). Hill, *English Bible*, explores the radical potential of the Bible for the earlier period. The issue of canonisation will be dealt with in J. Brewer and A. Bermingham (eds), *Word, Image and Object: Culture and Consumption in the Seventeenth and Eighteenth Centuries* (London: Routledge, forthcoming).

30. See, for example, T. A. Birrell, 'Reading as Pastime: The Place of Light Literature in Some Gentlemen's Libraries of the Seventeenth Century', in R. Myers and M. Harris (eds), *Property of a Gentleman* (Winchester: St Paul's Bibliographies, 1991), pp. 113–31.

31. N. Hans, *New Trend in Education in the Eighteenth Century* (London: Routledge & Kegan Paul, 1951); P. McCann (ed.), *Popular Education and Socialisation in the Nineteenth Century* (London: Methuen, 1977); J. H. Plumb, 'The New World of Children in Eighteenth-Century England', in McKendrick *et al.*, *Birth*, pp. 286–315; I. Michael, *The Teaching of English from the Sixteenth Century to 1870* (Cambridge: Cambridge University Press, 1987); J. Money, 'Teaching in the Market-Place', in Brewer and Porter (eds), *Consumption*, pp. 335–80.

32. R. Chartier, 'Culture as Appropriation: Popular Cultural Uses in Early Modern France', in S. Kaplan (ed.), *Understanding Popular Culture* (Berlin: Mouton, 1984), pp. 229–53; Chartier, *Cultural History: Between Practices and Representations* (Cambridge: Polity Press, 1988); M. Fissell, 'Readers, Texts and Contexts: Vernacular Medical Works in Early Modern England', in Porter (ed.), *Popularization*, pp. 72–96.

33. See above nn. 8 and 11, together with S. Hull, *Chaste, Silent and Obedient: English Books for Women 1475–1640* (San Marino: Huntington Library, 1982); N. Armstrong and L. Tennenhouse (eds), *The Ideology of Conduct* (New York: Methuen, 1987); C. Lucas, *Writing for Women: The Example of Women as Readers in Elizabethan Romance* (Milton Keynes: Open University Press, 1989); F. Nussbaum, *The Autobiographical Subject: Gender and Ideology in Eighteenth-Century England* (Baltimore: Johns Hopkins University Press, 1990); T. Krontiris, *Oppositional Voices: Women as Writers and Translators of Literature in the English Renaissance* (London: Routledge, 1992), amongst a growing number of studies.

34. J. P. Klancher, *The Making of English Reading Audiences 1790–1832* (Madison: University of Wisconsin Press, 1987); M. McKeon, *Origins of*

the English Novel 1600–1740 (Baltimore: Johns Hopkins University Press, 1987); S. Mullaney, *The Place of the Stage: License, Plays and Power in Renaissance England* (Chicago: University of Chicago Press, 1988); M. Elsky, *Authorizing Words: Speech, Writing and Print in the English Renaissance* (Ithaca: Cornell Univesity Press, 1989); J. Hunter, *Before Novels: The Cultural Contexts of Eighteenth-Century Fiction* (New York: W. W. Norton, 1990); S. Achinstein, 'Audiences and Authors: Ballads and the Making of English Renaissance Literary Culture', *Journal of Medieval and Renaissance Studies*, XXII (1992), pp. 311–26.

35. A. Aspinall, *Politics and the Press c. 1780–1850* (London: Home & Van Thal, 1949); F. S. Siebert, *Freedom of the Press in England 1476–1776* (Urbana: University of Illionois Press, 1952); C. Ginzburg, 'High and Low: The Theme of Forbidden Knowledge in the Sixteenth and Seventeenth Centuries', *Past and Present*, LXXIII (1970), pp. 28–41; G. Boyce, J. Curran and P. Wingate (eds), *Newspaper History from the Seventeenth Century to the Present Day* (London: Constable, 1978); A. Patterson, *Censorship and Interpretation* (Madison: University of Wisconsin Press, 1984); C. Hill, *Collected Essays*, 3 vols (Brighton: Harvester Press, 1985–6), espcially 'Censorship and English Literature' (I, pp. 32–71); Hill, *A Nation of Change and Novelty* (London: Routledge, 1990), especially Chs 3, 10–11; R. Cust, 'News and Politics in Early Seventeenth-Century England', *Past and Present*, CXII (1986), pp. 60–90; S. Lambert, 'Richard Montagu, Arminianism and Censorship', *Past and Present*, CXXIV (1989), pp. 36–60; T. Cogswell, 'Politics of Propaganda: Charles I and the People in the 1620s', *Journal of British Studies*, XXIX (1990), pp. 187–215; L. Schwoerer, 'Liberty of the Press and Public Opinion 1660–1695', in J. R. Jones (ed), *Liberty Secured: Britain before and after 1688* (Stanford: Stanford University Press, 1992), pp. 199–230; G. C. Gibbs, 'Press and Public Opinion: Prospective', in ibid., pp. 231–64.

36. See above n. 19, together with C. Webster, *The Great Instauration: Science, Medicine and Reform 1626–60* (London: Gerald Duckworth, 1975), and J. Morgan, *Godly Learning: Puritan Attitudes towards Reason, Learning and Education 1540–1640* (Cambridge: Cambridge University Press, 1986).

37. J. Brewer, *Party Ideology and Popular Politics at the Accession of George III* (Cambridge: Cambridge University Press, 1976); G. H. Jenkins, *Literature, Religion and Society in Wales 1660–1730* (Cardiff: University of Wales Press, 1978); D. M. Valenze, 'Prophecy and Popular Literature in Eighteenth-Century England', *Journal of Ecclesiastical History*, XXIX (1978), pp. 75–92; J. King, *English Reformation Literature* (Princeton: Princeton University Press, 1982); S. Pedersen, 'Hannah More meets Simple Simon: Tracts, Chapbooks and Popular Culture in Late Eighteenth-Century England', *Journal of British Studies*, XXV (1986), pp. 84–113; L. Colley, 'Whose Nation? Class and National Consciousness in Britain, 1760–1820', *Past and Present*, CXIII (1986), pp. 97–117; L. Bertelsen, *The Nonsense Club: Literature and Popular Culture 1749–64* (Oxford: Clarendon Press, 1986); L. B. Fallen, *Turned to Account : Forms and Functions of Criminal Biography in Late Seventeenth-*

and Early Eighteenth-Century England (Cambridge: Cambridge University Press, 1987); Collinson, *Birthpangs*; L. Potter, *Secret Rites and Secret Writing: Royalist Literature 1641–60* (Cambridge: Cambridge University Press, 1989); P. Monod, *Jacobitism and English People* (Cambridge: Cambridge University Press, 1989); P. Curry, *Prophecy and Power: Astrology in Early Modern England* (Cambridge: Polity Press, 1989); J. Holstun (ed.), *Pamphlet Wars: Prose in the English Revolution*, special edition of *Prose Studies,* XIV (Dec. 1991); Watt, *Cheap Print*; J. A. Mendelsohn, 'Alchemy and Politics in England 1649–1660', *Past and Present*, CXXXV (1992), pp. 30–78.

38. R. Williams, *Culture and Society, 1780–1950* (London: Chatto & Windus, 1958); Williams, *The Long Revolution* (London: Chatto & Windus, 1961); Williams, *Key Words* (Oxford: Oxford University Press, 1976); P. Rogers, *Grub Street* (London: Methuen, 1972); Rogers, *Literature and Popular Culture in Eighteenth-Century England* (Brighton: Harvester Press, 1985); K. MacDermott, 'Literature and the Grub Street Myth', in P. Humm, P. Stigant and P. Widdowson (eds), *Popular Fictions* (London: Methuen, 1986), pp. 16–28; Shiach, *Discourse*; I. Dyck, *William Cobbett and Rural Popular Culture* (Cambridge: Cambridge University Press, 1992); *Rural History*, IV (1993), No. 1.

39. M. J. Cullen, *The Statistical Movement in Early Victorian Britain* (Brighton: Harvester Press, 1975); P. Buck, 'Seventeenth-Century Polictical Arithmetic', *Isis*, LXVIII (1977), pp. 67–84; Buck, 'People who Counted: Political Arithmetic in the Eighteenth Century', ibid., LXXIII (1982), pp. 28–45; K. V. Thomas, 'Numeracy in Early Modern England', *Transactions of The Royal Historical Society*, 5th series, XXVII (1987), pp. 103–32.

40. Cressy, *Literacy*; A. Fletcher, *The Outbreak of the English Civil War* (London: Edward Arnold, 1981); P. Langford, *Public Life and the Propertiec Englishman* (Oxford: Clarendon Press, 1991), pp. 102–14.

41. L. Stone, *The Road to Divorce* (Oxford: Oxford University Press, 1990), pp. 121–8, summarises the issues and debates.

5. FROM REFORMATION TO TOLERATION *Martin Ingram*

1. Peter Burke, *Popular Culture in Early Modern Europe* (London: Temple Smith, 1978); Roger Chartier, 'Culture as Appropriation: Popular Cultural Uses in Early Modern France', in Steven L. Kaplan (ed.), *Understanding Popular Culture: Europe from the Middle Ages to the Nineteenth Century* (Berlin: Mouton, 1984), pp. 229–53. See also Bob Scribner, 'Is a History of Popular Culture Possible?', *History of European Ideas*, X (1989), pp. 175–91.

2. Natalie Zemon Davis, 'From "Popular Religion" to Religious Cultures', in Steven Ozment (ed.), *Reformation Europe: A Guide to Research* (St Louis: Center for Reformation Research, 1982), p. 322; Keith Thomas, *Religion and the Decline of Magic: Studies in Popular Beliefs in*

Sixteenth- and Seventeenth-Century England (London: Weidenfeld & Nicolson, 1971); Bob Bushaway, *By Rite: Custom, Ceremony and Community in England, 1700–1880* (London: Junction Books, 1982).

3. Donald A. Spaeth, 'Common Prayer? Popular Observance of the Anglican Liturgy in Restoration Wiltshire', in S. J. Wright (ed.), *Parish, Church and People: Local Studies in Lay Religion, 1350–1750* (London: Hutchinson, 1988), pp. 125–51.

4. Paradoxically the best recent introduction to these themes is a work that attempts to chart the erosion of religious culture: C. John Sommerville, *The Secularization of Early Modern England: From Religious Culture to Religious Faith* (Oxford: Oxford University Press, 1992).

5. Eamon Duffy, *The Stripping of the Altars: Traditional Religion in England, c.1400–c.1580* (New Haven: Yale University Press, 1992), and for an excellent brief survey, Imogen Luxton, 'The Reformation and Popular Culture', in Felicity Heal and Rosemary O'Day (eds), *Church and Society in England: Henry VIII to James I* (London: Macmillan, 1977), pp. 57–77.

6. Margaret Aston, *England's Iconoclasts*, vol. I: *Laws against Images* (Oxford: Clarendon Press, 1988); Patrick Collinson, *The Birthpangs of Protestant England: Religious and Cultural Change in the Sixteenth and Seventeenth Centuries* (London: Macmillan, 1988), pp. 115–21; but cf. Tessa Watt, *Cheap Print and Popular Piety, 1550–1640* (Cambridge: Cambridge University Press, 1991), Ch. 4.

7. Christopher Hill, *The English Bible and the Seventeenth-Century Revolution* (Harmondsworth: Allen Lane, 1993) (though this exaggerates the importance of the Geneva Bible and, more generally, underestimates conservative implications of Bible reading). For differing interpretations of literacy statistics, see David Cressy, *Literacy and the Social Order: Reading and Writing in Tudor and Stuart England* (Cambridge: Cambridge University Press, 1980); Margaret Spufford, *Small Books and Pleasant Histories: Popular Fiction and its Readership in Seventeenth-Century England* (London: Methuen, 1981), Ch. 2; Keith Thomas, 'The Meaning of Literacy in Early Modern England', in Gerd Baumann (ed.), *The Written Word: Literacy in Transition* (Oxford: Clarendon Press, 1986), pp. 101–3.

8. On the proliferation of religious literature, see C. John Sommerville, *Popular Religion in Restoration England* (Gainesville: University of Florida Monographs, Social Sciences, No. 59, 1977); Eamon Duffy, 'The Godly and the Multitude in Stuart England', *The Seventeenth Century*, I (1986), pp. 31–55; Ian Green, '"For Children in Yeeres and Children in Understanding": The Emergence of the English Catechism under Elizabeth and the Early Stuarts', *Journal of Ecclesiastical History*, XXXVII (1986), pp. 397–425; Watt, *Cheap Print*.

9. John Kenyon, *The Popish Plot* (London: Heinemann, 1972); Tim Harris, *London Crowds in the Reign of Charles II: Propaganda and Politics from the Restoration until the Exclusion Crisis* (Cambridge: Cambridge University Press, 1987).

10. Carol Z. Wiener, 'The Beleaguered Isle: A Study of Elizabethan and Early Jacobean Anti-Catholicism', *Past and Present*, LI (May 1971), pp. 27–

62; Robin Clifton, 'Fear of Popery', in Conrad Russell (ed.), *The Origins of the English Civil War* (London: Macmillan, 1973), pp. 144–67.

11. For a fuller discussion of these complex issues, see Collinson, *Birthpangs*, Ch. 1.

12. The background is explored in Ole Peter Grell, Jonathan I. Israel and Nicholas Tyacke (eds), *From Persecution to Toleration: The Glorious Revolution and Religon in England* (Oxford: Clarendon Press, 1991).

13. Sommerville, *Secularization of Early Modern England*, p. 1 and passim.

14. Green, '"For Children in Yeeres and Children in Understanding"', passim; Martin Ingram, *Church Courts, Sex and Marriage in England, 1570–1640* (Cambridge: Cambridge University Press, 1987), esp. Ch. 3.

15. Patricia Crawford, *Women and Religion in England, 1500–1720* (London: Routledge, 1993).

16. For a survey of work on the Catholic community see Alan Dures, *English Catholicism, 1558–1642* (London: Longman, 1983). On pre-Civil War sectarianism (offering a somewhat different view from that presented here), see R. J. Acheson, *Radical Puritans in England, 1550–1660* (London: Longman, 1990), Chs 1–4.

17. Nicholas Tyacke, 'Popular Puritan Mentality in Late Elizabethan England,' in Peter Clark, Alan G. R. Smith and Nicholas Tyacke (eds), *The English Commonwealth, 1547–1640* (New York: Barnes & Noble, 1979), pp. 77–92.

18. *Historical Manuscripts Commission: Report on Manuscripts in Various Collections*, vol. I (London, 1901), pp. 71–2; on the background to this case, see Ingram, *Church Courts, Sex and Marriage*, pp. 110–11.

19. Paul Seaver, *Wallington's World: A Puritan Artisan in Seventeenth-Century London* (London: Methuen, 1985), passim.

20. Wiltshire R[ecord] O[ffice, Trowbridge], D5/19/39, fol. 29.

21. Patrick Collinson, *The Religion of Protestants: The Church in English Society, 1559–1625* (Oxford: Clarendon Press, 1982), Ch. 5; Margaret Spufford, 'Puritanism and Social Control?', in Anthony Fletcher and John Stevenson (eds), *Order and Disorder in Early Modern England* (Cambridge: Cambridge University Press, 1985), pp. 41–57.

22. David Underdown, *Revel, Riot and Rebellion: Popular Politics and Culture in England, 1603–1660*. (Oxford: Clarendon Press, 1985), esp. Chs 1–5. For criticisms of the thesis and Underdown's response, see John Morrill, 'The Ecology of Allegiance in the English Revolution', *Journal of British Studies*, XXVI (1987), pp. 451–67, and David Underdown, 'A Reply to John Morrill', ibid, pp. 468–79; and see also A. J. Fletcher, 'New Light on Religion and the English Civil War', *Journal of Ecclesiastical History*, XXXVIII (1987), pp. 99–103.

23. Keith Wrightson and David Levine, *Poverty and Piety in an English Village: Terling, 1525–1700* (London: Academic Press, 1979); Martin Ingram, 'Religion, Communities and Moral Discipline in Late Sixteenth- and Early Seventeenth-Century England: Case Studies', in Kaspar von Greyerz (ed.), *Religion and Society in Early Modern Europe, 1500–1800* (London: George Allen & Unwin, 1984), pp. 177–93, and the references there cited; David Underdown, *Fire from Heaven: The Life of an English Town in the Seventeenth Century* (London: HarperCollins, 1992).

24. These themes are well illustrated in Collinson, *Religion of Protestants*, Chs 4–5; Underdown, *Fire from Heaven*, Chs 4–5.

25. Thomas, *Religion and the Decline of Magic*, Ch. 6.

26. B. Howard Cunnington, *Records of the County of Wilts: Being Extracts from the Quarter Sessions Great Rolls of the Seventeenth Century* (Devizes: George Simpson, 1932), p. 231; quoted in Thomas, *Religion and the Decline of Magic*, p. 171; Christopher Hill, *The World Turned Upside Down: Radical Ideas during the English Revolution* (London: Temple Smith, 1972), p. 181; J. F. McGregor and B. Reay (eds), *Radical Religion in the English Revolution* (Oxford: Oxford University Press, 1984), pp. 133–4. On the background, see Hill, *World Turned Upside Down*, p. 180.

27. Public Record Office, London, STAC 8/59/11, m.2; on Blagden's career, see Ingram, *Church Courts, Sex and Marriage*, pp. 118, 252–2, 255, 316, 361.

28. Michael Hunter, 'The Problem of "Atheism" in Early Modern England', *Transactions of the Royal Historical Society*, 5th series, xxxv (1985), pp. 135–57 (p. 148 for the quotation from Gibbens); cf. Thomas, *Religion and the Decline of Magic*, pp. 37, 161.

29. E.g. Cunnington, *Records of the County of Wilts*, p. 247.

30. Alan Macfarlane, *Witchcraft in Tudor and Stuart England: A Regional and Comparative Study* (London: Routledge & Kegan Paul, 1970), Ch. 3; J. A. Sharpe, *Crime in Early Modern England, 1550–1750* (London: Longman, 1984), pp. 54–6. Dr Sharpe is currently engaged on a major re-examination of witchcraft in early modern England.

31. Michael MacDonald, *Mystical Bedlam: Madness, Anxiety, and Healing in Seventeenth Century England* (Cambridge: Cambridge University Press, 1981), p. 107; Ingram, *Church Courts, Sex and Marriage*, pp. 113–14; Underdown, *Fire from Heaven*, pp. 78–9, 165. For examples of pricking and swimming, see Wiltshire RO, A1/110/1664E, no. 143; Cunnington, *Records of the County of Wilts*, pp. 279–80.

32. Wiltshire RO, D1/42/9, fol. 22. On the activities of cunning folk, see Thomas, *Religion and the Decline of Magic*, Ch. 8; Macfarlane, *Witchcraft in Tudor and Stuart England*, Ch. 8.

33. Thomas, *Religion and the Decline of Magic*, Chs 10–12; Patrick Curry, *Prophecy and Power: Astrology in Early Modern England* (Cambridge: Polity Press, 1989).

34. Thomas, *Religion and the Decline of Magic*, p. 5 and passim; John Aubrey, *Three Prose Works: Miscellanies, Remaines of Gentilisme and Judaisme, Observations*, ed. John Buchanan Brown (Fontwell: Centaur Press, 1972).

35. *The Workes of that Learned Minister of Gods Holy Word, Mr William Pemble* (3rd edn, London, 1635), pp. 558–9; cf. Giles Firmin, *The Real Christian, or a Treatise of Effectual Calling* (London, 1670), p. 162 (citing Pemble and referring to the story as 'very famous'). For modern citations, see Thomas, *Religion and the Decline of Magic*, pp. 163–4; Barry Reay, 'Popular Religion', in Barry Reay (ed.), *Popular Culture in Seventeenth-Century England* (London: Croom Helm, 1985), p. 98.

36. Christopher Haigh, 'The Church of England, the Catholics and the People', in Christopher Haigh (ed.) *The Reign of Elizabeth I* (Basingstoke:

Macmillan, 1984), pp. 212–13; cf. Thomas, *Religion and the Decline of Magic*, pp. 163–6. But see Duffy, 'Godly and the Multitude', pp. 31–40; Donald Arragon Spaeth, 'Parsons and Parishioners: Lay–Clerical Conflict and Popular Piety in Wiltshire Villages, 1660–1740', unpublished Ph.D. thesis, Brown University (1985), pp. 1–6.

37. Keith Wrightson and David Levine, 'Death in Whickham', in John Walter and Roger Schofield (eds), *Famine, Disease and the Social Order in Early Modern Society* (Cambridge: Cambridge University Press, 1989), pp. 161–2; Luxton, 'Reformation and Popular Culture', pp. 71–2. For related arguments see Peter Lake, 'Deeds against Nature: Cheap Print, Protestantism and Murder in Early Seventeenth Century England', in Kevin Sharpe and Peter Lake (eds), *Culture and Politics in Early Stuart England* (Basingstoke: Macmillan, 1994), pp. 257–83.

38. Watts, *Cheap Print*, p. 327 and passim; Duffy, 'Godly and the Multitude', pp. 41–8.

39. Cunington, *Records of the County of Wilts*, p. 14; Wiltshire RO, D1/43/6, fol. 15; Judith Maltby, '"By this Book": Parishioners, the Prayer Book and the Established Church', in Kenneth Fincham (ed.), *The Early Stuart Church, 1603–1642* (Basingstoke: Macmillan, 1993), pp. 118–28.

40. Ralph Houlbrooke (ed.), *Death, Ritual and Bereavement* (London: Routledge, 1989), Chs 1–4; Clare Gittings, *Death, Burial and the Individual in Early Modern England* (London: Croom Helm, 1984); Ingram, *Church Courts, Sex and Marriage*, p. 119.

41. Ingram, *Church Courts, Sex and Marriage*, pp. 98–9.

42. Oxfordshire RO, MS Oxford Archdeaconry Papers, Oxon. c. 12, fol. 279. The literature on this subject is now extensive; for some recent discussions, see Underdown, *Revel, Riot and Rebellion*, passim; Ingram, *Church Courts, Sex and Marriage*, pp. 100–6; Kenneth L. Parker, *The English Sabbath: A Study of Doctrine and Discipline from the Reformation to the Civil War* (Cambridge: Cambridge University Press, 1988), passim.

43. Ingram, *Church Courts, Sex and Marriage*, pp. 106–8; Jeremy Boulton, 'The Limits of Formal Religion: The Administration of Holy Communion in Late Elizabethan and Early Stuart London', *London Journal*, x (1984), pp. 135–54; Ian Archer, *The Pursuit of Stability: Social Relations in Elizabethan London* (Cambridge: Cambridge University Press, 1991), pp. 90–1; Nick Alldridge, 'Loyalty and Identity in Chester Parishes, 1540–1640', in Wright (ed.), *Parish, Church and People*, pp. 97–9; E. P. Knubley, 'Steeple Ashton Churchwardens' Accounts', *Wiltshire Notes and Queries*, VI (1908–10), p. 366.

44. Ingram, *Church Courts, Sex and Marriage*, p. 122; Maltby, '"By this Book"', passim. I am indebted to Dr Ian Green's unpublished researches for information on the metrical psalms; cf. Collinson, *Religion of Protestants*, pp. 236–9.

45. Reay, 'Popular Religion', p. 92; David Cressy, *Bonfires and Bells: National Memory and the Protestant Calendar in Elizabethan and Stuart England* (London: Weidenfeld & Nicolson, 1989), passim; Martin Ingram, 'Ridings, Rough Music and Mocking Rhymes in Early Modern England', in Reay (ed.), *Popular Culture*, pp. 181–2.

46. Underdown, *Revel, Riot and Rebellion*, pp. 30–3; Ingram, *Church Courts, Sex and Marriage*, pp. 111–12; Susan Dwyer Amussen, *An Ordered Society: Gender and Class in Early Modern England* (Oxford: Basil Blackwell, 1988), pp. 137–44; Alldridge, 'Loyalty and Identity', pp. 94–7. For wider context see Margaret Aston, 'Segregation in Church', in W. J. Sheils and Diana Wood (ed), *Women in the Church*, Studies in Church History, XXVII (Oxford, 1990), pp. 237–94.

47. Maltby, '"By this Book"', passim; Alldridge, 'Loyalty and Identity', passim; Jonathan Barry, 'The Parish in Civic Life: Bristol and its Churches, 1640–1750', in Wright (ed.), *Parish, Church and People*, pp. 152–78; Archer, *Pursuit of Stability*, pp. 82–92. See also the references cited in n. 45.

48. Thomas, *Religion and the Decline of Magic*, pp. 161–2; but cf. Ingram, *Church Courts, Sex and Marriage*, pp. 108–9.

49. West Sussex RO, Chichester Diocesan Records, Ep.I/17/15, fol. 107; Oxfordshire RO, MS Oxford Diocesan Papers d. 4, fol. 170.

50. Ingram, *Church Courts, Sex and Marriage*, pp. 109–11, 116, 119; Underdown, *Revel, Riot and Rebellion*, pp. 80–2; Wrightson and Levine, 'Death in Whickham', pp. 163–5.

51. Arthur Hussey, 'Visitations of the Archdeacon of Canterbury', *Archaeologia Cantiana*, XXVI (1904), p. 32; Buckinghamshire RO, MS Oxford Archdeaconry Papers, Bucks, c. 290, fol. 86; Ingram, *Church Courts, Sex and Marriage*, p. 106.

52. Oxfordshire RO, MS Oxford Archdeaconry Papers, Oxon, c. 12, fol. 35; Ingram, *Church Courts, Sex and Marriage*, pp. 89–90, 121.

53. Archer, *Pursuit of Stability*, p. 90; Ingram, *Church Courts, Sex and Marriage*, p. 121; Buckinghamshire RO, MS Oxford Archdeaconry Papers, Bucks, c. 290, fol. 77^v.

54. Wiltshire RO, D3/4/1, fols 222^v–3.

55. Patrick Collinson, 'The Cohabitation of the Faithful with the Unfaithful', in Grell, Israel and Tyacke (eds), *From Persecution to Toleration*, p. 72; Wiltshire RO, D1/42/30, fol. 124; *The Archdeacon's Court: Liber Actorum, 1584*, ed. E. R. Brinkworth (Oxford: Oxfordshire Record Society, XXIII–XXIV, 1941–2), II, p. xviii. Cf. for other parts of Europe and across the Atlantic, John Bossy, 'The Counter-Reformation and the People of Catholic Europe', *Past and Present*, XLVII (May 1970), pp. 55–6; David Warren Sabean, *Power in the Blood: Popular Culture and Village Discourse in Early Modern Germany* (Cambridge: Cambridge University Press, 1984), Ch. 1; David Hall, *Worlds of Wonder, Days of Judgment: Popular Religious Belief in Early New England* (New York: Alfred A. Knopf, 1989), pp. 156–62.

56. Michael Watts, *The Dissenters: From the Reformation to the French Revolution* (Oxford: Oxford University Press, 1978), Chs 2–3; McGregor and Reay (eds), *Radical Religion*; John Morrill, 'The Church in England, 1642–9', in John Morrill (ed.), *Reactions to the English Civil War, 1642–1649* (Basingstoke: Macmillan, 1982), pp. 89–114.

57. Watts, *Dissenters*, pp. 491–2. For a selection of local evidence, see *Bishop Fell and Nonconformity: Visitation Documents from the Oxford Diocese, 1682–83*, ed. Mary Clapinson (Oxford: Oxfordshire Record Society, LII,

1980), pp. xviii–xxi; Harris, *London Crowds*, pp. 62–73; Jonathan Barry, 'The Politics of Religion in Restoration Bristol', in Tim Harris, Paul Seaward and Mark Goldie (eds), *The Politics of Religion in Restoration England* (Oxford: Basil Blackwell, 1990), pp. 163–5.

58. William Stevenson, 'The Economic and Social Status of Protestant Sectarians in Huntingdonshire, Cambridgeshire and Bedfordshire (1650–1725)', unpublished Ph.D. thesis, Cambridge University (1990), Ch. 8: W. J. Sheils, 'Oliver Heywood and his Congregation', in W. J. Sheils and Diana Wood (eds), *Voluntary Religion*, Studies in Church History, XXIII (Oxford: Basil Blackwell, 1986), pp. 261–79; John D. Ramsbottom, 'Presbyterians and "Partial Conformity" in the Restoration Church of England', *Journal of Ecclesiastical History*, XLIII (1992), pp. 249–70; Barry Reay, *The Quakers and the English Revolution* (London: Temple Smith, 1985), passim; Richard Bauman, *Let Your Words Be Few: Symbolism of Speaking and Silence among the Seventeenth-Century Quakers* (Cambridge: Cambridge University Press, 1983).

59. Spaeth, 'Parsons and Parishioners', p. 187 and Ch. 6 passim; Harris, *London Crowds*, pp. 72–3; Wiltshire RO, D1/41/3/21, no. 21.

60. Morrill, 'Church in England'; Christopher Durston, *The Family in the English Revolution* (Oxford: Basil Blackwell, 1989), Ch. 4.

61. Wiltshire RO, D1/54/1/3, no. 27; *The Whole Works ... of Sir William Dawes, B[a]r[one]t*, 3 vols (London, 1732–3), III, pp. 263–7; Spaeth, 'Common Prayer?', pp. 132–9.

62. Spaeth, 'Common Prayer?' p. 144 and passim; Wiltshire RO, D1/41/3/23, no. 62.

63. These themes are well illustrated in Spaeth, 'Parsons and Parishioners', passim; see also Duffy, 'Godly and the Multitude', pp. 41–8.

64. *Bishop Fell and Nonconformity*, ed. Clapinson, pp. 22, 23.

65. G. V. Bennett, 'Conflict in the Church', in Geoffrey Holmes (ed.), *Britain after the Glorious Revolution, 1689–1714* (London: Macmillan, 1969), p. 163.

66. *The Rector's Book of Clayworth, Notts.*, ed. H. Gill and E. L. Guilford (Nottingham, 1910), passim.

6. THE PEOPLE'S HEALTH IN GEORGIAN ENGLAND *Roy Porter*

1. Patrick Curry, *Prophecy and Power: Astrology in Early Modern England* (Cambridge: Polity Press, 1989). More broadly see Peter Burke, *Popular Culture in Early Modern Europe* (London: Temple Smith, 1978); E. P. Thompson, *Customs in Common* (London: Merlin, 1991).

2. L. Guthrie, 'The Lady Sedley's Receipt Book, 1686, and other Seventeenth-Century Receipt Books', *Proceedings of the Royal Society of Medicine*, VI (1913), pp. 150–70; M. Chamberlain, *Old Wives' Tales: Their History, Remedies and Spells* (London: Virago, 1981), discusses remedy books.

3. For pluralism, see Dorothy Porter and Roy Porter, *Patient's Progress: Doctors and Doctoring in Eighteenth-Century England* (Cambridge:

Polity Press, 1989), esp. Chs 1 and 2. For the multiplicity of healing see
Mary E. Fissell, *Patients, Power and the Poor in Eighteenth-Century Bristol*
(Cambridge: Cambridge University Press, 1991).

4. For popular medical lore, see M. P. Tilley (ed.), *Dictionary of Proverbs
in England* (Ann Arbor: University of Michigan Press, 1950);
J. Obelkevitch, 'Proverbs and Social History', in P. Burke and R. Porter
(eds), *The Social History of Language* (Cambridge: Cambridge University
Press, 1987), pp. 43–72; Roy Porter, ' "Expressing Yourself Ill": The Lan-
guage of Sickness in Georgian England', in P. Burke and R. Porter (eds),
Language, Self and Society: The Social History of Language (Cambridge: Polity
Press Press, 1992), pp. 276–99.

5. See L. M. Beier, *Sufferers and Healers: The Experience of Illness in Seven-
teenth-Century England* (London: Routledge & Kegan Paul, 1987); J. Lane,
"The Doctor Scolds Me": The Diaries and Correspondence of Patients in
Eighteenth-Century England', in R. Porter (ed.), *Patients and Practitioners:
Lay Perceptions of Medicine in Pre-Industrial Society* (Cambridge: Cambridge
University Press, 1985), pp. 207–47; Andrew Wear, 'Puritan Perceptions of
Illness in Seventeenth-Century England', in ibid., pp. 55–99; Wear, 'Inter-
faces: Perceptions of Health and Illness in Early Modern England', in
R. Porter and A. Wear (eds), *Problems and Methods in the History of Medicine*
(London: Croom Helm, 1988), pp. 230–55.

6. J. R. Smith, *The Speckled Monster: Smallpox in England 1670–1970, with
Particular Reference to Essex* (Chelmsford: Essex Record Office, 1987).

7. Quoted from William Withering's *Account of the Foxglove* in
Chamberlain, *Old Wives' Tales*, p. 175. Cf. J. K. Aronson, *An Account of the
Foxglove and its Medicinal Uses, 1785–1985* (London: Oxford University
Press, 1985).

8. E. G. Thomas, 'The Old Poor Law and Medicine', *Medical History*, XXIV
(1980), pp. 1–19; J. Lane, 'The Provincial Practitioner and his Services to
the Poor 1750–1800', *Society for the Social History of Medicine Bulletin*, XXVIII
(1981), pp. 10–14; Thomas, 'A Provincial Surgeon and his Obstetric Practice: Thomas W. Jones of Henley-in-Arden, 1764–1846', *Medical History*,
XXXI (1987), pp. 333–48.

9. For medicalisation, see J.-P. Goubert, *La Médicalisation de la Société
Française 1770–1830* (Waterloo, Ontario: Historical Reflections
Press, 1982).

10. See, e.g., A. Maclaren, *Reproductive Rituals: The Perception of Fertility in England from the 16th Century to the 19th Century* (London: Methuen, 1984); J. Donnison, *Midwives and Medical Men: A History of
Interprofessional Rivalries and Women's Rights* (London: Heinemann Educational, 1977); Roy Porter, 'A Touch of Danger: The Man-Midwife as
Sexual Predator', in G. S. Rousseau and R. Porter (eds), *Sexual Under-
worlds of the Enlightenment* (Manchester: Manchester University Press,
1988), pp. 206–32. For female healers, see Roy Porter, 'Female Quacks
in the Consumer Society', *History of Nursing Journal*, III (1990), pp. 1–25;
A. L. Wyman, 'The Surgeoness: The Female Practitioner of Surgery,
1400–1800', *Medical History*, XXVII (1984), pp. 22–41; P. Crawford,
'Printed Advertisements for Women Medical Practitioners in London,

1670–1710', *Society for the Social History of Medicine Bulletin*, XXXV (1984), pp. 66–70.

11. V. M. Macdonald (ed.), *The Letters of Eliza Pierce (Eliza Taylor) 1751–1775* (London: F. Etchells & H. Macdonald, 1927), p. 89.

12. On the medical marketplace, see G. Holmes, *Augustan England: Professions, State and Society, 1680–1730* (London: George Allen & Unwin, 1982); I. S. L. Loudon, 'The Nature of Provincial Medical Practice in Eighteenth-Century England', *Medical History*, XXIX (1985), pp. 1–32; Loudon, *Medical Care and The General Practitioner 1750–1850* (Oxford: Clarendon Press, 1986); J. Lane, 'The Medical Practitioners of Provincial England in 1783', *Medical History*, XXVIII (1984), pp. 353–71; Juanita G. L. Burnby, *A Study of the English Apothecary from 1660 to 1760, Medical History*, Supplement No. 3 (London: Wellcome Institute for the History of Medicine, 1983).

13. T. Beddoes, *A Letter to the Right Honourable Sir Joseph Banks ... on the Causes and Removal of the Prevailing Discontents, Imperfections, and Abuses, in Medicine* (London: Richard Phillips, 1808), p. 100. On patient power, see N. Jewson 'Medical Knowledge and the Patronage System in Eighteenth-Century England', *Sociology*, VIII (1974), pp. 369–85; Jewson, 'The Disappearance of the Sick Man from Medical Cosmology, 1770–1870', *Sociology*, X (1976), pp. 225–44.

14. For medicine as trade, see W. F. Bynum and R. Porter (eds), *Medical Fringe and Medical Orthodoxy, 1750–1850* (London: Croom Helm, 1987); M. Pelling, 'Medical Practice in Early Modern England: Trade or Profession?', in W. Prest (ed.), *The Professions in Early Modern England* (London: Croom Helm, 1987), pp. 90–128.

15. See Roy Porter, 'Commerce and Disease in Eighteenth-Century England', in S. Halini (ed.), *Commerce(s) en Grande Bretagne au XVIIIe siècle* (Paris: Publications de la Sorbonne, 1990), pp. 55–73. On pharmaceuticals and their sales outlets, see Roy Porter and Dorothy Porter, 'The Rise of the English Drugs Industry: The Role of Thomas Corbyn', *Medical History*, XXXIII (1989), pp. 277–95; Hoh-cheung and L. Mui, *Shops and Shopkeeping in Eighteenth-Century England* (London: Methuen, 1987); Hilary Marland, *Medicine and Society in Wakefield and Huddersfield* (Cambridge: Cambridge University Press, 1987).

16. For advice literature see Ginnie Smith, 'Prescribing the Rules of Health: Self-Help and Advice in the Late Eighteenth-Century England', in Porter (ed.), *Patients and Practitioners*, pp. 249–82.

17. B. Capp, *Astrology and the Popular Press: English Almanacs, 1500–1800* (London: Faber & Faber, 1979).

18. V. Chancellor (ed.), *Master and Artisan in Victorian England* (London: Evelyn, Adams & MacKay, 1969), p. 95. Gutteridge is more fully discussed in Porter and Porter, *Patient's Progress*, Ch. 11. For Culpeper, see F. N. L. Poynter, 'Nicholas Culpeper and his Books', *Journal of the History of Medicine*, XVII (1962), pp. 155–67. And see more generally, David Vincent, *Literacy and Popular Culture: England 1750–1914* (Cambridge: Cambridge University Press, 1989).

19. Chancellor (ed.), *Master and Artisan*, p. 131.

20. On epidemics, see M. Dobson, 'Population, Disease and Mortality in Southeast England, 1600–1800' unpublished D. Phil. thesis, Oxford University (1982) L. Clarkson, *Death, Disease and Famine in Pre-Industrial England* (Dublin: Gill & Macmillan, 1975).

21. K. V. Thomas, *Religion and the Decline of Magic: Studies in Popular Beliefs in Sixteenth- and Seventeenth-Century England* (London: Weidenfeld & Nicolson, 1971). For the Continent see F. Loux, *Practiques et Savoirs Populaires: Le Corps dans la Société Traditionnelle* (Paris: Berger-Levrault, 1979); J. Devlin, *The Supersititious Mind: French Peasants and the Supernatural in the Nineteenth Century* (New Haven: Yale University Press, 1987).

22. J. Beresford (ed.), *The Diary of a Country Parson: The Rev. James Woodforde, 1758–1802*, 5 vols (Oxford: Oxford University Press, 1978–81), III, p. 253; R. Brookes, *The General Practice of Physick*, 2 vols (6th edn, London: T. Carnan & F. Newbery, 1771), I, p. 93.

23. The following instances of medical magic are conventional, and may be documented in such sources as Thomas, *Religion and the Decline of Magic*; J. Brand (ed.), *Observations on Popular Antiquities: Chiefly Illustrating the Origin of Our Vulgar Customs, Ceremonies and Superstitions* (London: Chatto & Windus, 1913); W. G. Black, *Folk Medicine: A Chapter in the History of Culture* (London: Folklore Society, 1883); and the pages of the journal *Folklore*.

24. For John Aubrey's medical magic, see M. Hunter, *John Aubrey and the Realm of Learning* (London: Gerald Duckworth, 1975), p. 106 and passim. It is disputable how far Aubrey believed such recipes or merely recorded them.

25. P. Linebaugh, 'The Tyburn Riot Against the Surgeons', in Douglas Hay, Peter Linebaugh, John G. Rule, E. P. Thompson and Cal Winslow (eds), *Albion's Fatal Tree* (London: Allen Lane, 1975), pp. 65–118.

26. On the herbal tradition, see Agnes Arber, *Herbals* (Cambridge: Cambridge University Press, 1938).

27. C. H. Josten (ed.), *Elias Ashmole (1617–1692): His Autobiographical and Historical Notes, His Correspondence*, 5 vols (Oxford: Clarendon Press, 1966), IV, p. 1680.

28. R. Burton, *The Anatomy of Melancholy*, ed. D. Floyd and P. Jordan-Smith (New York: Tudor, 1948; 1st edn, London: H. Cripps, 1621), p. 390.

29. For such examples, see Thomas, *Religion and the Decline of Magic*, p. 416; Brand (ed.), *Observations on Popular Antiquities*, p. 727; Michael MacDonald, 'Science, Magic and Folklore', in J. F. Andrews (ed.), *William Shakespeare: His World, His Work, His Influence*, I (New York: Charles Scribner's Sons, 1985), pp. 175–94.

30. For Clare see E. Robinson (ed.), *John Clare's Autobiographical Writings* (Oxford: Oxford University Press, 1983), p. 35.

31. For further discussion of magic and medicine more broadly, in the magazine, see Roy Porter, 'Lay Medical Knowledge in the Eighteenth Century: The Evidence of the *Gentleman's Magazine*', *Medical History*, XXIX (1985), pp. 138–68; Porter, 'Laymen, Doctors and Medical Knowledge in the Eighteenth Century: The Evidence of the *Gentleman's*

Magazine', in Porter (ed.), *Patients and Practitioners*, pp. 283–314. I have examined many manuscript recipe books from the fine collection in the Wellcome Institute for the History of Medicine, London. The same is true of household books such as Eliza Smith, *The Complete Housewife* (3rd edn, London: J. Pemberton, 1729).

32. For journals etc., see Roy Porter and Dorothy Porter, *In Sickness and in Health: The British Experience, 1650–1850* (London: Fourth Estate, 1988); Roy Porter, 'The Patient's view: Doing Medical History from Below', *Theory and Society*, XIV (1985), pp. 175–98; and the works cited above in n. 5. For the King's Evil, see M. Bloch, *The Royal Touch: Sacred Monarchy and Scrofula in England and France* (London: Routledge & Kegan Paul, 1973).

33. P. Gay, 'The Enlightenment as Medicine and as Cure', in W. H. Barber (ed.), *The Age of the Enlightenment: Studies Presented to Theodore Besterman* (Edinburgh: St Andrews University Publications, 1967), pp. 375–86; Roy Porter, 'Civilization and Disease: Medical Ideology in the Enlightenment', in J. Black and J. Gregory (eds), *Culture, Politics and Society in Britain 1660–1800* (Manchester: Manchester University Press, 1991), pp. 154–83; Porter, 'Was There a Medical Enlightenment in Eighteenth-Century England?', *British Journal for Eighteenth-Century Studies*, V (1982), pp. 46–63.

34. Thomas, *Medicine and the Decline of Magic*, p. 789.

35. Neil McKendrick, John Brewer and J. H. Plumb, *The Birth of a Consumer Society: The Commercialization of Eighteenth-Century England* (London: Europa, 1982); John Brewer and Roy Porter (eds), *Consumption and the World of Goods* (London: Routledge, 1992).

36. For nostrums, see Roy Porter, *Health for Sale: Quackery in England 1650–1850* (Manchester: Manchester University Press, 1989). For Goody Two Shoes, see C. Welsh, *A Bookseller of the Last Century: Being some Account of the Life of John Newbery, and of the Books he published, with a Notice of the later Newberys* (London: Griffith, Farran, Okeden & Welsh, 1885), p. 13.

37. See Roy Porter, 'The Language of Quackery in England, 1660–1800', in Burke and Porter (eds), *The Social History of Language*, pp. 73–103. The English Frenchified meant syphilitic.

38. See Porter, *Health for Sale*, passim; S. Billington, *A Social History of the Fool* (Brighton: Harvester Press, 1984).

39. For the rise of the G. P., see above, nn. 8 and 12.

40. Paul Slack, 'Mirrors of Health and Treasures of Poor Men: Uses of the Vernacular Medical Literature of Tudor England', in C. Webster (ed.), *Health, Medicine and Mortality in the Sixteenth Century* (Cambridge: Cambridge University Press, 1979), pp. 237–74; Andrew Wear, 'The Popularization of Medicine in Early Modern England', in Roy Porter (ed.), *The Popularization of Medicine, 1650–1850* (London: Routledge, 1992), pp. 17–41. The whole volume is relevant to the present discussion, especially Mary Fissell, 'Readers, Texts and Contexts: Vernacular Medical Works in Early Modern England', pp. 72–96. Other essays discuss the medical popularisation in France, Switzerland, Spain,

Hungary and North America, for which also see Lamar Riley Murphy, *Enter the Physician: The Transformation of Domestic Medicine, 1760–1860* (Tuscaloosa: University of Alabama Press, 1991).

41. John Wesley, *Primitive Physick: Or, an Easy and Natural Method of Curing Most Diseases* (London: T. Trye, 1747); George S. Rousseau, 'John Wesley's *Primitive Physick* (1747)', *Harvard Library Bulletin*, XVI (1968), pp. 242–56.

42. On the multifacetedness of popular culture, see J. M. Golby and A. W. Purdue, *The Civilization of the Crowd: Popular Culture in England, 1750–1900* (London: B. T. Batsford, 1984); and Roy Porter, 'Introduction', in Porter (ed.), *Popularization of Medicine*.

43. For the politics of health, see R. Cooter, 'The Power of the Body: The Early Nineteenth Century', in B. Barnes and S. Shapin (eds), *Natural Order: Historical Studies of Scientific Culture* (London: Sage Publications, 1979), pp. 73–92.

44. For Buchan, see C. Lawrence, 'William Buchan: Medicine Laid Open', *Medical History*, XIX (1975), pp. 20–35; C. Rosenberg, 'Medical Text and Medical Context: Explaining William Buchan's *Domestic Medicine*', *Bulletin of the History of Medicine*, LVII (1983), pp. 22–4.

45. W. Buchan, *Observations Concerning the Prevention and Cure of the Venereal Disease* (London: Chapman, 1796), p. iv.

46. Ibid., pp. xxii, xvii.

47. Ibid., p. xxvii.

48. W. Buchan, *Domestic Medicine, or a Treatise on the Prevention and Cure of Diseases by Regimen and Simple Medicines* (Edinburgh: Balfour, Auld & Smellie, 1769), pp. xxi–xxix.

49. For Beddoes, see D. A. Stansfield, *Thomas Beddoes M. D. 1760–1808: Chemist, Physician, Democrat* (Dordrecht: D. Reidel, 1984); Roy Porter, *Doctor of Society: Thomas Beddoes and the Sick Trade in Late Enlightenment England* (London: Routledge, 1991); especially Ch. 9, 'Instructing the People'.

50. Buchan, *Observations*, p. xxxiii.

51. Thomas Beddoes, *Hygëia: or Essays Moral and Medical, on the Causes Affecting the Personal State of our Middling and Affluent Classes*, 3 vols (Bristol: J. Mills, 1802), vol. 1, essay i, p. 54; see also 2. vi. 48. See Roy Porter, 'Reforming the Patient: Thomas Beddoes and Medical Practice', in Roger French and Andrew Wear (eds), *Medicine in the Age of Reform* (London: Routledge, 1991), pp. 9–44.

52. See A. D. Morris, *James Parkinson, his Life and Times* (Boston: Birkhauser, 1989).

53. James Parkinson, *The Villager's Friend and Physician, or a Familiar Address on the Preservation of Health and the Removal of Disease on its First Appearance, Supposed to be Delivered by a Village Apothecary, with Cursory Observations on the Treatment of Children, on Sobriety, Industry, etc. Intended for the Promotion of Domestic Happiness* (2nd edn, London: C. Whittingham, 1804), p. 66.

54. James Parkinson, *Medical Admonitions to Families Respecting the Preservation of Health and the Treatment of the Sick, also a Table of Symptoms Serving to Point out the Degree of Danger, and to Distinguish one Disease from*

Another (4th edn. London: C. Whittingham for H. D. Symonds, 1801), p. 5.

55. James Parkinson, *The Way to Health, Extracted from the Villager's Friend and Physician* (London: C. Whittingham for H. D. Symmonds, 1802), p. 63.

56. E. Robinson (ed.), *John Clare's Autobiographical Writings* (Oxford: Oxford University Press, 1983), p. 35.

57. E. J. Climenson (ed.), *Elizabeth Montagu, the Queen of the Blue Stockings: Her Correspondence from 1720–1761* (London: John Murray, 1906), I, p. 33. Drownings were common. Surprisingly few people could swim. See N. Orme, *Early British Swimming, 55BC–AD1719* (Exeter: University of Exeter, 1983).

58. H. W. Robinson and W. Adams (eds), *The Diary of Robert Hooke (1672–1680)* (London: Taylor & Francis, 1935), p. 205; J. Webb, 'The Development of First Aid', *Physiotherapy,* LVII (1971), pp. 365–9; E. W. A. 'First Aid 140 Years Ago', *British Medical Journal* (1944) I, p. 263.

59. Beresford (ed.), *The Diary of James Woodforde,* 28 August 1790, III, p. 210.

60. The medicine chest awaits its Ph.D. But see Roy Porter, 'The Patient in England, *c.* 1660–*c.* 1800', in Andrew Wear (ed.), *The Social History of Medicine* (Cambridge: Cambridge University Press, 1992), pp. 91–118.

61. W. Buchan, *Domestic Medicine,* p. 730. Apparently dead people, Buchan insisted, were often recoverable. Above all, they should be kept warm, and resuscitated. Buchan recommended 'a strong person may blow his own breath into the patient's mouth with all the force he can; or, what will generally succeed better, the smoke of tobacco may be blown into the lungs, by means of a pipe or funnel'.

62. Buchan, *Domestic Medicine,* pp. 718, 695. Regarding 'broken bones', Buchan noted that 'there is in most country villages some person who pretends to the art of reducing fractures. Though in general such persons are very ignorant, yet some of them are very successful; which evidently proves, that a small degree of learning, with a sufficient share of common sense and a mechanical head, will enable a man to be useful in this way': *Domestic Medicine,* p. 722.

63. Ibid., p. 705.

64. Ibid., p. 706.

65. James Parkinson, *The Villager's Friend and Physician.* Parkinson commended the methods promoted by the Humane Society. See Morris, *James Parkinson,* p. 57.

66. P. J. Bishop, *A Short History of the Royal Humane Society* (London: The Royal Humane Society, 1974); E. Thomson, 'The Role of the Physician in Humane Societies of the Eighteenth Century', *Bulletin of the History of Medicine,* XXXVII (1963), pp. 43–51. Inspired by the Humane society, newspapers began to carry advice for dealing with accident victims.

67. *Gentleman's Magazine,* XXXVII (1767), p. 488; XXXII (1762), p. 386; VIII (1738), p. 416; xix (1749), p. 407; XXII (1752), p. 318; C. Mullett, 'Hydrophobia: Its History in England to 1800', *Bulletin of the History of Medicine,* XVIII (1945), pp. 44–65.

68. Mary E. Fissell, *Patients, Power and the Poor in Eighteenth-Century Bristol* (Cambridge: Cambridge University Press, 1991), Ch. vii, 'Surgeons and the Medicalization of the Hospital'.

69. Fenwick Skrimshire, *The Village Pastor's Surgical and Medical Guide* (London: Churchill, 1838).

7. WOMEN, WORK AND CULTURAL CHANGE IN EIGHTEENTH- AND EARLY NINETEENTH-CENTURY LONDON *Patty Seleski*

The author wishes to thank the National Endowment for the Humanities, the American Historical Association/Bernadotte Schmidt award and the California State University Affirmative Action fund for funding the research and writing of this essay.

1. Mary Ann Ashford, *Life of a Licensed Victualler's Daughter* (London, 1844), pp. iii–iv.

2. Ibid., pp. iii–iv.

3. Ibid., p. iv.

4. J. J. Hecht, *The Domestic Servant Class in the Eighteenth Century* (London: Routledge & Kegan Paul, 1955), pp. 200–27; B. Hill, *Women, Work and Sexual Politics in Eighteenth-Century England* (Oxford: Basil Blackwell, 1989), pp. 125–47); D. Roche, *The People of Paris*, trans. by M. Evans (Los Angeles: University of California Press, 1987), pp. 66–9; C. Fairchilds, *Domestic Enemies: Servants and their Masters in Old Regime France* (Baltimore: Johns Hopkins University Press, 1984), pp. 112, 264n.; S. Maza, *Servants and their Masters in Eighteenth-Century France* (Princeton: Princeton University Press, 1983), pp. 210–27; L. Davidoff, 'Mastered for Life: Servant and Wife in Victorian and Edwardian England', *Journal of Social History*, VII (1973/74), p. 421.

5. T. McBride, *The Domestic Revolution* (New York: Holmes & Meier, 1976), p. 14; D. A. Kent, 'Ubiquitous but Invisible: Female Domestic Servants in Mid-Eighteenth-Century London', *History Workshop Journal*, XXVIII (1989), p. 112; L. D. Schwarz, *London in the Age of Industrialisation* (Cambridge: Cambridge University Press, 1992), p. 15. Figures are based on Kent's estimate that about 10 per cent of Londoners were servants.

6. Kent, 'Ubiquitous but Invisible', pp. 14–22; P. Earle, *The Making of the English Middle Class* (London: Methuen, 1989), pp. 218–19; Davidoff and Hall note that by 1850 approximately 82 per cent of servants in middle-class households were women. L. Davidoff and C. Hall, *Family Fortunes: Men and Women of the English Middle Class* (London: Hutchinson, 1987), p. 388.

7. Kent argues, for example, that models of service as a dependent occupation do not take women's comparative experiences into account and that service could represent a 'sufficiently attractive [occupation] for some women to choose it as a way of life': Kent, 'Ubiquitous but Invisible', p. 112. He is especially critical of Hecht, almost all of whose

attention is given to male domestic servants. Roche also uses male experience to document his conclusions about domestic service and he relies almost exclusively on men's *post mortem* inventories for his observations about domestic servants. Hecht, *Domestic Servant Class*, pp. 200–27; Roche, *People of Paris*, pp. 59–63, 73–7. Fairchilds and Maza, both of whom are concerned with the process of 'feminisation' of service and who therefore discuss women more consistently, raise some doubts about the 'trickle-down' theory. Fairchilds,*Domestic Enemies*, pp. 112–13; Maza, *Servants and Masters*, pp. 210–27.

8. Earle, *Making of the English Middle Class*, pp. 218–19.

9. P. Burke, *Popular Culture in Early Modern Europe* (London: Temple Smith, 1978), p. 28.

10. The literature on the making of the middle class and the making of middle-class culture grows daily. See, for example, Davidoff and Hall, *Family Fortunes*; Earle, *Making of the English Middle Class*; and T. Koditschek, *Class Formation and Urban Industrial Society: Bradford 1750–1850* (Cambridge: Cambridge University Press, 1990).

11. This is the central thesis of Davidoff and Hall in Part 3 of *Family Fortunes*, pp. 317–450. Some of the most important work in this regard has been done by feminist literary scholars. See N. Armstrong, *Desire and Domestic Fiction: A Political History of the Novel* (Oxford: Oxford University Press, 1987) and M. Poovey, *Uneven Developments: The Ideological Work of Gender in Mid-Victorian England* (Chicago: University of Chicago Press, 1988). For an essay that links historical and literary approaches to cultural studies on this issue see J. Newton, 'Family Fortunes: "New History" and "New Historicism"', *Radical History Review*, XLIII (1989), pp. 5–22.

12. Newton, '"New History" and "New Historicism"' pp. 16, 19; Davidoff and Hall, *Family Fortunes*, p. 13. With the exception of some consideration of governesses, both Poovey and Armstrong neglect servants entirely.

13. Davidoff and Hall, *Family Fortunes*, p. 392.

14. Davidoff, 'Mastered for Life', pp. 406–28. Although Davidoff seeks to align male and female servants as subordinate to the power of the master, she de-emphasises the real power of mistresses over servants by relegating them to the role of 'deputies' in the household. The result is to create a symmetry of subordination between servants and married women of every class. Davidoff makes the link explicit in a later article. See Davidoff, 'The Rationalization of Housework', in *Dependence and Exploitation in Work and Marriage*, ed. D. Leonard Barker and S. Allen (London: Longman, 1976), esp. pp. 138–43.

15. A. Kussmaul, *Servants in Husbandry in Early Modern England* (Cambridge: Cambridge University Press, 1981), pp. 26–7; C. Hall *White, Male and Middle-Class* (London: Routledge, 1992), p. 48.

16. Kent, 'Ubiquitous but Invisible', p. 112.

17. Earle, *Making of the English Middle Class*, p. 218.

18. P. S. Seleski, 'The Women of the Laboring Poor: Love, Work and Poverty in London, 1750–1820', unpublished Ph.D. thesis, Stanford University (1989), pp. 32–5.

19. D. Defoe, *Every-Body's Business is No-Body's Business; or, Private Abuses, Public Grievances* (London, 1725), p. 6. Defoe explored many of the same themes in *Augusta Triumphans* (London, 1729).

20. See the essays contained in L. Davison, T. Hitchcock, T. Keirn and R. B. Shoemaker (eds), *Stilling the Grumbling Hive: The Response to Social and Economic Problems in England, 1689–1750* (New York: St Martin's, 1992), especially those by J. Beattie, 'London Crime and the Making of the "Bloody Code", 1689–1718', pp. 68–9; N. Rogers, 'Confronting the Crime Wave: The Debate over Social Reform and Regulation', pp. 84–5; and R. B. Shoemaker, 'Reforming the City: The Reformation of Manners Campaign in London, 1690–1738', p. 110.

21. Rogers, 'Confronting the Crime Wave', p. 84.

22. E. Haywood, *A Present for a Servant Maid* (London, 1743), p. 4. Haywood echoes Defoe: 'I know my business, and don't fear a service; there are more places than parish churches'; Defoe, *Every-Body's Business*, p. 20.

23. Kent, 'Ubiquitous but Invisible', pp. 120–2. It is likely that settlement records overestimate the length of time that women spent in service. While most claimants to parish relief in the parish of St George the Martyr, Southwark, claimed to have served in one place for at least a year in order to establish a settlement and thus a right to relief, this year was frequently many years in the past and subsequent employments lasted for much shorter periods of time. Over half of the forty-eight single women questioned from 1798 to 1800 in the parish had gained their settlements by working as yearly hired servants for less than two years, but a majority of these women had not been employed anywhere else for more than a year at any time in the previous five years. Elizabeth Sadler, for example, gained settlement in the parish of Christ Church, Surrey, by virtue of serving there for a year with Mrs Fletcher, a parish householder. After she left Mrs Fletcher's service, however, she did not stay at any job for very long: she served a Mrs Hudson for three weeks at a wage of 1*s.*/6*d.* and then went to a Mrs Fernier for five weeks. At one point she found a position with a Captain Ayers in St George's parish at a yearly wage of five pounds. She stayed with Ayers about six weeks and received wages of 11*s.*/6*d.* Borough of Southwark, John Harvard Library, Southwark Local History Archives, St George the Martyr Settlement Examinations, 1798–1800.

24. GLRO/A/FH/A/7/2, 'Register of Servants', 1759–1772.

25. Anon., *Satan's Harvest Home* (London, 1749), p. 4. Again the echo is of Defoe: 'Thus many of them rove from place to place, from bawdy-house to service, and from service to bawdy-house again, ever unsettled, and never easy, nothing being more common than to find these creatures one week in a good family, and the next in a brothel. This amphibious life makes 'em fit for neither, for if the bawd uses them ill, away they trip to service, and if their mistresses gives 'em a wry word, whip, they're at a bawdy-house again'; Defoe, *Every-Body's Business*, p. 9.

26. J. Huntingford, *The Laws of Masters and Servants Considered* (London, 1790), pp. 101–4.

27. GLRO/A/FH/AH/7/2.

28. Davidoff and Hall, *Family Fortunes*, p. 392.

29. Westminster Abbey, Muniments Room, Westminster Coroners' Inquests, 1790. Hereafter cited as WA/MR/CI. Mistresses' lack of knowledge about their employees' names was not unusual, either in humble locales – Mrs Jacobs of Christ Church, Spitalfields, hired a women known only to her as Rachel – or in more fashionable households – Jane Lang, a coal merchant's wife in Allhallows in the City, employed a women whose entire name was unknown to her for two months. See GLRO/MJ/SP/1784 and CLRO/L/SP/1771.

30. WA/MR/CI/1790.

31. GLRO/A/FH/Petitions for Admission of Children/1792–1793.

32. WA/MR/CI/28/1804.

33. *Proceedings on the King's Commission of the Peace, Oyer and Terminer, and Gaol Delivery of Newgate, Held for the City of London and County of Middlesex at Justice Hall in the Old Bailey (OBSP)*, no. 347 (London, 1768–9), pp. 290–9. Defoe, *Augusta Triumphans*, p. 27.

34. GLRO/A/FH/Petitions for the Admission of Children/1822.

35. Haywood, *Present*, p. 39.

36. WA/MR/CI/17/1792.

37. GLRO/A/FH/Petitions for the Admission of Children/1811, 1812.

38. Literature directed at servants from the Restoration to the Victorian period is oppressively monotonous in its concerns with these issues. For a sampling of the complaints see: Defoe, *Every-Body's Business*, pp. 4–6; T. Broughton, *Serious Advice and Warning to Servants* (London, 1746), pp. 11–20; Haywood *Present*, pp. 8–50; Anon., *A Present for Servants from their Ministers, Masters or Other Friends* (London, 1787), pp. 73–4; Anon., *The Good Servant* (Otley, [1830]), pp. 2–8; Anon., *Household Work; or the Duties of Female Servants* (London, 1849), p. 4. Broughton went through repeated editions until 1818, while the anonymous *Present for Servants* was still being reissued after 1805.

39. 'Tea, sugar, wine, etc, or any such trifling commodities are reckoned no theft'; Defoe, *Every-Body's Business*, p. 10.

40. Haywood, *Present*, pp. 12–13.

41. *Household Work*, p. 4.

42. Revd. J. Trusler, *The London Adviser and Guide* (London, 1786), p. 47.

43. Anon., *Proposal for the Amendment and Encouragement of Servants* (London, 1752), pp. 1–2.

44. See, for example, *The Servant's Friend; or, the Master and Mistresses Best Gift to their Servants, Apprentices and Workmen* (London, 1750).

45. *Proposal for Amendment and Encouragement*, p. 12.

46. *A Plan of the Universal Register-Office Opposite Cecil Street in the Strand* (London, 1751), p. 8.

47. J. Reed, *The Register Office* (London, 1771), p. 20. James Huntingford perpetuated this piece of middle-class mythology in the 1790s, suggesting further that most servants who appeared before the Old Bailey for robbing their employers had been hired with false characters purchased from

a register office. Huntingford, *The Laws of Masters and Servants*, p. 99. Such was the case of Henrietta Radbourne, tried at the Old Bailey in 1787 for the murder of her mistress during a failed robbery attempt. At her trial, the prosecutor stressed the fact that Henrietta had been hired through a register office and had 'obtained a written and surreptitious [*sic*] character' there. He further argued that Radbourne's crime could have been predicted and thus prevented had her mistress known her *true* character. *London Chronicle*, 14–17 July, 1787.

48. Anon., *British Society for the Encouragement of Servants* (London, 1797), pp. 22–3, 89; *Journal of the House of Commons*, XLVI (1791), p. 299.

49. *Journal of the House of Lords*, XXXIX (1792), p. 490. Sometimes servants who did try to pass off falsified characters were caught. In 1796, the Society for Prosecuting Felons gave assistance to a householder who wished to expose Elizabeth Spink, 'the servant who was tried and convicted at the Sessions before last for robbing him[and who] had obtained a place'; CLRO, Misc. MSS 115.9, 17 June 1796.

50. A summary of the recent work on this idea can be found in J. Newton, ' "New History" and "New Historicism" ', pp. 5–22.

51. Anon., *The Accomplish'd Housewife; or, the Gentlewoman's Companion* (London, 1745), p. 10.

52. A. Martin Taylor, *Practical Hints to Young Females, on the Duties of a Wife, a Mother, and a Mistress of a Family* (8th edn, London, 1818), pp. v–vi. Women's efforts were a key component of their husband's ability both to provide for the family and to create national wealth: 'Vain are his labors to accumulate, if she cannot or will not, expend with discretion. Vain too are his expectations of happiness, if economy, order and regularity, are not to be found at home'; ibid., p. 18.

53. L. Child, *The Frugal Housewife* (London, 1832), p. 115.

54. See T. McBride, *Domestic Revolution*, pp. 18–33; and P. Branca, *Silent Sisterhood: Middle Class Women in the Victorian Home* (London: Croom Helm, 1975), pp. 22–37.

55. *Accomplish'd Housewife*, p. 428.

56. Anon., *A New System of Domestic Cookery* ([London?], 1812), p. xii; Mrs W. Parkes, *Domestic Duties; or Instructor to Young Married Ladies* (3rd edn, London, 1828), pp. 121–2. Another manual urged women to 'ask every *minute* question'. In fact, the author doubted that any method of hiring servants was any good; for if a servant was any good, no mistress would allow them to leave: 'all those who advertise for situations, should not meet with a moment's consideration – if they were *good* servants, their mistresses would willingly get them situations by private recommendations, – nay, it is but reasonable to suppose, that if they were worth anything, they would not part with them' (original emphasis); Anon., *The Book of Domestic Duties* (London 1835), p. 17.

57. London, Guildhall Library, MSS. 14,951, 1 (Diary of Elizabeth Tyrrell), May 1809.

58. Anon., *The Female Instructor; or Young Woman's Friend and Companion* (London, [1837]), p. 177; *Accomplish'd Housewife*, p. 62; *Book of Domestic Duties*, p. 32; Taylor, *Practical Hints*, p. 27.

59. *Book of Domestic Duties*, p. 25; S. Adams and S. Adams, *The Complete Servant; being a practical guide to the peculiar duties and business of all descriptions of servants* (London, 1825), pp. 12–13; *New System of Domestic Cookery*, p. vi.

60. Taylor, *Practical Hints*, pp. 27–8.

61. *Book of Domestic Duties*, pp. 18–19.

62. *Accomplish'd Housewife*, pp. 57, 427–8

63. *Female Instructor*, p. 178.

64. *Accomplish'd Housewife*, pp. 428–9.

65. *OBSP* (1793–4), p. 360.

66. *To the Right Honourable Lord Mayor, to the Worshipful Aldermen and to the Worthy Liverymen and Citizens of the City of London, The Ensuing Report of the Fatal Proceedings before their Recorder in the Case of Elizabeth Fenning and other Circumstances connected therewith* (London, 1815), pp. 5–55.

67. Davidoff, 'Mastered for Life', p. 421; Hill, *Women, Work and Sexual Politics*, pp. 143–5.

68. Parkes, *Domestic Duties*, pp. 51, 124.

69. L. Davidoff Lockwood, 'Domestic Service and the Working Class Life-Cycle', *Bulletin of the Society for the Study of Labour History*, XXVI (1973), p. 11.

70. Ibid., p. 11. The issue of the Foundling Hospital population is explored at some length in Seleski, 'Women of the Laboring Poor', pp. 37–147.

71. GLRO/WJ/SP/17781/May/42; Guildhall/MSS. 14,951/1/ October 1809. Even mistresses' guidebooks acknowledged that influence had its limits: 'It is painful to hear the incessant complaints to which this subject [servants' behaviour] gives rise, as they are strong indications of the continued level of depravity of the lower orders, notwithstanding the benevolent exertions of the last thirty years to banish ignorance, and vice as its offspring . . . nor ought the society to which most servants have been exposed to be forgotten: a well-inclined girl is frequently ruined by her neighbours, or the companions of her servitude, who are much less likely, in general to improve than to injure her. What wonder then, if, when we admit into our houses the children or associates of such, we find them incapable of using either their eyes, their ears, or understandings! Why should we expect to gather grapes of thorns, or figs of thistles?' Taylor, *Practical Hints*, pp. 36–7. Despite acknowledging these realities, Taylor still held mistresses accountable for servants' behaviour: 'It should also be remembered that servants, as well as children, suffer from the frequent absence of her whose duty it is to superintend them; acquiring habits of idleness and irregularity, which a mistress will find difficult to reprove, and still more difficult to correct, while thus remiss in her own department. When she quits the post at which she is stationed, and in which her own interest is so deep, it is not to be wondered at if servants quit theirs, in which they have no interest at all: nor is it likely they should be so skillful in their business, when the watchful eye of the mistress is so often removed. Where this neglect arises

from the love of dissipation and gaiety, she can scarcely be pitied when suffering from its inevitable effects'; ibid., pp. 111–12.

72. '. . . everything about the upper servants' position in Victorian society, including their sexual relations, must be seen in light of these specialized roles . . . especially their peculiar position in the elaboration of a distinctive class culture that, while not their own, had a powerful effect on their behavior and, to a lesser extent, their values'; J. Gillis, 'Servants, Sexual Relations, and the Risks of Illegitimacy in London, 1801–1900', *Feminist Studies*, v (1979), p. 153. The authors of one popular servant manual were themselves former upper servants who had bettered themselves. Samuel and Sarah Adams claimed over fifty years between them in service. Samuel started life as a footboy in 1770, rose to become a butler and then a housesteward; Sarah claimed that she had begun her life in service as a maid-of-all-work and ended her career as a housekeeper. Adams and Adams, *The Complete Servant*, pp. iii–iv.

73. Hecht, *Domestic Servant Class*, pp. 209–11, 223–4; Hill, *Women, Work and Sexual Politics*, p. 145. On the meaning of expenditures among the working classes, see J. Rule, *The Labouring Class in Early Industrial England, 1750–1850* (London: Longman, 1986), p. 213.

74. E. Higgs, 'Domestic Service and Household Production', in *Unequal Opportunities: Women's Employment in England, 1800–1918*, ed. A. John (New York: Basil Blackwell, 1986), pp. 137–45.

75. Ashford, *Life*, pp. 20, 40.

76. Ashford, *Life*, pp. 23–34, 53. Ashford's frequent changes of place were not abnormal. Hannah Cullwick, who was in service during the middle years of the nineteenth century and who kept a diary of her life in service, also records her continuous entry and exit from various situations at a similar pace. See H. Cullwick, *The Diaries of Hannah Cullwick, Victorian Maidservant*, ed. and introduced by L. Stanley (New Brunswick, NJ: Rutgers University Press, 1984), pp. 35–52.

77. Ashford, *Life*, pp. 35–6.

78. Anon., *Advice to Servants of Every Denomination* (London, [*c.*179?]), Guildhall Broadside 5.29, Guildhall Library, London.

79. Ashford, *Life*, p. 49.

80. Ibid., pp. 23–49.

81. Ibid.

82. Although Hill disputes the notion that female workers sought independence and resisted control in preference to security or betterment, Kent also argues that domestic servants were motivated in their choices by a desire for independence. Hill, *Women, Work and Sexual Politics*, p. 128; Kent, 'Ubiquitous but Invisible', pp. 120–1.

83. Ashford, *Life*, p. 38.

84. Ibid., pp. 62, 78–9.

85. Ibid., pp. 87–91.

86. See C. Hall, 'The Tale of Samuel and Jemima: Gender and Working-Class Culture in Early 19th-Century England', in *Popular Culture and Social Relations*, eds T. Bennett, C. Mercer and J. Woollacott (Philadelphia: Open

University Press, 1986), pp. 73–92; A. Clark, 'The Rhetoric of Chartist Domesticity: Gender, Language and Class in the 1830s and 1840s', *Journal of British Studies*, XXXI (1992), pp. 62–88.

8. AGAINST INNOVATION? *John Rule*

1. For some general comments see: P. Joyce (ed.), *The Historical Meanings of Work* (Cambridge: Cambridge University Press, 1987), pp. 20–1.

2. See M. Berg, *The Age of Manufactures, 1700–1820* (London: Fontana, 1985), pp. 164–7; S. Alexander, 'Women, Class and Sexual Differences in the 1830s and 1840s', *History Workshop Journal*, XVII (1984), pp. 125–49.

3. A. Charlesworth and A. J. Randall, 'Morals, Markets and the English Crowd in 1766', *Past and Present*, CXIV (1987), p. 206.

4. The examples of workplace customs in this and in the following paragraphs are taken from: John Rule, *The Experience of Labour in Eighteenth-Century Industry* (London: Croom Helm, 1981), Ch. 8, where the original sources are fully cited.

5. See especially for Birmingham, C. Behagg, 'Secrecy, Ritual and Folk Violence: The Opacity of the Workplace in the First Half of the Nineteenth Century', in R. D. Storch (ed.), *Popular Culture and Politics in Nineteenth-Century England* (London: Croom Helm, 1984), pp. 166–8.

6. C. R. Dobson, *Masters and Journeymen: A Prehistory of Industrial Relations 1717–1800* (London: Croom Helm, 1980), pp. 61–73; Rule, *Experience of Labour*, pp. 201–4.

7. Rule, *Experience of Labour* p. 201; Devon County Record Office, MSS. 146 B/ add Z1.

8. Rule, *Experience of Labour*, p. 195.

9. Ibid., pp. 195–6.

10. The rules of the journeymen hat-makers are printed in A. Aspinall (ed.), *The Early English Trade Unions* (London: Batchworth Press, 1948), pp. 105–11.

11. Cited in Rule, *Experience of Labour*, pp. 196–7.

12. Ibid., p. 197.

13. R. Colls, *The Pitmen of the Northern Coalfield: Work, Culture and Protest, 1790–1850* (Manchester: Manchester University Press, 1987), p. 48; John Rule, 'Attitudes towards Trade Unionism and Chartism among the Cornish Miners: A Configuration of Quietism?', *Tijdschrift voor Sociale Geschiedenis*, XVIII, Pt 2/3 (June 1992), pp. 248–62.

14. Behagg, 'Secrecy, Ritual and Folk Violence', pp. 163–4.

15. Aspinall (ed.), *Early English Trade Unions*, p. 128.

16. *Exeter Flying Post*, 16 May 1787.

17. Aspinall (ed.), *Early English Trade Unions*, p. 85.

18. See E. P. Thompson, *Customs in Common* (London: Merlin Press, 1992), pp. 519–20.

19. Aspinall (ed.), *Early English Trade Unions*, pp. 19, 10; Rule, *Experience of Labour*, pp. 187–8.

20. Cited in Rule, *Experience of Labour,* p. 194.

21. Cited in J. L. Hammond and Barbara Hammond, *The Skilled Labourer* (1919, reprinted London: Longman, 1979), p. 212.

22. Rule, *Experience of Labour,* pp. 95–119, for apprenticeship legislation and its repeal.

23. Ibid., pp. 124–35, for perquisite and theft and see also: P. Linebaugh, *The London Hanged: Crime and Civil Society in the Eighteenth Century* (London: Allen Lane, 1991), Ch. 7.

24. Examples cited in J. G. Rule, 'Some Social Aspects of the Cornish Industrial Revolution', in R. Burt (ed.), *Industry and Society in the South-West* (Exeter: Exeter University Press, 1970), pp. 76, 78–80.

25. See especially E. P. Thompson, 'Time, Work Discipline and Industrial Capitalism', in his *Customs in Common,* pp. 352–403.

26. M. Harrison, *Crowds and History: Mass Phenomena in English Towns, 1790–1835* (Cambridge: Cambridge University Press, 1988), pp. 119–26; D. A. Reid, 'The Decline of Saint Monday, 1766–1876', *Past and Present,* LXXI (1976) pp. 76–101.

27. Thompson, *Customs in Common,* pp. 57–63.

28. On the tramping system in England see the classic article by E. J. Hobsbawm, 'The Tramping Artisan', reprinted in *Labouring Men* (London: Weidenfeld & Nicolson, 1964), pp. 34–63, and R. A. Leeson, *Travelling Brothers* (London: Allen George & Unwin, 1979). But contrast Hans-Ulrich Thamer, 'On the Use and Abuse of Handicraft: Journeyman Culture and Enlightened Public Opinion in 18th and 19th Century Germany', in S. L. Kaplan (ed.), *Understanding Popular Culture: Europe from the Middle Ages to the Nineteenth Century* (Berlin: Mouton, 1984), pp. 275–300. For France see W. H. Sewell, *Work and Revolution in France: The Language of Labor from the Old Regime to 1848* (Cambridge: Cambridge University Press, 1980).

29. Hammond and Hammond, *Skilled Labourer,* p. 212.

30. For the Exeter woollen weavers see John Rule, 'Labour Consciousness and Industrial Conflict in Eighteenth-Century Exeter', in B. Stapleton (ed.), *Conflict and Community in Southern England* (Stroud: Alan Sutton, 1992), pp. 100–4.

31. Thompson, *Customs in Common,* pp. 9–10; E. P. Thompson, *The Making of the English Working Class* (Harmondsworth: Penguin, 1968), p. 594.

32. Charlesworth and Randall, 'Morals, Markets and the English Crowd', p. 212.

33. Verses cited in Thompson, *Customs in Common,* pp. 62–3.

34. *Commons Journals,* LXI, 17 July 1806.

35. For the campaigns of the woollen workers in the West Country see especially: A. Randall, *Before the Luddites: Custom, Community and Machinery in the English Woollen Industry, 1776–1809* (Cambridge: Cambridge University Press, 1991), pp. 149–220.

36. Cited in Hammond and Hammond, *Skilled Labourer,* pp. 64–5.

37. J. G. Rule, 'The Property of Skill in the Period of Manufacture', in Joyce (ed.), *Historical Meanings of Work,* pp. 105–6.

38. Randall, *Before the Luddites*, p. 89.

39. Adam Smith, *Wealth of Nations*, ed. E. Cannan ([1776] 1904, reprinted London: Methuen, 1961), I, pp. 74–5.

40. D. Levine and K. Wrightson, *The Making of an Industrial Society: Whickham, 1596–1765* (Oxford: Oxford University Press, 1991), pp. 394–426; J. A. Jaffe, *The Struggle for Market Power: Industrial Relations in the British Coal Industry 1800–1840* (Cambridge: Cambridge University Press, 1991).

41. Randall, *Before the Luddites*, pp. 10, 89. See also W. Reddy, *The Rise of Market Culture: The Textile Trade and French Society, 1750–1900* (Cambridge: Cambridge University Press, 1984), especially the Introduction.

42. The particular grievances of the Nottinghamshire Luddites were made clear by the Hammonds in 1919, *Skilled Labourer*, pp. 210–19.

43. Randall, *Before the Luddites*, p. 69. See also M. Berg, 'Workers and Machinery in Eighteenth-Century England', in J. G. Rule (ed.), *British Trade Unionism, 1750–1850: The Formative Years* (London: Longman, 1988), pp. 52–73.

44. This argument has been especially associated with E. J. Hobsbaw 'Custom, Wages and Workload in Nineteenth-Century Industry', in *Labouring Men*, pp. 344–70.

45. Rule, *Experience of Labour*, pp. 178–9, for these and other examples.

46. See n. 7 above.

47. E. J. Hobsbawm, Introduction to E. J. Hobsbawm and T. Ranger (eds), *The Invention of Tradition* (Cambridge: Cambridge University Press, 1983), pp. 2–3.

48. Behagg, 'Secrecy, Ritual and Folk Violence', p. 164; Randall, *Before the Luddites*, p. 118.

9. 'TACIT, UNSUSPECTED, BUT STILL IMPLICIT FAITH' Bob Bushaway

This paper has profited by discussion with several scholars but I should like to thank John Rule and Mick Reed whose original stimulation led to its writing. Any errors which remain should be lain at my door alone.

1. Rev. J. C. Atkinson, *Forty Years in a Moorland Parish: Reminiscences and Researches in Danby in Cleveland* (London: Macmillan, 1891), p. 63.

2. Ibid., p. 60.

3. Ibid., p. 61.

4. Ibid., p. 63.

5. For example, K. D. M. Snell, *Annals of the Labouring Poor: Social Change and Agrarian England 1600–1900* (Cambridge: Cambridge University Press, 1987); Alun Howkins, *Reshaping Rural England: A Social History 1850–1923* (London: HarperCollins Academic, 1991); Mick Reed and Roger Wells (eds), *Class, Conflict and Protest in the English Countryside 1700–1880* (London: Frank Cass, 1990); Howard Newby, *Country Life: A Social History of Rural England* (London: Cardinal, 1988); A. Charlesworth, *An Atlas of Rural Protest in Britain 1549–1900* (London:

Croom Helm, 1983); Alan Armstrong, *Farmworkers: A Social and Economic History 1770–1980*; (London: B. T. Batsford, 1988); Dennis R. Mills, *Land and Peasant in Nineteenth-Century Britain* (London: Croom Helm, 1980).

6. For a more detailed discussion of the dismantling of the customary framework of rural society, see: Bob Bushaway, *By Rite: Custom, Ceremony, and Community in England, 1700–1880* (London: Junction Books, 1982); Robert D. Storch (ed.), *Popular Culture and Custom in Nineteenth-Century England* (London: Croom Helm, 1982); Bob Bushaway, 'Rite, Legitimation and Community in Southern England 1700–1850: The Ideology of Custom', in Barry Stapleton (ed.), *Conflict and Community in Southern England: Essays in the Social History of Rural and Urban Labour from Medieval to Modern Times* (Stroud: Alan Sutton, 1992).

7. See, for example, James Obelkevich, *Religion and Rural Society: South Lindsey 1825–1875* (Oxford: Clarendon Press, 1978); Charles Phytian-Adams, 'Rural Culture', in G. E. Mingay (ed.), *The Victorian Countryside* (London: Routledge & Kegan Paul, 1981), ii, pp. 616–25; Ian Dyck, 'Towards the "Cottage Charter": The Expressive Culture of Farm Workers in Nineteenth-Century Rural England', *Rural History*, i (April 1990), pp. 95–111.

8. David Vincent, *Literacy and Popular Culture: England 1750–1914* (Cambridge: Cambridge University Press, 1989), p. 157.

9. Alfred William, *A Wiltshire Village* (1912, reprinted London: Gerald Duckworth, 1920), p. 283.

10. Thomas Hardy, *Far from the Madding Crowd* (1874, reprinted London: Macmillan, 1974), pp. 38–9.

11. See, for example, John Brand, *Observations on Popular Antiquities*, ed. Henry Ellis (London: various, 1813), pp. xviii–xix, where it is suggested that 'The Antiquities of the Common People cannot be studied without acquiring some useful knowledge of Mankind: and it may be truly said in this instance that by the chemical process of Philosophy, even Wisdom may be extracted from the follies and superstitions of our forefathers'. Gilbert White referred to the material as 'Superstitious prejudices ... sucked in ... with our mother's milk'. See Gilbert White, *The Natural History of Selborne* (1789, reprinted London: J. M. Dent, 1912), p. 173.

12. Contemporary writers stick to this terms with equal vigour. See, for example, the most recent collection that has been published, Iona Opie and Moira Tatem (eds), *A Dictionary of Popular Superstitions* (Oxford: Oxford University Press, 1989). See also Christina Hole (ed.), *Superstitions of the Countryside* (London: Arrow Books, 1978), *Superstitions of Death and the Supernatural* (London: Arrow Books, 1978) and *Superstitions of Love and Marriage* (London: Arrow Books, 1978). This series is a republication of Edwin and Moira Radford (eds), *The Encyclopaedia of Superstitions* (London: Hutchinson, 1948). The Folklore Society avoids the term and prefers 'religious folk-lore and the supernatural'. See Wilfrid Bonser, *A Bibliography of Folklore* (London: William Glaister, 1961), pp. 53–72. Many of its members, however, are comfortable with the more pejorative term. Other

terms are occasionally used, such as 'traditional' beliefs or the 'prior culture', but these are scarcely more acceptable. Such phrases are redolent of 'survivalism' and imply that older patterns of belief were replaced by newer ideas, whereas alternative belief remained simply an extant frame of reference for the rural labourer for much of the nineteenth century.

13. Edwin Sidney Hartland (ed.), *Country Folk-Lore: Printed Extracts: Gloucestershire* (London: D. Nutt, 1892), pp. 4–5.

14. Ibid., pp. 6–7.

15. That 'education' was inimical to 'popular superstition' was a common view which had a long history and from which contemporary social historians have not necessarily escaped. See White, *Natural History of Selborne*, p. 173.

16. Rev. S. Baring-Gould, *A Book of Folk-Lore* (London: Collins, n.d., c. 1910), pp. 9–10.

17. John Aubrey referred to 'Hermetick Philosophy'. See *John Aubrey: Miscellanies*, in John Buchanan-Brown (ed.), *John Aubrey: Three Prose Works* (Fontwell: Centaur Press, 1972), p. 6. See also Christopher Hill, *The World Turned Upside Down: Radical Ideas during the English Revolution* (London: Temple Smith, 1972), pp. 231–8, for the relationship between magic and science in early modern England. Yet by the beginning of the eighteenth century, Addison could refer to 'superstitious follies'. See *The Spectator*, 7(8 March 1710–11), in *The Spectator* (London: Henry G. Bohn, 1861), p. 11. See also Brand, *Observations on Popular Antiquities*, II, pp. 647–66.

18. William Hone (ed.), *The Year Book* (1831–2, reprinted London: William Tegg, 1864), p. 126.

19. Ibid., p. 127.

20. Ibid., p. 128.

21. Vincent, *Literacy*, pp. 193–4.

22. John R. Wise, *The New Forest: Its History and Scenery* (London: Smith, Elder, 1863), pp. 177–8.

23. See Edwin Sidney Hartland's introduction to Ella Mary Leather, *The Folk-Lore of Herefordshire* (Hereford: Jakeman Carver, 1912; reprinted Wakefield: E. P. Publishing, 1973), p. v.

24. Ibid., p. vi.

25. Brand, *Observations on Popular Antiquities*, I, pp. ix–x.

26. I. M. Lewis, *Social Anthropology in Perspective: The Relevance of Social Anthropology* (London: Penguin, 1976), pp. 68–9. This point has also been emphasised by Keith Thomas in his study of witchcraft in the early modern period. See Keith Thomas, *Religion and the Decline of Magic* (London: Penguin, 1973), p. 800.

27. Atkinson, *Forty Years in a Moorland Parish*, p. 62.

28. John Symonds Udal, *Dorsetshire Folk-Lore* (Hertford: Stephen Austin, 1922, reprinted Guernsey: Toucan Press, 1970), p. 226.

29. Quintin Hoare and Geoffrey Nowell Smith (eds), *Selections from the Prison Notebooks of Antonio Gramsci* (London: Lawrence & Wishart, 1971), p. 323.

30. Helen Mary Reynolds, 'Magic and Superstition in Contemporary British Society', unpublished M.Soc.Sci thesis, University of Birmingham (1978), synopsis. Twentieth-century Christianity continued to see itself as engaged in a conflict with 'superstition' in England. See, for example, Bede Frost, *Some Modern Substitutes for Christianity* (London and Oxford: A.R. Mowbray, 1949), pp. 9–22.

31. Reynolds, *Magic and Superstition*, p. 164.

32. Harry H. Marsh, 'An Empirical Exploration of the Occurrence of Superstitious Habits', unpublished Ph.D. thesis, University of Birmingham (1981), p. 83. See also Peter L. Berger, *A Rumour of Angels: Modern Society and the Rediscovery of the Supernatural* (London: Penguin, 1973), pp. 13–42.

33. Gustav Jahoda, *The Psychology of Superstition* (London: Penguin, 1970), p. 141.

34. Article on 'Folk Lore' by Ovidiu Birlea in Mircea Eliade (ed.), *The Encyclopaedia of Religion* (New York: Macmillan, 1987), v, p. 363. See also the article on 'Superstition' by Mary R. O'Neil, ibid., xiv, pp. 163–6. For an earlier approach, see Alice Gardner, 'Superstition' in James Hastings (ed.), *Encyclopaedia of Religion and Ethics* (Edinburgh: T. & T. Clark, 1921), xii, pp. 120–2.

35. See, for example, Thomas Hardy, *The Life and Death of the Mayor of Casterbridge: A Story of a Man of Character* (1886, reprinted London: Macmillan, 1974), p. 211, which describes Henchard's visit to 'Conjurer' Fall, and Thomas Hardy, Tess of the d'Urbervilles: A Pure Woman (1891, reprinted London: Macmillan, 1974), p. 172, in which Dairyman Crick discusses the merits of various local conjurors. Also Thomas Hardy's 'The Withered Arm', which first appeared in *Blackwood's Edinburgh Magazine* in January 1888, describes Conjuror Trendle's skills. See Thomas Hardy, *Stories and Poems*, ed. Donald J. Morrison (London: Dent, 1970), pp. 31–3. Witchcraft in England is usually dealt with by historians only for the period from the late middle ages to the end of the seventeenth century. See, for example, Christina Larner, *Witchcraft and Religion: The Politics of Popular Belief* (Oxford: Basil Blackwell, 1985), especially Ch. 5 'Witchcraft Past and Present', pp. 79–92. Also Alan MacFarlane, *Witchcraft in Tudor and Stuart England* (London: Routledge & Kegan Paul, 1970). An earlier work by C. L'Estrange Ewen, *Witch-Hunting and Witch Trials* (London: Kegan Paul, Trench, Trubner, 1929), considered the records of witch trials from the Home Circuit 1559 until the repeal in 1736 of the laws which made witchcraft an offence. Sir James G. Frazer's massive *The Golden Bough: A Study in Magic and Religion* (London: Macmillan, 1971) remains a starting point for all enquiry into magic rituals, in particular pp. 14–63, on sympathetic magic. The standard social anthropological perspective remains that of E. E. Evans-Pritchard, *Witchcraft, Oracles and Magic among the Azande* (Oxford: Clarendon Press, 1937).

36. D. H. Moutray Read, 'Hampshire Folklore', *Folk-Lore*, xxii (1911), pp. 314–15.

37. Marianna S. Hagen, *Annals of Old Ropley (Hampshire)* (Alton: C. Mills, 1929), p. 63.

38. Howard Coombs and Arthur N. Bax (eds), *Journal of a Somerset Rector: John Skinner, A.M., Antiquary* (London: John Murray, 1930), p. 238.

39. Lucy Mair, *Witchcraft* (London: Weidenfeld & Nicolson, 1969), p. 9.

40. See, for example, Charlotte M. Yonge, *An Old Woman's Outlook in a Hampshire Village* (London: Macmillan, 1896), p. 163. The herbalist Yonge describes from her personal experience was a baker by profession. She writes: 'He compounded drugs and gave his attendance and his medicines freely out of pure charity. It was really valuable doctoring in many simple cases'.

41. Atkinson, *Forty Years in a Moorland Parish*, p. 111.

42. See, for example, blacksmiths' rituals on St Clements Day (23 November) at Twyford and Hursley (Hampshire) reported in Moutray Read, 'Hampshire Folklore', p. 328. For horsemen, see Leslie F. Newman, 'Notes on some Rural and Trade Initiation Ceremonies in the Eastern Countries', *Folk-Lore*, LI (March 1940), pp. 32–47; Thomas Davidson, 'The Horseman's Word: A Rural Initiation Ceremony', *Gwerin*, I (December 1956), pp. 67–74.

43. Udal, *Dorsetshire Folk-Lore*, p. 215.

44. R. L. Tongue, *Somerset Folklore: County Folklore*, VIII, ed. K. M. Briggs (London: The Folk-Lore Society, 1965), p. 76.

45. M. K. Ashby, *Joseph Ashby of Tysoe, 1859–1919: A Study of English Village Life* (London: Merlin Press, 1974), p. 16.

46. Charlotte S. Burne, 'Folk-Lore: Legends and Old Customs', in Thomas Auden (ed.), *Memorials of Old Shropshire* (London: Bemrose, 1906), p. 121.

47. Rev. A. C. Smith 'On Certain Wiltshire Traditions, Charms and Superstitions', *The Wiltshire Archaeological and Natural History Magazine*, XIV (1874), pp. 322.

48. Ibid., p. 323.

49. For example, Thomas Hardy has Tess's mother refer to a volume called 'The Compleat Fortune-Teller' in his novel *Tess of the d'Urbervilles*, p. 50. Even in the twentieth century it was possible to obtain such volumes. As an example, see *The Complete Book of Fortune*, which was published by Associated Newspapers Ltd, even though it carries a disclaimer that 'the results obtained must be regarded as an indication of what *may* happen, and must not be accepted as conclusive evidence of what *will* happen – for you, yourself, are the master of your Destiny'.

50. For a brief account of the statute, see Richard Burn, *The Justice of the Peace and Parish Officer* (London: T. Cadell, 1780), IV, p. 403. The law removed the offence of witchcraft from prosecution but created the new offence of 'pretending to witchcraft'.

51. For Tring (Hertfordshire) see *Gentleman's Magazine*, XXI (1751), pp. 186, 198. Collective action of ducking was taken against a

presumed witch called 'Old Mother Osborne' who died as a result of the rough treatment. For Seend (Wiltshire) see *Reading Mercury,* 13 March 1773.

52. *Reading Mercury,* 13 March 1773.

53. See the account by George Morley, *Shakespeare's Greenwood: The Customs of the Country* (London: David Nutt, 1900), pp. 65–8.

54. Dorothy Amphlett, 'Worcestershire Folklore', in Francis B. Andrews (ed.), *Memorials of Old Worcestershire* (London: George Allen, 1911), p. 263.

55. Ibid.

56. A. L. Clark 'Some Wiltshire Folk-Lore', *Wiltshire Notes and Queries,* I (1895), p. 105.

57. Smith, 'On Certain Wiltshire Traditions', p. 326.

58. Ibid., p. 328.

59. Udal, *Dorsetshire Folk-Lore,* p. 32.

60. *Gentleman's Magazine,* CII (1832), p. 590.

61. Ibid., p. 591.

62. George Sturt, *A Small Boy in the Sixties* (Brighton: Harvester Press, 1977), pp. 136–7.

63. Ibid., pp. 135–6.

64. G. F. Northall, *English Folk-Rhymes* (London: Kegan Paul, Trench, Trubner, 1892), pp. 131–2.

65. Sturt, *A Small Boy,* p. 134.

66. S. G. Kendall, *Farming Memoirs of a West Country Yeoman* (London: Faber & Faber, 1944), p. 35.

67. J. Alfred Eggar, *Life and Customs in Gilbert White's, Cobbett's and Kingsley's Country* (London: Simpkin, Marshall, Hamilton, Kent, n.d. *c.*1912), p. 148.

68. Enid Porter, *Cambridgeshire Customs and Folklore* (London: Routledge & Kegan Paul, 1969), p. 181.

69. H. Colley March, 'Witched Fishing Boats in Dorset', *Somerset and Dorset Notes and Queries,* X (June 1906), p. 37.

70. Eggar, *Life and Customs,* p. 149.

71. Henry J. Moule, 'Dorset Folk-Lore', *Folk-Lore Journal,* VI (1888), p.116.

72. Udal, *Dorsetshire Folk-Lore,* p. 213.

73. E. E. Balch, 'In a Wiltshire Village: Some Old Songs and Customs', *The Antiquary,* XLIV (1908), p. 382.

74. See Northall, *English Folk-Rhymes,* pp. 167–8; Udal, *Dorsetshire Folk-Lore,* pp. 239–40; W. J. Brown, *The Gods had Wings* (London: Constable, 1936), pp. 275–6.

75. Udal, *Dorsetshire Folk-Lore,* pp. 180–8.

76. Moutray Read, 'Hampshire Folklore', pp. 320–2.

77. David Clark, *Between Pulpit and Pew: Folk Religion in a North Yorkshire Fishing Village* (Cambridge: Cambridge University Press, 1982), pp. 134–9.

78. W. Wells Bladen, 'Notes on the Folk-Lore of North Staffordshire, chiefly collected at Stone', *Transactions of the North Staffordshire Field*

Club, xxxv (1901–4), p. 157. The personal response to deliberate malice, witchcraft could be a considered counter-measure. See Charlotte S. Burne, 'The Folklore of Staffordshire', *Journal of The British Archaeological Association*, ii (1892), p. 25.

79. John Lloyd Warden Page, *An Exploration of Dartmoor and its Antiquities* (London: Seeley, 1892), pp. 32–3.

80. Lilias Rider Haggard (ed.), *I Walked by Night: The Life of the King of Poachers* (London: Ivor Nicholson & Watson, 1933), p. 18.

81. Auden (ed.), *Memorials of Old Shropshire*, p. 121.

82. Thomas de Quincy, *Essays on Christianity, Paganism and Superstition* (Boston: Houghton, Mifflin, 1877), p. 561.

83. Oliver Lawson Dick (ed.), *Aubrey's Brief Lives* (London: Penguin, 1972), p. 29.

84. J. Harvey Bloom, *Folklore, Old Customs and Superstitions in Shakespeare Land* (London: Mitchell Hughes & Clarke, 1930), pp. iii–iv.

85. William Howitt, *Rural Life of England* (Philadelphia: Carey & Hart, 1841), p. 483.

86. Alfred Williams, *Villages of the White Horse* (London: Gerald Duckworth, 1918), pp. 265–6. For local legend and popular culture see also Jacqueline Simpson, 'The Local Legend: A Product of Popular Culture', *Rural History*, ii (April 1991), pp. 25–35

Bibliography

1. PROBLEMATISING POPULAR CULTURE *Tim Harris*

The best general European overview is Peter Burke, *Popular Culture in Early Modern Europe* (London: Temple Smith, 1978 – revised edition Scolar Press, 1994).

For early modern England in particular, see: Barry Reay (ed.), *Popular Culture in Seventeenth-Century England* (London: Croom Helm, 1985); Eileen and Stephen Yeo (eds), *Popular Culture and Class Conflict 1590–1914: Explorations in the History of Labour and Leisure* (Brighton: Harvester Press, 1981); J. M. Golby and A. W. Purdue, *The Civilisation of the Crowd: Popular Culture in England 1750–1900* (London: B.T. Batsford, 1985); Hugh Cunningham, *Leisure in the Industrial Revolution c.1780–c.1880* (London: Croom Helm, 1980); Robert W. Malcolmson, *Popular Recreations in English Society 1700–1850* (Cambridge: Cambridge University Press, 1973); Robert D. Storch (ed.), *Popular Culture and Custom in Nineteenth-Century England* (London: Croom Helm, 1982); Bob Bushaway, *By Rite: Custom, Ceremony and Community in England 1700–1880* (London: Junction Books, 1982). Valuable insights can also be gleaned from: Keith Wrightson and David Levine, *Poverty and Piety in an English Village: Terling, 1525–1700* (London: Academic Press, 1979); Keith Wrightson, *English Society 1580–1680* (London: Hutchinson, 1980); Tessa Watt, *Cheap Print and Popular Piety, 1550–1640* (Cambridge: Cambridge University Press, 1991); E. P. Thompson, *Customs in Common* (London: Merlin, 1991); Peter Borsay, *The English Urban Renaissance: Culture and Society in the Provincial Town 1660–1770* (Oxford: Clarendon Press, 1989).

For some of the conceptual and methodological problems involved in the study of popular culture, see: Tim Harris, 'The Problem of "Popular Political Culture" in Seventeenth-Century London', *History of European Ideas*, x (1989), pp. 43–58; Bob Scribner, 'Is a History of Popular Culture Possible?', *History of European Ideas*, x (1989), pp. 175–91; Steven L. Kaplan (ed.), *Understanding Popular Culture: Europe from the Middle Ages to the Nineteenth Century* (Berlin: Mouton, 1984).

2. REGIONAL CULTURES? *David Underdown*

Popular Culture: General

John Aubrey, *Three Prose Works*, ed. John Buchanan-Brown (Fontwell: Centaur Press, 1972). Although chaotically arranged, Aubrey's works contain much interesting information about popular customs.

Peter Burke, *Popular Culture in Early Modern Europe* (London: Temple Smith, 1978).

Edwin O. James, *Seasonal Feasts and Festivals* (New York: Barnes & Noble, 1961).

Barry Reay (ed.), *Popular Culture in Seventeenth-Century England* (London: Croom Helm, 1985).

Bob Scribner, 'Is a History of Popular Culture Possible?' *History of European Ideas*, x (1989), pp. 173–91.

David Underdown, 'The Taming of the Scold: The Enforcement of Patriarchal Authority in Early Modern England', in Anthony Fletcher and John Stevenson (eds), *Order and Disorder in Early Modern England* (Cambridge: Cambridge University Press, 1985), pp. 116–36.

Regionalism and Culture

Richard Carew, *Carew's Survey of Cornwall* (London: T. Bensley, 1811). One of the best of the early antiquarian studies of individual counties; contains a famous description of hurling.

Alan Everitt, *Continuity and Colonization: The Evolution of Kentish Settlement* (Leicester: Leicester University Press, 1986).

John Morrill, 'The Ecology of Allegiance in the English Revolution', *Journal of British Studies*, xxvi (1987), pp. 451–67. A sceptical view of the argument for regional culture. See also Underdown's 'Reply to John Morrill', ibid., pp. 468–79.

Enid Porter, *Cambridgeshire Customs and Folklore* (New York: Barnes & Noble, 1969). One of many county folklore studies.

A. L. Rowse, *Tudor Cornwall: Portrait of a Society* (London: Jonathan Cape, 1941). A valuable supplement to Carew (above).

E. P. Thompson, *Whigs and Hunters: The Origin of the Black Act* (New York: Pantheon Books, 1975). A fine study of popular protest in the forests of southeastern England in the early eighteenth century.

David Underdown, *Fire from Heaven: Life in an English Town in the Seventeenth Century* (London: HarperCollins, 1992). Illustrates urban–rural tensions.

David Underdown, *Revel, Riot and Rebellion: Popular Politics and Culture in England 1603–1660* (Oxford: Clarendon Press, 1985).

Sport: General

Dennis Brailsford, *Sport and Society: Elizabeth to Anne* (London: Routledge, 1969).

Christina Hole, *English Sports and Pastimes* (London: B. T. Batsford, 1949).

Robert W. Malcolmson, *Popular Recreations in English Society 1700–1850* (Cambridge: Cambridge University Press, 1973).

Cricket

Rowland Bowen, *Cricket: A History of its Growth and Development throughout the World* (London: Eyre & Spottiswoode, 1970). Perhaps the most complete history of the game, but contains some dubious speculations about its origins.

Christopher Brookes, *English Cricket: The Game and its Players through the Ages* (London: Weidenfeld & Nicolson, 1978). Contains the best social history of the game before 1800.

John Nyren, *The Young Cricketer's Tutor*, ed. F. S. Ashley-Cooper (London: Gay & Bird, 1902). The classic description of the great Hambledon club of the 1770s. Selections often reprinted in cricket anthologies.

3. THE GENDERING OF POPULAR CULTURE IN EARLY MODERN ENGLAND   *Susan Dwyer Amussen*

Women and Gender

Susan Dwyer Amussen, *An Ordered Society: Gender and Class in Early Modern England* (Oxford: Basil Blackwell, 1988).

Judith Bennett, 'Misogyny, Popular Culture, and Women's Work', *History Workshop Journal*, XXXI (1991), 166–88.

Lindsey Charles and Lorna Duffin (eds), *Women and Work in Pre-Industrial England* (London: Croom Helm, 1985).

Alice Clark, *Working Life of Women in the Seventeenth Century* (London, 1919, reprinted London: Routledge & Kegan Paul, 1982): the classic work in the field, whose conceptual framework is still powerful.

Natalie Z. Davis, ' "Women's History" in Transition: The European Case', *Feminist Studies*, III (1976), pp. 83–103.

Lisa Jardine, *Still Harping on Daughters: Women and Drama in the Age of Shakespeare* (2nd edn, New York: Columbia University Press, 1989).

Joan Kelly, *Women, History, and Theory: The Essays of Joan Kelly* (Chicago: University of Chicago Press, 1984), esp. 'The Social Relations of the Sexes: Methodological Implications of Women's History' (pp. 1–18) and 'Did Women Have a Renaissance?' (pp. 19–50).

Katherine Usher Henderson and Barbara McManus (eds), *Half-Humankind: Texts and Contexts of the Controversy about Women in England, 1540–1640* (Urbana: University of Illinois Press, 1985).

Mary Prior (ed.), *Women in English Society, 1500– 1800* (London: Methuen, 1985).

Joan Wallach Scott, 'Gender: A Useful Category of Historical Analysis', in *Gender and the Politics of History* (New York: Columbia University Press, 1988), pp. 28–50.

Joy Wiltenburg, *Disorderly Women and Female Power in Early Modern England and Germany* (Charlottesville: University of Virginia Press, 1992).

Skimmingtons and Other Rituals

Natalie Davis, 'The Reasons of Misrule', in *Society and Culture in Early Modern Europe* (Stanford: Stanford University Press, 1975), pp. 97–123.

Martin Ingram, 'Ridings, Rough Music, and the "Reform of Popular Culture" in Early Modern England', *Past and Present*, CV (1984), pp. 79–113.

Martin Ingram, 'Le Charivari dans l'Angleterre du XVIe et du XVIIe siècle', in Jaques Le Goff and Jean-Claude Schmitt (eds), *Le Charivari: Actes de la table ronde organisée à Paris . . .* (Paris: Mouton, 1981), pp. 251–64.

E. P. Thompson, '"Rough Music": Le Charivari Anglais', *Annales: ESC*, XXVII (1972), pp. 285–312.

David Underdown, 'The Taming of the Scold: The Enforcement of Patriarchal Authority in Early Modern England', in Anthony Fletcher and John Stevenson (eds), *Order and Disorder in Early Modern England* (Cambridge: Cambridge University Press, 1985), pp. 116–36.

Popular Literature

Margaret Spufford, *Small Books and Pleasant Histories: Popular Fiction and its Readership in Seventeenth-Century England* (Cambridge: Cambridge University Press, 1981).

Roger Thompson (ed.), *Samuel Pepys' Penny Merriments* (New York: Columbia University Press, 1977): a selection which gives a flavour of the cheap ballad literature.

Witchcraft

John Demos, *Entertaining Satan: Witchcraft and the Culture of Early New England* (New York: Oxford University Press, 1982).

Anabel Gregory, 'Witchcraft, Politics, and "Good Neighbourhood" in Early Seventeenth-Century Rye', *Past and Present*, CXXXII (1991), pp. 31–66.

Marianne Hester, *Lewd Women and Wicked Witches: A Study of the Dynamics of Male Domination* (London: Routledge, 1992).

Clive Holmes, 'Popular Culture? Witches, Magistrates and Divines in Early Modern England', in Steven L. Kaplan (ed.), *Understanding Popular Culture: Europe from the Middle Ages to the Nineteenth Century* (Berlin: Mouton, 1984), pp. 85–111.

Carol F. Karlson, *The Devil in the Shape of a Woman: Witchcraft in Colonial New England* (New York: W. W. Norton, 1987).

Christina Larner, *Enemies of God: The Witch-Hunt in Scotland* (Baltimore: Johns Hopkins University Press, 1981).

Michael MacDonald, *Witchcraft and Hysteria in Elizabethan London: Edward Jorden and the Mary Glover Case* (London: Routledge, 1991).

Alan Macfarlane, *Witchcraft in Tudor and Stuart England* (London: Routledge & Kegan Paul, 1970).

Keith Thomas, *Religion and the Decline of Magic* (London: Weidenfeld & Nicolson, 1971). The classic work in the field.

4. LITERACY AND LITERATURE IN POPULAR CULTURE   *Jonathan Barry*

The standard work on literacy before 1700 is D. Cressy, *Literacy and the Social Order: Reading and Writing in Tudor and Stuart England* (Cambridge: Cambridge University Press, 1980). For the later period see D. Vincent, *Literacy and Popular Culture: England 1750–1914* (Cambridge: Cambridge University Press, 1989) and W. B. Stephens, *Education, Literacy and Society, 1830–1870* (Manchester: Manchester University Press, 1987). A brief overview is provided by D. Cressy, 'Literacy in Context: Meaning and Measurement in Early Modern England', in J. Brewer and R. Porter (eds), *Consumption and the World of Goods* (London: Routledge, 1993), pp. 305–19, while W. B. Stephens, 'Literacy in England, Scotland and Wales, 1500–1900', *History of Education Quarterly*, XXX (1990), pp. 545–71, reviews the literature of the last few decades. For international comparisons see R. A. Houston, 'Literacy and Society in the West 1500–1850', *Social History*, VIII (1983), pp. 269–93; Houston, *Literacy in Early Modern Europe* (Harlow: Longman, 1988); and Houston, *Scottish Literacy and Scottish Identity: Illiteracy and Society in Scotland and Northern England 1600–1800* (Cambridge: Cambridge University Press, 1985). Interdisciplinary debates about the nature and significance of literacy can be sampled in J. Goody (ed.), *Literacy in Traditional Societies* (Cambridge: Cambridge University Press, 1968); H. J. Graff, *Literacy and Social Development in the West: A Reader* (Cambridge: Cambridge University Press, 1981); B. V. Street, *Literacy in Theory and Practice* (Cambridge: Cambridge University Press, 1984). The most important recent articles on this period are T. W. Laqueur, 'The Cultural Origins of Popular Literacy in England 1500–1850', *Oxford Review of Education*, XI (1976), pp. 255–75; M. Spufford, 'First Steps in Literacy: The Reading and Writing Experiences of the Humblest Seventeenth-Century Autobiographers', *Social History*, IV (1979), pp. 407–35; K. Thomas, 'The Meaning of Literacy in Early Modern England', in G. Baumann (ed.), *The Written Word: Literacy in Transition* (Oxford: Clarendon Press, 1986), pp. 97–131; Thomas, 'Numeracy in Early Modern England', *Transactions of the Royal Historical Society*, 5th series, XXXVII (1987), pp. 103–32; B. Reay, 'The Context and Meaning of Popular Literacy: Some Evidence from Nineteenth-Century Rural England', *Past and Present*, CXXXI (1991), pp. 89–129. The debate on the impact of industrialisation can be traced through S. J. and J. M. Nicholas, 'Male Literacy, "De-skilling" and the Industrial Revolution', *Journal of Interdisciplinary History*, XXIII (1992–3), pp. 1–18. The place of literacy in education as a whole can be traced through R. O'Day, *Education and Society 1500–1800* (London: Longman, 1982), while key studies are T. W. Laqueur, *Religion and Respectability: Sunday Schools and Working-Class Culture 1780–1850* (New Haven: Yale University Press, 1976) and I. Michael, *The Teaching of English from the Sixteenth Century to 1870* (Cambridge: Cambridge University Press, 1987).

An excellent introduction to popular literature is provided by B. Capp, 'Popular Literature', in B. Reay (ed.), *Popular Culture in Seventeenth-Century England* (London: Croom Helm, 1985), pp. 198–243, while an overview of the types of literature involved is given by V. Neuburg, *Popular Literature: A History and a Guide* (Harmondsworth: Penguin, 1977). The best guide to the early part of the period is now T. Watt, *Cheap Print and Popular Piety 1550–1640* (Cambridge: Cambridge University Press, 1991). Other important studies include L. B. Wright, *Middle-Class Culture in Elizabethan England* (new edn, Cornell: Cornell University Press, 1958); L. Stevenson, *Praise and Paradox: Merchants and Craftsmen in Elizabethan Popular Literature* (Cambridge: Cambridge University Press, 1984); N. Wurzbach, *The Rise of the English Street Ballad 1550–1650* (Cambridge: Cambridge University Press, 1990). For the middle part of our period see C. J. Sommerville, *Popular Religion in Restoration England* (Gainesville: University of Florida Presses, 1979); B. Capp, *Astrology and the Popular Press: English Almanacs 1500–1800* (London: Faber & Faber, 1979); M. Spufford, *Small Books and Pleasant Histories: Popular Fiction and its Readership in Seventeenth-Century England* (London: Methuen, 1981). For the eighteenth century see V. Neuburg, *Popular Education in Eighteenth-Century England* (London: Woburn Press, 1971); P. Rogers, *Literature and Popular Culture in Eighteenth-Century England* (Brighton: Harvester Press, 1985); S. Pederson, 'Hannah More meets Simple Simon: Tracts, Chapbooks and Popular Culture in Late Eighteenth-Century England', *Journal of British Studies*, xxv (1986), pp. 84–113; J. Raven, *Judging New Wealth: Popular Publishing and Responses to Commerce in England 1750–1800* (Oxford: Clarendon Press, 1992). Raven's book also provides the best introduction to recent studies of publishing and bookselling, for an overview of which see J. Feather, *A History of British Publishing* (London: Routledge, 1988). A useful collection of essays is R. Myers and M. Harris (eds), *Spreading the Word: The Distribution Networks of Print 1550–1850* (Winchester: St Paul's Bibliographies, 1990).

The classic studies of readership are R. K. Webb, *The British Working-Class Reader 1790–1848: Literacy and Social Tension* (London: George Allen & Unwin, 1955) and R. D. Altick, *The English Common Reader: A Social History of the Mass Reading Public 1800–1900* (Chicago: University of Chicago Press, 1957); a helpful critique and updating of these is provided by J. Rose, 'Re-Reading the English Common Reader: A Preface to the History of Audiences', *Journal of the History of Ideas*, III (1992), pp. 47–70. An illustration of new approaches is provided by R. Chartier (ed.), *The Culture of Print* (Cambridge: Polity Press, 1989) and M. Fissell, 'Readers, Texts and Contexts: Vernacular Medical Works in Early Modern England', in R. Porter (ed.), *The Popularization of Medicine 1650–1850* (London: Routledge, 1992), pp. 72–96. Examples of their application to popular literature, as read by women, are D. Dugaw, *Warrior Women and Popular Balladry 1650–1850* (Cambridge: Cambridge University Press, 1989) and J. Wiltenburg, *Disorderly Women and Female Power in the Street Literature of Early Modern England and Germany* (Charlottesville: University Press of Virginia, 1992). For the implications of such work for the definition of literature see P. Rogers, *Grub Street* (London: Methuen, 1972); K. MacDermott, 'Literature and the Grub Street Myth', in P. Humm, P. Stigant, and P. Widdowson (eds), *Popular Fictions* (London: Methuen, 1986), pp. 16–28; J. P. Klancher,

The Making of English Reading Audiences 1790–1832 (Madison: University of Wisconsin Press, 1987); S. Achinstein, 'Audiences and Authors: Ballads and the Making of English Renaissance Literary Culture', *Journal of Medieval and Renaissance Studies*, XXII (1992), pp. 311–26. On censorship see C. Hill, *Collected Essays*, 3 vols (Brighton: Harvester Press, 1985–6), especially 'Censorship and English Literature' (I, pp. 32–71); Hill, *A Nation of Change and Novelty* (London: Routledge, 1990), especially Chs 3, 10–11; L. Schwoerer, 'Liberty of the Press and Public Opinion 1660–1695', in J. R. Jones (ed.), *Liberty Secured; Britain before and after 1688* (Stanford: Stanford University Press, 1992), pp. 199–230; G. C. Gibbs, 'Press and Public Opinion: Prospective', in ibid., pp. 231–64.

Finally, any work on literature and culture owes an inevitable debt to the work of Raymond Williams. For a brilliantly sympathetic critique and revision of his work, notably in the light of recent gender studies, see M. Shiach, *Discourse on Popular Culture: Class, Gender and History in Cultural Analysis, 1730 to the Present* (Cambridge: Polity Press 1989).

5. FROM REFORMATION TO TOLERATION *Martin Ingram*

Studies of the religious history of this period are legion, but few are couched specifically in terms of popular culture. Barry Reay, 'Popular Religion', in Barry Reay (ed.), *Popular Culture in Seventeenth-Century England* (London: Croom Helm, 1985), is a lively, wide-ranging recent survey, while Imogen Luxton, "The Reformation and Popular Culture", in Felicity Heal and Rosemary O'Day (eds), *Church and Society in England; Henry VIII to James I* (London: Macmillan, 1977), was when it appeared a highly innovative piece focusing on the shifting balance between words and symbols, and still repays careful attention. Sir Keith Thomas's magisterial *Religion and the Decline of Magic: Studies in Popular Beliefs in Sixteenth- and Seventeenth-Century England* (London: Weidenfeld & Nicolson, 1971) was written before the term 'popular culture' became fashionable, but the sub-title suggests a closely related conceptual framework. This giant of a book is far and away the best introduction to popular religious cultures, and has been enormously influential. However, its concentration on witchcraft, magic, astrology, popular superstition and religious ignorance, indifference and scepticism perhaps gives an exaggerated impression of their significance, while at the same time privileging 'religion' over 'magic' as an intellectual and philosophical system. Another view which has had a substantial impact is that of Keith Wrightson, presented most succinctly in his *English Society, 1580–1680* (London: Hutchinson, 1982), Ch. 7, but developed in other works including Keith Wrightson and David Levine, *Poverty and Piety in an English Village: Terling, 1525–1700* (London: Academic Press, 1979). This interpretation, based on a contrast between the 'godly' minority of pious believers and the less religious 'multitude', relates religious change to a more general model of social and cultural polarisation. However, its terms of reference derive from the writings of contemporary Puritan moralists and are inevitably compromised by their partisan vision, while the social and cultural model is essentially a bipolar one that does not do justice to the complexities and subtleties of contemporary English religious cultures, in particular by underemphasising unspectacular orthodoxy.

An attempt to redress the balance in favour of the conforming majority, and also to reassert the centrality of religious beliefs and practices within the broad framework of the official church, may be seen in Martin Ingram, *Church Courts, Sex and Marriage in England, 1570–1640* (Cambridge: Cambridge University Press, 1987), esp. Ch. 3. The importance of the 'reality of religion' for the 'ordinary villager' had earlier been stressed in Margaret Spufford, *Contrasting Communities: English Villagers in the Sixteenth and Seventeenth Centuries* (Cambridge: Cambridge University Press, 1974), which also provides an interesting discussion of Cambridgeshire dissent. John Morrill's 'The Church in England, 1642–9', in John Morrill (ed.), *Reactions to the English Civil War* (London: Macmillan, 1982) argues for enduring attachment to the Anglican church during the Civil Wars and Interregnum. The importance of the parish church in the religious culture of the sixteenth and seventeenth centuries – and indeed of earlier and later periods too – is also the theme of Susan Wright (ed.), *Parish, Church and People: Local Studies in Lay Religion, 1350–1750* (London: Hutchinson, 1988), which among other valuable contributions includes Donald Spaeth's essay on the under-explored topic of late seventeenth-century popular Anglicanism.

Numerous works, with varying emphases on popular religious culture (however defined), may be consulted on specific topics and periods. The best evocation of pre-Reformation religious culture is Eamon Duffy, *The Stripping of the Altars: Traditional Religion in England, c.1400–c.1580* (New Haven: Yale University Press, 1992), but it is less satisfactory on the process of change. Moreover it says virtually nothing about the current of self-conscious dissent known as Lollardy, on which see Anne Hudson, *The Premature Reformation: Wycliffite Texts and Lollard History* (Oxford: Clarendon Press, 1988). The 'Reformation', as a term and as a topic, is now highly contentious. A. G. Dickens, *The English Reformation* (London: B. T. Batsford, 1964; revised edition, 1989) argues for a groundswell of dissatisfaction with the late medieval church. The contrary view, which presents that church as 'unchallenged', 'Reformation' as a set of changes contingent on political circumstances, and the outcome of these developments as the partial failure of Protestantism at the popular level, is vigorously argued in Christopher Haigh, *English Reformations: Religion, Politics and Society under the Tudors* (Oxford: Clarendon Press, 1993). One feature of the impact of the Reformation on English culture – popular and otherwise – is imaginatively explored by Margaret Aston, *England's Iconoclasts, Vol. I: Laws against Images* (Oxford: Clarendon Press, 1988); another by

Christopher Hill, *The English Bible and the Seventeenth-Century Revolution* (Harmondsworth: Allen Lane, 1993). Tessa Watt, *Cheap Print and Popular Piety, 1550–1640* (Cambridge: Cambridge University Press, 1991) charts the emergence of a post-Reformation popular culture in ballads, prints and chapbooks; David Cressy, *Bonfires and Bells: National Memory and the Protestant Calendar in Elizabethan and Stuart England* (London: Weidenfeld & Nicolson, 1989) deals with yet another dimension of cultural change. The most interesting book on a controversial subject is John Bossy, *The English Catholic Community, 1570–1850* (London: Darton, Longman & Todd, 1975), but for a briefer introduction and judicious survey of the debates, see Alan Dures, *English Catholicism, 1558–1642* (London: Longman, 1983); unfortunately neither work pays as much attention to the lower ranks of society as might be wished. The essential guide to Puritanism is Patrick Collinson. Of his various works perhaps the most directly relevant to popular religion is *The Religion of Protestants: The Church in English Society, 1559–1625* (Oxford: Clarendon Press, 1982), especially Ch. 5; but see also *The Birthpangs of Protestant England: Religious and Cultural Change in the Sixteenth and Seventeenth Centuries* (London: Macmillan, 1988); *Godly People: Essays on English Protestantism and Puritanism* (London: Hambledon Press, 1983); and *The Elizabethan Puritan Movement* (London: Jonathan Cape, 1967). Excellent insights into the life of a Puritan layman of relatively low status are provided by Paul Seaver, *Wallington's World: A Puritan Artisan in Seventeenth-Century London* (London: Methuen, 1985), which is based closely on Wallington's personal writings. For a different and highly stimulating view of Puritanism, which contrasts it with variants of parish Anglicanism, tries to relate it to regional cultural patterns, and argues for the importance of cultural conflicts in the Civil Wars, see David Underdown, *Revel, Riot and Rebellion: Popular Politics and Culture in England, 1603–1660* (Oxford: Clarendon Press, 1985); some of these themes are further explored in a particular local context in the same author's *Fire from Heaven: The Life of an English Town in the Seventeenth Century* (London: Harper Collins, 1992). On the explosion of religious sects in the 1640s and 1650s see J. F. McGregor and B. Reay (eds), *Radical Religion in the English Revolution* (Oxford: Oxford University Press, 1984). The standard introduction to post-Restoration dissent is Michael Watts, *The Dissenters: From the Reformation to the French Revolution* (Oxford: Clarendon Press, 1978), Pt III, but see also the important findings of Tim Harris, *London Crowds in the Reign of Charles II: Propaganda and Politics from the Restoration until the Exclusion Crisis* (Cambridge: Cambridge University Press, 1987). The background to the Toleration Act is explored in Ole Peter Grell, Jonathan I. Israel and Nicholas Tyacke (eds), *From Persecution to Toleration: The Glorious Revolution and Religion in England* (Oxford: Clarendon Press, 1991). By 1689, of course, the role of religion in England was in many respects different from what it had been 150 years earlier: the problem for the historian of culture is how best to conceptualise these changes. For one provocative solution, see C. John Sommerville, *The Secularization of Early Modern England: From Religious Culture to Religious Faith* (Oxford: Oxford University Press, 1992).

6. THE PEOPLE'S HEALTH IN GEORGIAN ENGLAND *Roy Porter*

There is a dearth of good recent scholarship on the history of folk medicine in Britain; nothing has yet superseded W. G. Black, *Folk Medicine: A Chapter in the History of Culture* (London: Folklore Society, 1883). On the more magical dimensions, see K. V. Thomas, *Religion and the Decline of Magic: Studies in Popular Beliefs in Sixteenth- and Seventeenth-Century England* (London: Weidenfeld & Nicolson, 1971), and M. Chamberlain, *Old Wives' Tales: Their History, Remedies and Spells* (London: Virago, 1981); for astrology and healing, now see Patrick Curry, *Prophecy and Power: Astrology in Early Modern England* (Cambridge: Polity Press, 1989). Herbalism is handled in Agnes Arber, *Herbals* (Cambridge: Cambridge University Press, 1938) and B. Griggs, *Green Pharmacy: A History of Herbal Medicine* (London: Jill Norman & Hobhouse, 1981).

A recent collection of essays – Roy Porter (ed.), *The Popularization of Medicine, 1650–1850* (London: Routledge, 1992) – examines the simplification of elite medicine for wider audiences, in Britain, France, Central Europe and North America. In that volume, Andrew Wear's 'The Popularization of Medicine in Early Modern England' deals with religious aspects, and Mary E. Fissell's 'Readers, Texts and Contexts: Vernacular Medical Works in Early Modern England' examines chapbooks, almanacs and other writings for the barely literate. For forms of alternative medicine see Roy Porter, *Health for Sale: Quackery in England 1650–1850* (Manchester: Manchester University Press, 1989), and the essays in W. F. Bynum and Roy Porter (eds), *Medical Fringe and Medical Orthodoxy 1750–1850* (London: Croom Helm, 1986).

The world of fertility pills and abortifacient potions is illuminated in Angus MacLaren's *Reproductive Rituals: The Perception of Fertility in England from the 16th Century to the 19th Century* (London: Methuen, 1984).

7. WOMEN, WORK AND CULTURAL CHANGE IN EIGHTEENTH- AND EARLY NINETEENTH-CENTURY LONDON *Patty Seleski*

Domestic servants, especially pre-Victorian servants, have received a curiously small amount of attention from historians. The best place to start for information about English servants before the Victorian period is still J. J. Hecht, *The Domestic Servant Class in the Eighteenth Century* (London: Routledge & Kegan Paul, 1955), although readers should beware of its bias towards the servants of the gentry and the aristocracy. Further, Hecht relies almost exclusively on printed sources: he makes great use of memoirs, printed handbooks and household manuals, and contemporary literature. French servants have been served much better. Both C. Fairchilds, *Domestic Enemies: Servants and their Masters in Old Regime France* (Baltimore: Johns Hopkins University Press, 1984) and S. Maza, *Servants and their Masters in Eighteenth-Century France* (Princeton: Princeton University Press, 1983) provide good coverage of the major issues surrounding domestic service, albeit in a French context, and employ a wide range of sources, both archival and printed, in making their arguments. In recent years, B. Hill, *Women, Work and Sexual Politics in Eighteenth-Century England* (Oxford: Basil Blackwell, 1989), J. Gillis 'Servants, Sexual Relations, and the Risks of Illegitimacy in London, 1801–1900', *Feminist Studies,* v (1979) and D. A. Kent, 'Ubiquitous but Invisible: Female Domestic Servants in Mid-Eighteenth-Century London', *History Workshop Journal,* xxviii (1989), have looked at eighteenth- and early nineteenth-century domestic service as an occupation, and they have applied questions of gender construction and difference to women's experience of domestic service. Hill relies heavily on Hecht and additional printed sources, but both Kent and Gillis suggest creative ways of finding out about these 'invisible' workers in philanthropic, administrative and legal records.

Equally neglected have been questions of class and cultural relations between servants and mistresses/masters. The most important work on middle-class formation only briefly addresses the issues. L. Davidoff and C. Hall, *Family Fortunes: Men and Women of the English Middle Class* (London: Hutchinson, 1987) is surprising in this regard, especially because of the centrality of gender to its thesis. P. Earle, *The Making of the English Middle Class* (London: Methuen, 1989) also provides important information about the cultural transformation of the middle class without engaging the gender issues raised in this essay. L. Davidoff's 'Mastered for Life: Servant and Wife in Victorian and Edwardian England', *Journal of Social History,* vii (1973/74) suggests one way of looking at mistress/servant relations, while P. Seleski's, 'The Women of the Laboring Poor: Love, Work and Poverty in London, 1750–1820' unpublished Ph.D. thesis, Stanford University (1989), forms the basis of the argument made here. Literary critics have done much of the exploration of emerging middle-class domestic ideology. M. Poovey, *Uneven Developments: The Ideological Work of Gender in Mid-Victorian England* (Chicago: University of Chicago Press, 1988) and *The Proper Lady and the Woman Writer: Ideology as Style in the Works of Mary Wollstonecraft, Mary Shelley and Jane Austen* (Chicago, 1984); and N. Armstrong, *Desire and Domestic Fiction: A Political History of the Novel* (Oxford: Oxford University Press, 1987) have had the most influence among historians, though their virtual silence on the question of servants has been noted in the text. Armstrong and Poovey's 'new historicist' approaches and their relation to the work of Hall and Davidoff have been explored by J. Newton, 'Family Fortunes: "New History" and "New Historicism"', *Radical History Review,* xliii (1989) in a valuable essay that suggests new avenues for research.

8. AGAINST INNOVATION? *John Rule*

John Rule, *The Experience of Labour in Eighteenth-Century Industry* (London: Croom Helm, 1981) is a detailed study of most of the issues and provides information on sources. Adrian Randall, *Before the Luddites: Custom,*

Community and Machinery in the English Woollen Industry 1776–1809 (Cambridge: Cambridge University Press, 1991), is a major recent work. The important work on the Birmingham trades of Clive Behagg has now been brought together in *Politics and Production in the Early Nineteenth Century* (London: Routledge, 1990). For the London trades, especially on the issue of customary perquisites, P. Linebaugh, *The London Hanged: Crime and Civil Society in the Eighteenth Century* (London: Allen Lane, 1991) is challenging, but essential reading. Edward Thompson's seminal work on the popular culture of the eighteenth century has been brought together with some important revisions and additions in *Customs in Common* (London: Merlin, 1992). His influential article 'Time, Work Discipline and Industrial Capitalism' is included. It originally appeared in *Past and Present*, XXXVIII (1967), pp. 56–97. On the same subject is D. A. Reid, 'The Decline of Saint Monday, 1766–1876', *Past and Present*, LXXI (1976), pp. 76–101. Maxine Berg, *The Age of Manufactures, 1700–1820* (London: Fontana, 1985), has much of relevance, especially on rural manufacturing, and also provides a broad economic and social background. Her contribution to P. Joyce (ed.), *The Historical Meanings of Work* (Cambridge: Cambridge University Press, 1987), looking at 'Women's Work, Mechanisation and the Early Phases of Industrialisation in England', is valuable, while that of J. G. Rule, 'The Property of Skill in the Period of Manufacture' in the same collection is also useful. A collection of studies of early trade unionism is provided in J. G. Rule, (ed.), *British Trade Unionism 1750–1850: The Formative Years* (London: Longman, 1988), while on this subject, E. P. Thompson, *The Making of the English Working Class* (1963, reprinted Harmondsworth: Penguin, 1968) remains essential. So too do some of the early writings of E. J. Hobsbawm, conveniently reprinted in *Labouring Men* (London: Weidenfeld & Nicolson, 1964).

9. 'TACIT, UNSUSPECTED, BUT STILL IMPLICIT FAITH?' *Bob Bushaway*

The historiography of alternative belief is rich and varied for the late medieval and early modern period but is much scantier for rural culture in the eighteenth and nineteenth centuries. Much of the theoretical framework for the historian of alternative belief is provided by the work of social anthropologists.

General

Peter L. Berger, *A Rumour of Angels: Modern Society and the Supernatural* (London: Pelican, 1971).

Judith Devlin, *The Superstitious Mind: French Peasants and the Supernatural in the Nineteenth Century* (New Haven: Yale University Press, 1987).

E. E. Evans-Pritchard, *Witchcraft, Oracles and Magic among the Azande* (Oxford: Clarendon Press, 1937).

J. G. Frazer, *The Golden Bough: A Study in Magic and Religion* (abridged edn, London: Macmillan, 1922).

Gustav Jahoda, *The Psychology of Superstition* (London: Penguin, 1970).

J. M. Lewis, *Social Anthropology in Perspective: The Relevance of Social Anthropology* (London: Penguin, 1976).

Lucy Mair, *Witchcraft* (London: Weidenfeld & Nicolson, 1969).

Pre-1700

Christina Larner, *Witchcraft and Religion: The Politics of Popular Belief* (Oxford: Basil Blackwell, 1984).

C. L'Estrange Ewen, *Witch-Hunting and Witch Trials* (London: Kegan Paul, Trench, Trubner, 1929).

Alan MacFarlane, *Witchcraft in Tudor and Stuart England* (London: Routledge & Kegan Paul, 1970).

Keith Thomas, *Religion and the Decline of Magic* (London: Weidenfeld & Nicolson, 1971; reprinted London: Penguin, 1973).

Hugh Trevor-Roper, *The European Witch-Craze of the 16th and 17th Centuries* (London: Pelican, 1969).

Post-1700

Rev. J. C. Atkinson, *Forty Years in a Moorland Parish: Reminiscences and Researches in Danby in Cleveland* (London: Macmillan, 1891).

Bob Bushaway, *By Rite: Custom, Ceremony and Community, 1700–1880* (London: Junction Books, 1982).

David Clark, *Between Pulpit and Pew: Folk Religion in a North Yorkshire Fishing Village* (Cambridge: Cambridge University Press, 1982).

James Obelkevich, *Religion and Rural Society: South Lindsey 1825–1875* (Oxford: Clarendon Press, 1978).

J. S. Udal, *Dorsetshire Folk-Lore* (Hertford: Stephen Austin, 1922; reprinted 1970).

David Vincent, *Literacy and Popular Culture: England 1750–1914* (Cambridge: Cambridge University Press, 1989).

Alfred Williams, *Villages of the White Horse* (London: Gerald Duckworth, 1918).

Notes on Contributors

Jonathan Barry is a Lecturer in History in the Department of History and Archaeology, University of Exeter. He has written many articles on the social, cultural and urban history of early modern England and is the editor of *The Tudor and Stuart Town* (London: Longman, 1990), (with Joe Melling) *Culture in History* (Exeter: University of Exeter Press, 1992) and (with Chris Brooks) *The Middling Sort of People* (Basingstoke: Macmillan, 1994). He is currently completing a study of the cultural life of early modern Bristol for Oxford University Press.

Bob Bushaway's doctoral thesis for the University of Southampton was published as *By Rite: Custom, Ceremony and Community in England, 1700–1880* (London: Junction Books, 1982). He has published several articles on English rural custom and collective ritual and on the popular culture of the Great War. He works as a university administrator and is Associate Member of the Department of Modern History at the University of Birmingham. He is a Fellow of the Royal Anthropological Institute and a Fellow of the Royal Historical Society. His most recent published work is 'Name upon Name: The Great War and Remembrance', in Roy Porter (ed.), *Myths of the English* (Cambridge: Polity Press, 1992).

Susan Dwyer Amussen is a member of the core faculty of the Graduate School, The Union Institute, Connecticut, and is the author of *An Ordered Society* (Oxford: Basil Blackwell, 1988), and numerous articles. She is currently working on a book provisionally entitled *Women, Gender and Society in Early Modern England.*

Tim Harris, formerly a Research Fellow at Emmanuel College, Cambridge, is now Associate Professor of History at Brown University, Rhode Island. His publications include *London Crowds in the Reign of Charles II* (Cambridge: Cambridge University Press, 1987), *Politics under the Later Stuarts* (London: Longman, 1993), and (co-edited with Paul Seaward and Mark Goldie) *The Politics of Religion in Restoration England* (Oxford: Basil Blackwell, 1990). He is currently working on a study of politics, power and ideology in Britain during the 1680s.

Martin Ingram was supervised at Oxford by Sir Keith Thomas, moved to a research fellowship at King's College, Cambridge, and subsequently worked at the University of East Anglia and the Queen's University of Belfast. Since 1989 he has been a Fellow, Tutor and University Lecturer in Modern History at Brasenose College, Oxford. His publications include *Church Courts, Sex and Marriage in England, 1570–1640* (Cambridge: Cambridge University Press, 1987) and a number of articles on crime and the law, sex and marriage, and popular customs. He has also published on the history of climate.

Roy Porter is Professor in the Social History of Medicine at the Wellcome Institute for the History of Medicine. He is currently working on the history of hysteria. Recent books include *Mind Forg'd Manacles: Madness in England from the Restoration to the Regency* (London: Athlone Press, 1987); *A Social History of Madness* (London: Weidenfeld & Nicolson, 1987); *In Sickness and in Health: The British Experience, 1650–1850* (London: Fourth Estate, 1988); *Patient's Progress* (Cambridge: Polity Press, 1989) – these last two co-authored with Dorothy Porter; and *Health for Sale: Quackery in England 1660–1850* (Manchester: Manchester University Press, 1989).

John Rule is a Professor of History at the University of Southampton. He has published widely in the area of labour history of the eighteenth and early nineteenth centuries. He has recently (1992) published a two-volume social and economic history of Hanoverian England: *The Vital Century: England's Developing Economy 1714–1815* and *Albion's People: English Society 1714–1815* (both published London: Longman, 1992).

Patty Seleski is Assistant Professor of History at California State University, San Marcos. She is completing a manuscript about women in domestic service titled *Good Characters: Women and the Drama of Domestic Service in London, 1750–1830* and is at work on a biography of the late Irish jurist and human rights activist, Sean MacBride.

David Underdown is Professor of History at Yale University. His most recent books are *Revel, Riot and Rebellion* (Oxford: Clarendon Press, 1985) and *Fire from Heaven* (London: HarperCollins, 1992).

Index